Forerunner of the 'Precedents', a Ramsbottom 'Newton' Class 2-4-0 No 2004 Witch, *at Manchester London Road (afterwards named 'Piccadilly')* (Author's collection).

Up Irish Mail passing Penmaenmawr hauled by 'Renown' Class 4-4-0 No 1968 Cumberland *and 'Prince of Wales' Class 4-6-0 No 833* Suvla Bay *(Rail Archive Stephenson, photo F.R. Hebron).*

GREAT LOCOMOTIVES
OF THE LMS

O.S. Nock

PSL
Patrick Stephens Limited

First published in 1989

British Library Cataloguing in Publication Data

Nock, O.S. (Oswald Stevens), 1905-
  Great locomotives of the LMS.
  1. Great Britain. Railway services: London,
  Midland and Scottish Railway. Steam
  locomotives. to 1987
  I. Title
  625.2'61'0941

  ISBN 1-85260-020-9

Note
At the time the LMS ceased to exist in January 1948, and became part of British Railways, the art of railway photography in colour had barely started. The colour pictures in this book were all taken after this change and show LMS locomotives either in their working days in post-nationalization colours or restored to their former glory on some of the country's many preserved railways.

Patrick Stephens Limited is part of the Thorsons Publishing Group, Wellingborough, Northamptonshire, NN8 2RQ, England.

Printed in Great Britain by Butler & Tanner Limited, Frome, Somerset
Typeset by MJL Limited, Hitchin, Hertfordshire

10 9 8 7 6 5 4 3 2 1

Contents

Preface

Forty years after the Company itself ceased to exist, I find it not a little difficult to write of the LMS and its locomotives, and particularly those of its constituents, without apparently becoming strongly partisan. But in the intervening years since the Grouping of the British railways took place in 1923, much technical evidence has come to light, not to mention my own widening experience as a professional civil and mechanical engineer mainly concerned with railway work over 45 very eventful years, and this has consolidated my views on certain aspects of pre-LMS history that I now feel are not partisan at all, but are the facts of locomotive history. My field of study in this particular book has left me with a degree of wonderment at the astonishing contrast between the post-Grouping locomotive history of the LMS and that of the other three Groups; how nearly all that had gone before was cast on one side, and that the casting on one side was followed by a period of such indecision and muddle that the top management was compelled to bring in a complete outsider to 'scrap the lot' and begin again!

This is not to say all was well in the locomotive departments of some of the constituents of the LMS. On the Lancashire and Yorkshire, Horwich was only just emerging from a very bad patch. On the Glasgow and South Western, so far as the principal main-line engines were concerned, they were still reaping the whirlwind from the Manson era of light structural work on frames and attachments, while the neighbouring Caledonian had recently built four of the most ineffective big engines to run in these islands. On the Midland, one of the most affluent of pre-Grouping companies, the locomotive department was under the iron hand of the top management and was compelled to work the traffic with a swarm of undersized, though superbly maintained, little engines. And what of the North Western? Some writers have made merry over the shortcomings of the Webb three-cylinder compounds, but while the 'Experiments' were more or less poor tools, the 'Dreadnoughts' and the 'Teutonics' were far otherwise, and, in their nigh on twenty years of main-line express work, their mileage, double manned, very far exceeded that of all their contemporaries, in England, Scotland and elsewhere. Nor was their demise, in the Whale era, so ignominious as some people have made out. It should not be forgotten that their much revered rivals at Doncaster, the Stirling 8-footers, after a much lower mileage record, were going to the scrap heap just as rapidly as, sometimes even more so than, the 'Dreadnoughts' and the 'Teutonics' around 1905.

As to the later Crewe express passenger engines

I have emphasized in Chapter 13 the outstanding everyday performance of the 'George the Fifth' Class 4-4-0s, and the effectiveness of the Joy valve gear in comparison with the performance of much more recent locomotives under carefully observed maximum test conditions. Of course, after Grouping the Joy valve gear was apparently beneath consideration, even though, in addition to the Crewe thousands, only a small minority of Lancashire and Yorkshire engines had valve gear other than the Joy. I have often wondered what the results might have been if, under other leadership, a team of dedicated engineers had been set up to modernize the Joy, as Churchward did with the Stephenson and the Walschaerts on Great Western locomotives. It must not be forgotten that despite Stanier's 'scrap and build' mandate from 1932 onwards, there were still many hundreds of ex-LNWR 0-8-0s, with Joy valve gear, still doing yeoman work for British Railways in the 1950s. As for the removal of the central bearing on the driving axle of the 'Prince of Wales' and 'George the Fifth' express engines as related in Chapter 18, it was as near to partisan sabotage as one likes to think!

'Picking up the bits' from 1932 onwards, Stanier did a great job. Of course, he enjoyed what his predecessors never really had, the whole-hearted and enthusiastic backing of the top management; while his own personality quickly ensured the strong support of every man of his own workforce from end to end of the line. But in the flood-tide of his career, with the many honours both academic and national that were bestowed upon him, he never forgot the 'Alma Mater' down in the West Country where he had learned his trade. I was privileged to meet him many times during the late afternoon of his career, sometimes at the Institution of Mechanical Engineers and later in his beautiful home near Rickmansworth when I was writing a biography of his engineering life. One evening over tea prior to a meeting of the Institution of Locomotive Engineers in company with one or two other ex-Swindon men, he caused a storm of laughter by remarking to me 'We've all still got GWR embroidered on the seats of our trousers!' While my own sentiments have not yet reached the stage of embellishment of my most personal underwear, my feelings for 'the other place', as it would be expressed in the highest academical circles, will have been apparent to all who have read thus far; and I have included as an Appendix to this book the text of an address I delivered at the 64th Crewe Dinner on Friday 7 May 1971, when I had the honour of proposing the toast of Crewe Men Past and Present.

Of those who have helped me with information for

this book, in addition to Sir William Stanier I must mention H.G. Ivatt, V.R. Bowen Cooke, and his sisters, to whom Crewe and the LNWR were favourite topics for a hearty discussion over the tea cups in their drawing room overlooking Falmouth harbour. Then of course there was Robin Riddles, and my great personal friend from the other side of the partisan fence, Roland Bond, trained at Derby and staunchly Midland in his early days. Kenneth Cantlie, pupil of Bowen Cooke, was a mine of information, and across the Border, W. Barr, late of the Caledonian, and a power in the land as far back as when McIntosh was in the chair at St Rollox, reminisced fascinatingly when I visited him in his retirement in the 1950s. My best thanks are due to them all, and to the many who have provided photographs and details of train running.

O.S. Nock

1. LNWR: Webb's pocket masterpieces

When Francis W. Webb succeeded Ramsbottom as Chief Mechanical Engineer of the London and North Western Railway in 1871, the locomotive position of this, already acknowledged as the premier railway of Great Britain, was very sound. In Ramsbottom's time, the physical extent and manufacturing potential of Crewe Works had been greatly expanded, and in 1871 Webb was able to take over one of the foremost engineering establishments, not only in Great Britain, but in the whole world. Many new locomotives were immediately needed for the ever-increasing traffic of the railway, and for the passenger business Webb at first continued building, with no change in design, the two Ramsbottom standard 2-4-0 classes, the 'Newtons', with 6-ft 7-in coupled wheels, and the much smaller 'Samsons', with 6-ft wheels. With these later additions, twenty in the first case and forty in the second, the 'Newtons' eventually mustered a total of 96 engines, and the 'Samsons' ninety. In Ramsbottom's time at Crewe, the seal was set on the mass production of main-line locomotives, with the building of no fewer than 943 0-6-0s of the 'DX' Class in 15 years. These splendid little engines, together with the two classes of passenger 2-4-0s, formed the basis on which Webb developed his own early design practice.

His first new class could be described as a smaller-wheeled version of the 'DX', with a larger firebox and a higher boiler pressure of 140 psi as against 120. Machinery-wise, the two classes were identical, with 17-in by 24-in cylinders and the Stephenson link motion, as on all Ramsbottom's engines. The '17-inch Coal Engines', as they became known, were, like the 'DXs', an immediate success, and from their first introduction in 1873 continued to be built at Crewe until 1892, by which time the class totalled 500. It was a remarkable example of the way class standardization was practised at Crewe; from the time the 17-inch coal engine was first produced, two additional valve gears were introduced for inside-cylindered locomotives, and yet there was not any suggestion that the Allan straight link motion or the

Joy radial gear might be substituted for the Stephenson curved link motion on the later examples of the class.

While the immediate demands of the traffic department were being met by construction of further Ramsbottom-type passenger engines, the first 2-4-0s of Webb's own highly original design were being built at Crewe. The importance and significance of these engines can scarcely be over-estimated. As if to underline this significance, Mr Webb named the first of the small-wheeled variety *Precursor*, and the larger-wheeled one *Precedent*. The two designs were identical, save in the diameter of the coupled wheels, and *Precursor* was the first to appear. With the Scottish expresses timed at no more than 42 mph between Preston and Carlisle, the intention was to provide an engine of enhanced nominal tractive effort that would climb the banks at higher speeds than the 'Newtons' did, and obviate the need for fast running downhill, with its attendant increases in wear and tear. Before deciding on the relatively small wheel diameter of 5 ft 6 in, a trial had been made by removing the leading coupling rods of a 5-ft 6-in McConnell 0-6-0 goods engine, and apparently this engine ran quite freely at the express speeds of the day. But although the use of 5-ft 6-in coupled wheels in *Precursor* attracted a great deal of attention at the time, there were other features of the design that seem considerably more important in the light of subsequent history, and these features were common to both 'Precursors' and 'Precedents'. It is evident that Webb had most clearly in view the object of keeping running and maintenance costs to a minimum, and the layout of the front end seems to have been developed from a desire to provide large bearing surfaces for the driving axle boxes. This feature is particularly mentioned in contemporary descriptions of the engines, and it was done by removing the slide valves from their conventional positions between the cylinders, and bringing the cylinders themselves closer together, with their centre lines only 24 in apart.

The valve faces were inclined; the steam chest in

LNWR locomotives: valve gear variations

'17-in Coal' 0-6-0	'Precedent' 2-4-0	'Whitworth' 2-4-0	18-in fast goods 0-6-0
Stephenson link motion	Allan link motion	Allan link motion	Joy radial gear
500 built, 1873-92	Original class: 70 built, 1874-82	Replacement of 'Samsons': 90 built, 1889-96	310 built, 1880-1902
	Improved replacement 'Newtons': 96 built, 1887-94		

Top *One of the contemporary 'Samson' Class 6-ft 2-4-0s, No 764* Shap (F. Moore's Rail Photos).

Above *One of the early Ramsbottom 'DX' express goods engines No 578* (Loco Publishing Co).

Right *No 3121, one of the 500 'DX' engines as rebuilt by Webb and fitted with a vacuum brake for passenger train working. More than 200 of these engines were still in service in 1914* (H.W. Burman).

cross-section was V-shaped, and the valve spindles were considerably above the centre-line of the cylinders. This inclining of the valve faces had been adopted in the McConnell 'Patent' engines of 1852, and it seems very likely that it was this point in the design that led to the choice of the Allan valve gear instead of the Stephenson. It would not have been easy to fit in the ordinary link motion under the boiler with the cross-shaft and lifting link above the expansion link, and the Allan had a very neat and compact layout. But quite apart from the valve setting, Webb had provided very short and direct steam passages, and a very large steam chest volume. This latter point is of great importance for an express engine. When running fast, pressure of the steam always has a tendency to drop during the admission, and this is sometimes attributed wholly to the throttling or 'wire-drawing' effect of the steam passing through the valve ports. As Swindon has shown, however, its effect can be greatly lessened by having a large reservoir of steam on the boiler side of the valve; the larger this reservoir, the less will be the drop in pressure as each successive 'gulp' of steam is taken by the cylinders. The large steam chest volume was a very big contributory factor in the fast running of the 'Precedents'. The two cylinders, together with the steam chests and the smokebox saddle, were combined in a single casting—a very fine piece of foundry work. By its use, erection was simplified and weight reduced by the absence of flanged faces and the bolts necessary with the method of construction, then usual in Great Britain, of having separate castings for each cylinder.

Externally, the 'Precursors' and 'Precedents' followed in the style of the modernized 'Newtons' and 'Samsons', except that the running plates were straight. Mr Webb continued for a time the drop-down smokebox doors, though the sand boxes were

The first of the celebrated Webb 'Precedent' Class 2-4-0s, No 2175 Precedent *in 'shop grey' (British Railways).*

placed below the running plate. The boilers were of the same design as those on the 17-inch coal engines. *Precursor* was completed in April 1874, followed by 19 further engines of the class; *Precedent* came out in December 1874, and she, too, was the first of a batch of twenty. As previously mentioned, the 'Precursors' were intended for the Crewe-Carlisle section, though as it happened their stay on the Scotch expresses was very short. According to Ahrons, it was said that they knocked themselves to pieces, through their coupled wheels being too small for express work. In passing on this explanation of their early withdrawal from the service for which they were designed, Ahrons admits he found it hard to believe. I do, too. Timings between Preston and Carlisle were very easy, and Webb himself stated that when *Precursor* was stripped down after 11 months' running, the amount of wear in the motion and driving boxes was very small. The failure of the 'Precursors' was, I think, much more likely due to insufficient boiler power. The nominal tractive effort was 12 per cent greater than that of the 'Precedents', but tractive effort is no use if the boiler cannot produce the steam. It is just possible that the Shap incline proper might be rushed by mortgaging the boiler, but nothing can make up for boiler capacity on the long climb from Carlisle to Summit.

The 'Precedents' of 1874-1882 were:

2175	*Precedent*	2182	*Giraffe*
2176	*Robert Benson*	2183	*Antelope*
2177	*Edward Tootal*	2184	*Reynard*
2178	*Pluck*	2185	*Alma*
2179	*Patience*	2186	*Lowther*
2180	*Perseverance*	2187	*Penrith Beacon*
2181	*Buffalo*	2188	*Chillington*

2189	*Avon*	919	*Nasmyth*
2190	*Beatrice*	1170	*General*
2191	*Snowdon*	1173	*The Auditor*
2192	*Caradoc*	1183	*Plynlimmon*
2193	*Salopian*	1187	*Chandos*
2194	*Cambrian*	1193	*Joshua Radcliffe*
857	*Prince Leopold*	1194	*Miranda*
858	*Sir Salar Jung*	619	*Mabel*
860	*Merrie Carlisle*	789	*Breadalbane*
861	*Amazon*	477	*Caractacus*
862	*Balmoral*	478	*Commodore*
863	*Meteor*	480	*Duchess of Lancaster*
864	*Pilot*	482	*Pegasus*
865	*Envoy*	506	*Sir Alexander*
866	*Courier*		*Cockburn*
867	*Disraeli*	512	*Lazonby*
868	*Condor*	514	*Lawrence*
869	*Llewellyn*	945	*Humphry Davy*
870	*Fairbairn*	253	*President Garfield*
871	*Prosperine*	254	*President Lincoln*
872	*Wizard*	256	*President Washington*
883	*Phantom*	257	*Duke of Albany*
890	*Sir Hardman Earle*	260	*Duke of Connaught*
1105	*Hercules*	262	*Wheatstone*
1177	*Princess Louise*	264	*Buckland*
1189	*Stewart*	265	*Thomas Carlyle*
193	*Rocket*	364	*Henry Pease*
517	*Marathon*	955	*Charles Dickens*
749	*Mercury*		

In their early days the 'Precedents', curiously enough, gave very little indication of their outstanding worth. The seventy engines comprising the true 'Precedent' Class had ⅞-in thick plate frames, and a boiler pressure of 140 psi. On the basis of early timings, the 7-ft 'Bloomers' 'could run rings round them', uphill and down, and even on moderate loadings their coal consumption of about 30 to 32 lb per mile was very heavy in relation to the work done. Ahrons is inclined to condemn them as being too small for the job, and certainly the runs he has set on record do not compare with those enjoyed by Rous-Marten at a somewhat later period. The revolution that seemed to take place in their working can, I think, be attributed to both engineering and psychological factors; first to the use in later years of steel, for rails and tyres, that was much harder than the steel, or wrought-iron, previously used, and secondly that the North Western enginemen had acquired the art of running fast. After so long a spell of 40 to 45 mph schedules, the art of hard running could not be mastered in a few days, or even weeks.

The subsequent history of the Webb 2-4-0 express passenger engines makes fascinating reading. It began in 1887, and resulted in the building of 186 entirely new engines between that year and 1895, and the rebuilding of all the original 'Precedents' with new frames and new boilers. It is generally believed that the 186 'new' engines were 'accountants' rebuilds' of the Ramsbottom 'Newton' and 'Samson' Classes, 96 and 90 engines respectively, since the new engines carried the same numbers, names and dates as the engines they replaced. In that monumental register of all the locomotives of the London and North Western Railway first compiled by C. Williams in 1912, and subsequently revised by him, the dates of the new 2-4-0s built from 1887 onwards are given as those on the engine number and name plates, for example No 633 *Samson* as May 1863. The 'Newtons'

One of the most famous of the 'Precedents', No 955 Charles Dickens. *Built in 1882 and stationed at Longsight, it worked between Manchester and Euston daily until it had clocked two million miles of express running by 5 August 1902, when it was replaced by a larger engine* (British Railways).

were renewed as 'Improved Precedents', with 1-in thick main frames, instead of ⅞-in as on the original 'Precedents', and boilers carrying a pressure of 150 psi, instead of 140. Their names and numbers, in order of their original construction, were:

The 10 am Anglo-Scottish express on Bushey water troughs hauled by a 'Lady of the Lake' Class 2-2-2 Eunomia, *and a 'Precedent', No 871* Proserpine *(British Railways).*

394	*Eamont*	308	*Booth*
395	*Scotia*	2001	*Henry Crosfield*
396	*Tennyson*	2002	*Madge*
271	*Minotaur*	2003	*Alecto*
275	*Vulcan*	2004	*Witch*
276	*Pluto*	2005	*Lynx*
295	*Penmaenmawr*	2006	*Princess*
304	*Hector*		

1480	*Newton*	1666	*Ariadne*
1481	*The Duke of Edinburgh*	1667	*Corunna*
1482	*Herschel*	1668	*Dagmar*
1483	*Newcomen*	1669	*Ilion*
1484	*Telford*	1670	*Ganymede*
1485	*Smeaton*	1671	*Shamrock*
1486	*Dalton*	1672	*Talavera*
1487	*Faraday*	1673	*Lucknow*
1488	*Murdock*	1674	*Delhi*
1489	*Brindley*	1675	*Vimiera*
1513	*Shakespeare*	1676	*The Nile*
1514	*Scott*	1677	*Badajos*
1515	*Milton*	1678	*Airey*
1516	*Byron*	1679	*Bunsen*
1517	*Princess Helena*	1680	*Livingstone*
1518	*Countess*	1681	*Minerva*
1519	*Duchess*	1682	*Novelty*
1520	*Franklin*	1683	*Sisyphus*
1521	*Gladstone*	1684	*Speke*
1522	*Pitt*	1685	*Gladiator*
1523	*Marlborough*	1744	*Magdala*
1524	*Wolfe*	1745	*John Bright*
1525	*Abercrombie*	1746	*Bevere*
1526	*Drake*	1747	*John Mayall*
1527	*Raleigh*	1748	*Britannia*
1528	*Frobisher*	1749	*Hibernia*
1529	*Cook*	379	*Sedgwick*
1530	*Columbus*	380	*Quermore*
1531	*Cromwell*	381	*Patterdale*
1532	*Hampden*	382	*Buckingham*
		393	*Brougham*

The twenty further engines of the class built by Webb were as follows:

1872		**1873**	
1211	*John Ramsbottom*	403	*Isabella*
1212	*Pioneer*	696	*Director*
1213	*The Queen*	787	*Clarendon*
1214	*Prince Albert*	790	*Hardwicke*
1215	*Albion*	941	*Blenkinsop*
1216	*Premier*	942	*Shah of Persia*
1217	*Florence*	974	*Richard Cobden*
1218	*Phaeton*	1020	*Wordsworth*
1219	*Lightning*	1132	*North Western*
1220	*Belted Will*	1141	*S. R. Graves*

It is a great pity that the London and North Western dynamometer car of Webb's days was not used to record the work of the 'Improved Precedents', because, of the 2-4-0s with 17-in by 24-in cylinders, they were incomparable. They may have been heavy coal burners, but the work they did was prodigious. The layout of the front end made them exceedingly free-running engines, and as universal favourites with the Running Department there was no doubt why so many of them were kept in first class condition when so many engines of other contemporary designs were scrapped. I began my regular travelling on the line, and photographing from the lineside, in 1921; from then until well into 1926, several years after the LNWR had been absorbed by the LMS, I was travelling in first class main-line express trains on which these splendid little 2-4-0s still formed part of the motive power. I well remember some individual engines I saw and travelled behind in those years: the up Perth express, due into Euston at 7.30 pm, with *Delhi* pilot from Carlisle to Crewe and *Perseverance* onwards with a 450-ton load; then the up morning 'Scotsman', after combining the Glasgow and Edinburgh portions, leaving Crewe with a red-painted 'Prince of Wales' 4-6-0 piloted by *Caractacus*. On the 1.30 pm down 'West Coast Corridor', before it was named the 'Midday Scot', I logged *Vimiera* as pilot to a 'Claughton', *Vindictive*, and *Hector* as pilot to another red 'Prince', *Lucknow*. But I could gossip for pages upon pages of my recollections of those fascinating old engines, and I must now pass on to their 6-ft 3-in confreres, the 'Whitworths', as the replacements of the old Ramsbottom 'Samsons' became known.

The 'Whitworths', even more than the 'Improved Precedents', were absolutely new engines from 1889 onwards. While the latter engines certainly had the same cylinder dimensions as the 'Newtons', though different in almost all other respects, the 'Samsons' originally had cylinders 15¼ in by 20 in, and carried a boiler pressure of no more than 120 psi. The 'Whitworths', like the 'Improved Precedents', had 17-in by 24-in cylinders, and 150-psi pressure, and because of their smaller coupled wheels had a higher tractive effort than the 'Precedents'.

The latter engines in their hey-day were essentially West Coast Main Line engines, while the 'Whitworths', although doing a great deal of West Coast work, were also used on the important cross-country main line between Manchester and Leeds. In the days of the Webb compounds, the gentlemen who compiled logs of the running of the fast trains between Crewe and Carlisle almost invariably found the finest running was made not by any combination of engines in which the compounds of any class were involved, but by a pair of 2-4-0s, often a 'Whitworth' and a 'Precedent' together. At the turn of the century the loads were heavy, and two engines were usually required on the most important West Coast trains. The 'Whitworths', in order of construction at Crewe, were as follows:

1889	September	1045	*Whitworth*
	November	731	*Croxteth*
	November	748	*Waterloo*

1890	January	633	*Samson*
	January	635	*Zamiel*
	January	733	*Chimera*
	June	231	*Firefly*
	June	632	*Ostrich*
	June	738	*Terrier*
	July	828	*Tubal*
	August	642	*Bee*
	October	35	*Talisman*
	October	36	*Thababa*
	October	901	*Hero*
	November	444	*Typhon*
	November	604	*Narcissus*
1892	January	81	*Greystoke*
	January	735	*Charon*
	January	757	*Banshee*
	January	821	*Diomed*
	January	829	*Turk*
	March	479	*Mastodon*
	March	752	*Glowworm*
	March	934	*North Star*
1893	February	830	*Trent*
	March	124	*Marquis Douro*
	March	285	*Phalaris*
	March	634	*Ellesmere*
	March	724	*Eden*
	March	739	*Sutherland*
	March	742	*Spitfire*
	March	758	*Hardman*
	March	763	*Violet*
	March	764	*Shap*
	March	795	*Falstaff*
	March	817	*Constance*
1893	April	418	*Zygia*
	April	445	*Ixion*
	April	609	*The Earl of Chester*
	April	628	*Tartarus*
	April	819	*Puck*
	May	636	*Eclipse*
	May	832	*Sanspareil*
	May	902	*Onyx*
	May	935	*Planet*
	June	434	*St Patrick*
	June	446	*Siren*
	June	469	*St George*
	June	485	*Euxine*
	June	486	*Skiddaw*
	June	792	*Theorem*
	June	794	*Woodlark*
	June	805	*Caliban*
	June	824	*Adelaide*
	June	1126	*Saddleback*
	June	2150	*Atlas*
	June	2153	*Isis*

Left *One of the 'Whitworth' Class 6-ft 3-in 2-4-0s, originally No 742* Spitfire, *transferred to the civil engineers department and seen here named* Engineer Liverpool *(Author's Collection).*

Right *A 6-ft 6-in 'Jumbo' (officially 'Precedent' Class) No 477* Caractacus *on an up Central Wales through express near Kenton (C. Laundy).*

Below right *One of the 'Whitworths', formerly 793* Martin, *as* Engineer Watford *on a ballasting train near Bushey (F.R. Hebron).*

1894	May	404	*Zopyrus*
	May	736	*Memnon*
	May	737	*Roberts*
	May	793	*Martin*
	May	2154	*Loadstone*
	May	2159	*Shark*
	June	90	*Luck of Edenhall*
	June	401	*Zeno*
	June	419	*Zillah*
	June	468	*Wildfire*
	June	647	*Castor*
	June	814	*Henrietta*
	June	2152	*Sybil*
	November	2151	*Baltic*
1895	January	732	*Hecla*
	January	2156	*Sphinx*
	January	2158	*Serpent*
	February	852	*Kestrel*
	February	995	*Medea*
	February	1163	*John O'Gaunt*
	February	1164	*Odin*
	July	424	*Sirius*
	July	773	*Centaur*
	August	209	*Petrel*
	August	263	*Pheasant*
	August	487	*John O'Groat*
	September	414	*Prospero*
	November	2155	*Liver*
	December	2157	*Unicorn*
1896	January	631	*Hotspur*
	January	885	*Vampire*
	January	1166	*Wyre*
	January	1168	*Cuckoo*

Like the 'Precedents', or the 6-ft 6-in 'Jumbos', as they became more usually known to twentieth-century railwaymen and enthusiasts, the smaller-wheeled engines had an immense variety of names. Most of them were not in themselves original, having been inherited from the early Trevithick-Allan 2-2-2s and 2-4-0s, all of which, goods and passenger alike, were named. Many of the names of both the 6-ft and 6-ft 6-in classes were obvious enough, though not in association with each other in a series of names for the same type of locomotive. Nor was there any symmetry in the titles of the 'Old Crewe' engines from which they were derived. Take, for example, those borne by the seven 'Whitworths' built in June 1894: *Zeno, Wildfire, Henrietta, Castor, Zillah, Sybil,* and *Luck of Edenhall*! Some of the most obscure and exotic might well have made the subjects for a railway quiz game, except that as the 'Jumbos' became withdrawn and were replaced by the modern express engines of Whale or Bowen Cooke design some of the old names were not perpetuated, like *Luck of Edenhall*. As time went on, some of the old names were combined in new guises; once in 1924 I travelled northwards behind *Miranda* and *Samson*, a 6-ft 6-in 'Jumbo' piloting a new 'Prince of Wales' Class 4-6-0 that carried the name borne by successive Crewe engines since 1848!

Apart from the immortal *Hardwicke*, about which I have written much in my book *The Railway Race to the North*, there are two final memories of the last members of the 6-ft and 6-ft 6-in classes that I saw personally. The first was at Penrith in 1931, on a Sunday morning when I visited the shed and found old

No 628 (then LMS 5095) *Tartarus*, browsing in a side road. Buffer to buffer with her was the celebrated 6-ft 6-in *The Queen*, which partnered *Hardwicke* night and night about in the exciting August of 1895. But the last 6-ft 6-in I saw, and actually travelled behind, was *Talavera*, old 1672 and LMS 5018, on a local train from Northampton to Rugby.

In 1879, before he built any of the later 2-4-0s, Webb was planning a large express goods engine. The traffic department of the railway was developing a service of long freight runs between the major traffic centres, making lengthy non-stop runs, and a considerably more powerful engine than the Ramsbottom 'DX' was required. Webb settled at once for 18-in cylinders, and with a grate area of 17 sq ft and a boiler pressure of 140 psi, the nominal tractive effort of the new engines would be enhanced over that of the 'DX' by 30 per cent. It was at this stage that David Joy entered upon the North Western scene. In his diaries he tells how throughout the winter of 1878-9 he was working on a big model of his new radial valve gear, which resulted in a patent dated 8 March 1879. Quoting from his diary of the period:

'The Advantages of this system are —

First: That it is simpler, lighter and less costly than 'Link' gear by about 25 per cent. This is stated on the authority of the Barrow Shipbuilding Co, who made the weights come out for 'Link' gear 5 tons 6 cwt 0 qrs 25 lb against the new gear 4 tons 0 cwt 1 qr 27 lb saving being 1 ton 5 cwt 2 qr 26 lb, being about 25 per cent in favour of the new.

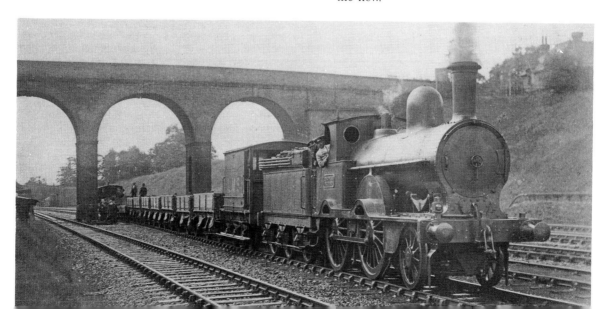

'Second: It favours the shortening of the engine, so saving 25 per cent length of engine room, by placing the valve chests and valve gear on the transverse centre line of each cylinder. The cylinders are placed close together, instead of being spread as with 'Link' gear, where the valve chests are between the cylinders. This also shortens the crank shaft, allowing the employment of four large bearings instead of six small ones.

'Third: The improvement of the distribution of the steam, which is almost mathematically correct, for both top and bottom of the cylinder; but by 'setting' with a little more lead at the bottom, the steam admissions, or 'cut-offs', may be arranged in the proportions of, say, 65 per cent up and 62 per cent down, or any similar proportions. So in overhead engines, allowing a perfect balance of the strokes up and down. Also, as the movement transmitted to the valve is the result of the combination of the vertical movement, with its vibrating motion, when the two are acting in the same direction, the movement of the valve is very rapid, and this occurs at lead and for the opening of the port. Then follows a time when the two movements are opposed, resulting in a slow action, almost a 'dwell' holding the port steadily full open; when, again, by a combination of the movements, the port is quickly closed.'

Now we come to the memorable day 25 May 1879; it proved to be not only a 'red letter day' in Joy's career, but even more so a turning point in London and North Western locomotive history. On that day, Joy was granted an interview by F.W. Webb, and it may be stated that the 'great man' fairly swooped on it. While Joy naturally dilated upon the advantage quoted previously, from Webb's immediate point of view the outstanding feature was the elimination of the eccentrics used in both Stephenson and Allan link motion. This cleared the way for very large bearings on the driving axle of the new express goods engine he was planning. The adoption of the Joy radial valve gear was evidently a sufficiently forward step at Crewe for Webb to seek the LNWR directors' permission to incorporate it in the new 0-6-0, for experimental purposes. But for all practical reasons the gear was as good as 'sold'. Furthermore, Webb seems to have gone out of his way to publicize it. The summer meeting of the Institution of Mechanical Engineers was to be held at Barrow-in-Furness in 1880, and it was doubtless through Webb's influence that Joy was invited to read a paper on his new valve gear. Webb supported him magnificently by arranging for the 0-6-0 so fitted to be taken up to Barrow for exhibition; but strangely enough, other than Webb himself, none of his fellow locomotive engineers on British

railways took part in the discussion on his paper.

The illustrations in the published account of the meeting in Barrow, in the Proceedings of the Institution of Mechanical Engineers, Part Three, of 1880 were superb, some of which are reproduced herewith. The plan and cross-sectional views show particularly how the absence of eccentrics enabled large driving axle bearings to be accommodated, and the centre-lines of the cylinders to be brought closer together. One engine only was built at first, No 2365, dated June 1880, and doubtless it was subjected to very searching tests. In the meantime, in 1881 a start had been made on rebuilding the Ramsbottom 'DX' express goods engines with new boilers of the same dimensions as those of the 17-inch coal engines. Eventually 500 of the 'DX' Class were so treated, but they were not so powerful as the new 18-inch engine with Joy valve gear. Another nine of the latter, Nos 2464-2472, were built at Crewe in October-November 1882, but a further five years elapsed before more of the 18-inch goods class were built. By that time, Webb was obviously convinced of the merits of the Joy valve gear because before he had embarked on the second production batch of 18-inch goods he had built no less than sixty new three-cylinder compounds, thirty 'Experiments' and thirty 'Dreadnoughts' with Joy valve gear for both high- and low-pressure cylinders. There were twenty of the second batch of 18-inch 0-6-0s in 1887, with scattered numbers in the usual Crewe style, and another batch of only ten in 1892.

In view of Webb's principles of standardization in other respects, it was remarkable that he retained, for new construction, three different valve gears simultaneously. The last batches of the 17-inch coal engines, with the Stephenson link motion, were not built until 1892, but there was the even more anomalous case of the 'Whitworths', or 6-ft 'Jumbos', and the replacements for the 96 2-4-0s of the Ramsbottom 'Newton' Class. Both series were virtually new engines, and although their construction did not begin until 1887, one might have thought, with Webb's partiality to the Joy valve gear, it might have been used on these new engines. Evidently, however, with much other new design work in the drawing office, Webb felt it was wise enough to let well alone and use the front end that had proved successful on the 'Precedents', with the Allan straight link motion. In consequence, Crewe built 186 new 2-4-0s with Allan gear from 1887 onward, while quantity production of the 18-inch 0-6-0 express goods with Joy valve gear began in real earnest from 1895. The class was multiplied to a total of 310 in 1902, the last engine being No 2502, completed at Crewe in May of that year.

In these engines Webb had reverted to a running plate curved over the coupled wheel bosses as in the

VALVE GEAR.

London & North Western Goods Engine with Joy's Gear, Plan.

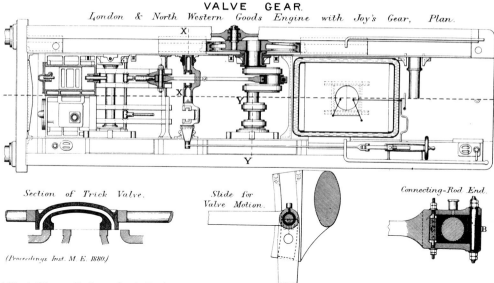

Section of Trick Valve.

Slide for Valve Motion.

Connecting-Rod End.

(Proceedings Inst. M.E. 1880.)

'London and North Western Railway Goods Engine, with Joy's Gear', from the Proceedings of the Institution of Mechanical Engineers, 1880.

VALVE GEAR.

London and North Western Goods Engine, with Joy's Gear.

Valve Gear.

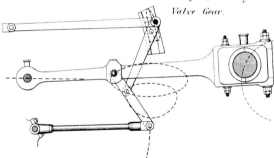

Half Cross Sections along XX and YY

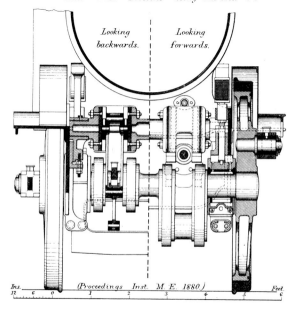

Looking backwards.

Looking forwards.

(Proceedings Inst. M.E. 1880.)

'Samsons' and 'Newtons'; they had the company's coat of arms on the driving wheel splashers and on this account were sometimes known as the 'Crested Goods', though it was the men who coined the nickname that has lasted for 70 years, the 'Cauliflowers'. As the main-line goods traffic became heavier in the present century, they were gradually moved to lighter duties, and to branches where their light axle loading enabled them to be run without restriction. At one time, the Cockermouth, Keswick and Penrith line was very much of a last stronghold of the Webb 2-4-0 passenger engines, and after they had gone, in 1932, the 'Cauliflowers' reigned in almost complete possession for another 18 years. In 1950, I had the privilege of making some footplate trips on one of the survivors, No 58396—old No 38—built in February 1900. Like the majority of those that remained for any length of time under LMS ownership, she had a Belpaire firebox and pop safety valves. That apart, she was very much a Webb engine.

At the risk of digressing too far into the twentieth century, one of these trips is well worth mention. The road is something of a terror, with 4½ miles at 1 in 68 to 1 in 62½ straight off the platform end at Threlkeld, including the sharp reverse curve when nearing Troutbeck. From Keswick to Penrith we had a load of 155 tons gross—actually four non-corridors and a van, packed to the last inch on the Saturday before August Bank Holiday; this would be roughly equal to 15 six-wheeled main-line coaches in the early days of the 'Precedents'. When I joined the driver

Above *One of the very celebrated 18-in 0-6-0 express goods engines, nicknamed the 'Cauliflowers', No 684, built at Crewe in May 1902 (H. Gordon Tidey).*

Below *One of the 'Cauliflowers' on British Railways service in 1950 at Penrith (O.S. Nock).*

and fireman at Keswick, they told me that the engine was not steaming too well, and that we might have some trouble on the bank; actually, we did quite well. From Keswick, amid the lovely scenery of the Greta gorge, on gradients stiffening from 1 in 88 to 1 in 76, we sustained 22 mph, and ran the 3.7 miles to Threlkeld in 9 min 57 sec start to stop. Pressure dropped to 130 psi during this short but heavy spell, and we got away on the 1 in 68 with the reverser in full forward gear and the regulator five-eighths open. After nearly half a mile of this terrific pounding, and with the gradient changing from 1 in 68 to 1 in 62½, the driver linked up to about 35 per cent cut-off. With pressure held at about 130-132 psi, speed rose to 21 mph, though as we mounted high on to the moorland, and looked away northwards to the great ridges of Saddleback, the grade began gradually to take its toll. The curves pulled us down to 16 mph at one point, but although pressure was now falling, the little engine fought her way back to 20 before we reached Troutbeck, though with a lengthening of the cut-off to 40 or 42 per cent pressure had dropped to 120 psi and, by the time we topped the bank, the water was 2 in down in the glass. The 4.9 miles from Threlkeld took 17 min 5 sec, start to stop, though I estimate that the engine was developing about 450 drawbar horsepower on the way up.

On the down grades into Penrith, old '38' rode very smoothly; we had a maximum speed of 46 mph between Penruddock and Blencow, but on the last stage we were checked by signal. Returning later in the day with a lighter train of about 125 tons gross ('12½ coaches' by old reckonings), pressure did not drop below 135 psi on the toilsome 1 in 70 out of Penrith, and speed was steadily held at 21 to 22 mph. Later we had quite a smart run, mostly on easy gradients, from Penruddock to Troutbeck, two miles in 5 min 13 sec start to stop, and then, down the bank, although she was restrained a little over the curving stretches, the engine elsewhere ran freely up to 57 mph, and without any suggestion of rough or wild riding. After this experience I can readily believe accounts of how, in their prime, these engines ran up to 75 mph, and some of them in much later years as well. One amusing memory of this trip is of cinders falling on my head! Starting away from Threlkeld I stood back on the tender footplate, so as to get a good view of both scenery and mileposts, when, to my consternation, I discovered I was just in the line of fire of the stuff thrown sky-high from the chimney, and which, at the slow speed we were going, came almost vertically down!

2. David Jones on the Highland

When, in September 1853, Alexander Allan resigned his position at Crewe as 'Foreman of the Locomotives' on the Northern Division of the London and North Western Railway, he became Locomotive Superintendent of the Scottish Central Railway. At that time, the Highland Railway, or rather its original constituents, were in process of formation, and Allan was consulted about a likely man to act as Locomotive Superintendent. He recommended his nephew William Barclay, and to assist him, in 1858, a young engineer named David Jones, from Manchester, went to Inverness. It soon became apparent that the sport-loving Barclay was leaving most of the work to his youthful assistant. Of course, at that time no one at Inverness had any responsibility for the design of the locomotives. That duty devolved upon Alexander Allan, and the Highland adopted various of the 'Old Crewe' designs, to which he was partial. So David Jones, as assistant, became thoroughly familiar with all the features and peculiarities of the Allan style of design, with results that benefitted the Highland Railway for more than sixty years.

It was just after he had transferred from the LNWR to the Scottish Central that Allan invented his celebrated 'Straight Link' motion. This had more working parts than the Stephenson gear, but it had the big advantage that the expansion links were straight, and were thus more readily manufactured by the equipment then available than the curved links of the Stephenson. Moreover, as will be seen from the accompanying drawing, the mechanism involved

the minimum of headroom beneath the boiler and this was thus one of the major points that commended it to F.W. Webb when he adopted it for his 'Precedent' Class 2-4-0s on the LNWR in 1874. All that, however, was many years ahead when Allan first designed his straight link gear in 1855. Like David Joy, 24 years later, Allan also read a paper before the Institution of Mechanical Engineers, in his case in 1856, accompanied by a fine working model which he presented to the Institution. Before even the date of that meeting, the straight link gear had been installed on the very first engines built for the Highland lines, and so it continued for the ten years that Barclay was in charge of the locomotive department. By that time, 55 engines were in service, all, except for four diminutive tank engines, of the Crewe type, 2-2-2s or 2-4-0s of Allan's design.

In May 1865 occurred the incident that led to the dismissal of Barclay. Although David Jones had been in the service of the railway since 1855 and was then 31 years of age, the directors felt he was too young for the job, and advertised it. Out of 30 applicants they were fortunate in choosing William Stroudley, who was on the Edinburgh and Glasgow Railway; for while a considerable number of locomotives of Allan design had been added to the stock in 1862-4, and Highland Railway finances did not permit of any new departures in design, his four-year sojourn at Inverness was invaluable in getting the stock into first rate order and providing some moral support for David Jones. When, in 1869, Stroudley secured the appoint-

Allan 'Straight Link' motion.

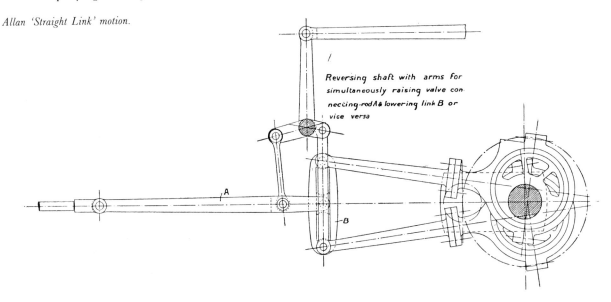

Reversing shaft with arms for simultaneously raising valve connecting-rod A & lowering link B or vice versa

ment of Locomotive Engineer to the Brighton Railway, the Highland once again advertized for a Locomotive Superintendent, and this time Jones was successful in getting the job as from 1 February 1870. In his previous assignments at Inverness, first as Foreman of Locomotives and then as assistant to Barclay, he had amassed an unrivalled familiarity with the Allan type of locomotive, and he seems to have had no reason to change his own developing practice.

In August 1870, the 'Dingwall and Skye' railway was opened throughout from Dingwall Junction to Strome Ferry. To cope with the very severe gradients, the locomotives first employed were of the small-wheeled Allan 2-4-0 type, but Jones found that it was not so much the gradients as the incessant curvature of the track that tried the locomotives almost to breaking point. The Highland main line, both north and south of Inverness, had a relatively good alignment for a mountain route, but the 'Dingwall and Skye' was another matter. In 1873, Jones took one of the earliest Allan 2-4-0s, No 10 *Westhall*, and rebuilt it with 17-in by 24-in cylinders instead of the original 16-in by 22-in, lengthened the frames and added a leading bogie. This latter was of W. Adams's design. At the time of this rebuilding, the engine was renamed *Duncraig*.

The modification of the front end of engine No 10 could be seen as the prototype of David Jones's first main-line passenger engines for the Highland, the very noteworthy '60' or 'Duke' Class. These retained

the characteristic Allan style of front-end framing, but incorporating still larger cylinders than the *Duncraig*, 18 in by 24 in, with coupled wheels of 6-ft 3-in diameter. An order for ten of the new engines was awarded to Dübs & Co, and they were delivered promptly between June and August 1874. Numbered from No 60 to 69, seven of the ten were originally named after Highland counties, though not in any south to north geographical sequence. The remaining three were named after personalities. The original tally was as follows, although in the earlier days of the company all were subsequently renamed.

60	*Bruce*	65	*Nairnshire*
61	*Sutherlandshire*	66	*Ross-shire*
62	*Perthshire*	67	*The Duke*
63	*Inverness-shire*	68	*Caithness-shire*
64	*Morayshire*	69	*The Lord Provost*

Engine No 60 was named after the Hon C.T. Bruce, Chairman of the Highland Railway Company, while No 67 was the Duke of Sutherland.

Technically, the 'Duke' Class was outstanding among later Victorian locomotive practice. Dimensionally, with cylinders of 18-in diameter and 24-in stroke, 6-ft 3-in coupled wheels and 140 psi boiler pressure, they were the most powerful passenger engines in the country at that time. But dimensions can count for nothing if other factors are not right, and in those other respects David Jones excelled. The boiler was beautifully proportioned; the Highland always bought the finest steam coal in Scotland, and the Allan straight link motion gave an admirable distribution of steam in the cylinders. The ten locomo-

One of David Jones's Class 'F' 4-4-0s introduced in 1874, but a later example built at Inverness in 1883, No 71 Clachnacuddin *(F. Moore's Rail Photos).*

tives of this class were originally used on the southern part of the main line, between Inverness and Perth, despite some of their names, and they quickly became very popular with their drivers and firemen. As traffic developed it was not surprising that more engines of the class were built, not by contractors in this instance but at the Highland Railway's own works at Lochgorm, Inverness. The seven engines built thus, with the dates of construction, were:

1876	July	4	*Ardoss*
1883	December	71	*Clachnacuddin*
1884	July	72	*Bruce*
1885	January	73	*Thurlow*
	September	74	*Beaufort*
1886	October	75	*Breadalbane*
1888	December	84	*Dochfour*

Of the above, the name that will arouse much speculation is undoubtedly *Clachnacuddin*, particularly as it was a revival of a name used on an Allan 2-2-2 of 1863, which was renamed *Kingussie* to make the name available for this new 4-4-0 in 1883. It was neither a director's estate, nor a topographical feature of the line, but a large stone by the river on which the washerwomen of Inverness rested their tubs. The Gaelic name is 'Clach na cudainn', the 'stone of the tubs'. It was, however, one of the landmarks of the burgh, and was later placed on the Exchange at the Town Hall; today it rests at the foot of the old Mercat Cross.

Names apart, a most distinctive feature of these first Jones 4-4-0s, and indeed of every other class of main-line engines that he built for the Highland Railway, was the louvred chimney. This was, in fact, a double chimney, one inside the other, and it was the outer one only that contained the louvres. These induced an air current in the annular space between, the effect of which was to carry the exhaust steam from the chimney high and clear over the cab. It is sometimes said that the purpose of this arrangement was to prevent the exhaust from drifting down and obscuring the driver's view when the engine was steaming lightly, but having regard to the height of the chimney and its relative nearness to the cab front I can hardly believe this was the real reason. Some years ago, when I read a paper to a joint meeting of the Institutions of Locomotive and Railway Signal Engineers—'Signalling from the driver's point of view'—and the question of obscuring the lookout was under discussion, a very different explanation was given! The Highland Railway ran through much forest country, and, as on many early railways, fires were caused by red-hot cinders thrown back from the locomotives. The effect of the louvres was to ensure that the exhaust was thrown as high and as vertically

as possible, with the idea that the higher the sparks were thrown the cooler they would be when they came down, thus less likely to cause damage. Even so, it was strange to see the louvred chimney used also on David Jones's pretty little 4-4-0 yard shunting tank engines used for so many years after Grouping at Inverness.

A further distinctive feature of these first Jones 4-4-0s of the Highland Railway was their colour. During the short time he was at Inverness W. Stroudley invented his celebrated 'Improved Engine Green'. As every Brighton enthusiast knows, this was not green in the ordinary sense, but a rich yellow ochre having no more than a hint of green in certain lights. No more than a few Highland engines were painted thus in Stroudley's time; but David Jones adopted it for the engines he was repairing and rebuilding at Inverness, and when the contract was awarded to Dübs & Co for the first ten engines of the '60' Class, in 1874, this style was also specified. As with the Brighton locomotives, the photographic plates of those days were not very sensitive to colour rendering, and few of the pictures of Highland engines of that period give a true impression of the brilliant spectacle they presented. Around 1885, however, Jones changed to an equally brilliant pea green, and this was specified for the series of eight 4-4-0s built by the Clyde Locomotive Co in 1886.

About the pea green livery there is a good story to be told. In addition to the 'Clyde Bogies', it was used on all the subsequent main-line engines of David Jones's design—'Straths', 'Skye Bogies', the memorable 'Jones Goods', and the 'Lochs'. When the first of the 'Big Goods' was withdrawn from active service and set aside for preservation in 1934, *The Railway Magazine* commissioned a noted artist of the day, M. Secretan, to prepare a colour plate showing engine No 103 as it originally was. The result was magnificent. I was doing some work for the magazine at the time and took the earliest opportunity to call on the Editor, the inimitable Aberdonian W.A. Willox, to express my appreciation. But he pulled a wry face in response, and told me how, full of pride, they had shown the picture to David Jones's surviving daughter. She had said, 'Very nice, but it's the wrong colour!' Shamefully they tried to press her for what the true colour was; but she would not be drawn. The episode remained behind the portals of 33 Tothill Street until some years later, when it transpired that the 'grape-vine' had borne some fruit.

Another of Willox's friends who had been let into the guilty secret was that most erudite of engineering historians, John Nevil Maskelyne, then Editor of *The Model Engineer*. When the engine was painted yellow in 1959 and caused consternation among older enthusiasts, who all believed that Stroudley's 'green'

One of the celebrated 'Skye Bogies', No 32, used for the line to the Kyle of Lochalsh (F. Moore's Rail Photos).

had been banished from the Highland Railway some years before the 'Big Goods' were built, he unearthed from his personal archives a large photograph of No 103 taken from the signal box at Stanley Junction on the occasion when the Highland was taking delivery of her as a brand new engine. It is believed that Nos 103 and 104 and possibly No 105 were delivered in yellow, after which the pea green colour was resumed. Maskelyne commented at the time: 'Yellow is a non-actinic colour from the photographic point of view, and none but what were known in the 1890s as 'authochromatic' plates (or films) were even faintly sensitive to it; but those 'auto' plates were fairly sensitive to green.' On this basis it seems safe to assume than when No 103 had her photograph taken at Stanley Junction on that Sunday morning in 1894 she was *not* painted pea green; in monochrome, that colour would have come out a lighter tone than is seen in the photograph.

Returning to the history of the Jones locomotives, in chronological order and following the first of the Lochgorm-built series of the '60' Class, No 4 *Ardross*, and preceding by 18 months the next of them, the memorable *Clachnacuddin*, there was a smaller-wheeled 4-4-0, a development of the two early Allan 2-4-0s that Jones had rebuilt with leading bogies, Nos 7 and 10. The new engine, No 70, was considerably more powerful than the rebuilds, having 18-in by 24-in cylinders and 150 psi boiler pressure. No 70 was actually the first of the celebrated 'Skye Bogies', and though built at Lochgorm Works, Inverness, in May

1882, it was not until ten years later that further engines of the class were built. By that time, the remaining examples of the Lochgorm series of Class '60', the eight 'Clyde Bogies', and the 12 more powerful 'Straths' were at work. Before dealing with these latter, however, it will be convenient to refer in more detail to those wonderful little engines, the 'Skye Bogies'.

It was in June 1893 that the extension of the 'Dingwall and Skye' line, from Strome Ferry to the Kyle of Lochalsh was authorized, and in anticipation of increased traffic, and even more because of the continuous and exceedingly severe curvature of the extension line, more bogie engines were needed. Four additional 'Skye Bogies' were built at Lochgorm Works from 1892 to 1895, numbered 85 to 88, and, like the original engine of the class, were unnamed. It was at about that time that Jones had a serious accident while riding on the footplate, so serious indeed that the resulting disability led to his resignation. He was succeeded by Peter Drummond, who, while immediately making plans for new locomotives in his own family tradition, added another four 'Skye Bogies'. He altered the design by eliminating the double chimney with the distinctive louvres and dispensing with the compensated springing of the driving wheels. I take leave to doubt, however, if these relatively small changes in design resulted in a 30 per cent reduction in the cost of the engine as has been claimed by a writer in a book published about ten years ago! As far as I know there was little difference, if any, between the working of the original five of these engines and those built by Peter Drummond. The performance was uniformly excellent.

The last engine of the class, built at Lochgorm Works as late as December 1901, had a strange episode in its early career. It was in 1903 that a long legal battle with the North British over the ill-starred Invergarry and Fort Augustus Railway ended with an agreement that the line should be worked by the Highland Railway. In North British hands, this offshoot of the West Highland could have been a dagger pointed straight towards Inverness, but actually it was such an unremunerative proposition as to be a millstone round anyone's neck, rather than an asset. Anyway, by the agreement of 1902, confirmed by an Act of 1903, the Highland opened the train service, and Peter Drummond sent one of the Class 'P' 'Yankee' 4-4-0 tanks, No 52, to run the line. Later she was replaced by this last of the 'Skye Bogies', No 48. I have often wondered how those Highland engines were transferred from their own system to the Invergarry and Fort Augustus line. The shortest rail route would have been via Perth, Crieff, Balquhidder and the Callander and Oban line to Crianlarich, and then up the West Highland of the North British to Spean Bridge, a total mileage for an engine based at Inverness of 229 before it could do any revenue earning on the Invergarry and Fort Augustus line itself. The thought occurs to me that it might have been cheaper to transfer them by barge along the length of Loch Ness, because it is only 28 miles from Inverness to Fort Augustus.

Apart from this brief excursion to foreign parts on behalf of one of its members, the 'Skye Bogies' remained on the Kyle road for almost all their lives. When I first visited the Highland line in 1927, however, some of them had been withdrawn and replaced on the hardest duties by the Cumming 4-6-0 goods engines. But one day, when I was with my parents motoring west of Garve and it was about time for the midday train up from the Kyle, I persuaded them to wait a while at a good photographic spot above Loch Luichart. To my delight, when the train came pounding up the bank, it was hauled by a 'Skye Bogie', No 14284 (old No 7). At that time it was usual for the engine that had worked up from the Kyle to pilot the 3.45 pm up mail from Inverness up to the Slochd summit; and I saw both Jones and Cumming goods 4-6-0s thus engaged. I have often wondered if that resplendent red 'Skye Bogie' that I photographed was so used that day. She would have made a brave sight piloting a 'Castle' or a 'Clan'.

The 'Clyde Bogies', built in Glasgow in 1886 and numbered from 76 to 83, were no more than a detailed development of Jones's '60' Class. The working pressure was advanced to 160 psi, and the grate area was enlarged to 18.83 sq ft from 16.2 sq ft; but the external feature that distinguished them from the earlier engines, indeed from those built at the Loch-gorm Works only a year earlier, was the two-ring boiler barrel, instead of three, which resulted in the dome being set back towards the cab to a noticeable degree compared to the position it occupied on the older engines. The 'Clyde Bogies' were named as follows:

76	*Bruce*	80	*Stafford*
77	*Lovat*	81	*Colville*
78	*Lochalsh*	82	*Fife*
79	*Atholl*	83	*Cadboll*

Like the earlier 4-4-0s, they proved excellent and long-lived engines, remaining in main-line traffic, on piloting duties, until 1923. One of them, No 82, survived to acquire an LMS number 14278 and be painted Midland red. It had been renamed *Durn* in 1900, but yielded up that name in 1917 to one of the new Cumming superheater 4-4-0s. It survived on the Fochabers branch until 1930.

The next Jones development, and the last survival of the Allan style of front-end framing on the Highland, was seen in the 'Strath' Class of 1892. These characteristically handsome 4-4-0s had the same machinery and chassis as the 'Clyde Bogies' but slightly larger boilers, with a combined total heating surface of 1,242 sq ft, against 1,140 sq ft. All 12 engines of the class were built in the early summer of 1892 by Neilson & Co. There was some exchanging of names in the first few weeks of the engines' existence, but apart from the case of No 90, which for the first five years of its life was named *Tweeddale*, the rest were:

89	*Sir George*	95	*Strathcarron*
90	*Grandtully*	96	*Glentilt*
91	*Strathspey*	97	*Glenmore*
92	*Strathdearn*	98	*Glentruim*
93	*Strathnairn*	99	*Glentromie*
94	*Strathtay*	100	*Glenbruar*

Engine No 89 was named after Sir George Macpherson-Grant, of Ballindalloch Castle, who was in 1892 Deputy Chairman of the Company.

The 'Straths', like all David Jones's engines, were very popular with the footplate men. They steamed freely, and had an excellent turn of speed. Naturally, the Allan link motion had been retained, and the good distribution of steam made them economical despite the hard work they had to perform. They replaced the '60' Class and the 'Clyde Bogies' on the south main line between Inverness and Perth, though naturally a number of the older engines had to be retained for banking duties, from Blair Atholl up to the County March and from Forres up to Dava Moor. In later years, when six-coupled engines had become the principal motive power on the south main line,

Right *A 'Skye Bogie' in Midland red, No 14284, on the up morning mail train from Kyle of Lochalsh near Lochluichart* (O.S. Nock).

Below *One of the 'Clyde Bogies' built by the Clyde Locomotive Works in 1886, No 76* Bruce, *seen here as one of the bank engine pilots at Blair Atholl with tender cab for working tender first* (Author's Collection).

Bottom *'Strath' Class 4-4-0 No 93* Strathnairn, *built by Neilson & Co in 1892* (F. Moore's Rail Photos).

One of the Jones goods engines of 1894, the first 4-6-0s ever to be built in Great Britain. Engine No 108 is seen here on a northbound goods train at Blair Atholl (Author's Collection).

A train of locomotive coal for Inverness approaching Stanley Junction hauled by Jones Goods 4-6-0 No 109 (Author's Collection).

The original Jones Goods No 103 as preserved in working order and painted in the original yellow livery, at Stranraer in 1963 (Derek Cross).

five of the 'Straths' were themselves stationed at Blair Atholl, and another four at Forres for this same duty. In the last years of the Highland Railway, of the rest of the class one was at Helmsdale and the other two at Wick. It was noteworthy that at that time the 'Straths' were still the most powerful engines stationed in these northern fastnesses. The other 4-4-0s were one 'Clyde Bogie', No 83 *Cadboll*, at Wick, and one other of the same class, No 79 *Atholl*, at Thurso, and that was all! By that time, of course, the new Cumming superheater 4-4-0s *Snaigow* and *Durn* were regularly working the mail trains throughout between Inverness and Wick, and both engines were shedded at Inverness.

After the 'Straths', the next Jones design, the 'Big Goods' of 1894, was instantly, and in retrospect, one of the most remarkable in British locomotive history. In sheer size, as the first ever 4-6-0, it took the breath away from those who first saw it emerge from Sharp, Stewarts Works in Glasgow. Dimensionally, with 20-in by 26-in cylinders, 5-ft 3-in coupled wheels, and a boiler working first at 170 and then at 175 psi, it had by far the highest nominal tractive effort of any main-line passenger or mixed traffic engine then running in the country, namely 24,850 lb. Although termed 'Big Goods', they came to take an important share of the heavy summer tourist traffic before the introduction of the 'Castle' Class 4-6-0s. The boiler was a large one, of 4-ft 7-in diameter, with the barrel 13 ft 9 in long, having 211 tubes of 2-in diameter, and providing 1,559 sq ft of heating surface, to which was added 113.5 sq ft in the firebox. The grate area was 22.5 sq ft, with the forward part inclined and the rear part horizontal. The large size of the cylinders precluded the use of the traditional Allan style of front-end framing, but the Allan straight link motion was retained with beneficial results to the performance.

In view of the many innovations incorporated in the design of these engines, even size alone, it might have seemed venturesome in the extreme for the Highland Railway to have placed a first order for no less than fifteen engines with Sharp, Stewart & Co in February 1894—fifteen! And the astonishing thing was that, despite everything, there were no teething troubles at all. The huge new engines rolled off the production line like modern automobiles, five in September 1894, seven in October, and the last three in November. The Highland enginemen, used to nothing larger than 2-4-0s and 4-4-0s, were inclined to look askance at these very long engines; but they soon took the measure of them and found that, despite their smaller wheels, the Allan valve gear made them so free running that they could run up to 60 mph and more with passenger trains. They had been fitted with the vacuum automatic brake from the outset.

By the time the summer season of 1895 was approaching, the 4-6-0 engines were able to be used to take an important share in the heavy tourist traffic on the south main line. By their use, double heading that had been needed throughout from Perth to Aviemore was limited purely to banking assistance from Blair Atholl to the County March summit. It was the same with the southbound autumnal rush from Forres up to and over the summit on Dava Moor. When I first visited the Highland line, in 1927, I was interested to see one or two of the 'Jones Goods' 4-6-0s still in their old green livery, though by that time precious little of the 'green' was left in it. It was, however, common knowledge on the railways of Scotland that engines painted with the care and diligence of Lochgorm Works lasted a very long time. When I photographed 4-6-0 No 113 on a southbound goods at Culloden Moor in September of that year, she was going well with no steam escaping from her glands. When I returned south by the 3.45 pm mail from Inverness, another 'Jones Goods', the engine that had come up from the Kyle earlier was our pilot up to the Slochd. This happened to be the pioneer of the class, which is now preserved. By that time, this engine, old No 103, had been repainted LMS black and renumbered 17916. She made a fine sight double-heading *Brahan Castle*; and with a gross load of 345 tons, they took 49¾ minutes to reach the summit. On the longest stretch of 1 in 60, between Culloden Moor and Daviot, the lowest speed was 22 mph.

The 'Jones Goods' 4-6-0s were long-lived engines. All 15 survived their 35 to 40 years of existence without being rebuilt further than having their louvred chimneys replaced by the Drummond type, and having the smokebox wing plates removed. Even so, not all of the class had their louvred chimneys replaced. Engines 105, 106, 108, 109 and 115 retained the original type to the end, and the others were not altered till after 1930, doubtless because the original ones were wearing out. Apart from No 103, which as LMS No 17916 was withdrawn for preservation in July 1934, the remaining 14 engines of the class were withdrawn as follows:

Engine No	Year Scrapped
104/17917	1939
105/17918	1933
106/17919	1934
107/17920	1932
108/17921	1930
109/17922	1929
110/17923	1935
111/17924	1934
112/17925	1940
113/17926	1939
114/17927	1936

The largest Jones express passenger engine: 'Loch' Class No 133 Loch Laoghal, built by Dübs & Co 1896, seen on the turntable at Inverness (F. Moore's Rail Photos).

No 132 Loch Naver *on a northbound express on the Caledonian line near Luncarty (Author's Collection).*

After the grouping : 'Loch' Class No 14392 Loch Naver, *having been renumbered and painted in Midland red, leaving Perth (Author's Collection).*

Engine No	Year Scrapped
115/17928	1933
116/17929	1936
117/17930	1939

The 'Jones Goods' 4-6-0s were the progenitors of the equally distinguished 'Castle' Class express passenger 4-6-0s; but although these were undoubtedly the conception of David Jones, as they were not built until four years after he resigned, they are dealt with in a later chapter of this book.

Jones's last design, the 4-4-0s of the 'Loch' Class, was a logical development of his earlier engines, though considerably more powerful. As with the 'Big Goods' 4-6-0s, the Allan type of front-end framing was not used. With 19-in diameter cylinders, and a boiler pressure of 175 psi, they, like their predecessors of 1874, ranked among the most powerful British passenger engines of the day. They were superb engines in traffic. All 15 of them were built by Dübs & Co in a single batch between July and September 1896, though three more were built as a wartime emergency at the end of 1916, to identical drawings. In the ordinary way, the main batch of 1896 would have been the last Highland engines to have the special louvre chimney which was discontinued by Peter Drummond; but the wartime engines were needed in such a hurry that there was apparently no time to amend the drawings. The original 15 'Lochs' were as follows:

119	*Loch Insh*	127	*Loch Garry*
120	*Loch Ness*	128	*Loch Luichart*
121	*Loch Ericht*	129	*Loch Maree*
122	*Loch Moy*	130	*Loch Fannich*
123	*Loch An Dorb*	131	*Loch Shin*
124	*Loch Laggan*	132	*Loch Naver*
125	*Loch Tay*	133	*Loch Laoghal*
126	*Loch Tummel*		

While some of the names might perplex a traveller not familiar with the intricacies of Highland top-ography, the majority were well known, even though lochs Insh and Garry, passed on the main line, would not be readily identifiable by some, and Laggan, An Dorb, Maree and Naver, while lying some distance from any part of the main line, are sufficiently well known in themselves. The real tongue-twister, however, was the name of engine No 133. This was one Gaelic version of the Norse name for a law hill, 'laga-fjall'; the phonetic pronunciation is 'loyal', and this is the name usually printed on maps, and in guide books. The name is also used for the fine 'Ben' that overlooks the loch; and when, in Peter Drummond's time, the Highland Railway added a series of 'Bens' to their locomotive stud, they chose the easy way out and named engine No 15 *Ben Loyal*. Incidentally, in browsing through some nineteenth-century Scottish guides, I was amused to find the mountain rendered as 'Ben Royal'! But this was nothing to what the painters at Kilmarnock did to poor old 133 when it was decked in LMS red after Grouping; as No 14393, the name was rendered *Loch Laochal*!

The three engines built during the war were also named, the first after the small loch of the same name alongside the Dingwall and Skye line just before reaching Garve station, but the other two, *Ashie* and *Ruthven*, were little-known lakes scarcely more than a mile long, in each case in the hills east of the Great Glen, both of them barely ten miles from Inverness. It so happens, however, that I have stirring memories of two out of the three 1916 'Lochs' from my first visit to the Highland line 11 years later. One afternoon, when I was photographing near Daviot, the 'Royal Highlander' came up in great style hauled by *Loch Ruthven* as pilot to *Gordon Castle*, both engines then in Midland red; then, on a visit to Kyle of Lochalsh, having travelled from Inverness behind a Cumming goods 4-6-0, I left the family at the waterside, went exploring, and found *Loch Garve* in the rock-girt locomotive yard so supremely turned out that she might have been decked for the Royal Train! Treasure trove indeed.

3. Lancashire and Yorkshire: the creation and development of Horwich

In mid-Victorian times, the Lancashire and Yorkshire was rather a 'hotchpotch' of a railway. In his famous series of articles in *The Railway Magazine* on 'Locomotive and Train Working in the latter part of the Nineteenth Century', E.L. Ahrons had many humorous passages about its shortcomings in its early days, and being a Bradfordian at the tail-end of one of its inconceivably awkward track layouts, he was in a good position to judge! The railway assumed its familiar name in 1846 when a number of smaller lines were amalgamated with the Manchester and Leeds; but the consummation of the mid-Victorian 'hotchpotch' came in 1859 with the absorption of the East Lancashire Railway. Then the amalgamated 'Lancashire and Yorkshire Railway' became possessed of two works, neither of them very well laid out or efficient, at Miles Platting and Bury, a swarm of small running sheds, and an unbelievable assortment of ageing and effete locomotives. To add to this, the track layouts at the key points on the line had clearly been laid out with no conception as to the way the traffic would very soon develop. So, added to the bad running of the ineffective locomotives was congestion at many busy junctions.

The appointment of W. Barton Wright as Locomotive Superintendent in 1875 certainly began to get

A Barton Wright 4-4-0 engine built in 1880 by Sharp, Stewart & Co; note the four-wheeled tender (Author's Collection).

some order into the department, and plans for a range of standard designs were formulated. But for some years, the locomotive department, from end to end of the line, was starved of capital investment; and although the dividend on the ordinary shares had not dropped below 5 per cent in 1882 from the peak of 9 per cent in 1872, there was general dissatisfaction among the shareholders, and in 1883 a resolution was passed that the newly appointed Chairman should be a full-time Chief Executive. The gentleman in question was John Pearson, a colliery owner, who very quickly set to work to tie up the commercial and financial side of the railway, but needed guidance in the realms of engineering. Fortunately, there was near at hand an engineer of renown, namely John Ramsbottom. He had retired in poor health, at the relatively early age of 57 years, from the well-nigh Herculean task of putting the great Works at Crewe into good order after the somewhat leisurely management of Francis Trevithick. But the 12 years of virtual retirement in his beautiful home at Alderley Edge in the Cheshire countryside had worked wonders with his health, and at 69 he was once again bursting with energy. So, when the Chairman of the Lancashire and Yorkshire Railway approached him and asked him to accept a year's appointment as 'Consulting Engineer in matters relating to the Locomotive Department', he jumped at the opportunity.

From the outset he got on well with Barton Wright.

Together they toured the whole line, visiting not only the two Works but every single running shed, however remote. He studied and whole-heartedly approved Wright's proposals for four or five standard designs of locomotive to replace the numerous old and ineffective units that had up till then been relied upon, but most important of all, in a report submitted to the Board in February 1884, he recommended the establishment of a central works at which the repair of all the locomotives on the line could be efficiently done, instead of having patched up jobs as well as the local fitters could contrive with the facilities available. The Board accepted his report, and a virgin site, then in open country a mile north-eastwards off the main line from Bolton to Chorley, at Horwich, was purchased, and preparations made for a miniature version of Crewe. Even today, the Locomotive Works is still bounded by open country on its southern side, while on its first establishment a branch line had been built to connect the works and the town that grew up alongside to a triangle junction with the main line at Blackrod. Horwich was then a village with a population of barely 4,000 people, but Ramsbottom's experience at Crewe now became invaluable, not only in his advice as to the works layout but equally in respect of possible civic developments. By then, having completed two years as Consulting Engineer, he was appointed to the Board, and took over the Chairmanship of the Rolling Stock and the Locomotive Workshops Committees.

By the spring of 1886, the new era of the Locomotive Department was getting well into its stride. New standard locomotive designs, 4-4-0, 0-6-0 and 0-4-4 tanks, had been prepared and contracts placed with outside builders, while under Ramsbottom's guidance large orders had been awarded to suppliers of machinery for the Works at Horwich. Then, when all was apparently going so well, Barton Wright received a very tempting offer to return to India, whence he had come previous to his present appointment. When money was concerned, the hard-headed directors of the LYR were not men to dissuade anyone from a big promotion, and indeed, while advertising for a successor, they gave Barton Wright a handsome gratuity to cover any expenses he was likely to incur while finishing off any projects then uncompleted. As to a successor, Ramsbottom, as the director mainly responsible for the appointment, naturally consulted Webb at Crewe. Among various applicants for the job, John A.F. Aspinall, the Locomotive Superintendent of the Great Southern and Western Railway of Ireland, was soon on the short list. Eleven years earlier, Webb had recommended him, although then no more than 23½ years of age, to be assistant to Alexander McDonnell at Inchicore, and when that engineer left to go to the North Eastern at Gateshead,

Aspinall was his natural successor. He was then 31 years of age and had already made his mark, albeit as an assistant, on Irish locomotive practice. But Aspinall was a Lancastrian by birth and instincts, and the chance of getting back was more than he could resist, particularly as the vacant post on the LYR held out considerably more in professional status than that then offered to locomotive engineers in Great Britain and Ireland; for in June 1886, the Board resolved to advertise for a 'Chief Mechanical Engineer'. As far as I can trace, Webb was the only other British or Irish railwayman to have that title at the time. Aspinall was appointed at the very next Board meeting on 14 July.

At that time, delivery was still being taken of Barton Wright's new standard 4-4-0s, which had 17½-in by 26-in cylinders, 6-ft 0-in coupled wheels, and a boiler pressure of 140 psi. From 1880, successive batches had been built by Sharp, Stewart & Co, Neilson & Co, Kitsons, and finally by the Vulcan Foundry, by which time, 1887, there were 110 engines in the class. The last 16, which were built after Aspinall had taken over, had boilers carrying a pressure of 160 psi, and the American type of swing-link bogie. The Lancashire and Yorkshire Railway at the time when Aspinall joined it could not be called an express line in any sense of the word. The original trans-Pennine route was direct enough and had no serious gradients once the immediate exit from Manchester had been surmounted. But the trains were timed very slowly and punctuality was not good. West of Manchester, the line to Liverpool was carried via Bolton and Wigan, and the inter-city service was virtually non-existent—nothing to compete with the excellent hourly service of fast trains by both the London and North Western and the Cheshire Lines. The LYR trains to the coastal towns of Blackpool and Southport were also very slow. In these conditions, passenger engines with coupled wheels of no more than 6-ft diameter were adequate.

Aspinall was quite satisfied with the way his predecessor's engines were doing the job, even though there was not the dash and determination about the running that he was used to in Ireland. That was to come later on the Lancashire and Yorkshire. His major task was to get Horwich Works going, and organize the repair of locomotives on a fully efficient basis. In the meantime, he was pleased with the way the drawing office staff had settled down in their new surroundings, under the newly appointed Chief Draughtsman, Zachariah Tetlow. This was a good augury for future progress. There was, however, an important question to be answered on valve gears. One batch of the standard Barton Wright 4-4-0s built by Neilson & Co was fitted with Joy radial valve gear. Aspinall had been very interested in this gear since it was taken up so enthusiastically by his old mentor at Crewe, F.W. Webb; and once on to the Lancashire and Yorkshire, he instituted a methodical examination of the performance of those Neilson-built Joy 4-4-0s, in comparison with the others from the same builder which had the ordinary link motion. He found that whereas the latter engines ran an average of 51,319 miles between works repairs, the Joys ran 62,344 miles. To what extent the design of those Neilson 4-4-0s was changed otherwise I cannot say.

The overriding advantage of the Joy valve gear, as discussed in Chapter 1 of this book in respect of the Webb 18-inch express goods 0-6-0s of the London and North Western Railway, was that with the absence of eccentrics it was possible to get in larger bearing surfaces for the driving axles. Aspinall himself, explaining why he came to choose the Joy as his future standard, said: 'I do not think that it is better than the ordinary link motion, but with the former it is possible to get in much larger axle-boxes and bearing surfaces.' From this decision, the Joy valve gear became standard on the Lancashire and Yorkshire Railway, even on George Hughes's massive, but not very successful, four-cylinder 4-6-0s of 1908. Aspinall did not follow Crewe to the extent of adding a central bearing on the driving axle. When the gear was to be standardized on the LYR, Joy had a telling note in his diary for 30 September 1887: 'To Horwich, where I had a fearful go at a bargain with J.A.F. Aspinall. I could never hold my own at a bargain!'

The first class of locomotives to be built new at Horwich can be reckoned one of the most successful of all Aspinall's achievements in engine design; it was, of course, the 2-4-2 radial tank of which the pioneer, one of a batch of ten, steamed out of the erecting shop on 20 February 1889. It was Horwich's No 1 engine, but it carried the running number 1008. The design was interesting in its great simplicity. At that time in British locomotive history, opinion seemed more or less evenly divided as to the relative merits of the 2-4-2 against the 0-4-4 type for short-distance passenger working, with the bias tending to shift slightly in favour of the 0-4-4. Aspinall had already had experience of the latter on the Great Southern and Western in Ireland, while Barton Wright had plenty of them on the Lancashire and Yorkshire. Aspinall had a marked dislike of unguided driving wheels, despite Stroudley's famous advocacy of them, even for express passenger engines; but before making up his mind to use the 2-4-2, he consulted some of his fellow Locomotive Superintendents. Webb, of course, was all for the 2-4-2, having already made good use of his own radial axle-box on several types of engine. But apparently what convinced Aspinall most of all was the opinion of James Holden on the Great Eastern who gave a glowing account of what the Worsdell 2-4-2s were doing on the Liverpool Street suburban service.

So Aspinall put Tetlow and his draughtsmen to work on a 2-4-2 tank, to have Webb's radial axle-boxes fore and aft, Joy's valve gear, and, although carrying the same sized cylinders as Barton Wright's 0-4-4s, the boiler and firebox were larger and worked at a higher pressure, 160 against 140 psi. The boiler itself was to be an Aspinall standard used alike on his new 0-6-0 goods and later on his 7-ft 3-in express passenger 4-4-0s. It is interesting to set down the relative basic dimensions of the three 2-4-2 tank designs that may have influenced Aspinall in making his decision. All four designs used the Joy valve gear.

The first Aspinall 2-4-2 type tank engine No 1008, and the first locomotive to be built at Horwich, February 1889 (British Railways).

Date introduced	Railway	Coupled wheel diameter (ft in)		Cylinders diameter × stroke (in)	Boiler pressure (psi)
1884	Great Eastern	5	4	18 × 24	140
1886	North Eastern	5	7	18 × 24	160
1889	Manchester, Sheffield and Lincolnshire	5	7	18 × 24	160
1889	Lancashire and Yorkshire	5	8	18 × 26	160

Aspinall used a larger boiler and firebox than any of the others, having a total heating surface of 1,216 sq ft and a grate area of 18¾ sq. ft. Notable also was the point that when Webb himself built 5-ft 6-in 2-4-2 tank engines from 1890 onwards, they were less powerful than Aspinall's, having 18-in by 24-in cylinders, the same as those of the non-LYR designs included in the above table.

Horwich built a first batch of ten of the 2-4-2 tanks in 1889. An interesting story of their first introduction was told by Aspinall himself in 1910, when he was President of the Institution of Mechanical Engineers. The occasion was his taking of the Chair for a paper by his next-but-one successor at Horwich, George Hughes, on 'Compounding and Superheating in Horwich Locomotives'. Aspinall was winding up, from the Chair, and said 'that one thing which struck him with regard to the Paper the author had read was that it became very necessary for the kind of experiment, to which reference had been made, to be spread over a much larger area if average reliable results were to be obtained. In connection with another branch of the subject, he would say that many years ago, about 1887, he built ten radial tank-engines for working local traffic in a certain district in Lancashire, and they were sent to take the place of ordinary tender-engines in the same district. There was nothing special about their construction; they were plain, simple, straightforward engines, with no patented appliances upon them, or anything else that could be said to be novel. After a while he inquired how they were doing their work and was informed that they were saving 7 lb of coal to the mile. At first he did not believe it, but after going to the district and investigating the subject he found the statement was perfectly true. If those engines had, for the sake of argument, been superheated engines, or compound engines, or had some particular device on them which he thought would prove of an extremely economical character, he would in all probability have said 'What a wonderful result has been obtained by this new method'; but that incident had taught him the lesson that he was now always extremely sceptical about results.'

The new engines, indeed, went into traffic with next to no teething troubles, and they met with general acclaim from the traffic department. At the time, of course, the locomotive running was wholly within the jurisdiction of the Chief Mechanical Engineer, and surveying the line as a whole, with its many branches, Aspinall became convinced that other than the relatively few longer-distance trains, as from Manchester to the Yorkshire towns, and the important services that carried the Manchester businessmen to their seaside residences on the Fylde coast and to Southport, he could run the entire passenger traffic of the railway with his new 2-4-2 tank engines. Multiplication of the class started in earnest in 1890, with twenty more built; and from 1892 to 1898, the yearly output of this one class alone was 40, 20, 20, 40, 20 and 40 engines, all to exactly the same drawings. In only one year of this period was production halted, namely 1894. By the end of 1898 there were 210 of the class at work, and their activities and their attributes had spread to almost every shed on the line.

This was not all. By the year 1898, Aspinall had envisaged the use of these engines on longer-distance residential trains, and before the end of that same year construction had started on further batches of these engines with increased water-carrying capacity. The water tanks of the first 210 carried 1,340 gallons; the later engines carried 1,540 gallons. From the outset, however, all Aspinall's 2-4-2 tank engines had water pick-up apparatus. He had patented a scoop including a two-way pick-up to enable tank engines to replenish their tanks in both directions of running. This patent was dated 1888, before the first 2-4-2 tank engine was completed at Horwich, and all engines of the class were so equipped. The Lancashire and Yorkshire Railway, despite its gradients, was, like the London and North Western, lavishly provided with water troughs. On the fastest running main line, between Manchester and Liverpool, there were sets at Walkden and Kirkby, with a further set at Hoscar for trains diverging at Hindley Junction for Southport. On the Blackpool route there were sets at Lostock Junction (north of Bolton), and near Lea Road, while a surprising provision was near Rufford, about 18 miles out of Liverpool, on the cross-country line from Walton Junction towards Blackburn and Accrington. On the main line east of Manchester, there were sets at Smithy Bridge (east of Rochdale), near Sowerby Bridge, and about a mile short of Wakefield. Aspinall seemed to be making sure his engines did not run short of water!

Construction of locomotives to the original design

A later example of the Aspinall 2-4-2 tank engine built at Horwich in 1893, in service until 1930 (E. Mason).

Hughes's second development of the Aspinall standard 2-4-2 tank : No 1526, built in January 1910 (E. Mason).

Left *Aspinall's 7-ft 3-in 4-4-0 designed for the fastest express trains, first built in 1891 (Real Photo Co Ltd).*

Right *One of Aspinall's 7-ft 3-in 4-4-0s, No 455, attached to a 9-coach train for coastal services from Manchester (British Railways).*

of 1889, apart from their having enlarged water tanks, continued until February 1901, even though Aspinall had stepped up to be General Manager of the railway, and had been succeeded as Chief Mechanical Engineer by H.A. Hoy in July 1899. By February 1901, there were 260 2-4-2s at work; and from their general popularity and use over the entire Lancashire and Yorkshire Railway system, they could in every way be ranked as among the great locomotives of British railway history. In later years, 63 of the true Aspinall engines of 1889 design were rebuilt, some merely with Belpaire fireboxes, and others with superheaters, and some notes on these changes and the development of the class under George Hughes are added later. In the meantime, Aspinall might have been proud to have built, entirely in the Company's own works at Horwich, such a fleet of useful and efficient workhorses, of which 197 remained unchanged throughout their long lives. In the 1920s, my own journeys on the former L & Y line were not many; but one night in December 1927, travelling north for Christmas, I did have the experience of riding behind one of the non-superheater engines of 1895 on an express from Manchester to Preston, engine No 1275, then LMS No 10724. After mounting the adverse gradients to Bolton, she skipped along merrily with a load of 190 tons until slowing down to stop at Chorley. The maximum speed near Adlington was 54 mph.

Turning now to power for the longer-distance passenger services, when Aspinall took over, the latest 4-4-0s built to Barton Wright's design by Beyer, Peacock in 1888 were holding the fort until the construction of the deviation lines began, which by-passed Bolton and Wigan and gave a clear uninterrupted run, with no intermediate speed restrictions anywhere

between Manchester and Liverpool. The faster running thus required west of Manchester required something more attuned to high speed than the 'Peacocks', as the latest 6-ft 4-4-0s were nicknamed. Although it became the practice to detach one or two coaches for the westward run to Liverpool in keeping with the reduced passenger loading, it was no real solution. Neither was the other temporary expedient of using on these lighter trains the old Ramsbottom type 2-4-0s which the London and North Western Railway had built for the LYR at Crewe in the early 1870s before Barton Wright arrived. Aspinall was well satisfied with the general performance of the 'Peacocks', particularly with their excellent steaming boiler. So, for faster running and competitive schedules with the rival routes between Manchester and Liverpool, he planned a 4-4-0 with much larger coupled wheels and the higher boiler pressure he had used on the 2-4-2 tanks and his 0-6-0 goods engines. Actually, the boilers and fireboxes were standard between the three classes.

The first five of the new 4-4-0s, with coupled wheels of a diameter as large as 7 ft 3 in, were completed at Horwich in March and April 1891. With a similar boiler to that of the 'Peacocks', but pitched higher to clear the larger wheels, they were handsome engines, particularly in the graceful curving of the splashers over those huge driving wheels. A further 15 of the class were built at Horwich later the same year, and with their establishment a marked change in the locomotive workings began. Engine changing at Manchester on the through trains from Liverpool to the Yorkshire towns became a thing of the past. With four of the new engines allocated to Sandhills and a further three to Low Moor, these trains were

henceforth worked through by the same engine between Liverpool and Leeds. The 7-ft 3-in Aspinall 'flyers', as they were at first called, were also put on to the Manchester-Blackpool run, while, in addition to those allocated to the through Leeds to Liverpool service, a further ten engines were sent to Low Moor shed. When Professor Foxwell and Lord Farrer collaborated in writing their monumental railway statistical book *Express Trains English and Foreign* in 1884, their standard for an express train was one that maintained an average of 40 mph exclusive of stops. At that time, the Lancashire and Yorkshire, working over the original main line from Liverpool to Manchester via Bolton, could not manage more than four runs at, or above, that average, the fastest being from Manchester to York at only 41½ mph exclusive of stops—35½ mph including them.

After the direct line was opened and the Aspinall 'flyers' got into their stride, the non-stop time over the 36 miles between Liverpool and Manchester was fixed at first at 45 minutes, an average speed of 48 mph maintained by an express every hour in each direction. Some of these spurs were the opening or concluding runs of longer-distance expresses bound for Leeds, York or still further afield. Another twenty engines of the class were built at Horwich in January to April 1894, at an average of five or six a week. The newer arrivals were sent to Low Moor to reinforce the stud there, to Newton Heath, and to provide for the service between Manchester and York. Excellent though the general performance of these engines was, Aspinall was keen to study the finer points of the running, not so much in respect of power output as such, but with regard to the extraneous fac-

tors that affected train running. Using at first engine No 1112, the very comprehensive series of tests began that led eventually to his memorable paper to the Institution of Civil Engineers on 'Train Resistance' which he presented on 26 November 1901. At first, on the Manchester-Southport run, he was concerned only with engine performance; but the investigations convinced him that there were far more variables in train resistance than the 'unknowns' in the locomotives themselves, and this led him on to the very elaborate programme he set up later.

When Aspinall was in Ireland and H.A. Ivatt, also from Crewe, joined him and eventually became his chief assistant at Inchicore, a lasting friendship between their two families grew up. Furthermore, professional consultations continued after Aspinall was well established at Horwich and Ivatt had gone from Inchicore to Doncaster, after the death of Patrick Stirling. Both engineers were thinking in terms of bigger engines, and by the year 1897 both had settled for the 'Atlantic' type, rather than the 4-6-0. While Ivatt, determining upon cylinders as small as 18½ in, mounted them outside, unlike all his previous practice Aspinall built on the solid and sure foundation of his 4-4-0 'flyers', as far as the front end was concerned. Both of them, however, were constantly comparing notes on progress, and Ivatt gave serious consideration to the use of the Joy valve gear. To help him, Aspinall loaned him one of the 7-ft 3-in 4-4-0s, but as water troughs were rather sparingly used on the Great Northern main line, the visitor had to be

Aspinall 'Atlantic' No 1419, attached to a train of 6-wheeled coaches (Author's Collection).

One of the 'Atlantics', No 1394, fitted with outside bearings to the trailing wheels (Real Photo Co Ltd).

fitted with a standard Ivatt tender. At that time, the first set of water troughs out of London were those at Werrington Junction, 80 miles from King's Cross. Despite this trial, however, Ivatt was not converted to the use of the Joy valve gear.

When the actual task of building the first 'Atlantic' engines began, while Ivatt ventured on to no more than a single prototype, Aspinall placed an order with Horwich Works for no fewer than twenty; and although Ivatt had his one engine completed at Doncaster first, and thus had the distinction of building the first ever British 'Atlantic', Aspinall had the production line at Horwich tooled up for quantity building of the new mammoths—as they were dubbed by the railway press of the day. The first engine, No 1400, was steamed in February 1899, and the remaining 19 followed each other out of the erecting shop, works numbers 632 to 650, between March and October of that year. It was a remarkable record to outshop twenty engines of a new and very much larger design in eight months. The general rate of production was three per month. The remarkable thing about the introduction of so relatively novel a project was that there were almost insignificantly few of what are sometimes called 'teething troubles'. The entire twenty rolled out of the erecting shop as if it was a well-proved repeat order. It was a triumph not only for Aspinall himself but also for Tetlow and the drawing office staff and for Hoy, his Works Manager.

While the front end of the new engines was based

on the successful layout of the 7-ft 3-in 4-4-0s, certain improvements were incorporated, apart from the increase in cylinder diameter from 18 to 19 inches. The steam chests, immediately above the cylinders, were arranged to provide the free flow of exhaust steam to the blast pipe, while the Joy valve gear ensured a very accurate distribution of the steam. In later years, particularly on the London and North Western Railway in the sad years after the war, and especially after incorporation into the LMS, there was a concerted attempt by certain groups of partisans to denigrate the Joy valve gear, primarily because the drilling of a hole in the middle of the connecting rod caused fracture in one or two cases of appallingly bad maintenance; one or two cases, in more than twenty years of use by two major railways on over three thousand engines! No—the Joy valve gear still stands four square as a major cornerstone in the development of British locomotive practice. The only significant changes in design came as a result of reports about rough riding; and with this Aspinall had to seek some personal experience on the footplate before he authorized any change. Two changes were eventually made, not immediate so far as the whole class was concerned. Outside bearings on the trailing wheels were fitted on some engines by way of a trial; while the swing-link bogie, which Aspinall had inherited from his days at Inchicore from McDonnell's practice, was superseded by the Adams type, spring centred.

It was, however, the then-enormous boiler and its height above rail level that created most attention. Actually, the barrel was not nearly as long as it looked externally, because the front tube plate was some distance inside what appeared to be barrel and was

Above *Aspinall's 0-8-0 heavy goods engine, No 500, first built in April 1900 and having the same boiler as the 'Atlantics'* (British Railways).

Below *Leeds-Liverpool express near Mytholmroyd, hauled by an unidentified 'Atlantic'* (F.E. Mackay).

No 1098, one of Hughes's rebuilt superheater versions of Aspinall's standard 4-4-0 — a very successful modernization (British Railways).

3 ft 10 in in rear of the centre-line of the blast pipe. This feature can be appreciated from a study of the accompanying cross-sectional drawing of the locomotive. Even so, the boiler was very large by contemporary standards, being of 4-ft 10-in diameter, 15 ft 0 in between the tube plates, and having a Belpaire firebox with a grate area of 26 sq ft. The heating surface was 1,877 sq ft in the tubes, plus 175.8 sq ft in the firebox. The working pressure was 175 psi. As originally built, these engines had steam reversing gear; but this was the one item of equipment that the men disliked, and Aspinall, always sensitive to the feelings of the footplate, eventually took it off and substituted a hand-controlled screw gear. A further twenty of these engines were built at Horwich in 1902, three years after Aspinall had received the prestigious promotion from Chief Mechanical Engineer to General Manager of the Railway.

In view of his personal acquaintance with the locomotive engineers of the British railways and of his keen following up of the exploits of any new type, it is remarkable to find that Charles Rous-Marten virtually ignored the Lancashire and Yorkshire Railway and its engines throughout his authorship of the famous monthly feature 'British Locomotive Practice and Performance' in *The Railway Magazine*. There was plenty of interesting material for him to work on, particularly after the introduction of the 'Atlantics' and the quickening of the Manchester-Liverpool run from 45 to 40 minutes—an average speed of 54½ mph. Certainly his successor in the authorship of

those articles, R.E. Charlewood, lost no time in filling the gap, for after no more than three months after taking over, the new author published some interesting notes on the working of those fast trains. Not the least striking was the way they got away westward from Victoria Station, Manchester. The line, far from straight, includes one severe restriction through Salford station, yet the 'Atlantic' drivers used to tear away, piling on every ounce of speed before reaching the foot of the Pendlebury bank. Although that point was no more than two miles from the start, the speed often reached about 55 mph!

This, dynamically, would have been understandable with the three-coach trains often worked on these services, but it was another matter with the corridor restaurant car trains necessary on the through services between Liverpool and Newcastle. These trains were made up alternately with LYR and North Eastern Railway stock and usually loaded to about 200 tons. With one coach less, Charlewood recorded a fine run westbound from Manchester behind engine No 1399. He did not note the maximum speed before the Pendlebury bank, but it must have been well over 50 mph, for the first five miles took no more than 8¾ minutes, and speed had fallen to 37½ mph on the bank itself. At Walkden troughs, where F.E. Mackay took some memorable photographs, speed was 67 mph and it rose to 78 mph in the dip between Hindley and Pemberton. On the steep succeeding climb to Orrell Tunnel, much of it as severe as 1 in 91, speed did not fall below 40 mph. This fine running made unnecessary any exceptional speed on the racing final descent towards Liverpool, where the maximum often reached 85 mph; and nothing higher than 72 mph saw the completion of this inter-city journey, in 8 seconds inside the 40-minute schedule.

Charlewood noted a run by one of the 7-ft 3-in 4-4-0s on the same service, but with no more than three coaches, a load of 80 tons. Time was kept precisely, with the intermediate running times almost exactly the same as those of the 'Atlantic' with double the load.

My own travelling on the Lancashire and Yorkshire section of the LMS came too late for me to record any appreciable performance of these fine 'Atlantic' engines. In any case, the 40-minute schedule between Manchester and Liverpool, and vice versa, was not restored after the First World War. Before the decelerations of 1917, Lancashire and Yorkshire train timings on the non-competitive express routes were far less exacting than those between Manchester and Liverpool, and a run I had on one of the Blackpool trains in 1927 was typical of both pre-war and post-war demands on the motive power. It was an afternoon express leaving Preston at 2.59 pm and running non-stop to Salford, 30½ miles in 51 minutes. The route is certainly an awkward one, climbing steeply from its junction with the West Coast Main Line at Euxton Junction, and then having to negotiate the sharply curved link from Horwich Fork Junction to where it joins the Liverpool to Manchester main line at Dobbs Brow Junction. With a good load of 260 tons, the 'Atlantic' engine No 1411, then renumbered LMS No 10326, did well to cover this first 17.6 miles to Dobbs Brow Junction in 30¾ minutes, and could then run the rest of the journey with relatively easy steam to arrive at Salford 2 minutes early. I was sorry to learn that the engine was scrapped later that same year.

I write of the post-Aspinall era at Horwich with somewhat mixed feelings. I have referred earlier to the paper George Hughes presented to the Institution of Mechanical Engineers on 'Compounding and Superheating in Horwich Locomotives'; but the period was more lightly touched upon in the discussion following a paper read before the Institution of Locomotive Engineers in 1946, when a speaker with strong Derby affiliations said: 'At Horwich they had gone scientific; they talked in 'thous' even though their work was often to the nearest half-inch'! Hughes built a series of 2-4-2 tanks with Schmidt superheaters in 1911. They were fitted with 20½-in cylinders and larger big end bearings. But the running department rather overreached themselves with these engines, using them on main-line express trains that involved running at 60 mph and more. The result was a disaster. It happened on 21 June 1912, when one of them was working the 2.25 pm from Manchester to Leeds, booked non-stop from Rochdale to Halifax. Descending from Summit Tunnel and rounding the Charlestown curve, on which there was a permanent speed restriction to 45 mph, the train took it at an estimated 60 mph and literally 'burst the road'. The track was forced bodily out of alignment for nearly 200 yards and displaced up to 5 inches. The whole train was derailed and many lives were lost. As a result, the new superheated 2-4-2 tanks were all taken off express passenger work on the main line. This must have been a great disappointment to Hughes, because these engines were the first real success the Locomotive Department had achieved since Aspinall had left Horwich. Of the huge, ungainly Hoy 2-6-2 tanks, and the four-cylinder 4-6-0s as originally built, the less said, the better!

4. LNWR: the Webb compounds

A connoisseur browsing through long-past volumes of *The Railway Magazine* and coming in May 1915 upon one of the inimitable contributions by E.L. Ahrons on 'Locomotive and Train Working in the latter part of the Nineteenth Century' might well be wondering how a chapter on the Webb compounds could find a place in a book devoted to 'Great Locomotives of the LMS'; because the inference that could be drawn from that Ahrons article of 1915 was that those engines were very far from great. On mature reflection, however, it seems that the article in question was no more than a racy journalist exercise by a writer who was then constrained as to space. The contrast can be seen in the same author's scholarly discourse on the same subject of the Webb three-cylinder compounds in his splendid book *The British Railway Steam Locomotive from 1825 to 1925*. But it is extraordinary how the sentiments of that original article have survived, and been duly embellished by some recent scribes who appear to write for effect, rather than to have any serious thought for the subject.

But why in the first place did Webb go in for compounding in such a big way? Many of his contemporaries on British railways would not touch it; those that did mostly built one or two experimental engines, and then dropped the idea like a red-hot coal! In nineteenth-century Britain, of course, the principle of compounding had everything to commend it, theoretically. Physicists and engineers of a hundred years ago, analyzing the performance of steam engines and writing weighty treatises about it, referred to the discrepancy between the boiler pressure as registered on the pressure gauge, and the pressure on entry to the cylinders as could be recorded on an indicator diagram, when one was taken, as 'The Missing Quantity'. It was sufficiently serious for my old teacher at Imperial College, Professor W.E. Dalby, to devote nearly thirty pages of his monumental 750-page tome *Steam Power* to discussing it. He wrote: 'The range of expansion may be considerably increased without proportionately increasing the "missing quantity" if the expansion is carried out in a series of stages in separate cylinders. Or put in another way, the "missing quantity" corresponding to a given rate of expansion in a single cylinder is reduced if the expansion is carried out in stages in separate cylinders. Although losses are incurred by the transference of the steam from cylinder to cylinder in the series as expansion goes on, yet these losses are small in comparison with the gain in efficiency when the initial pressure is high.' Professor Dalby went on to describe how marine engine practice had developed to the almost universal use of triple-expansion engines for large vessels.

So far as the new LNWR engines were concerned, one is inclined to think that David Joy had quite a hand in their design. Since the introduction of the '18-inch goods' he was very much in Webb's confidence, and after his first successful meeting with him in 1879, Joy had sent a design for a two-cylinder compound, very much on the lines of that which T.W. Worsdell afterwards adopted on the North Eastern. Webb's final scheme, however, was much closer to an earlier proposal of Joy's dated 1866, when the latter had schemed out a four-cylinder compound, with the high- and low-pressure cylinders driving separate uncoupled wheels; the two pairs of wheels were of different sizes! Webb eventually produced a very neat and compact engine in No 66 *Experiment*, completed at Crewe in 1882; the boiler was of the same design as that on the 'Precedents', and a direct comparison in running costs was no doubt intended, though the boiler pressure in the Experiment was increased to 150 psi. On the trial engine, the high-pressure cylinders, outside, and driving the rear pair of 6-ft 6-in wheels, were 11½-in diameter by 24-in stroke, while the one inside cylinder was 26-in by 24-in stroke. Separate sets of Joy valve gear were used for the high- and low-pressure cylinders with independent control from the footplate. The high-pressure steam chests were underneath the cylinders, and the valves, which were of the Allan trick-ported type, dropped from their seats when steam was shut off. This feature was intended to provide for free running in 'coasting' conditions. But there was precious little else conducive to free running in these engines!

Experiment is stated to have been successful; so successful indeed that the decision was taken to build 29 more, though with larger high-pressure cylinders of 13-in diameter. Why this decision was taken defies explanation, because they seem to have been unsurpassed as sluggards. Rous-Marten, writing in 1901, said: 'It took a tremendous lot of hard flogging to get much over 50 or 55 miles an hour out of them. Anything over 60, even down the most tempting descent, was rare. I tried them with all sorts of expresses, sometimes travelling on the footplate, sometimes behind them. Setting aside one failure through a slight mishap to the machinery, I found the work consistently respectable, but never brilliant.' That flogging to get 55 mph tells its own tale, and I think there can be no doubt that the ratio of low- to high-pressure cylinder volumes was much too small. On the run, the low-pressure cylinder was not large enough to deal with the steam exhausted from the high-pressure. Unfortunately, Rous-Marten has left no details as to

Above *Webb's first and least successful three-cylinder compounds: 'Experiment' Class No 1104* Sunbeam (Author's Collection).

Below *The first of the 'Dreadnoughts' in shop grey, with Webb himself on the footplate, somewhat obscured* (British Railways).

how the engines were driven on his footplate trips, but if the relative cylinder volumes are compared with those of other famous compounds, a great difference is at once apparent:

Railway	Engine Class	Ratio of LP to HP cylinder volume
LNWR	'Experiment'	1.99
Midland	Class '4', No 1000	2.44
GWR	'La France'	2.74
NER	4-cyl 730 and 731	2.39

The above relates to the 'Experiment' Class, with 13-in high-pressure cylinders. The original No 66, with 11½-in cylinders, had a ratio of 2.55, but was so feeble in starting that something had to be done about it. With the class as a whole, it seemed that no amount of careful enginemanship could strike the right balance and get them really going. Even with No 66 *Experiment* it was usual, so Webb said in his paper, to keep the low-pressure cylinder in full gear, and to link up the high pressure so as to do the work with the least amount of steam. It was also necessary to avoid choking the receiver and the low-pressure cylinder with too much steam, though this point did not seem to be fully appreciated at the time, and Webb was assailed for trying to run with too low a receiver pressure. This may have been theoretically correct, but that sluggishness points inexorably to a restricted flow of steam somewhere; the lack of coupling rods, and consequent lack of synchronization between high- and low-pressure cylinders, has been blamed, but the same sluggishness reappeared in the four-cylinder compounds of the 'Jubilee' Class, which were coupled. It was unfortunate for the 'Experiments' that in the very year that many of them were built, there were some considerable accelerations. The down day 'Irish Mail', for example, was quickened to do Euston-Bletchley, 46.7 miles, in 59 minutes, and Bletchley-Rugby, 35.9 miles, in 44 minutes, and whereas on other accelerated trains the 'Precedents' rose most nobly to the occasion, the 'Experiments' could not, and from almost the outset of their career earned for themselves a bad name.

The full list was as follows, in order of construction:

66	Experiment	520	Express
300	Compound	311	Richard Francis Roberts
301	Economist	315	Alaska
302	Velocipede	321	Servia
303	Hydra	333	Germanic
305	Trentham	323	Britannic
306	Knowsley	353	Oregon
307	Victor	363	Aurania
519	Shooting Star	365	America
366	City of Chicago	1111	Messenger
310	Sarmatian	1115	Snake
1120	Apollo	1116	Friar
1102	Cyclops	1117	Penguin
1104	Sunbeam	374	Emperor
1113	Hecate	372	Empress

Nos 300 to 520 were built in 1883, and those from 311 onwards in 1884. Most of the names were subsequently used on 4-4-0s of the 'Precursor' Class.

However well the 'Precedents' may have risen to the occasion in 1884, larger engines were needed, and before the year was out Webb had built the first of the 'Dreadnought' Class of three-cylinder compounds. These were decidedly larger and heavier engines in every way, and from the compound point of view much more promising. The high-pressure cylinders were of 14-in diameter, and the low-pressure no less than 30-in, giving a ratio of 2.29 low-pressure to high-pressure volumes. It seems to have been realized that the sluggishness of the 'Experiments' was not due to the size of the driving wheels, and in the 'Dreadnoughts' Webb went smaller still, to 6 ft 3 in. The boiler was a very good one, with 1,242 sq ft of tube heating surface, 175 psi pressure and 20.5 sq ft of grate area. With the driving wheels still uncoupled, they played much the same tricks in starting as the 'Experiments' did, though to a lesser degree; the adhesion weight on the rear pair of drivers was greater, and in starting they were helped by the transference of weight that occurs, and which in later years made 4-6-0s so much better in starting than 'Pacifics'. Of course, this same weight transference took place with the 'Experiments', but with a lighter engine its effect was not so pronounced. Once they were on the run, the 'Dreadnoughts' had a good turn of speed; the cylinder proportions were much more favourable, and maximum speeds in excess of 70 mph were recorded with them. There was a difference in the controlling of the valve gear. Although at the time the 'Experiments' were built Webb thought it was better in the interests of simplicity to have two separate reversing gears, in the 'Dreadnoughts' he introduced a mechanism whereby the gear for both high- and low-pressure cylinders could be adjusted simultaneously or independently as the driver wished.

The first two engines of the class were completed in 1884; 18 more followed in 1885, another ten in 1886, and a final ten in 1888. The full list was as follows:

503	Dreadnought	509	Ajax
508	Titan	510	Leviathan
504	Thunderer	511	Achilles
507	Marchioness of Stafford	513	Mammoth
		515	Niagara

685	*Himalaya*	545	*Tamerlane*
2055	*Dunrobin*	659	*Rowland Hill*
2056	*Argus*	1353	*City of Edinburgh*
2057	*Euphrates*	1370	*City of Glasgow*
2058	*Medusa*	1379	*Stork*
2059	*Greyhound*	1395	*Archimedes*
2060	*Vandal*	637	*City of New York*
2061	*Harpy*	638	*City of Paris*
2062	*Herald*	639	*City of London*
2063	*Huskisson*	640	*City of Dublin*
2064	*Autocrat*	641	*City of Lichfield*
2	*City of Carlisle*	643	*Raven*
173	*City of Manchester*	644	*Vesuvius*
410	*City of Liverpool*	645	*Alchymist*
		647	*Ambassador*
437	*City of Chester*	648	*Swiftsure*

A 'Dreadnought' in the smart turn-out characteristic of all LNWR express engines, No 643 Raven *(British Railways).*

The only names that were not used on the Whale engines were *Marchioness of Stafford* and *City of New York*. An interesting change was to be noted in the speed at which these engines were built. While many of the 'Experiments' went into service at intervals of three or four days in 1884, with the 'Dreadnoughts' it was not until the batch beginning at 2055 that Crewe really got into its customary stride. Then, in December 1885, they turned out the whole 2055-2064 series. Rous-Marten recorded a number of really good runs with them, which may be summarized in the following table:

Run no	Engine name	Load (tons tare)	Route	Distance (miles)	Time (min) actual	Time (min) net	Net average speed (mph)	Time gained
1	*Raven*	190	Willesden-Rugby	77.2	85½	83	55.8	—
2	*Raven*	190	Rugby-Crewe	75.5	78¾	77	58.8	+ 8
3	*Achilles*	220	Crewe-Preston	51.0	—	59	51.8	—
4	*Achilles*	160	Preston-Carlisle	90.1	100	100	54.0	+ 5
5	*Harpy*	165	Euston-Rugby	82.6	97¾	92¾	53.5*	+ 7½
6	*Autocrat*	200	Rugby-Willesden	77.2	86½	—	53.5†	
7	*City of London*	270	Bletchley-Willesden	41.3	50	—	49.5††	
8	*Stork*	203	Crewe-Nuneaton	61.0	69	—	53.0	—
9	*Mammoth*	249	Rugby-Willesden	77.2	88	—	52.7	—

* First 81 miles covered in 88 min net   † 4 minutes early on arrival   †† On time, so no hurry from Tring

On No 4 run, Shap Summit, 58.7 miles, was passed in 69 min 22 sec and the time up from Tebay was 9 min 8 sec. On No 8 run, *Stork* climbed from Crewe to Whitmore in 15 min 50 sec. These were all very good runs, especially those of *Raven* and *Achilles*. On yet another trip, No 2 *City of Carlisle* took a load of 202 tons up Shap without assistance, averaging 30½ mph from Tebay to the top.

Ahrons records that he found the 'Dreadnoughts' variable, on occasions doing well, and on others losing small amounts of time. His timings are likely to be the more impartial of the two, since on many occasions Rous-Marten was either on the footplate, or recording for some purpose for which the driver had been given special instruction. His runs are therefore an exposition of what the engines could do rather than what they regularly did in ordinary service. At the same time, one would not take too much notice of odd minutes lost. Unless the psychological side of engine driving has changed vastly, there was probably then, as now, a proportion of men who would scrape along barely on time, and who would regard 30 seconds or a minute late in arriving as 'on time', even though their engine was easily capable of faster running. Nevertheless, although the 'Dreadnoughts' were vastly better than the 'Experiments' and could take heavy loads along, they were far from satisfactory engines. Against the theoretical soft blast of a compound, due to the more complete expansion of the steam and low back pressure, the two exhausts per revolution were more like muffled explosions, and in fire-throwing they yielded nothing to the 'Precedents'. This all goes to suggest that they were still restricted in steam flow and exhaust, and it is not surprising that their coal consumption averaged 35 to 38 lb per mile. This was heavy, even for fine running such as that in the foregoing table; but being an average, it included a good deal of less onerous work, too.

At Crewe, in March 1889, the famous 7-ft three-cylinder compound No 1301 *Teutonic* was completed. This engine had the same boiler and cylinder dimension as the 'Dreadnoughts'; but in addition to the 7-ft driving wheels, there was another very important difference from the earlier engines—Joy's valve gear for the low-pressure cylinder was discarded, and a single loose eccentric substituted. This was not incorporated at first, neither in *Teutonic* herself, nor in *Oceanic*. Originally they had the same gear as the 'Dreadnoughts', but only for a short time. This loose eccentric, which was at first included in No 1305, was mounted on the crank axle and free to turn on that axle into the correct position for either forward or backward gear. The eccentric was connected to the low-pressure valve spindle by means of a rocking lever; it was driven by a pin projecting from the side of the crank web, and engaged in a slotted plate forming part of the eccentric. The practical result of this arrangement was that the low-pressure cylinder was always worked in full gear; the port openings both for admission and exhaust remained all the time at their maximum, and it did seem that at last Crewe had realized the value of the freest possible flow of steam through the low-pressure cylinder. Both high-pressure and low-pressure valves had longer travel in full gear than in the 'Dreadnoughts'—3½ in for high pressure. In the low-pressure cylinders, the lead was increased to ½ in and a small amount of exhaust lap was provided, ostensibly to give a cushioning effect to obviate the surging action that was felt throughout the train, and which was characteristic of all the Webb three-cylinder compounds. This 'cushioning' did not appear to affect the freedom of running at

Finest of all the Webb three-cylinder compounds, the 'Teutonic' Class, exemplified by No 1312 Gaelic *(Loco Publishing Co).*

high speed, and in view of the larger port openings to the low-pressure cylinder, consequent upon the use of longer valve travel, it would indeed seem that here more than anywhere else was the place at which steam flow had been most seriously restricted in the earlier compounds. The proof seemed to lie in the speedworthiness of the 'Teutonics'. Where the 'Dreadnoughts' had touched the seventies, the 'Teutonics' worked easily into the eighties, and they pulled as well as, if not better than, the 6-ft engines.

After *Teutonic* herself came two more, in May and June 1889, that were in the nature of experiments, 1302 *Oceanic* and 1303 *Pacific*. Engine No 1302 started life with 28-in diameter low-pressure cylinders, and as such, no doubt, was a relative failure; No 1303 had a mysterious beginning as a continuous expansion engine. It was not until March 1890 that more were built, and then they were to the original dimensions,

to which 1302 and 1303 were also converted. The remaining seven engines of the class were:

1890	March	1305	*Doric*
	June	1306	*Ionic*
	June	1307	*Coptic*
	June	1309	*Adriatic*
	June	1311	*Celtic*
	June	1312	*Gaelic*
	July	1304	*Jeanie Deans*

All except No 1304 were named after liners of the White Star Atlantic fleet in connection with which the LNWR worked many special trains between Euston and Liverpool. The immortal *Jeanie Deans* was stationed at Camden from the time of her construc-

The most famous of all Webb compounds, No 1304 Jeanie Deans *of the 'Teutonic' Class (Loco Publishing Co).*

tion; all the rest were at first stationed at Crewe.

While the loose eccentric and the consequent running of the low-pressure cylinder all the time in full gear was, I feel sure, the predominating factor in the success of the 'Teutonics', these engines were just as troublesome in starting as the 'Experiments' and 'Dreadnoughts'; they had, in addition, an amusing peculiarity of their own. After an engine had backed on to its train, the loose eccentric would be in the reverse position; it could not be changed over to 'forward' until the engine had started away with the train and moved the wheels forward the few feet necessary to bring the automatic change-over mechanism into action. To ensure that exhaust steam from the high-pressure cylinders did not reach the low-pressure steam chest before the eccentric had been reversed, there was a bypass valve in the smokebox by which the driver could turn the exhaust from the high-pressure cylinders straight to the chimney. Like most smokebox valves, this one occasionally stuck, and then, if the high-pressure driving wheels spun round without moving the train at all, and the admission port to the low-pressure cylinder happened to be open, one might see the comical sight of the rear pair of driving wheels slipping in the forward direction and the leading pair slipping in the opposite. Nevertheless, the loose eccentric, coupled with the enlarged steam ports to the low-pressure cylinder, seems to me to have been the main reason for the free running of the 'Teutonics', as compared with the foregoing class, and many of the 'Dreadnoughts' had this arrangement fitted in later years. It would be interesting to know how many of the engines responsible for the good runs recorded below had the loose eccentric.

No 1304 *Jeanie Deans* worked the 2 pm 'Corridor' from Euston to Crewe, returning with the corresponding up express at 7.32 pm from Crewe, continuously from January 1891 until August 1899, except during the times she was at Crewe for general overhaul. She was a 'star' engine in every way, and

her coal consumption was less than that of the others in her class. In general, they averaged about 35 lb per mile, though *Jeanie Deans,* during the first 135,000 miles of her life, averaged only 32.4 lb. This was a vast improvement over previous Webb compounds, for the speeds were higher and the load of the 'Corridor' varied between 250 and 300 tons. Furthermore, the 'Teutonics' ran a much higher mileage between general repairs than any LNWR engines that had preceded them. Bowen Cooke quotes the figures relating to engines 1309 *Adriatic* and 1307 *Coptic* at one period as 86,579 and 88,179 respectively. This was typical of the class between 1890 and 1900. There did not seem much deterioration in their work as the time for general overhaul approached; in April 1893, No 1307 *Coptic,* having run 85,000 miles since last in the shops for repairs, was on the down 8 pm 'Tourist' express from Euston, and, with a load of 204 tons tare, made some fast running on the Trent Valley line, including an average of 73 mph over the 12¾ miles from Nuneaton to Tamworth. Shortly after the great record set up in August 1895 during the 'Race to the North', the driver and fireman who had done so well with *Hardwicke* were chosen to make an experimental run non-stop from Euston to Carlisle with engine No 1306 *Ionic.* The load was not a heavy one, amounting to no more than 151 tons tare behind the tender, but the run was successfully made at an average speed of 51 mph. Euston was left at 8.45 am, Crewe was passed at 11.50 am and Carlisle was reached at 2.38 pm—299.2 miles in 353 minutes. The standard North Western tenders of the day carried 4 tons of coal, and even if this had all been used the consumption could not much have exceeded 27 or 28 lb per mile. Probably the tender was stacked up after the fire had been lit at Camden. But even so it was a fine effort, and a fitting counterpart to Driver Ben Robinson's effort with *Hardwicke* a fortnight earlier.

So far as the ordinary performance of the 'Teutonics' was concerned, the table below gives the details of various recordings.

Run no	Engine name	Load (tons tare)	Route	Distance (miles)	Time (min)	Average speed (mph)
1	*Teutonic*	'19'	Willesden-Rugby	77.2	88¼	52.7
2	*Teutonic*	'19'	Rugby-Crewe	85.5	88¾	51.2
3	*Teutonic*	'17'	Carlisle-Preston	90.1	97	55.7
4	*Ionic*	151	Euston-Carlisle	299.1	353	51.0
5	*Adriatic*	224	Euston-Crewe	158.1	174	54.7
6	*Coptic*	207	Euston-Crewe	158.1	172¼	55.0
7	*Ionic*	220	Rugby-Crewe	75.5	82¼	55.1
8	*Gaelic*	255	Rugby-Crewe	75.5	85	53.2
9	*Jeanie Deans*	326	Nuneaton-Willesden	91.7	101¾	54.0

On No 8 run, a severe side gale made the going much heavier than it would have been otherwise, but no time was lost. Run No 3 with *Teutonic* must have been a particularly fine one, though it is naturally the performance of *Jeanie Deans* that attracts most attention. In 1901 Rous-Marten wrote: 'Over and over again I have travelled behind No 1304 on the Scottish corridor-diner, and in no case did she ever lose a minute of time either way between Euston and Crewe when I was on the train; although the absolutely smallest loads I noted were 256 and 264 tons, respectively, each on one occasion only, while in all other cases the loads equalled or exceeded 300 tons.' This is certainly a fine record, and a tribute to her two regular drivers, David Button and Jesse Brown of Camden shed. It is somewhat significant, however, that when *Jeanie* was off the job, the train had to be double-headed.

Reviewing the overall performance of the 'Teutonics', with their lower coal consumption, their ability to work really heavy trains, and the high mileages they ran between general overhaul, one feels that Webb was within a hair's breadth of securing a real triumph with these engines. All that seemed necessary was to add coupling rods, which would have eliminated all their peculiarities in starting, and probably cured the surging troubles. It seems fairly safe to add, with twentieth-century experience of high speed, that coupling rods would not have limited their maximum speed capacity. North Western locomotive history, however, includes one or two 'near misses' of this kind, and Webb's ideas were unfortunately running in a totally different direction after he had built the rest of the 'Teutonics' in 1890. In the *English Mechanic* of 2 October 1891, a correspondent using the pen name of 'Chillington' revealed 'that they have just turned out of the shops at Crewe a new locomotive of colossal size on eight wheels. The engine weighs about 60 tons, is handsome, and is, I should think, the largest tender locomotive running in

England'. Such was one of the earliest news items concerning No 2053 *Greater Britain*, which bore the date October 1891. That this engine created a first class sensation goes almost without saying; but although many onlookers were suitably impressed by the sheer size of the boiler and by the unorthodox wheel arrangement, the design as a whole now appears more as a freak than anything else, and there is no point in discussing the dimensional details.

The Engineer of 20 November 1891 referred to No 2053 as the most remarkable engine built in England for several years, and upheld the coal consumption of 73 lb per sq ft of grate area per hour as an example to American railways of the day, which, it was said, could not get below 100 lb in the haulage of heavy trains. *Greater Britain* proved a very smooth-riding engine, and, if space on the footplate was severely restricted, this feature was certainly approved by the firemen, as the distance between the shovelling plate of the tender and the firehole door was much reduced. The reason for the attenuated cab was that the overall length of the engine and tender would otherwise have exceeded the maximum that the turntables could accommodate. A second engine of the class, No 2054 *Queen Empress*, was completed in May 1893, and was sent to the Chicago Exhibition later that year. She did not go into ordinary service on the North Western itself until February 1894, and the remaining eight engines of the class were turned out in time for the summer traffic of that year. Their names and numbers were:

525	*Princess May*	767	*William Cawkwell*
526	*Scottish Chief*	772	*Richard Trevithick*
527	*Henry Bessemer*	2051	*George Findlay*
528	*Richard Moon*	2052	*Prince George*

The first of the long-boilered compounds, No 3292 Great Britain, *with Webb himself on the footplate* (British Railways).

The names were all 'double-barrelled' ones, so that one half could go on to each splasher. Of the personalities concerned, Sir George Findlay had just retired from the General Managership of the line, and William Cawkwell had been his predecessor. Sir Richard Moon had retired two years earlier, while, of course, Prince George and Princess May, after whom engines 2052 and 525 were named, became our beloved King George V and Queen Mary.

The 'Greater Britain' Class engines were normally stationed at Crewe, and worked to both Carlisle and Euston. On the crack trains it was not uncommon to change from one to another of the class at Crewe. They were fast runners, and, like the 'Teutonics', could exceed 80 mph in favourable circumstances. They fairly captured popular imagination by their vast length, though when it came to really hard slogging they did not seem anything like as good as the 'Teutonics'. When No 1304 *Jeanie Deans* was away from Camden for repairs, her place on the 'Corridor' was taken by a 'Greater Britain'; but the train was then more often than not double-headed, a thing never heard of with the 'Teutonic'. With lighter loads the big engines ran very well, but in relation to the loads hauled they were never economical.

At the time of the Diamond Jubilee, the North Western symbolized popular enthusiasm for and consciousness of the growing significance of the British Empire by the painting of its two magnificently named express engines, *Greater Britain* and *Queen Empress*, in special colours. No 2053 was decked out in Post Office red, with yellow and black lining, while No 2054 appeared in a creamy white, with brass bands around the boiler. There was a suggestion that a third engine, the 'Dreadnought' Class three-cylinder compound No 507 *Marchioness of Stafford*, was to be painted blue to complete the patriotic trio, but this latter proposal was not carried out.

The first of the 6-ft long-boilered compounds, the 'John Hick' Class, was turned out in February 1894 — that is, before the last eight of the 'Greater Britains'. This engine, No 20, was intended for the Crewe-Carlisle section, on which certain trains like the down morning mail leaving Crewe at 11.15 am had quite smart timings, and with frequent stops required rapid acceleration from rest. No 20 *John Hick* had almost a monopoly of this train for some time, and it was not until four years had elapsed that further engines of the class were built. Poor 'John Hick'! No contemporary writer seems to have had one good word to say for them. In 1915 E.L. Ahrons wrote: 'As for the "John Hicks", the less said about them the better. They had the same-sized wheels, 6 ft 3 in, as the "Dreadnoughts", all the faults of the latter, but none of their virtues. They were employed principally between Crewe and Carlisle.' And that was that! Now

it is a very strange thing that two such eminently practical locomotive engineers as George Whale and C.J. Bowen Cooke, who were, above all, running men, should have allowed the 'John Hicks' to remain the last survivors of the Webb three-cylinder express compounds. The 'Experiments', the 'Dreadnoughts', the 'Greater Britains' and the 'Teutonics' were all scrapped in Whale's time; the 'John Hicks' came last, very likely because they were the last to be constructed, but with five left at the beginning of 1910, Mr Bowen Cooke seemed in no desperate hurry to cut up the rest, and No 1505 *Richard Arkwright* survived until 1912.

It is, however, part of the mystery and fog surrounding the working of these engines that I should be writing of their decease before I have said anything of their career. Like the 'Greater Britains', they had 'double-barrelled' names, and except for No 20 were all constructed in 1898:

20	*John Hick*	1536	*Hugh Myddleton*
1505	*Richard Arkwright*	1548	*John Penn*
1512	*Henry Cort*	1549	*John Rennie*
1534	*William Froude*	1557	*Thomas Savery*
1535	*Henry Maudslay*	1559	*William Siemens*

The 1898 batch differed from No 20 and from the 'Greater Britains' in having piston valves. But a point that seems of great interest is that these engines were built after Webb had begun experimenting with the four-cylinder 4-4-0 passenger locomotives.

The only log I have been able to turn up behind one of them on a main-line job was one compiled in 1901 by the late R.E. Charlewood, on the 5.15 am from Euston between Wigan and Penrith. In his record, Mr Charlewood stated that 2 minutes of the loss was by adverse signals, though it is not

LNWR: 10.30 am, Wigan-Penrith

Engine 2-2-2-2 1505 *Richard Arkwright*
Load 190 tons tare, 205 tons full

Distance (miles)		Schedule time (min)	Actual time (m s)	Speed* (mph)
0.0	Wigan	0	0 00	
15.1	Preston	20	21 00	43.1
36.1	Lancaster	43	46 43	49.0
42.4	Carnforth	50	53 15	57.9
55.2	Oxenholme	65	68 55	49.1
62.3	Grayrigg	74	80 03	37.7
68.3	Tebay	81	86 35	55.0
73.8	Shap Summit	90	96 00	35.0
87.3	Penrith	105	110 10	—

* Averages from station to station

Left *One of the last survivors of the Webb three-cylinder compounds, No 1505 Richard Arkwright of the 'John Hick' Class, working from Shrewsbury until 1912 and, as this picture shows, still magnificently turned out (Author's Collection).*

Right *One of the Webb three-cylinder compound 0-8-0 heavy goods engines, with a 6-ft 3-in 'Whitworth' Class 2-4-0 No 404 Zopyrus 'intruding' on the right (Loco Publishing Co).*

Below right *One of the four-cylinder compound 0-8-0 heavy freight engines, No 2024 (Loco Publishing Co).*

Bottom right *Webb compounds on vital war work : a four-cylinder compound climbing Shap with a load of South Wales coal for the Grand Fleet based in Northern Scotland (F.E. Mackay).*

possible from the log to detect just where the check took place. The scheduled time uphill from Oxenholme to Grayrigg was very severe, requiring an average speed of 46 mph, but it will be seen that no time was lost between Grayrigg and Shap Summit, and, despite a reputation for rough riding, a minute was regained from Summit down to Penrith. Incidentally, the famous 2 pm 'Corridor' was scheduled at 49 minutes from Lancaster to Shap Summit until 1917, and this time was kept by the 'John Hick'.

Like some of the 'Teutonics', the 'John Hicks' eventually went to Shrewsbury, and put in a good deal of work on stopping trains over the joint line from there to Hereford. On occasions, the 'Teutonics' worked on the West to North expresses, piloted when necessary by 'Jumbos'; but by the time the 'John Hicks' arrived, sufficient of the four-cylinder compounds had been displaced from the main line by new 'Precursors' to make it unnecessary to use the 2-2-2-2s on fast trains. It is, however, very pleasing to hear eye-witnesses recall the superb condition in which these three-cylinder compounds were kept, even in their last years. Whatever the shortcomings of the 'John Hicks' and the 'Greater Britains' may have been, they were grand and imposing engines to look at, and after Webb's retirement the ignominy of a coating of grime was not added to their indifferent reputation.

It has been said that the Webb three-cylinder compounds formed one of the most spectacular 'near misses' to real greatness in British locomotive history. Certainly this was so in the case of the 'Teutonics'; but then, strangely enough, Webb seemed to begin to wander off into other fields. The huge eight-wheeled three-cylinder compounds were a curiosity

rather than a logical development, quite apart from the sudden departure from traditional Crewe valve gears and use once again of the Stephenson link motion. Then, in the year following the second 'Race to the North', in which Rugby-based engines of the 'Teutonic' Class shared the glory won by the 6-ft 6-in 'Precedents' in making record times from Euston to Carlisle, there came the disastrous smash on the Preston curve involving the very train that had taken part in the racing of the previous year. In the subsequent inquiry, it appeared that the underlying reason was not reckless engine driving but culpable running shed management at Crewe North shed, seeing that neither driver on the two 2-4-0s allocated to haul that very fast train had ever worked it previously, and neither of them had driven an express train required to pass through Preston without stopping.

Some strong views were expressed at the time, notably in a leading article in *The Engineer* questioning the continued use of engines without bogies on fast trains. Many commentators felt that despite the excessive speed, the train might have negotiated the curve safely if the engines had been bogie equipped. So far as the casualty list was concerned, the North Western on this occasion escaped its traditional ill-luck, and although the whole train was wrecked, and the coaches scattered far and wide, there was only one person killed. It can only remain a matter for conjecture as to how far the general hue and cry after bogies, following the Preston accident, had any effect upon Mr Webb; but the fact remains that the very next new design prepared at Crewe had what was termed officially a 'Double radial truck'. This, of course, was the first of the four-cylinder engines, which was completed at Crewe in June 1897. There

A 'Jubilee' Class four-cylinder compound 4-4-0, No 1929 Polyphemus (Loco Publishing Co).

are several general points about this new design which are obviously interconnected, though it is a little difficult to decide which were the primary and which were the secondary factors. If the changeover to four cylinders was indeed the primary feature, then the use of a bogie seems a natural corollary, to carry the additional weight at the front end. But in a paper read before the Institution of Civil Engineers in June 1899, Webb made a big point of getting large bearing surfaces in the 'Jubilee' engine, mentioning particularly that the use of Joy's gear and the resultant absence of eccentrics enabled him to introduce a central bearing on the driving axle. This, of course, would not have been possible with a three-cylinder engine. Then there was the layout of the valve gear, for in the new four-cylinder compound simultaneous linking up of high-pressure and low-pressure cylinders was reverted to, and a derived gear for the high-pressure cylinders introduced. In arranging this gear, Webb chose to set all the cylinders in line, and all driving on to the leading pair of coupled wheels. Thus, coupling rods were essential.

Why Webb reverted to simultaneous linking up in this engine will remain for ever a mystery. Presumably he wished to avoid four sets of valve gear, but this feature was fatal to the free running of the engines, particularly as it was associated with a low-pressure cylinder volume less than that of the 'Teutonics', despite the larger high-pressure cylinders. The ratio of low-pressure to high-pressure volume in the latter engines was 2.3 to 1, against 1.69 to 1 in the *Black Prince*. The linking up of the low-pressure valves would result in restricted port openings at speed, and reintroduce the serious restriction which had been

successfully overcome in the later three-cylinder compounds by use of loose eccentric gear. Low-pressure cylinders of 20½-in diameter as used on later engines of the class were, no doubt, the largest that could be got in, while keeping the central bearing on the driving axle, but even this increase did not bring the low-pressure to high-pressure volume ratio up to more than 1.87 to 1. But there is no point in discussing further the details of the four-cylinder compounds. In their original state they were very far from being 'great locomotives'. May I close this chapter instead by referring again to those fascinating 'near misses', the 'Teutonics'.

In his celebrated book *British Locomotives*, written in 1893 when he was Outdoor Assistant in the LNWR Locomotive Department and based at Rugby, C.J. Bowen Cooke described some fast runs that had been made recently by those engines. One of these, by engine No 1307 *Coptic*, involved hauling a train of 201 tons tare over a stretch of 12¾ virtually level miles at an average speed of 73 mph, while engine No 1309 *Adriatic*, working a somewhat lighter train of 170 tons, must have reached nearly 90 mph on the very gradual descent from Whitmore towards Stafford, because the average speed between Standon Bridge and Norton Bridge was 87 mph. But perhaps an even more impressive example of 'Teutonic' performance was on the celebrated 2 pm West Coast 'Corridor' train from Euston, not on the memorable lengthy innings of No 1304 *Jeanie Deans*, but further north when No

One of the later series of four-cylinder compound 4-4-0s, 'Alfred the Great' Class No 1955 Hannibal *(Loco Publishing Co).*

1312 *Gaelic* had to tackle a train of ten corridor bogies, 277 tons tare and 295 tons full, on the 72.2-mile run from Preston over Shap to Penrith in 89 minutes. The log of this splendid run is appended, but its merit is notably enhanced when its uphill times from Carnforth to Shap Summit are compared with what the Whale 'Experiment' Class 4-6-0s were doing with comparable loads some 15 years later. The three 4-6-0 performances are taken from the recordings of Cecil J. Allen.

From this table it will be seen that as far as Tebay the 'Teutonic' was handsomely leading the field, with a passing time from Carnforth of 34 min 5 sec, against the fastest 'Experiment' time of 34 min 55 sec.

LNWR: The West Coast 'Corridor', 1893

Engine three-cylinder compound No 1312 *Gaelic*
Load 10 corridor bogies, 277 tons tare, 295 tons full

Distance (miles)		Actual time (m s)	Average speed (mph)
0.0	Preston	0 00	—
4.8	Barton	8 00	—
27.3	Carnforth	30 25	60.2
31.8	Burton	35 30	53.1
34.6	Milnthorpe	38 25	57.7
40.1	Oxenholme	45 30	46.6
47.2	Grayrigg	57 20	36.1
53.2	Tebay	64 30	50.2
58.7	Shap Summit	76 00	28.7
60.7	Shap	78 40	45.1
68.0	Clifton	85 15	66.5
72.2	Penrith	89 15	—

LNWR: Carnforth—Shap Summit

Engine No		1312	1020	565	887
Engine name		*Gaelic*	*Majestic*	*City of Carlisle*	*Fortuna*
Engine type		2-2-4-0	4-6-0	4-6-0	4-6-0
Load (full)		295	285	285	310
Distance point to point (miles)		Time (m s)	Time (m s)	Time (m s)	Time (m s)
7.3	Carnforth-Milnthorpe	8 00	7 35	7 55	8 10
5.5	Milnthorpe-Oxenholme	7 05	7 20	8 35*	7 25
7.1	Oxenholme-Grayrigg	11 50	13 20	12 15	13 10
6.0	Grayrigg-Tebay	7 10	7 00	6 50	6 50
5.5	Tebay-Shap Summit	11 30	10 10	11 00	11 20
31.4	Total time pass to pass	45 35	45 05	46 35	46 55

* signal check at Hincaster Junction

5. S.W. Johnson on the Midland

Matthew Kirtley, the Locomotive Superintendent of the Midland Railway ever since its formation in 1844, died in office 29 years later, leaving a stud of locomotives that must be regarded as second to none on British railways at that time. His successor coming over from the Great Eastern Railway had an excellent foundation on which to build, and with constantly increasing traffic and a management whose enterprise then knew no bounds, there was certainly scope for development in the field of locomotive practice. Johnson had already shown himself an artist, so far as locomotive lineaments were concerned, by his skilful rebuilding of some of the Sinclair single-wheelers of the Great Eastern; but the final Kirtley design for the Midland, the 1070-1089 series of 6-ft 2½-in 2-4-0s was too far advanced in construction by Sharp, Stewart & Co at the time of Kirtley's death for Johnson to implant any of his own features of adornment, except his own pattern of chimney. But more passenger engines were needed at once. The far-famed Settle and Carlisle line was about to be opened for through traffic, and Johnson's first engines for that hilly road were very similar to the Kirtley '1070' Class, in having 6-ft 2½-in coupled wheels. But while the latter did well on the Derby-Manchester line, the later engines, built at Derby Works, were not liked north of Leeds.

This was not an auspicious beginning to Johnson's long stay on the Midland Railway; but there were other changes to design other than the Johnson style of boiler mountings. I believe that there were changes in the details of the motion; and those would have been instantly detectable by the drivers who had to run them, and had probably led to their unpopularity when working on the Carlisle road. No such stigma had been attached to their immediate predecessors of the '1070' Class, so similar in every other way. As renumbered 127 to 146 under the 1907 reclassification, most of them remained on the Derby-Manchester line until their ultimate withdrawal, whereas Johnson's No 1 Class locomotives were banished from Skipton, where they were first shedded, to second-rate work in the east Midlands after no more than three or four years' work on the Scotch Expresses to Carlisle. On the other hand, I personally had an express run behind No 144, formerly No 1087, piloting a new LMS compound, No 1099, and it participated in an excellent performance with a heavy Christmastide load of 335 tons in December 1927.

Johnson's No 1 Class was, however, no more than an unfortunate first start; because all the other 2-4-0s he designed were uniformly excellent, if not necessarily very powerful. Until the very end of his career, he did not introduce any express passenger engines that would rank among the biggest in the country; his aim, it appeared, was to provide ample dimensions that made for high nominal tractive effort, but with relatively small boilers. Thus it was essential to steam the engines lightly, avoiding any suspicion of thrashing, and thus work at maximum economy. Kirtley's 2-4-0s, as well as his own, were beautifully maintained and brought up to date with his own pattern boiler mountings, and when the complete renumbering of the locomotive stock took place in

Left *A posed photograph near Millers Dale of Johnson 7-ft 2-4-0 No 102 (of the '101' Class built in 1877) with a 10-coach train* (British Railways).

Right *Johnson standard 0-6-0 engine No 2073 forming part of the Hellifield snow-plough team* (British Railways).

Midland Railway: Johnson 2-4-0 locomotives

1907 numbers	Original numbers	Coupled wheel diameter (ft in)	Original location	Date first built	Works
147-156	1,9,10,13,70,71 73,74,96,146	6 2½	Skipton	1876	Derby
157-186	1282-1311	6 6	Manchester	1876	Dübs & Co
187-191	50-54	6 6	Sheffield	1876	Derby
192-196	55-59	6 8½	Skipton	1876	Derby
197-206	101-110	7 0	Skipton Saltley	1877	Derby
207-216	1400-1409	6 8½	Leeds	1879	Derby
217-221	111-114,89	6 6	Sheffield	1880	Derby
222-271	1472-1491, 1502-1531	6 8½	Leeds	1880	Derby
			Nottingham	1880-1	Neilson
272-281	1492-1501	7 0	Leicester	1881	Derby

1907, the 2-4-0s, then designated Class I, formed a solid block of 281 engines, Kirtley 1 to 146, and Johnson 147 upwards. All the Johnson 2-4-0s had the same-sized boiler, with 223 tubes of 1¾-in diameter, and providing a heating surface of 1,115 sq ft; the firebox added 110 sq ft. The other proportions of the various batches of 2-4-0 were as given in the accompanying table; but all except the ill-starred No 1 Class of 1876 had cylinders with a stroke of 26 inches.

Apart from the first ten engines in this series, which were built before Johnson had developed his true artistry in locomotive styling, I always consider that engines 157 to 281, collectively, form the most beautiful passenger engines that have ever run on the railways of this country. The drivers may have had their preferences between units of different batches, but

taken as a whole, wherever they were used, they were generally very popular. As to their allocation, it has not been possible, in tabular form, to show the full extent of their use, because they ran almost all over the Midland Railway, from London to Carlisle and Derby to Bristol, while the Skipton engines had many turns to Lancaster and Carnforth, as well as to Carlisle and south to Normanton. It will be realized from this that Skipton was then a major depot. While the many new Johnson engines took their turns on the ever-increasing passenger services operated by the Company, the Kirtley engines continued to play an important part. At Carlisle, for example, when the new Anglo-Scottish service over the Midland route began in 1876, none other than Kirtley express locomotives were shedded at Durran Hill, Carlisle, and the men infinitely preferred them to the new

Johnson No 1 Class. No such preferences were sustained, however, when the Skipton men got a few of the 1282-1311 class that were not required on the Derby-Manchester line. Engines 1302-1311 worked the fastest Scotch Expresses over the Carlisle road for upwards of ten years, with great satisfaction to all concerned.

Johnson was not only an 'artist in metal', as one of my oldest friends in the locomotive world termed it. This particular friend was actually speaking of Patrick Stirling at the time, extolling the graceful lines of his 8-ft bogie single-wheelers on the Great Northern; but he might well have been referring, with even more emphasis so far as I am concerned, to all the Johnson 2-4-0s on the Midland. The artistry extended even more so to the painting. Kirtley's engines were finished in a medium shade of blue-green, with the underframes and wheels in the same colour. On taking over at Derby, Johnson retained this at first, but he changed to a lighter green, with more yellow in it, for his own 2-4-0s introduced in 1876. Mentioning yellow, however, this is not to suggest that he tried out on the Midland the same experiment in which he had indulged while on the Great Eastern. In rebuilding two of the famous 7-ft Sinclair 'singles' with leading bogies and characteristic Johnson boiler mountings, he painted them in Stroudley yellow! The style of his first Midland 2-4-0s was beautifully captured by a fine coloured plate of engine No 1400 in the *Locomotive Magazine* of 1913, though as was the way with colour reproductions at that time, when the firm included the picture in one of their delightful coloured postcards, the tone of the green was more like Kirtley's than Johnson's.

One of the Johnson '1400' Class 6-ft 9-in 2-4-0s of 1879, as renumbered 260, and with a Fowler-type chimney (Loco Publishing Co).

The green livery on the Midland lasted beyond the time when Johnson ceased building 2-4-0s, though one writer referred to the experimental 'brick red' that he first tried, and which was first applied to a 7-ft 2-4-0 of the last class he built of that type, the 1492-1501 series. The true 'Derby red', that magnificent crimson lake that virtually deified Midland engines in the eyes of some of their most ardent supporters, was introduced at the end of 1884; and the infinite care bestowed on the painting of *all* engines, not only the express passenger stud, recalls the light-hearted summary of Midland motive power activities at just about the time of the Grouping, made, moreover, by a Midland man: 'The nice little engines were made pets of. They were housed in nice clean sheds, and they were never overloaded.' While the locomotives in Johnson's day were not given the extremely lavish treatment bestowed on the coaches, which were given 17 coats of paint and varnish—yes, 17!—the locomotives received two coats of lead grey, four coats of purple brown, followed by one coat of crimson; then five coats of varnish finished the job. The way in which they were turned out was legendary, even after a somewhat simpler form of livery had been adopted in Deeley's time; though when I personally came to see Midland engines in the North Country, from 1916 onwards, I regret to say that many of them looked as if they had not seen a cleaner's rag for weeks. It was certainly the case when I travelled in a train hauled by a Johnson compound No 1004 when my mother and I joined an up Scotch Express at Hellifield to journey to Leeds, though at that late stage in the war there was some excuse.

In 1876, Johnson began constructing 4-4-0s, though the earliest batches of these seemed to be nothing more than copies of the 2-4-0s with leading bogies. The second lot of these, twenty built by Dübs & Co in 1877, have a particular association for me. They, like the Kitson-built engines of 1876, were the only Johnson 4-4-0s that escaped the drastic rebuilding of all other small-boilered 4-4-0s that took place at Derby between 1904 and 1907. It may have been no more than a coincidence, but those Dübs-built engines of 1877 had the largest boilers of any fitted to Johnson 4-4-0s until the introduction of the much larger 'Belpaires' in 1900. Until 1898, the various successive batches of 4-4-0s had standard fireboxes with 110 sq ft of heating surface, but then the coupled wheelbase was increased from 8 ft 6 in to 9 ft and the fireboxes were enlarged to 117 sq ft. The tube heating surface was not increased. In his retirement, from 1904 onwards, Johnson confided to E.L. Ahrons some of his thoughts on locomotive design, some of which concerned proportions of boilers and fireboxes. He held the view that a large firebox was preferable to a marked increase in tube heating surface, and he followed this theory through 18 years of building 4-4-0

One of the '2183' Class 7-ft 4-4-0s of 1892, No 2201 (Loco Publishing Co).

engines, during which time the cylinder diameter increased from 18 to 19½ inches, and the boiler pressure went up to 170 psi; and still the tube heating surface remained at around 1,100 sq ft. But I must revert to the Dübs engines of 1877, which were the exceptions to the whole sequence.

The twenty original engines of this class, numbered 1327-1346, had the then-standard firebox, providing 110 sq ft of heating surface but a larger boiler with 1,203 sq ft of tube heating surface. The coupled wheels were of 7-ft diameter, but the boiler pressure was only 140 psi in accordance with usual Midland practice of those days. The cylinders were 18 in by 26 in. The original use of those engines appears to have been mainly on the Manchester expresses, both north and south of Leicester. At that time there did not seem to be any inhibitions about using engines with coupled wheels as large as 7 ft on the very hilly road between Derby and Manchester, despite the earlier allocation of 2-4-0 engines having coupled wheels no larger than 6 ft 2½ in specially for that service. The last five engines of the original 4-4-0 class, Nos 1341-1346, were originally allocated to Leeds; but these were not at first used on the Scotch Expresses over the north road to Carlisle, but rather on the faster running lines southward to Leicester and Birmingham. The purist for the English language may have noticed once or twice in this chapter that I have used the term 'Scotch Express'. When writing of Midland Railway matters, 'Scotch' it has to be. In the public timetables, and the display sheets

One of the '150' Class 7-ft 4-4-0s of 1896, No 1670 (Author's Collection).

at large stations, any Anglo-Scottish train was prominently marked 'Scotch Express', and the practice persisted for many years after the railway itself became the Midland Division of the LMS.

In later years, when the smaller-boilered 4-4-0s were rebuilt, those Dübs engines of 1877, then numbered 310 to 327, were mostly found north of Leeds, many of them stationed at Hellifield. In the tragic early morning of Christmas Eve, 1910, an overworked signalman's error led to the midnight express from St Pancras running down two light engines between the Moorcock and Shotlock Hill tunnels. It caught fire, and in the ensuing Board of Trade report on the disaster it was noted that no fewer than four engines of the 310-327 class, Nos 312, 313, 314 and 317, were at Hawes Junction after double-heading northbound expresses from Hellifield. Incidentally, three other down trains had been piloted up to Aisgill on that fateful morning, all by 2-4-0s, not to mention the ill-fated 'midnight' from St Pancras, the leading engine of which, a Kirtley 2-4-0, had to be scrapped because of the damage sustained in the collision. When I was at Giggleswick from 1916 onwards, I saw those Hellifield engines frequently, sometimes piloting Scotch Expresses, but more frequently on the locals to Carnforth or to Lancaster. That excellent railway artist, the late Jack Hill, painted a beautiful picture of the last survivor of the class coming up the bank towards Clapham Junction with a train from Lancaster for

one of my earlier books, *The Golden Age of Steam*.

Turning now to the main body of the Johnson small-boilered 4-4-0s, Nos 328 to 562 in the 1907 renumbering, I find it is with a pang of sadness that I write of their all too brief history, in their original condition. While the earliest of them dated from 1882, some 160 were not introduced before 1892 and the last, the '2591' series of 7-ft engines, were not built by Neilson, Reid & Co until 1901. The first of this latter class, indeed, was evidently considered sufficiently notable to form the firm's major exhibit at the Glasgow Exhibition of 1901. Yet all of them, the 235 engines numbered from 328 to 562, had all been rebuilt with larger boilers and look unrecognizable compared with their old selves by the end of 1907. But the process of rebuilding and the 'new look' that the Midland 4-4-0 engines then assumed are discussed in a later chapter of this book. For the present, I join in the praise given to them in their original condition by E.L. Ahrons, Charles Rous-Marten and other contemporary writers. I am taking for detailed examination the last batch, and by common consent the finest of them all, the ten built by Neilson, Reid & Co in 1901, Nos 2591-2600. It is interesting to compare their proportions with those of other 4-4-0s of that vintage, by means of the accompanying table.

4-4-0 locomotives, *circa* 1902

Railway	Designer	Class	Cylinders diameter × stroke (in)	Coupled wheel diameter (ft in)	Total heating surface (sq ft)	Firebox heating surface (sq ft)	Boiler pressure (psi)	Total engine weight (tons)
Midland	Johnson	'2591'	19 × 26	7 0	1,193	128	170	45¾
Caledonian	McIntosh	'Dunalastair III'	19 × 26	6 6	1,540	138	180	51¾
L & SW	Dugald Drummond	'T9'	18½ × 26	6 7	1,500	148	175	48.9
LB & SC	R. Billinton	'B4'	19 × 26	6 9	1,635	126	180	49
Great Western	Dean, Churchward	'Atbara'	18 × 26	6 8½	1,663	125	180	51½
North Eastern	Wilson Worsdell	'R'	19 × 26	6 10	1,527	144	200	51¾

The first engines of the so-called '60' Class were built at Derby in 1898. They had even larger fireboxes than earlier engines, made possible by the spacing of the coupled axles no less than 9 ft 6 in apart. The firebox heating surface was 128 sq ft, against the earlier 117 sq ft. But Johnson rather overreached himself in putting cylinders of no less than 19½-in diameter on this batch, and this was afterwards reduced to 19 in on subsequent ones, including the final ten built by Neilson, Reid & Co in 1901 and featured in the accompanying comparative table of dimensions. This table shows very clearly the way Johnson had fallen behind in the matter of tube heating surface in his boilers, though from all accounts the '2591' Class in particular did very good work on the road, not only those run at speed with light trains, but also the batch stationed at Leeds and used on the Carlisle road. Rous-Marten, making one of his special tests, recorded a time of 111½ minutes over the 99 miles from St Pancras to Leicester with a load of 300 tons, while Ahrons several times noted exceptionally fast starts by the 4.02 pm Scotch Express southbound from Leeds, loaded to between 250 and 270 tons. But it was more than could be expected that such standards of performance could be a regular thing with boilers having so little tube heating surface, and such a run as that which Rous-Marten recorded from St Pancras to Leicester must have been 'one in a thousand'.

By that time Johnson was fitting his main-line engines with piston valves. It was evident from a paper presented to the summer meeting of the Institution of Mechanical Engineers at Newcastle in July 1902 that for some years previously, liaison between the staffs at Gateshead and Derby had been intimate and cordial. The celebrated Chief Draughtsman of the North Eastern Railway, Walter Mackersie Smith, in presenting the paper, acknowledged the help he had received from Derby in developing the successive types of valve that had been used on both Midland and North Eastern locomotives. It seemed that the troubles in the original stages of the development

had been largely duplicated at Gateshead and Derby, and when a form of valve that was generally satisfactory had been evolved it was fitted to one engine of Wilson Worsdell's 'M' Class 4-4-0s in 1893, and was adopted as a standard on the Midland by the time the first examples of the '60' Class 4-4-0s were built at Derby in 1898. The North Eastern 'R' Class followed a year later, and one may be fairly certain that the success of these latter, and the excellent trouble-free mileages obtained from them, spurred Johnson on to bigger boilers on his own 4-4-0s. Before dealing with these developments, however, I must retrace my steps to the year 1887 to give some account of the new era of the single-wheeler on the Midland Railway.

In the early 'eighties, the Company was one of the most enthusiastic users of the Westinghouse air brake. Indeed, at one time it seemed likely that it would be standardized, and if this had happened, with the influential position the Midland held among British railways, there was the likelihood that the air brake, and not the vacuum, would have been the general favourite for the future. But then Mr Holt, Works Manager at Derby, devised a scheme for blowing sand on to the rails to minimize slipping, and naturally he used the power most readily to hand, compressed air from the brake pump. To test the effectiveness of his pump, the coupling rods were removed from one or two of the 2-4-0 engines then stationed at Hellifield, and working over the Settle and Carlisle line, and they ran as single-wheelers. The experiment was such a success that Johnson began to make plans for new single-wheelers, of modern design. But when the Westinghouse Brake Company heard what was going on, an almighty row blew up. They strongly objected to the air compressed in their pumps being used for any purpose other than braking, and threatened the direst penalties for its misuse! The Midland Railway were quick to take the message and lost no time in developing their own *steam* sanding gear.

When Johnson began to build his own single-wheelers, he chose a wheel diameter of 7 ft 4 in to

start with. The boilers had a total heating surface of 1,240 sq ft, with the firebox contributing 117 sq ft. This was the first time that this size of grate had been used on the Midland, because the then-standard coupled wheel spacing of 8 ft 6 in precluded anything larger than a firebox heating surface of 110 sq ft, to contemporary Derby designs. It was not until some fifty 4-2-2 singles had been built that the building of 4-4-0 engines, with the enlarged coupled wheel base of 9 ft, enabled fireboxes of equal size to those of the singles to be used on a new range of 4-4-0s in 1892. By that time, Johnson had increased the wheel diameter of his singles to 7-ft 6 in, and the cylinders, which had been 18 in by 26 in on the 7-ft 4-in engines, to 18½ in by 26 in. The boiler pressure remained at 160 psi. By 1893, sixty of those handsome engines were at work, 18 of them of the 7-ft 4-in class. Apart from the rectangular panel which supported the cab, and which was like that of the 0-6-0 goods engines in this respect, the singles would have equalled the 4-4-0s in being the most beautiful eight-wheeled engines in Britain at the time.

From the time of their introduction, the new singles, both 7-ft 4-in and 7-ft 6-in, were ranked as top-line express engines, and apart from four of the larger-wheeled variety, all the first batches built up to 1891 were put on to the London expresses southwards from Leicester and Nottingham, shedded variously at Kentish Town and the two south Midland sheds. The four exceptions were allocated to the level stretch of the Cheshire Lines to run the competing service from St Pancras to Liverpool which at one time included the old-style American Pullman cars. The singles worked eastwards from Liverpool to Marple, where they joined the Manchester portion of the London trains. The short route to the south via Cheadle Heath, Hazel Grove and the long Disley Tunnel was not then open, and through trains from Liverpool were routed through Stockport and Romiley to Marple. Those four engines, numbered from 1907 as 620-623, were still on the Cheshire Lines working the Liverpool portions of the London expresses right up to the First World War. The last thirty of the 7-ft 6-in singles were built at Derby in 1892-3, and most of them were sent to the West of England main line and shedded at Saltley and Bristol.

They needed help up the Lickey Incline, as of course did every other steam locomotive that has ever run over the route; but other than that, they did well.

Eye-witnesses of those days, and of course the experienced observers like Rous-Marten, have testified to the extreme popularity of the singles with their crews; and equally to their economy in working. Johnson designed his express passenger engines to work on a light rein, for the boilers would not stand thrashing in the North Western style. Furthermore, throughout Johnson's time on the Midland there were no water troughs. At the turn of the century there were quite a number of lengthy non-stop runs made by expresses timed at start-to-stop average speeds of 50 to 54 mph, and although this did not involve haulage of very heavy loads, mostly less than 200 tons, it required first class enginemanship to maintain time on runs like those between St Pancras and Leicester, Cheltenham and Derby (avoiding Birmingham by the Camp Hill line), and Skipton and Carlisle. The locomotives had simply *got* to be economical to make those runs without taking water intermediately. There were also the Nottingham runs, to and from St Pancras; although these mostly included a stop at Kettering, there would be precious little opportunity to get anything of a fill-up during the one-minute station stop then scheduled. Though not involving use of the singles over the northern part of the journey, some of the Manchester trains made exacting non-stop runs to and from Marple, avoiding a stop at Derby. Those from Leicester used the goods avoiding line beside the main Derby purlieu, but those from Nottingham used the circuitous route via Trowell and the Erewash valley main line to Codnor Park, striking off westwards through Butterley to reach Ambergate.

In 1896, Johnson built the first five of the enlarged singles, having 7-ft 9-in driving wheels, 19½-in diameter cylinders and the enlarged firebox giving 128 sq ft of heating surface as used on the '60' Class 4-4-0s. These were beautiful engines to look at, and no less excellent in their performances. Ahrons always said they were among the finest single express engines ever constructed. Ten more of them were built in 1899. Aesthetically, I did not approve of the enlargement of the bogie wheels to 3ft 9½ in for a quite frivolous reason. I was having an 0-gauge model of No 117 of this class made for my railway, and we found that with scale bogie wheels there was insufficient internal clearance on curves. The bogie wheels fouled the rather deep running plate which was continued to the fore end, and we had to make some unorthodox adjustments to the design in this neighbourhood. The enlarged singles were distributed at the various sheds dealing with the fastest running south and south-west of Derby. Everywhere they were

treated as absolutely top express passenger engines, and in the many photographs of them showing double-headed trains, invariably one sees the single as the train engine with a 4-4-0 or a 2-4-0 as the assistant.

In the following year, Johnson went one step even further with his single-wheelers, producing the '2601' Class of ten engines with 19½-in by 26-in cylinders, 7-ft 19½-in driving wheels and 180 psi boiler pressure. But the boilers were even smaller than the '115' Class, with only 1,217 sq ft total heating surface, though the firebox was much larger, providing 147 sq ft. It seemed as if Johnson reached his limit in small boilers and large fireboxes with these engines, because at the very next breath, as it were, he introduced the seemingly enormous—for the Midland—Belpaire 4-4-0s. Like the new 'Belpaires', the '2601' Class, of which the prototype was named *Princess of Wales*, was fitted with huge bogie tenders with a tank capacity of 4,000 gallons. The tenders, indeed, were heavier than the engines! There was a purpose in this, because while No 2601 was on exhibition in Paris, Nos 2602, 2603 and 2604, stationed at Kentish Town, were used to inaugurate through engine workings between St Pancras and Leeds. Even so, it seems that the '2601' Class were not the most popular of the singles. It may or may not have been significant that this last series was the first to go, *en bloc*, to the scrap heap. While odd individual engines of earlier batches were condemned for various reasons, the whole group numbered from 685 to 694 went soon after the First World War. I shall always remember my last sight of one of them. It was a gloomy wet November evening. We had been playing Rugby football at Harpenden, and were making our way to the station to return to London. Through a curtain of sleety rain I saw a down train just leaving; silhouet-

The first of the '2601' Class 'singles' of 1900 with the large bogie tender, No 2601 Princess of Wales *(British Railways).*

ted against the station lights I recognized at once the profile of a '2601' Class, as she slipped her halting way to the north.

Studying the details of Johnson's career on the Midland Railway, it becomes clear that he was, heart and soul, an express passenger engine man. These notes of mine have so far been exclusively about passenger classes. The variations in design, many of them small, it is true, are enough to show the intense personal interest he maintained. Yet despite the teeming goods and mineral traffic of the railway, he introduced no more than two freight engine designs throughout his whole career, both within a few years of his taking office. These were the standard goods, with coupled wheels of 4-ft 10-in diameter, of which 120 were built in 1875-6 and the 'express goods' class, with 5-ft 2-in coupled wheels, of which the first were built in 1878. While Johnson did not do much for the advancement of Midland freight motive power, he certainly rebuilt the Kirtley outside-framed 0-6-0s, giving them a much longer lease of life, and fitted them for their lengthy 'second innings' as pilot engines to the main-line mineral trains. Returning now to the express engines, it is interesting to recall that the very first article in the famous series 'British Locomotive Practice and Performance' in *The Railway Magazine* in October 1901, under the authorship of Charles Rous-Marten, discussed this very topic, the remarkable change in design policy made by Mr Johnson in 1900:

'The boilers of those standard Midland engines were scarcely adequate for dealing with the huge modern loads which have to be hauled at speeds as high as those of seventeen years ago—when the trains were 25 to 30 per cent lighter—and sometimes higher. In respect of many classes of Midland express duty, the boilers have proved equal to all requirements, but this has not been so in every case, and the fact has been frankly recognised by Mr Johnson in an entirely practical way—that is to say, by the introduction of a wholly novel type of Midland locomotive for the heaviest and fastest express service.

'This new type has virtually come in with the new century, and is a complete departure from Midland tradition in several respects. Its exponents are Nos 2606-2610 and 800-804. In the first place, the boiler is greatly enlarged, alike in diameter and in heating surface. Secondly, the Belpaire firebox is used. Thirdly, the driving wheel diameter of 6-ft 9-in is reverted to after an interval of eighteen years. A fourth change is the removal of the safety valves from the dome, and the substitution of the round-topped dome-cover seen on most other railways in place of the special Midland type. Next, the old style of safety-valve is abolished, and the Ramsbottom pattern substituted. Also the continuous splasher, dipping in a graceful curve between the two coupled wheels, is abandoned, and a single splasher placed over the driving-wheel, while the coupled trailing-wheel is under an extension of the cabside. It will be

recognised from these particulars that the newcomer is new in many respects, and that its advent constitutes an epoch in Midland, if not also in British, locomotive practice.

'With cylinders 19½ in by 26 in and coupled wheels 6 ft 9 in in diameter, these engines can excize a tractive effort of 122 lb for every 1 lb of effective steam pressure in the cylinders. The boiler pressure is 180 lb per square inch, and as the firebox has an exceptionally large share in the duty of steam generation, the efficiency of the machine is proportionately enhanced. The total heating surface is 1,520 square feet, and the weight of the engine is 51 tons 12 cwt, of which the amount available for adhesion is 34 tons 2 cwt. The tender, like those of the '2601' Class of single-wheeler, is placed upon two bogies, and weighs 51 tons 7 cwt in working order, so that the aggregate weight of engine and tender is no less than 102 tons 19 cwt.'

It was surprising, in view of the innovation involved, that several months elapsed after the completion at Derby of the first of the new 4-4-0s before any illustration appeared in the leading railway papers of the day, and then only a gloomy, unglamorous side-view of an unpainted engine that looked as if it had been taken in the pouring rain It was not until Rous-Marten's second article appeared, nearly a year after engine No 2606 left the Derby erecting shop, that an attractive picture of No 2609 was published, in all the traditional Midland finery. Even so, one senses that there was something of a move to 'play down' the advent of the new engines

An unidentified '2601' Class 'single' on a down Scotch express near Mill Hill in 1905 (Dr T.F. Budden).

at first. After all, delivery was still being taken from contractors of the very popular 19-in version of the '60' Class small-boilered 4-4-0s, and Derby Works had only just finished building the '2601' Class 4-2-2 singles before they turned at once to the 'Belpaires'. The first batch of these latter, after running in, was sent to Leeds for working on the Carlisle road, with results that in certain cases were spectacular in the extreme. But before referring to one such instance, the likeness of the design of the 'Belpaires' to the North Eastern 'R' Class, and the friendly association between Derby and Gateshead, must be further commented upon.

The basic dimensions of these two 4-4-0 classes are tabulated herewith. On the basis of nominal tractive effort there was little difference, because the higher boiler pressure of the 'R' Class was largely offset by the larger cylinders and slightly smaller coupled wheels of the Midland engines. The really significant difference lay in the design of the fireboxes—not so much in the use of the Belpaire shape on the Midland engine as in the size of the grate. The North Eastern engine was designed with a deep, narrow firebox in which a very thick fire would be used. The Gateshead top-link express engines of the day were fired mostly on soft Tyneside coals which gave good results in those conditions, whereas many of the best Midland runs relied on hard Yorkshire or Nottinghamshire coals which could be fired quite thinly on the grate. Johnson was continuing his attention to economical working, and a large grate thinly covered with top-grade hard coal gave excellent results.

One of the later Belpaire 4-4-0s, No 756, in original form, non-superheated but in the later painting style, at Kentish Town in 1914 (W.J. Reynolds).

	Midland Railway '2606' Class	North Eastern Railway 'R' Class
Coupled wheel diameter (ft in)	6 9	6 10
Cylinders, diameter × stroke (in)	19½ × 26	19 × 26
Adhesion weight (tons)	34.1	35.2
Boiler Barrel diameter (ft in)	4 8	4 7¾
Heating surfaces (sq ft)		
Tubes	1,374	1,383
Firebox	145	144
Total	1,519	1,527
Grate area (sq ft)	25	20
Boiler pressure (psi)	180	200
Total weight, engine only (tons)	51.6	51.7

The Midland 'Belpaires' soon established themselves as very speedy engines. There was a report of one of them attaining a maximum speed of 96 mph while descending from Blea Moor towards Settle Junction, but the circumstances were not disclosed. While the speed was fully accepted as authentic, privately, in railway engineering circles, it was a time when scaremongering about high train speeds was rife in the daily press, and this particular Midland feat was not publicized in any way. But a further exploit of one of the 'Belpaires' in its very early years came to light in 1913, when Cecil J. Allen was describing current performance over the Settle and Carlisle line. After detailing many runs in the post-1907 era when loads were restricted and piloting was frequent, he appended a run made in 1902 on the 9.30 am Scotch Express from St Pancras, with the second of the 'Belpaires', No 2607, when the train was heavy enough at 320 tons to require a pilot from Hellifield to Aisgill. The recorder was a Mr W.C.H. Church of Newcastle, a close friend of Charles Rous-Marten and an equally expert train timer. What happened on that occasion after the train engine had put off its pilot is best summarized by the log of the following startling run down to Carlisle.

Miles		Time (m s)	Average speed (mph)
0.0	Aisgill Box	0 00	
3.5	Mallerstang Box	5 18	39.6
6.8	Kirkby Stephen	7 57	74.0
10.0	Crosby Garrett	10 19	82.0
15.1	Ormside	13 55	85.1

Miles		Time (m s)	Average speed (mph)
17.5	Appleby	15 42	81.1
20.4	Long Marton	17 52	80.3
24.9	Culgaith	21 16	79.4
28.6	Langwathby	24 03	79.6
30.0	Little Salkeld	25 08	77.8
33.1	Lazonby	27 22	83.2
38.3	Armathwaite	32 13	65.2
44.4	Cumwhinton	37 30	70.0
48.3	Carlisle	41 55	—

A speed of 80 mph was reached before Kirkby Stephen, and a full 90 at Smardale Viaduct. A slackening off took place over the easier gradient north of Crosby Garrett, but the maximum of 90 mph was renewed at Ormside Viaduct. In any case, as the log shows, an average speed of 81.5 mph was maintained over the 26.3 miles from Kirkby Stephen to Lazonby.

Unhappily, this kind of running was to prove a false overture to twentieth-century locomotive working on the Midland Railway. It is true that the first of the Johnson compounds had yet to come, bringing with them promise of an even more brilliant era. The beginnings of the compound saga must be reserved for a further chapter of this book; but unfortunately, as will be told later, policies other than those of straightforward mechanical engineering came to swamp the activities of the Locomotive Department at Derby, and it was not until after the Grouping in 1923 that the Midland compounds began to take their true place in British locomotive history.

6. The Caledonian 'Dunalastair' family

Nigh on one hundred years ago, in the mid-'eighties of last century, Dugald Drummond could be set down as one of the greatest 'thinkers' in the entire profession of locomotive engineering. Nurtured on Clydebank, then probably one of the greatest centres of marine engineering anywhere in the world, where all ships of any size were powered by at least double, and very often by triple, expansion compound steam reciprocating engines, young Drummond was indoctrinated at an early stage in life with all the pros and cons of compounding. Even at that early stage he may have pondered upon the apparent reluctance of railway locomotive men to adopt compounding when the increased thermal efficiencies resulting from it were apparent in marine practice. After some varied early experience, he secured the job of Foreman-Erector in the Highland Railway works, and thus came under the influence of Stroudley. Within two years he had been promoted to Works Manager. There can be no doubt that the precepts and practice of that master engineer carried Drummond along for some time, after he had followed Stroudley to Brighton, and when he had secured his first major appointment, that of Locomotive Superintendent to the North British Railway at Cowlairs, in 1875.

When, seven years later, he was chosen to succeed George Brittain in the similar, but rather more prestigious, post on the Caledonian Railway at the neighbouring works at St Rollox, the date, 1882, was somewhat significant. He assumed command of motive power for all the Scottish end of the West Coast Main Line at the very time when his fellow engineer at Crewe, the mighty F.W. Webb, was embarking upon his momentous course in compound propulsion. It was unlikely that two men with such autocratic and dictatorial temperaments would ever consult together, or even compare notes on points of mutual interest in locomotive practice. On the contrary, at almost the same time as the first Webb three-cylinder compound express passenger engine was built at Crewe, Neilsons, in Glasgow, delivered the first Drummond 4-4-0 to the Caledonian Railway. Superficially these new Scottish engines were in the direct line of succession to the North British 4-4-0s he had built in 1876 for the Waverley Route and which did such good work thereon for upwards of twenty years; but the new Caledonian engines of 1884 were in many ways the most advanced design seen on British railways up till that time—and for many years thereafter. For in these engines, Drummond incorporated practices of cylinder design that were in many cases the precursors of the precepts of Churchward on the Great Western, and indeed of Chapelon.

It is interesting, however, that what may be called the more intimate details of the cylinder design were not published until some years after Drummond had left the Caledonian Railway. Certainly he read his paper to the Institution of Civil Engineers in 1890; but apart from the relatively few members who were present on that occasion, the membership in general, and the engineering public at large, had to wait until the script of the paper was published in the Proceedings for the session 1896-7, after Drummond himself had gone to the London and South Western

The famous Caledonian 4-2-2 'single', originally No 123, in her last years as working traffic department engine LMS No 14010 at Perth in 1932 (O.S. Nock).

Railway. Reverting to the Caledonian, however, Drummond's paper to the 'Civils' was titled 'An Investigation into the Use of Progressive High Pressures in Non-Compound Locomotive Engines'. At the time it was a thinly veiled counterblast to what Webb was doing at Crewe, for Drummond maintained that to make a true comparison between simple and compound working, the boiler pressures had to be equal; and that was what Webb was not doing in his LNWR engines. In his new Caledonian engines of 1884, Drummond used the usual pressure of the day, 150 psi; but for his tests of 1889, which were the subject of his paper to the 'Civils', four new engines of the same class were specially fitted with boilers, one with the usual 150 lb pressure, one with 175 lb and two with no less than 200 psi.

For the standard engines of the class, 16 of which were built by Neilson & Co in 1884-5, the cylinders were of 18-in diameter by 26-in stroke, and the coupled wheels were 6 ft 6 in, as on the preceding North British engines. The design of the cylinders was a departure from the normal arrangement of a central valve face. The steam ports were moved to the cylinder ends, and the slide valve was divided, each section having its own exhaust port. In this way, the port clearance was reduced to a minimum and a reduction in back pressure was effected. The weight of the valve, however, was increased by 70 per cent. The exhaust passages were increased so that the belt from the lower and top valves extended along the whole length of the cylinder, thus forming an exhaust-steam-jacketed cylinder. The blast pipe, which was of the Vortex type, had likewise a large exhaust capacity with a nozzle equal to a 5-in opening. The design of the cylinders of these engines was derived from Stroudley's practice, with divided steam ports, while steam leaving the lower part of the exhaust port passed round the cylinder in a cast passage before joining the steam from the upper portion at the base of the blast pipe. The new engines, like their North British forerunners, were very successful; but in 1889 Drummond was aiming for something far higher, as he explained in his paper to the 'Civils'.

On the four engines built for the trials of 1889, the steam ports, instead of being towards the centre of the valve face, were moved to the ends, giving a very short and direct passage. Furthermore, separate exhaust ports were provided at each end of the valve face, and the total port area for the exhaust was doubled. The tests, which were made at the beginning of November 1889, were confined to a single round trip per engine, on the 4.30 pm West Coast Express from Carlisle to Edinburgh, and returning the next day on the 10.15 am from Edinburgh to Carlisle. One intermediate stop was made, at Strawfrank Junction, to detach and attach coaches from farther north. Apparently the time of the trials was not particularly fortunate from the point of view of fuel consumption, because there was a coal strike at the time, and the only supplies were from stacks 12 months old, and containing a high proportion of slack. The normal coal supplied to the top-link Caledonian express passenger engines was capable of evaporating 8 lb of water per pound of coal, but a test made with the first engine to be put through its trials showed that the actual evaporation was 6 lb or even less. Consequently, while the actual coal consumption figures were not in any way representative for comparing with those of other railways, the comparison made between the locomotives with different boiler pressures was certainly significant.

Drummond 6-ft 6-in 4-4-0 No 124, built in 1886 (British Railways).

Caledonian Railway: 4.30 pm Carlisle-Strawfrank Junction

Engine No	Boiler pressure (psi)	Train weight (tons)	Carlisle (min)	Lockerbie (min)	Beattock (min)	Summit (min)	Strawfrank (min)
76	200	150	0	30	45	62	89
77	175	140	0	34	51	71	95
78	150	170	0	33	48	74	100½
79	200	140	0	32	46	64½	88

The accompanying table has been prepared to show the relative work on the hardest part of the round trip, including the ascent of the Beattock Bank, with the maximum load. Unfortunately, the records of the coal consumption were not detailed section by section, but given as the total consumed by each engine on the complete round trip, Carlisle to Edinburgh and back, thus including a mixture of severe and relatively easy work. Referring to the table again, note should be taken of the ascents of the Beattock Bank by the 200 lb engines, particularly as all the test runs were made in very stormy autumn weather. A complete set of indicator diagrams was taken throughout the tests with all four engines, and those with the 200 lb engines included some remarkable manifestations of tractive power from two such relatively small engines. The following is a selection of performances from engine No 79:

Speed (mph)	Regulator opening	Cut-off (per cent)	Indicated horsepower
65½	Full	19	553
65	Full	22	770
57½	Full	21	766
51	Full	27	940
37	Full	33	856
33¼	Full	33	806

Although Drummond had recorded economies ranging up to nearly 30 per cent in fuel consumption by the 200 lb engines over the one 150 lb engine, the tests clearly left him with something of an open mind. In the concluding paragraphs of his paper he wrote:

'During part of the running of engine No 76, five expansions were made, the efficiency increasing to the highest point. As the whole question of engine-economy resolves itself into the number of times steam can be expanded, and as in this case five expansions were within the economical limit in a single cylinder, compounding within this limit appears to be unnecessary. If, however, the thermal and dynamical conditions of the non-compound are superior to those of the compound engine, how is it that those who favour the latter system have attained superior results? The reply must be that the two systems have not been compared on a fair basis. In the first place, the boiler pressure of the compound locomotive has been usually higher. In the second place, the driver of the compound engine is obliged to keep up the boiler pressure, as there must be considerably less range of mean cylinder-pressure than in the non-compound engines which can expand steam as low as one-and-a-quarter times, and all starting from stations is so done—whereas the compound locomotive cannot expand less than two-and-a-half times. This reduction of range in the power of the latter engine is undoubtedly the cause of reduced coal consumption over what is due to higher pressure. Other things being equal, coal consumption is the measure of the work done by an engine, and if the compound engine cannot run so fast in express traffic, or has to be assisted on up-gradients, the result should not be credited to increased efficiency. The Author is of the opinion that in a comparative trial of the simple and compound systems, the boiler pressure should be alike. The minimum number of expansions should be alike; and the low-pressure cylinder of the compound engine should be equal to the combined areas of the non-compound cylinders. On this common basis only should the trials be conducted, and no analysis offers greater advantages than the one adopted here. He suggests that such a test should be made with engines on the compound principle against non-compound engines say for a month's duration, in order that their respective merits may be tested in a way that will settle doubts existing on the question.'

At the same time he evidently did not consider that the results he had obtained with engines 76 and 79 were realizable in everyday running. He found difficulty in getting his drivers to work with short cut-offs, and in such circumstances much of the advantage of high boiler pressures was thrown away. Evidently, on the Caledonian in the 'eighties of the last century, it was not considered possible to educate the enginemen, as Churchward so successfully did on the Great Western some years later, and Drummond concluded:

'Viewing the question of steam pressures broadly, the Author has come to the conclusion that for the present, until drivers appreciate the value and take advantage of higher pressures for ordinary locomotive engines working main line traffic economically in all respects, the pressure should not be less than 150 lb nor more than 170 lb per sq in. Pressures of 200 lb per square inch can, he believes, only be economnically used with engines working heavy suburban passenger-traffic, whereby speed can be got up quickly when leaving stations.'

It was one of the great misfortunes of nineteenth-century locomotive history that in 1890 Dugald Drummond was tempted by the offer of a post in Australia to resign from the job he had been filling with such distinction, and at a relatively high salary, on the Caledonian. His paper to the 'Civils', though ending on something of a disappointing note, showed that he was nevertheless on the threshold of a career of unexampled progress and scientific development, that could, if eventually continued on the Caledonian Railway, have had immense influence on future LMS practice. As it was, with the Australian project a nonstarter and his short foray in commercial engineering having somewhat soured his outlook, his return to normal railway work in the south of England was ultimately not as distinguished as his earlier work promised it might be. At St Rollox he was succeeded by John Lambie, an out-and-out running man, and he certainly played safe when more express passenger engines were needed by using the standard Drummond design, but increasing the boiler pressure from 150 to 160 psi. An incidental detail, however, which at once marked the change from the Drummond to

Lambie 4-4-0 No 14 photographed at the head of a corridor dining car express for Euston outside Princes Street station, Edinburgh (British Railways).

the Lambie batches, was the removal of the safety valve from the top of the dome to the more conventional place above the firebox.

It was perhaps significant that the general arrangement drawing of the Lambie 4-4-0, which incorporated the steam-jacketed cylinders, Vortex blast pipe and other features of Drummond practice, bore the initials R.W.U.—that was Robert Urie, who was then Chief Draughtsman at St Rollox, and who afterwards became Works Manager as well before he left to rejoin Dugald Drummond on the London and South Western Railway in 1897. Engines of both Drummond and Lambie batches covered themselves with glory in the 1895 'Race to the North'. In general terms, 60 mph had been the recognized speed for a British express train on level track until the 1890s, with spurts of 70 to 75 mph downhill. There were, of course, exceptions, but not many. But these Caledonian 4-4-0s were tearing along the level stretches north of Perth at 75 mph as well as making remarkable speed on the adverse gradients northwards from Carlisle. The refinements of the Drummond front-end design were being used to excellent effect, even though 'D.D.' could not get his drivers to use a wide-open regulator. In his paper to the 'Civils', Drummond did not instance a case of any indicator diagrams being taken at speeds of 75 mph or over, though a maximum speed of 82 mph was registered with one of the two engines then carrying a boiler pressure of 200 psi.

Lambie died in 1895, and was succeeded by the redoubtable John Farquharson McIntosh. Like his predecessor he was a 'running man', but very much aware of the increasing demands that heavier rolling-stock and improved facilities for passengers were going to make on the locomotive department. So he immediately set the St Rollox drawing office to work on an enlarged version of the Lambie 4-4-0. The front end was virtually unchanged, except for a very small

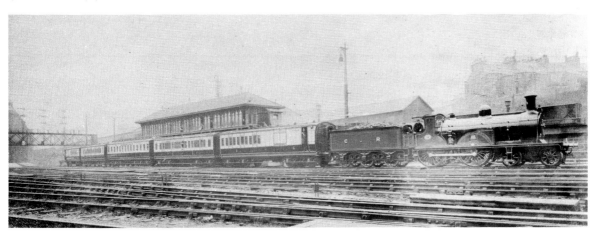

increase in cylinder diameter from 18 in to 18¼ in and the retention of the steam-jacketed cylinders and the Vortex blast pipe. But McIntosh demanded a much larger steaming capacity, and the St Rollox drawing office gave it in full measure, as will be seen from the comparative boiler proportions:

Engine Class	**Lambie**	**'721'**
Boiler		
Tube heating surface (sq ft)	1071.5	1284.45
Firebox heating surface (sq ft)	112.45	118.78
Total (sq ft)	1184.12	1403.23
Grate area (sq ft)	19.5	20.63
Tubes		
Number	238	265
External diameter (in)	1⅜	1¾
Length between tube plates (ft in)	10 7	10 7
Barrel, mean outside diameter (ft in)	4 6¼	4 8¾

The centre-line of the boiler was pitched 6 in higher above rail level, and this, with the resulting reduced height of chimney and dome, gave a considerably more massive appearance, which caught popular fancy in Scotland to a remarkable extent. The fact that the first engine of the new class was named *Dunalastair* increased the interest, but among the countless enthusiasts, English as well as Scottish, who came to worship at the shrine of the 'Dunalastairs', and of their successively more powerful derivatives, I wager not one in a hundred could tell the origin of the name, or where it is. Motoring southwards towards Beattock Summit one day, it must be nearly 30 years ago, I noticed a by-road in one of the Upper Clydesdale villages, I believe it was Crawford, named Dunalastair Terrace. This could only have been in honour of the locomotives that went streaking by, not the way towards the Chairman's residence; so, with another leisurely motoring holiday in prospect, having located it on a large-scale map of Perthshire, somewhere between the head of Loch Tummel and Kinloch Rannoch, my wife and I set out to pay a visit. Eventually, the cottages proved so scattered that when we reached the 'centre' of the clachan, the post office, there was not another house or building of any kind within sight. Such is fame!

Reverting to the year 1896, if the 'Dunalastairs' made a great impression upon members of the public, that welcome was mild compared to that which they received from the top-link enginemen. In Drummond and Lambie days it had, in modern popular parlance, been 'really something' to be an express driver on the Caledonian, and at joint stations like Perth and Carlisle it is to be feared that these great characters displayed a terrific superiority complex towards their counterparts on other railways. This was particularly so at Carlisle. All the Drummond 4-4-0s had their regular drivers, and no other, and of Tom Robinson—one of the heroes of the 1895 'Race to the North'—it was said that when he was in the Citadel station with engine No 78 he would hardly deign to acknowledge, let alone to fraternize with, enginemen of other railways, even those of his ally in the 'Race', the LNWR! In other respects, Robinson was a great-hearted soul, but professional etiquette and pride took possession of him once he was on No 78! Many of the other Carlisle and Pol-

madie men were the same. They had certainly engines to be proud of in 1895, and they justified that pride by their epic performances on the road. Imagine, then, their feelings when the first 'Dunalastairs' arrived, to supersede the Lambies and Drummonds!

All 15 engines of the class were turned out from St Rollox Works between January and May 1896, and the allocation by sheds was Polmadie: 721, 734 and 735; Perth: 722-725; Aberdeen: 726; Carlisle: 727-730, 732 and 733; Edinburgh: 731. The pioneer engine, *Dunalastair* herself, was immediately put on to the famous West Coast Corridor, 2 pm from Glasgow to Carlisle, and returned with the corresponding down train. The one Edinburgh engine worked the 10.15 am London express to Carlisle, returning with the 4.30 pm as was the case with the engines tested by Drummond in 1889. The new engines, although worked hard while on the road, led a fairly sheltered existence as far as aggregate mileages were concerned; and they were tended and nursed like pets by their regular crews. There was one exception to the utilization of these engines on a very strenuous single-home turn worked alternatively by Carlisle and Perth sheds. This was on the 8 pm sleeping car express from Perth to Carlisle, returning with the celebrated 2.17 am 'Tourist' express. This involved a round trip of 302 miles, and on the northbound run the 117.8 miles from Carlisle to Stirling were booked to be run *non-stop* in 125 minutes, an average speed of 56.5 mph, over Beattock Summit! The loads were usually around 170 to 200 tons, and no driver of a 'Dunalastair' would dream of taking a banker up to Beattock in those days.

The remarkable booked speeds of the night Scottish expresses of that year were the aftermath of the 'Race to the North' in the previous summer, but the 'Tourist' express ran to its fast schedule only for the three months of the summer service. At the very opening of that season, however, on 18 July 1896, that very train had come to grief on the curve north of Preston; and although the circumstances, as related in Chapter 4 of this book, were not directly related to fast running, the accident itself had a very bad effect upon the increase of railway speeds in general, quite apart from the terrible avalanche of scaremongering that was let loose in the popular press. Some general deceleration of the fastest West Coast expresses took place in the autumn of 1896. Fortunately, however, the very fast night run of the down 'Tourist' train remained throughout the season, and both Carlisle and Perth enginemen with their new 'Dunalastairs' seemed to revel in showing by how much they could improve upon the 56.5 mph booking from Carlisle to Stirling. Not only Rous-Marten, but also fellow enthusiasts like the Rev W.J. Scott and A.C.W. Lowe, spent night after night logging the train in the early hours of the morning.

The amazing feature of that glorious three months of nocturnal Caledonian speeding was that the Carlisle drivers, in particular, who had so distinguished themselves with the Drummond 4-4-0s in the previous summer, with loads less than 100 tons on the fastest night of the 'Race', were making equally spectacular times in 1896, with the 'Dunalastairs' and all but double the loads. Outline times of three runs, in the table below, bear this out.

With the prospect of heavier loads rather than higher speeds, McIntosh put his drawing office on to the design of an 'improved Dunalastair', with enlarged cylinders, a longer boiler barrel and a higher boiler pressure. With the enlarged cylinders, unfortunately,

Left *One of the first 'Dunalastairs', No 724* Jubilee, *built in 1896* (F. Moore's Rail Photos).

Caledonian Railway: Carlisle-Stirling

Engine No	90	728	733
Engine class	Drummond	'Dunalastair'	'Dunalastair'
Load (tons)	75	170	180
Distance	Time	Time	Time
(miles)	(m s)	(m s)	(m s)
0.0 Carlisle	0 00	0 00	0 00
8.6 Gretna Junc	10 15	8 58	8 53
25.8 Lockerbie	27 00	25 59	25 50
39.7 Beattock	39 30	37 50	38 23
49.7 Summit	53 00	53 33	53 30
66.9 Symington	68 00	67 44	68 24
73.5 Carstairs	74 00	72 46	73 40
89.9 Holytown	89 30	89 17	89 46
109.7 Larbert	109 00	109 22	110 10
117.8 Stirling	116 30	116 53	117 40

went some of Drummond's front-end design refinements, such as the steam-jacketed cylinders and the Vortex blast pipe. St Rollox practice thenceforward took the line of increased steam production, and with decreasing attention to overall thermal efficiency. The provision of large bogie tenders, with an increased water-carrying capacity from 3,500 to 4,125 gallons, was a significant step. The successive advances in 4-4-0 express passenger locomotive building at St Rollox may be tabulated thus:

Dunalastair locomotive dynasty

Loco prototype	766	900	140
Date introduced	1897	1899	1904
Cylinders, diameter × stroke (in)	19 × 26	19 × 26	19 × 26
Boiler Mean diameter, outside (ft in)	4 9¼	4 9¼	4 11½
Length of barrel (ft in)	11 1	11 1	11 2
Steam pressure (psi)	175	180	180
Tubes Number	265	269	276
Length between tube plates (ft in)	11 4½	11 4½	11 6
Heating surfaces (sq ft)			
Tubes	1,381·2	1,402	1,470
Firebox	118.78	138	145

Above *The first 'Dunalastair III', No 900, approaching Beattock summit with an up West Coast express* (M.W. Earley).

Loco prototype	766	900	140
Total	1,500	1,540	1,615
Grate area	20.63	22	21
Total weight of engine (tons)	49	51.6	54.5
Total weight of tender (tons)	45	49.5	53

It will be seen from the foregoing table that there was little increase in tractive effort between the second and fourth series of 'Dunalastairs', and a decrease in grate area between the third and fourth. The principal change was the increase in firebox heating surface. The 'engine' proper remained the same throughout. The machinery was massive, and contributed in no small measure to the reliability of Caledonian engines in service, no matter how severely they were thrashed. All three classes of improved 'Dunalastairs' were beautiful-looking engines, particularly to my mind the third, or '900' Class. These were the last of the range that were painted in the

Top right *Engine No 769 of the 'Dunalastair II' Class, showing the proportions of the engine and the huge bogie tender* (Author's Collection).

Above right *Two 'Dunalastair II' Class 4-4-0s, No 779 Breadalbane and an unidentified engine in the light blue livery* (British Railways).

Right *A 'Dunalastair III', No 902, in the original dark blue livery* (British Railways).

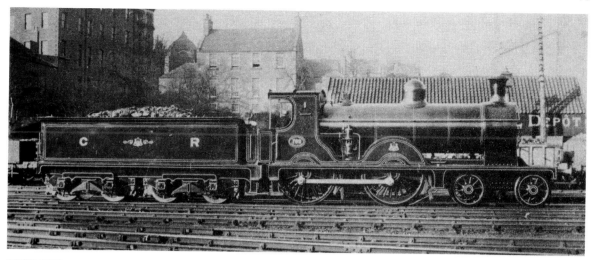

The first of the final batch of the non-superheater 'Dunalastair IV' Class, No 136, built in 1910 (British Railways).

'Dunalastair IV' Class No 148 approaching Beattock summit with a very heavy southbound Anglo-Scottish express (Author's collection).

Left *The first 'Dunalastair' to be built with a superheater, No 139 of the fourth class, built at St Rollox in 1910* (Loco Publishing Co).

Right *A Pickersgill 4-4-0, originally No 83 built by Armstrong Whitworth & Co in 1921, in the first LMS style of Midland red livery* (British Railways).

original dark blue. Magnificent they must have looked, with the valances, steps and tender underframes in crimson lake; but the lighter blue, with a proportion of white mixed with the basic Prussian blue, was equally acceptable, and became the traditional 'Caley Blue' known only to those enthusiasts of my age and younger who did not know the earlier style. The '140' Class, newly turned out in the light blue, and maintained thuswise, were certainly breathtaking in their splendour.

Of the 'Dunalastair II' Class there were 15 engines, with the numbers running from 766 to 780. The first six were built in 1897 and the rest in 1898. The pioneer engine, No 766, was not originally named; the title *Dunalastair 2nd* was added in 1898, a somewhat curious use, reminding us of schoolboy designations to distinguish those of the same surname. The '900' Class, 16 engines in all, were built in 1899-1900. The first three were Nos 900-2, and thereafter the numbers began at 887, running upwards to 899. It was interesting to see how the tender capacity, or rather the tender weight, increased over successive batches of this family of locomotives. While the coal capacity remained constant throughout at 4½ tons, and the water was increased only from 4,125 gallons on series 'II' and 'III' to 4,300 gallons on the 'Dunalastair IV', or '140' Class, the loaded weight of the tenders went up from 45 tons on 'II', and 49½ on 'III' to no less than 53 tons on series 'IV', the last named being almost as heavy as the locomotives! There is a good story to be told about the tenders of the 'Dunalastair IV', and the appetite for coal of the engines themselves when those engines were on the strenuous single-home night run from Perth to Carlisle and back. To appreciate this story to the full, it must be explained that 'lum' is the Scots vernacular for chimney. Well, on the run south with a heavy

train they had used a good proportion of the nominal 4½ tons carried on those big tenders, and in preparing for the homeward run the Perth driver got the coal man at Kingmoor shed, Carlisle, to put box after box of fresh supplies on to the tender, until indeed there was a stack almost up to the limit of the loading gauge! Then, when he shouted he'd got enough, the coal man replied, 'Back a bit,' and, as the engine moved, he yelled, 'Stop!' The Perth driver asked what was the matter, and the coal man replied, 'Take a box down the b— lum and you'll maybe have enough!'

The introduction of superheating on the 'Dunalastair IV' Class in 1910 wrought an amazing difference in the coal consumption of those engines. Up till that time, 16 engines of the class had been built and were giving every satisfaction. In that era no one, least of all on the Caledonian, minded about burning a lot of coal, and the 'Dunalastair IV' Class were great favourites wherever they went. Then, in 1910, an order was given to St Rollox Works for a further four of these engines, and, as if they were not big enough already, the tenders for them had an increased capacity to carry 4,600 gallons of water and no less than 6 tons of coal. When fully loaded they weighed 56 tons. Three of the new engines, Nos 136, 137 and 138, were of the standard 'Dunalastair IV' design, but No 139 was equipped with a Schmidt superheater, and was in fact the first superheater engine to run in Scotland. The extent of redesign was considerable, because the frames had to be altered to accommodate a smokebox longer than usual, though not to the extent seen on some contemporary Midland 4-4-0s. The cylinders were larger, and instead of the traditional St Rollox front end with direct-action Stephenson link motion actuating slide valves between the cylinders, engine No 139 had 8-in

piston valves vertically above the cylinders, with a rocker arm drive. At first the boiler pressure of the superheater engine was 165 psi against the 180 lb of the standard 'Dunalastair IVs'.

Engine No 139, in company with the new non-superheater engine No 138, was allocated to Perth shed, and as soon as they were both thoroughly run in, some coal trials were carried out on the strenuous night single-home run to Carlisle and back. But the down 'Tourist', leaving Carlisle at 2.20 am, was a very pale shade of what it had been in the halcyon days of 1896, because the start-to-stop time for the 117.8 miles from Carlisle to Stirling was 143 minutes, against the very exciting 125 minutes of 14 years earlier. I have not got the timing of the 9 pm up 'sleeper' from Perth to Carlisle.

Caledonian Railway: 1910 coal trials, Perth-Carlisle-Perth

Engine No	138	139
Type	Saturated	Superheated
Average trailing load (tons)		
Southbound	265	220
Northbound	220	235
Total coal, for three return trips (tons)	19.0	14.95
Coal consumption (lb per train mile)	47.5	37.2
Total water evaporation (gallons)	27,495	22,138

Having regard to the relatively moderate loads, these were not particularly impressive for a superheater engine, even though Beattock Bank was taken without any assistance. With heavier trains from Carlisle, in which pilot assistance was taken from the start, it was noticeable, even with superheater engines, that the drivers took advantage of the stop at Beattock Summit, while detaching their pilots, to replenish their tender tanks when continuing northwards to Perth.

Following the favourable results of the trials with engine No 139 in 1910, four more were built with Schmidt superheaters in 1911, but after that St Rollox changed to the Robinson type, and 17 more of the superheater 'Dunalastair IVs' were built between 1912 and 1914. Although McIntosh had introduced his great 4-6-0s, in limited numbers for prestige duties, the 'Dunalastair IVs' remained the principal express passenger workhorses of the line, and they were universally popular. They stayed the course remarkably well. Except for the ill-fated No 121, which was damaged beyond repair in the catastrophic disaster at Quintinshill in 1915, the remaining 21 engines of the class survived till after the Second World War, most of them later even than 1955, and the last one, BR No 54441 (CR No 132) was not scrapped until May 1959, at the ripe old age of 48 years. More than that, two of the engines built as non-superheaters in 1907-8 were afterwards rebuilt and assimilated into the '139' Class. One of these, CR No 923, BR No 14438, lasted until 1955, while sister engine No 924 proved to be the patriarch of the whole class, because she was not scrapped until August 1958, more than fifty years after construction. The only change in her appearance, apart from the painting, was the loss of the great bogie tender. The 'Dunalastair IVs' may not have been the most economical of engines, but in longevity they paid off handsomely.

7. LNWR: the Whale era

The twentieth century opened with what was to be a sad consummation in the personal life of F.W. Webb. In the early 'nineties he seemed to be striding like a colossus over the entire field of railway mechanical engineering; his latest three-cylinder compound express engines, the 'Teutonics', were doing some brilliant work, and the earlier shortcomings of his compounds had been successfully surmounted by use of the loose eccentric. Then, instead of building upon the prowess of the 'Teutonics', he began to branch into fresh and untried fields, with eventually disastrous results to his own reputation. No one doubted the pulling power of the four-cylinder compound 4-4-0s. They were splendidly and massively constructed, and they steamed well; but as *express* engines they were not far removed from a real dead loss. They were hopelessly sluggish. Without knowing all the considerations that influenced Webb in the selection of cylinder proportions on these engines, one would suggest that they were doomed to failure from the start. On the 'Teutonics', the ratio of low-pressure to high-pressure cylinder volume was 2.3 to 1, which was much the same as on the successful Smith-Johnson compounds on the Midland Railway, whereas the first series of Webb four-cylinder compounds had a ratio of no more than 1.87 to 1. Then, having put forty engines of the 'Jubilee' Class on the road, he produced the 'Alfred the Great' Class, with larger boilers and still larger high-pressure cylinders of 16-in diameter. The low-pressure cylinders, inside, could not be enlarged beyond the 20½-in diameter of the 'Jubilees', and the volume ratio became the still less propitious 1.69 to 1.

At this distance in time, it would be all too easy to pontificate upon the folly of ruining these otherwise superbly built 4-4-0 engines with a fundamental error in their cylinder proportions; and the error was intensified by the magnitude of the orders placed with Crewe Works—forty 'Jubilees' (including the two experimental ones of 1897) and forty of the 'Alfred the Great' series. Nevertheless, Webb himself seems to have realized his mistake in enlarging still further the diameter of the high-pressure cylinders on the 'Alfred the Great' Class, introduced in 1901, because even before the second ten of those engines were built, in the following year, the first batch, engines 1941-1950, were having their high-pressure cylinders lined up to make them of 15-in diameter. An engineer, recalling events of his five years' apprenticeship at Crewe between 1897 and 1902, and writing of the time in *The Railway Magazine* some twenty years later, has a diverting account of the process adopted, in which he, a tough young fellow, assisted personally. He wrote:

'After skimming the cylinders out to get them true, a gang of men at the run dragged lengths of white-hot rails from the boiler shop smithy adjacent and placed them in the cylinder to expand it a bit. When it was well hot, the liner, turned all over to size, was entered in the rear end of the cylinder and pulled into place with an enormous nut and bolt (about 2½-in diameter) with heavy bearers, one across the liner and the other across the far end of the cylinder. It took three gangs of men in turn on a heavy spanner to tighten up the nut, while other hefty individuals assisted the liner in by beating on the bolt head with a heavy hammer. Why the liner was not constructed with a light flange to fit over the cylinder end and turned an easy fit so that a pair of men could fit it in and bolt it up in about ten minutes, was one of life's mysteries to me; but seeing that I assisted at several of the above operations, it must have been the official way of doing it.'

Before even the first batch of these engines was fully into its stride, however, in October 1901, what was virtually the death knell of the four-cylinder compound 4-4-0s as top-line express passenger engines was issued, not by the CME but by the General Manager's office at Euston, ordering that any train loaded to '17 coaches', or more, must be double-headed. The tonnage system of calculating passenger train loads had not then been introduced on the LNWR, and a rough and ready method then sufficed, by which any six-wheeler counted as '1', any eight-wheelers '1½', and the twelve-wheelers as '2'. While there was much variation in the actual weights of individual vehicles, those who took detailed notes of train running, like Charles Rous-Marten and R.E. Charlewood, reckoned that the 'equal to 17' rule meant around 270 tons tare, while admitting that, prior to its introduction, many of the crack North Western trains had been worked without pilot engines carrying loads of 320 tons or more. This was certainly the case with the afternoon 'Corridor' expresses between Euston and Glasgow, in the days of *Jeanie Deans*, and the Irish boat train for Fleetwood, with the 'Jubilee' compounds, was frequently loaded up to 12 or 13 bogies. What Webb himself thought of the 'equal to 17' rule one does not like to imagine; but another ten of the 'Alfreds' were being built at Crewe in 1902, and another twenty at the time when Webb was somewhat unceremoniously hustled out of office in the early months of 1903. These last thirty

of the class had 15-in diameter high-pressure cylinders from the outset.

Apart from the compounding, Webb introduced an interesting and lasting constructional feature into the four-cylinder compound 4-4-0s. They were the first of his compound engines to have both high-pressure and low-pressure cylinders driving on to the same axle; and, particularly in view of the still higher boiler pressure used on these engines, 200 psi, special consideration had to be given to the pressures in the journals of the main bearings. After his brief reversion to the use of the Stephenson link motion on his eight-wheeled three-cylinder compounds of the 'Greater Britain' and the 'John Hick' Classes, he returned to the Joy valve gear on the 'Jubilees', and on these engines, no eccentrics being needed, Webb introduced the novel feature of a central bearing on the driving axle. While a third bearing involved some precision methods in lining up, Crewe Works was well adapted to procedures of that kind, and no difficulties were experienced—in fact, the constructional method was used on all subsequent inside-cylinder passenger engines built at Crewe during the ensuing twenty years.

With George Whale as Chief Mechanical Engineer designate, even before the official date of retirement of Mr Webb, it is not surprising that he immediately put the drawing office on to what was the most urgent matter of the day. As a running man he would have been well aware of the feature that made the 'Teutonics' far and away the most successful of all the Webb compounds, the loose eccentric controlling the steam admission to the low-pressure cylinder. While he could not improve the cylinder proportions already built into the 'Alfreds', there was a means of freeing up the flow of steam in which the new engines, and equally the 'Jubilees', were most restricted. Taking the relatively new engine No 1952 *Benbow*, the rocking shafts, through which the high-pressure cylinder valves were operated from tail rods on the low-pressure valve stems, were taken out, and a separate set of Joy valve gear fitted, outside as in the 'Teutonics', for the high-pressure cylinders. This enabled the driver to notch up the high-pressure valves without similarly adjusting the low-pressure.

The effect of the modifications made to engine No 1952 was shown on some trial runs made between Crewe and Stafford on 27 September 1903, with a train of 13 vehicles and the dynamometer car, 372 tons tare. On the first round trip, Crewe to Stafford and back, the high-pressure and low-pressure valves were linked up simultaneously, as with the original design. With this method of working, to avoid choking the engine, the regulator was only partially opened. On the second round trip, the low-pressure valves were left in full gear the whole time, and the

high-pressure linked up as required. With this method it was possible to use full regulator. The results as tabulated herewith speak for themselves, and before the end of November a start had been made on modifying other engines of the class. Engine No 1958 *Royal Oak* was the second to be treated.

LNWR: Trials with modified No 1952 *Benbow*

Crewe-Stafford

Location	Simultaneous linking up		New method	
	Speed (mph)	Indicated horse-power	Speed (mph)	Indicated horse-power
Milepost 156	30	756	34	880
Betley Road	32	815	40	938
Milepost 151	28	621	38	923
Milepost 149	32	739	41	940
Milepost 148	35	531	45	906
Time, Crewe to Whitmore (10.5 miles)	22 min		18 ½ min	
Time, Crewe to Stafford (24.5 miles)	38 ½ min		34 ¼ min	

Stafford-Crewe

Location	Distance from start (miles)	Simultaneous linking up		New method	
		Speed (mph)	Indicated horse-power	Speed (mph)	Indicated horse-power
Milepost 135	1.4	35	693	36	903
Milepost 138	4.4	40	663	50	949
Milepost 141	7.4	40	662	51	775
Milepost 144	10.4	44	754	50	760
Milepost 146	12.4	45	756	50	786
Milepost 147	13.4	43	705	48	769
Milepost 148	14.4	43	581	48	769
Time, Stafford to Whitmore (12 miles)		22 ½ min		19 ½ min	
Time, Stafford to Crewe (24.5 miles)		34 min		30 min	

The improved tractive power of the 'Benbows', as the modified engines became known, led to the 'equal to 17' rule being waived in their case, but of course there were not many of them at the start. As a dis-

'Alfred the Great' four-cylinder compound 4-4-0 No 1947 Australia *as modified to the 'Benbow' series* (W.H. Whitworth).

tinguishing feature, *Benbow* ran for some little time in plain grey. As the last batch of the 'Alfreds', Nos 1971-80, were similarly turned out from Crewe, there were rumours that a new livery was contemplation, following the change in Chief Mechanical Engineers; but reflecting on the personality of the new Chief, I should imagine that nothing was further from his thoughts! The 'Benbows', however, did have a further mark of change in the form of the canopied cab. A writer of seventy years ago once stigmatized the older North Western cabs as 'a disgrace to humanity'! Certainly there was not much in the way of 'creature comfort' in the Webb cabs, as I noted for myself in climbing aboard an 18-inch 0-6-0 in the little yard at Penrith, and then transferring my attentions to an ex-NER 'C' Class goods that was alongside. The contrast was breathtaking. Reverting to the year 1903, however, the cab fitted to the 'Benbows' was of course the prototype of that used on all subsequent Crewe tender engines, till their designs were superseded by those of the LMS.

In turning to entirely new work, George Whale had an excellent design staff headed by J.N. Jackson, the Chief Locomotive Draughtsman, and Tommy Sackville, the leading hand on new design work. One could well imagine Whale, as an out and out running man, giving these two men a broad specification: 'Give me a 4-4-0 with 19-in by 26-in cylinders that will steam as freely as a 'Precedent': Joy valve gear, with three bearings on the driving axle; and for goodness sake be quick about it, because I want 100 of them in traffic within two years!' Little more than nine months from the time he took over from Webb, at the end of May 1903, Whale had the first of his new engines completed at Crewe. 'Precursor' indeed! With the vast resources at his disposal, this period of nine months would not have been unduly short if

nothing more than an experimental prototype had been involved; if it had been built by what are sometimes called 'knife and fork' methods, leaving the outlay on tools for quantity production until the prototype had been proved by extended trials. But *Precursor* was in every way a 'production job'. Nevertheless, deep though the confidence of the higher management lay in Mr Whale, there had been so many disappointments in recent years in North Western express passenger motive power that there was naturally a certain time-lag between the successive completions of the first small batches, to observe whether fulfilment was in accordance with promise. Five engines of the new design were turned out in March-April 1904, and another five in June. But their performance during the heavy summer traffic of 1904 settled all doubts, and in the early autumn of 1904 Whale was instructed to build another hundred of them as quickly as he could. Those hundred engines were turned out in 76 weeks!

It is of particular interest to recall the names of those first ten 'Precursor' Class 4-4-0s, because they showed the way the wind was blowing with regard to the older engines of the LNWR:

New engine No	Name	Engine replaced (Class)
513	*Precursor*	'Precursor' 2-4-0
1395	*Harbinger*	'Precursor' 2-4-0
1419	*Tamerlane*	'Dreadnought'
2023	*Helvellyn*	'Precursor' 2-4-0
2164	*Oberon*	'Precursor' 2-4-0
2	*Simoom*	'Precursor' 2-4-0
7	*Titan*	'Dreadnought'
412	*Alfred Paget*	'Lady of the Lake'
510	*Albatross*	'Precursor' 2-4-0
659	*Dreadnought*	'Dreadnought'

Left *One of the first 'Precursor' 4-4-0s, No 659* Dreadnought *(British Railways).*

Right *'Precursor' Class 4-4-0 No 1309* Shamrock *on the 2 pm West Coast 'Corridor' express near Kenton* (Author's Collection).

That the 'Dreadnought' compounds were being scrapped as early as 1904 was significant; but I shall have more to say about the scrapping of historic locomotives, and not only North Westerns, later in this chapter.

Although *Precursor* was indeed the precursor of an entirely new era at Crewe, she could nevertheless be described as a thoroughly standard North Western job. There was nothing novel or untried in her basic design, or in any of the fittings. The boiler was a much larger version of that of the 'Cauliflowers'. At the same time they had a rather old-fashioned, but most efficient, type of deep firebox. Apart from the ease of firing, there is another point about deep fireboxes that is perhaps not so greatly appreciated, and that is the depth of fire actually in contact with the water space. Much of the trouble with leaking stays can arise from abrupt changes in temperature, and a great deal of Churchward's highly scientific development work on the Great Western, which led to the perfecting of his particular form of taper boiler, was centred upon the avoidance of local 'hot spots', which could give rise to unequal expansion, and consequent leakage, at tubes and stays. Experience had shown that far less trouble in this respect occurred with deep fireboxes and thick fires than with the new types with shallow grates that had to be worked with thin fires. Moreover, the 'Precursor' firebox was something with which the men were immediately familiar. Though larger, it was proportioned exactly the same as that of a 'Jumbo' or a 'Cauliflower', and it could be fired in just the same way.

The boiler itself was admirably proportioned to sustain a high rate of evaporation; the tubes were of $1\frac{7}{8}$-in outside diameter, with a distance of 12 ft $2\frac{1}{4}$ in between the tube plates. Originally, the tube heat-

ing surface was no less than 1,848.4 sq ft, but at a later date the upper rows of tubes were omitted, together with two vertical rows of five on each side, and this reduced the heating surface slightly to 1,728.5 sq ft. The grate area was 22.4 sq ft, but the very deep firebox provided a firebox heating surface of no less than 161.3 sq ft. Thus, originally, *Precursor* had no less than 2,009.7 sq ft of heating surface. The original general arrangement drawing, signed by Whale and initialled by both Jackson and Sackfield, shows a working pressure of 185 psi at the safety valve, and this figure is also quoted on a drawing of the 19-inch 4-6-0 goods which was published in the *Locomotive Magazine*. But, in actual practice, the valves were set to blow off at 175 psi, and this latter figure was always quoted in all technical descriptions of the locomotives published at the time they were first built.

Turning now from the boiler to the machinery, the main journals were of 8-in diameter by 9-in long, while the centre bearing was of $7\frac{1}{4}$-in diameter. The absence of any eccentrics enabled the entire available space to be taken up with the massive built-up crankshaft. Although this latter, and the bearings provided for it, were of a most generous proportion, the main frames—for an engine designed to develop so high an output of power continuously—were on the light side. The frame-plates were only 1 in thick, and there was a curious feature in the design of the frames, the origin of which may not be generally appreciated. The maximum length of main frame that could be slotted out at Crewe was about 28 ft, so that any engine longer than this had to have an extension spliced on. In practice, this meant that all types from 4-4-0s upwards had to have this splicing, and Crewe made a virtue out of this necessity by making the splice come between the point of attachment of the

cylinders to the frame and the motion plate. The distance between the frame-plates was 4 ft 2 in, rearwards from the motion plate, and 4 ft 0 in between the forward extensions, between which were fixed the cylinders.

The cylinder and valve design, though conventional in some respects, was excellent in the provision it made for getting large volumes of steam through the inlet and exhaust ports. The Webb 'Jumbos' were generally acknowledged to be among the fastest-running engines on the North Western, though the three-cylinder compound 'Teutonics', with a loose eccentric gear for their low-pressure cylinder, were very fast engines and frequently exceeded 85 mph. But in view of the reputation of the 'Jumbos', it is interesting to compare certain of their cylinder proportions with those of the 'Precursors'. The basic dimensions were 17-in diameter by 24-in stroke, against 19-in diameter by 26-in stroke, an increase, in the 'Precursor', of 35 per cent. But the maximum steam port area was more nearly doubled, from 13.125 sq in to 23.44—an increase of 79 per cent. The valve gear had the following dimensions:

Travel of valve in full gear	5 in
Lap of valve	$1^{1}/_{16}$ in
Lead of valve	$^{3}/_{16}$ in
Inside clearance	nil

At a time when the majority of British express locomotives, including such famous contemporaries of the 'Precursors' as the Great Eastern 'Claud Hamiltons' and the North Eastern 'R' Class, had maximum valve travels of 4-in or even less, the 'Precursor' valve gear, combined with the very large port openings it gave, represented a distinctly

advanced design. It had the great merit of enabling large volumes of steam to be got into and out of the cylinders, with consequent high output of power. Taken all in all, George Whale in the specification he had laid down, and Jackson in the way he had worked it out, had produced a modern express locomotive of admirable proportions, intended for very hard work on the road. A boiler that proved a prolific steam raiser, and a good cylinder layout, were combined with a series of 'home-made' fittings such as the Ramsbottom regulator and Webb injector that worked without fail. In giving the new regime all the credit they deserve for the fame the 'Precursors' subsequently earned, one must not overlook how much of their basic design was 'pure Webb'. Only the 'fads' were discarded, like the water-bottom to the ashpan. Otherwise, the 'Precursor' could be closely described as a much enlarged 4-4-0 version of the 'Cauliflower', with the four-wheeled radial truck from the 'Jubilees' and 'Alfreds'. The new regime made no startling innovations. They built an engine that was in every way a synthesis of what was best in the practice of Webb; and they built it in record time using the magnificent organization and plant that Webb had established at Crewe. In one respect, however, Whale did break fresh ground, in that the tender was of an entirely new design with steel frames. It is astonishing to recall that Webb was using wood-framed tenders to the very end of his time at Crewe.

The 'Precursors' were an outstanding success from the very outset. Rarely had there been a new locomotive design that was so completely right from the word 'go'. However, in the first months after their introduction, the impact of the new engines upon the train working as a whole was not great. To some extent, Whale was the victim of his own drive. With the

Left *The up day Irish Mail near Colwyn Bay, hauled by an unidentified 'Precursor' (Author's Collection).*

Below *Up 2-hour Birmingham express at the south end of Watford Tunnel hauled by 'Precursor' Class 4-4-0 No 2585* Watt *(Author's Collection).*

Bottom *Whale's 4-4-2 type of 1906 with 6-ft 3-in wheels for fast residential trains around the larger centres (British Railways).*

Below right *Whale's Class 'D', predecessor of the celebrated 'Super D', as the later superheater 'G1' and 'G2' Class was popularly known (British Railways).*

building of the 'Precursors', confident in the imminent authorization of the hundred further engines of the class he needed, he had also commenced a vigorous scrapping programme, which incidentally left the running department seriously short of express engines for a while. The scrapping of the Webb three-cylinder compounds has made excellent copy for some journalists who like to dwell upon the less satisfactory features of Webb's great career, but in referring to the relatively short life of the 'Experiment' and 'Dreadnought' compounds, one should take a broader view of happenings further afield than those on the LNWR, and include its great rival of 1895, Doncaster. No nineteenth-century express locomotives were more revered by their supporters than Patrick Stirling's bogie 8-ft singles, yet most of these preceded the Webb three-cylinder express engines to the scrap heap, some after considerably shorter lives, while on the Midland, as will be discussed in a later chapter of this book, all but a handful of the supremely graceful small-boilered Johnson 4-4-0s, 234 engines in all, had been rebuilt out of all recognition by the end of 1907. Beside such a slaughter, Whale's replacement of the Webb three-cylinder compound express engines must seem a relatively gentlemanly procedure.

It is of interest that the names of the 'Experiment' and 'Dreadnought' were used again in all but a few instances; but such was the rate of 'Precursor' building in 1904-6 that the rate of scrapping of the compounds was not nearly enough to furnish all that was needed for the new engines. Twenty-two former 'Experiment' names, and 26 from 'Dreadnoughts', were used on the 'Precursors'. Of the remainder of these Webb classes, four more from 'Experiments' were used on the new 'Experiment' Class 4-6-0, and this class took 11 further of the 'Dreadnought' names.

Only seven of those seventy compound names were not used again, four from 'Experiments', namely *Compound, Economist, Rich. Francis Roberts* and *City of Chicago,* and three from 'Dreadnoughts', *Marchioness of Stafford, City of New York* and *Raven.* It is interesting to note the titles that were discarded, particularly the two from American cities. *Compound* and *Economist* were obvious deletions, while I have no idea who *Rich. Francis Roberts* was. The picturesque name *Marchioness of Stafford* was down for revival on one of the four-cylinder 4-6-0s of the 'Claughton' Class in 1922, but further naming was halted by the imminence of the railway amalgamations.

As part of his modernization of North Western motive power, Whale needed a 4-6-0 to deal with the heavy gradients of the line north of Carnforth. The Crewe drawing office evolved a design that was to form the solid basis of a range of no fewer than 520 standard 4-6-0 locomotives. There was no question of building for prestige, or 'one-upmanship', over fellow Chief Mechanical Engineers. Whale and his men produced a solid dividend earner that had a very high route availability over the entire North Western system. It stemmed from a very soundly worked out design, so sound that it remained unchanged, save for the addition of superheaters and piston valves, for 17 years. Delivery of the last engines of the type was taken in April 1922. Yet alongside the universal acclaim that greeted the introduction of the 'Precursors' in 1904, the advent of Whale's 4-6-0s a year later was distinctly lukewarm. In producing the compact 4-6-0 version of the 'Precursor', the three pairs of 6-ft 3-in coupled wheels were pitched at no more than 6-ft 9½-in centres. The firebox backplate was actually ahead of the rearmost pair of coupled wheels, so that the injector, in its usual place on the back of the ashpan, was just ahead of the rear coupled axle. The

Left *The Glasgow portion of the 10 am Scotch express from Euston at Shap Summit behind engine No 1357* City of Edinburgh *('Experiment' Class) (R.J. Purves).*

Below *'Experiment' Class 4-6-0 No 2646* Boniface *(E. Mason).*

Bottom *One of the very successful 19-inch mixed traffic 4-6-0s, No 2188 introduced in 1906 (Author's Collection).*

Below right *An up sleeping car express on Bushey troughs hauled by 'Experiment' Class 4-6-0, No 507* Sarmatian *(British Railways).*

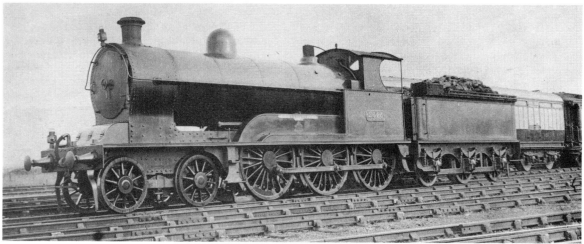

shape of the firebox was virtually dictated by the position of the coupled axles, and the result was a shallow level grate, with an area of 25 sq ft. The factor that most heavily prejudiced the early performance of the 'Experiments' was the technique needed in firing that very shallow grate. It was something entirely new on the North Western, and involved shooting the coal almost horizontally from the firedoor in order to keep the front part of the grate covered. Firemen found it difficult to see the effects of what they were doing, and they would allow holes to develop in what was, of course, the hottest part of the fire. In course of time they discovered that the most effective way to keep a good, even fire in the forward part of the grate was so to inject the coal that it hit the tube plate and then fell back on to the grate. To do this successfully required a certain knack, and an engineer who was trained at Crewe once made this comment to me: 'The shovel was a long narrow one, with a long handle, and the secret was to bang that shovel, held level, on the firehole doorplate, the while sliding the shank smartly through the guiding hand. Once this had been mastered there was nothing to fear.' It must be admitted, however, that my friend was referring to days when there were not only the 105 'Experiments', but also hundreds of the superheated 'Prince of Wales' 4-6-0s running. The knack was a well-known technique on the LNWR. It was very different when the first 'Experiments' came out in 1905; then, not even the locomotive inspectors knew the trick, and I do not suppose the men in the drawing office who designed that firebox could give much help either!

The first of the new engines, No 66 *Experiment*, was completed at Crewe in April 1905 and four more were turned out in June, namely No 306 *Autocrat,* No 353 *Britannic,* No 372 *Germanic* and No 507 *Sarmatian.* During the summer and autumn of that year these five

engines were almost exclusively on the Carlisle road. They took the Glasgow portion of the 10 am from Euston and the down 'Corridor' (2 pm from Euston), and from these two trains the return workings were the 8.42 pm and 1 am from Carlisle. They also had the 4.12 pm up 'Corridor', probably working north on the sharply-timed morning semi-fast from Crewe in order to pick up this important return working. Despite the enthusiasm of Rous-Marten, that other very experienced and critical observer, R.E. Charlewood, was not at all impressed. He used to contribute an article to *The Railway Magazine* at the close of each year, commenting upon the train services and locomotive performance of the past summer on the LNWR. Concerning the results from 1905, he wrote, 'It must be admitted that it was thanks to the fast downhill speed, rather than to any wonderful hill-climbing abilities, that the 'Experiments' performed the most exacting of their tasks.' The ascent to Shap from the Carlisle side could be just as exacting, even though the maximum steepness of the gradient was not more than 1 in 125. Starting 'cold' from Carlisle, with a fire that could easily be a bit 'green', that ascent could be a laborious affair, as when *Experiment* herself, on the 8.42 pm up with 350 tons, took 54½ min to pass Shap summit, 31.4 miles.

Thirty more 'Experiments' were built at Crewe during 1906 and another ten in the autumn of 1907. With more of these new engines available, some were drafted on to Southern Division duties. On the heaviest trains they were considered 'one coach better' than a 'Precursor', and engine No 1987 *Glendower* was allocated to the 'show-piece' of the entire line—the 2 pm down 'West Coast Corridor' express, between Euston and Crewe. *Glendower* was shared by two famous Camden drivers, David Button and Peter Jarvis, and from 1908 onwards to see that engine turned out for the

10am Euston to Glasgow and Edinburgh express on Bushey troughs hauled by 4-6-0 No 1412 Bedfordshire (H. Gordon Tidey).

'Corridor' was to appreciate the full dignity and majesty of a black engine, and just what the term 'Premier Line' meant in that spacious decade.

The thirty new 'Experiments' turned out in 1906 were followed in December by the mixed traffic version, with 5-ft 2-in coupled wheels, usually known as the '19-inch Goods'. They were the same as the 'Experiments' except that advantage was taken of the lower coupled axles to provide a slightly deeper firebox, with 144 sq ft of heating surface against 133 sq ft. The '19-inch Goods' was another great success for Crewe, and eventually 170 were built. Reverting to the express passenger engines, although there were occasions of exceptional loading in the Northern Division on which the 'Experiments' required double heading, they became widely appreciated as a general service passenger engine, and an order for sixty more of them was put in hand at Crewe in the autumn of 1908. This order had barely been started when Mr Whale retired at the end of the year, and only the first two engines of the new series had been completed. Whale was succeeded by C.J. Bowen Cooke, who had previously been Running Superintendent of the Southern Division, with his headquarters at Rugby. In that office he had been in a particularly good position to appreciate the practical working efficiency of the various types of locomotives on the line. Furthermore, unlike Whale, he was not only a running man, but an engineer of very wide interests. So one can be fairly sure that if he had harboured any doubts about the usefulness of the 'Experiments' he would have taken early steps to curtail or cancel altogether the locomotives of that large order for sixty

which had not been started. It seems certain, however, that Bowen Cooke was quite content to add this large number of 'Experiments' to the locomotive stock of the LNWR.

In the meantime he had been carrying out exchange trials with locomotives of friendly companies, and on the strength of the performance of Earle-Marsh's Class '13' 4-4-2 tank engine on the 'Sunny South Special' between Brighton and Rugby, as described in my *Great Locomotives of the Southern Railway*, Bowen Cooke decided to build a superheated version of the 'Precursor'. But then, before the new engine had completed even its preliminary trials, there was drawn across the scene what could well be described as the biggest 'red herring' in British locomotive history, the interchange trials between a LNWR 'Experiment' 4-6-0 and a Great Western 'Star'. Never, surely, in the history of technical journalism has there been built up such a mountain of false deduction, based originally on some ill-informed jumping to conclusions. In the first place, one could understand the touch-line commentators of 1910 imagining that its origin lay with Bowen Cooke, as a continuation of the series of interchanges he had sponsored in the previous summer. But had those contemporary observers really stopped to think, they could have been sufficiently perplexed at an event so completely out of context with what was currently happening at Crewe as to realize that there was something about it that did not ring true, at any rate so far as the LNWR was concerned. Before describing what happened, we must go back to the basic origins of the affair, which were due to storms that had begun to develop round the Board Table of the Great Western Railway at Paddington in 1903. Bowen Cooke, Crewe and the LNWR were dragged into it, all unwittingly, to provide the dramatic *dénouement*.

A bitter rift in the management structure of the Great Western Railway had developed over the proposals of the General Manager, James Inglis, to bring the engineering departments directly under his control, and certain directors, fastened on to the autonomy in financial matters enjoyed by the spending departments to start a campaign of awkward questioning of costs. Churchward's new locomotives became a major target. Some directors, with friends on other boards, did some shopping around, and by some means of building the 'Experiment' Class 4-6-0s at Crewe were obtained, and laid on the table at Paddington. Churchward was asked to produce corresponding figures for his 'Stars', and, having done so, to explain why they were so much higher than those of the LNWR engines. In the 'cut and thrust' of controversy around the GWR Board Table, tempers were apt to be short and, although his reply may have improved in the telling, the story goes that he explained the difference in the homely words, 'because one of mine could pull two of their bloody things backwards!' Then, with consummate diplomatic skill, he suggested an interchange trial. One is inclined to doubt if Bowen Cooke would ever have agreed to this interchange if he had realized at the outset the extent to which the whole question was 'loaded'. On the one hand he was quite happy to try a 'Star' between Euston and Crewe, because it was the nearest English equivalent to the big 4-6-0 he had already begun to plan; but sending an 'Experiment' to the Great Western was another thing altogether, especially during a week in August, when the West of England loadings were at their heaviest.

On the LNWR it would seem that the visiting engine *Polar Star* and her crew were committed to a policy of coal dodging, and certainly their running, apart from the quietness of the exhaust, was not impressive in its timekeeping. But on the GWR the unfortunate 'Experiment', No 1471 *Worcestershire*, was sacrificed to make a 'Roman holiday'. It is doubtful if senior running officers of the LNWR fully appreciated what their engine and its crew were in for. The driver and fireman were very soon under no delusions. It was not so much the disparity in trac-

tive effort, nor the awkward physical character of the West of England road that had to be learned by a strange driver, as the question of water supply. The North Western had made a lavish provision of water troughs to avoid the need for large tenders, and the dead weight that would have been involved in hauling them. Whale's tenders had a water capacity of only 3,000 gallons, and by comparison with the distance run by the Cornish Riviera Express, in the 230 miles run from Euston to Lancaster there were troughs near Bushey, Castlethorpe, Rugby, Hademore, Whitmore, Moore and Brock, distances of 15, 54, 84, 113, 149, 179 and 218 miles respectively from Euston, an average spacing of around 30 miles. The Great Western had only four sets between Paddington and Plymouth, at Aldermaston, Westbury, Cogload Junction and Starcross. While the fact of the GWR standard tenders carrying only 3,500 gallons of water was a mark of the working efficiency of the locomotives, this was no consolation to a strange engine crew who could hardly acquire in a fortnight's visit the technique to eke out their own supply.

Consequently, the North Western driver was running easily to conserve water, and on all his runs to the West of England except the last he had to stop at Savernake to top up the tank. Of course, all this simply played into Churchward's hands, and one had the feeling that, not for the only time in locomotive interchange trials, the men of the Great Western tended to 'rub it in' a little more roughly than was generous. Then the more popular organs of the national press waded in, and produced some highly coloured and characteristically inaccurate stories of *Worcestershire's* failures. It was the 'silly season', and some of them might otherwise have been short of copy! In this strange way, Churchward's critics on the Great Western Board were silenced; but while in 1910 no public riposte came from either Crewe or Euston, within a few years Bowen Cooke's new locomotives were hitting the headlines in the railway press to such an extent as to push Churchward, and other British locomotive engineers, completely 'off the front page'.

8. 4-6-0s of the Caledonian

When Dugald Drummond went to the Caledonian Railway, his major concern was with express passenger motive power. His predecessor, George Brittain, had introduced some admirable small-wheeled 4-4-0s in 1882, for the heavily graded Callander and Oban line, that were remarkably similar in their general proportions to the celebrated 'Skye Bogies' of the Highland Railway. In fact, Brittain's Oban 4-4-0s, built by Dübs & Co, preceded the Highland engines because all ten of the Caledonian engines were delivered in 1882, whereas only one of the 'Skye Bogies' was built in that year and the rest of them did not follow until 1892 and even later. By that time, of course, Brittain's 'Oban Bogies' were well established, to such an extent that successive locomotive superintendents of the Caledonian Railway had no concern about what was happening west of the junction at Dunblane, or so it appeared. But the new century, with its burgeoning tourist traffic, and through carriages from farther afield, put a new complexion on matters west of Callander, and McIntosh put the St Rollox drawing office on to the design of a much larger engine.

By use of the 4-6-0 wheel arrangement, greater adhesion was obtained without exceeding the axle-load limit of the Oban line, while the use of 19-in by 26-in cylinders in conjunction with coupled wheels of no more than 5-ft diameter and a boiler pressure of 175 psi gave the high nominal tractive effort of 23,269 lb. The boiler proportions on these engines were interesting. The barrel was considerably longer than on any of the 4-4-0 classes, and provided 1,800 sq ft of heating surface in the tubes. On the other hand, the grate area was no larger than that of the first 'Dunalastairs', and the firebox heating surface was no more than 100 sq ft. Here was a clear case of designing to suit the road. None of the very severe banks on the Callander and Oban line was of very long duration; an all-out effort was needed in spells of 10 minutes or a quarter-of-an-hour at the most, and in between times there would be far longer spells when the engine would be steaming lightly or coasting. For such duty, the long boiler and small firebox were ideal. The boiler could be used as a reservoir for building up a large head of steam in readiness for a big, though brief, effort, while the small firebox ensured the minimum of coal consumption in light steaming conditions, when coal could be wasted merely in keeping the bars covered! These Oban 4-6-0s were a great success, not only climbing well, but running at up to 60 mph on favourable stretches of line. The nine engines of the '55' Class, built

Left *'Oban Bogie' 5-ft 6-in 4-6-0 No 53* (Author's Collection).

Right *One of the Oban 4-6-0s of 1902, rebuilt with a larger boiler, seen here at Balquhidder in 1937* (O.S. Nock).

between 1902 and 1905, handled all the heaviest traffic of the line, both passenger and goods, for twenty years.

Although the main line, both north and south of Glasgow, included some lengthy and severe gradients, the Caledonian was by tradition a high-speed railway, and the 4-4-0 type of express locomotive continued, even into the twentieth century, to be the mainstay of the motive power stud. The zenith of express train speed had been the summer of 1896 when the 'Tourist', loaded up to 200 tons behind the tender, had been passing Beattock Summit in less than 54 minutes from the start at Carlisle. With the heavy corridor dining car trains on the daytime Anglo-Scottish services, loading to 300 tons or more, nothing approaching such speeds was likely to be attempted, but to McIntosh and his men the aim became to run those big trains without any need for assistance, up Beattock Bank in particular. When certain other railways introduced locomotives of greatly enhanced nominal tractive power to cope with exceptional demands, all too often the result was a massive, shapeless thing that looked as though the drawing office had been hard put to it to accommodate the proportions within the loading gauge. Setting alongside the comparative dimensions of the 'Dunalastair III' Class 4-4-0s and the new express passenger 4-6-0s of 1903, one might have imagined that the draughtsmen at St Rollox had been in a similar situation until one saw the elegantly graceful outline of Nos 49 and 50:

Engine type	'Dunalastair III'	4-6-0 Nos 49 and 50
Cylinders, diameter × stroke (in)	19 × 26	21 × 26
Total heating surface (sq ft)	1,540	2,323
Grate area (sq ft)	22	26
Boiler pressure (psi)	180	200
Total engine weight (tons)	51.7	70
Nominal tractive effort at 85 per cent of boiler pressure (lb)	18,411	24,990

There were no half measures about this advance in power; Nos 49 and 50 were in fact the most powerful locomotives in Great Britain at the time of their construction. And what superbly proportioned locomotives they were! As if to increase the impression of vastness, the initials CR on their great tenders were made nearly twice the normal size and the coat

McIntosh 4-6-0 of 1903, No 49, at Kingmoor shed with the semaphore headcode for the Holytown route used by the 2 pm West Coast Express from Euston (R.J. Purves).

of arms was ringed with gilt thistles and leaves instead of the usual scrolls. It is amazing to recall that these two locomotives, with their tenders, were built for no more than £3,100 apiece, which, even when the difference in price levels today is taken into account, is a mightily low figure! These engines did excellent work from their very inception, but for the servicing facilities then available they were ahead of their time. For one thing, the length of engine and tender over buffers was 65 ft 6 in, and there were no turntables large enough to take them. At Glasgow they were run round the Cathcart Circle, but at Carlisle engine and tender had to be uncoupled.

In the scheming out of these great engines, McIntosh and the élite of the drawing office at St Rollox had, one gathered, the gratuitous assistance of one of the most prominent Scottish locomotive enthusiasts of the day, Norman Doran MacDonald. Professionally he was an advocate, practising in Edinburgh, but he was an ardent locomotive 'buff' whose forthright manner and charming personality apparently gave him the entrée to the personal enclaves of many leading railway managers and engineers of the day. Pre-eminently, from 1896, he had been a Caledonian supporter, though from some of his utterances in the railway press of the day one gathers that he plagued Sir George Gibb, the General Manager of the North Eastern Railway, urging reform in certain directions. Many years later, when he was apt to fire off what he termed his 'self-recoiling boomerangs' in letters to the press, he recalled how he spent some enjoyable hours in the drawing office at St Rollox, planning the ever-larger Caledonian 4-6-0s. The part he played in the actual designing was never disclosed,

and unfortunately those closest to McIntosh never wrote any reminiscences!

The great engines 49 and 50 were originally intended to climb the Beattock Bank unassisted with the normal load of the 2 pm West Coast 'Corridor' train from Euston to Glasgow, and as early as the August 1903 issue of *The Railway Magazine*, readers were not only presented with a coloured plate of engine No 50 in the handsome lithographed style of the period, but also a graphic account of Charles Rous-Marten's first experiences in the trains travelling behind both the new engines. As a sequel to some of the topics discussed in the previous chapter of this book, I may add that he travelled north from Euston by the 'Corridor' and, with a load of 390 tons, it was naturally double-headed by a 2-4-0 'Jumbo' and the first of the 'Alfred the Great' 4-4-0 compounds as far as Crewe. Then, with an unchanged load as far as Preston, two 'Jumbos' made a fast run. After detaching certain through carriages, the load was still as much as 330 tons, and the two little engines, *Marathon* and *Ilion*, covered the remaining 90 miles to Carlisle in 5 seconds less than 103 minutes—a splendid run. Evidently the advent of the Caledonian 4-6-0s had aroused intense interest in Carlisle, because Rous-Marten noted that when No 50 backed on to the train, there was such a crowd of admiring sightseers that they had to be kept within bounds by a policeman! The load remained at 330 tons and this was taken without assistance. The engine made excellent time out to Beattock, covering this initial 39¾ miles in 43¼ minutes, but then the ten miles of the bank itself proved troublesome and occupied no less than 23 minutes, with a minimum speed of 22 mph. Thus the time to passing Beattock Summit from Carlisle was 66¼ minutes, and, with every allowance for the difference in train load, this performance by No 50 does not compare well with those of the first 'Dunalastairs' hauling the 180-ton 'Tourist' express of 1896.

On a later occasion, with a considerably heavier load of 390 tons, good time was also made out to Beattock by engine No 49 but there, understandably, a stop was made for a bank engine. The run from Carlisle was made in 44½ minutes, but it took 3 minutes to attach the 'pusher', and although the actual ascent of the bank took no more than 18½ minutes, the total time from Carlisle to passing the summit was 66 minutes. At that time, doubts were frequently expressed as to the ability of any six-coupled passenger engine to attain speeds comparable with those of a four-coupled, or even a single-wheeler. But the very first journeys Rous-Marten made behind engines 49 and 50 seemed to disprove any ideas in that direction. His second journey was on the up 2 pm 'Corridor' which had a very easy timing of 2 hr 15 min non-stop for the 102¼ miles from Glasgow Central to Carlisle. Because of some special traffic, however, the train was subjected to some considerable delay in the middle part of the run and lost 11 minutes in running, and it was in making up time from this that a fine speed exhibition was given south of Lockerbie. On the 1 in 200 gradient leading towards Gretna, the speed was worked up to 79 mph and the total time from Glasgow was exactly as booked, or, allowing for the delays, 124 minutes net. This was a fine performance with a heavy load of 395 tons behind engine No 49. Rous-Marten had yet another good run on his return to London with the 10.45 pm 'sleeper' when those trains were timed considerably faster than we were accustomed to in the inter-war years. In 1903, that train was allowed only 2 hr 10 min from Glasgow to Carlisle, including an 8-minute stop at Carstairs to attach the Edinburgh portion. With the full load, only 80 minutes was allowed to run the 73½ miles to Carlisle, an average of 55 mph.

Engine No 50, with the reduced load of 280 tons from Glasgow, had done well from the start, but it was after the train had been made up to its maximum of 384 tons that the work became really grand. From the restart at Carstairs, the 23.8 miles up to Beattock Summit took only 31¼ minutes, while the remaining 49¾ miles to Carlisle took only 47 minutes inclusive of two signal checks. Rous-Marten dilated somewhat upon the weight of the huge tenders

attached to the 4-6-0 locomotives 49 and 50, which weighed 55 tons when fully loaded. Comparing this to the standard timber-framed tenders fitted to the latest Webb compound engines of the LNWR, which weighed only 26 tons, as Rous-Marten put it, the new Caledonian engine on this occasion was hauling a load equivalent to one of 414 tons behind a standard North Western tender. One can sense the urgings of MacDonald in the decision of the Caledonian Board to install 70-ft turntables at the sheds where Nos 49 and 50 were being serviced, because more equally large engines were being planned. Eventually, of course, no more than five more 4-6-0s with the huge 55-ton bogie tenders were built, and the outlay on turntables at Kingmoor, Polmadie, Balornock, Perth and Aberdeen at that time seemed questionable for the very few engines making use of their exceptional length. In the Grouping era, of course, with both LMS and LNER using 'Pacifics', it paid off.

I would like to inject a personal memory of those great engines of 1903, dating back to the autumn of 1923. At that time, some nine months after Grouping, it was generally understood that Midland lake was to be the colour for all LMSR passenger locomotives; but it was surprising what large stocks of the old colours seemed to be on hand at the various works, and none of the constituents was anxious to accelerate the change! Nevertheless, by that time change was definitely in the air, even on the Caledonian. At that time, the working of the afternoon express to Euston had been changed. It still conveyed the Liverpool and Manchester portions, but instead of running non-stop to Carlisle, as of old, a stop was made at Symington, and there remarshalling took place with the corresponding train from Edinburgh. Because of this working there was little chance in those post-war years of seeing one of the big engines on the up 'Corridor'; but the 4.10 pm express to Liverpool and Manchester nearly always had a 4-6-0, more usually one of the Pickersgill '60' Class. On the afternoon in question, I was bound for Rothesay, and although my train left before the express for the south, there was usually time to cross over to the long No 8 platform which, extending far beyond the short suburban platforms and the Cathcart engine siding, provided a grandstand from which the main-line departures could be seen with little or no interruption. While I watched, there came into sight far across the Clyde bridge a light engine coming tender first towards the station. Even at that distance there was no mistaking what it was! No other Caledonian engines had such huge tenders, and it only remained to see if it was one of the 'Cardeans', or 49 or 50. It proved to be No 50, and whatever falling off there might have been in other directions, this engine, still

Left *Pickersgill '60' Class 4-6-0 No 62 approaching Carlisle with a Glasgow to Euston express* (F.E. Mackay).

Below left *The famous McIntosh 4-6-0 No 903* Cardean *with the semaphore headcode for the southbound run from Glasgow, via Motherwell* (F. Moore's Rail Photos).

Bottom left *The 2pm up West Coast 'Corridor' express near Polmadie shed hauled by 4-6-0 No 907* (Author's Collection).

a monster even in 1923, was gloriously turned out. After she had coupled on, standing there at No 2 platform in the full afternoon sun against the dark buildings in the background, she made a picture that a railway enthusiast never ceases to delight in recalling. I nearly missed my train to Wemyss Bay.

In 1930, I was on holiday with my parents at Stonehaven, and for a fortnight I saw the comings and goings of Caledonian and North British locomotives on the line to Aberdeen. Then, one day, when I was too far from the line to get a photograph, the 12 noon from Glasgow came up the bank hauled by No 49, or No 14750 as she was then, painted in unlined black! The engine of that train, I had previously noted, returned to Perth on the 5.30 pm, the train that was later given the old title 'The Granite City', and in 1930, sure enough, No 49 came back as expected. We had some shopping to do in Aberdeen next day, and returning by the 5.30 pm to Stonehaven I was delighted to see No 49 again on the job. The load was not heavy, only 225 tons, and the great old engine sailed up the bank past Cove Bay in almost complete silence; then, once over the crest at milepost 234, she ran like a stag, touching 69 mph at Muchalls, breasting the 2 miles at 1 in 103 at 56 mph, and reaching 69 mph again before stopping at Stonehaven. She was obviously in good form; indeed, it was not until three years later, thirty years after her construction, that she and her sister engine No 50 were scrapped.

It was in 1906 that the five larger-boilered express passenger 4-6-0s were built, Nos 903-907. The boilers, although larger in diameter, had a re-arrangement of the tubes to give improved circulation of the water, and the tube heating surface was slightly less. Also, the cylinder diameter was reduced to 20 in. Whatever doubts anyone might have had about the success of Nos 49 and 50, there was no room for any lurking suspicions about the '903' Class. It can be well and truly said that these huge but wonderfully graceful engines represented the summit point of McIntosh's work as an engine designer. There was a subtle point to be noted about them which they shared with Nos 49 and 50. As originally built, they had no brake hoses on the front buffer beams. The folks at St Rollox evidently considered they would never need to be double-headed!

They, more than any other class on the line, epitomized the twentieth-century splendour of the Caledonian, and the regular daily working of the afternoon West Coast corridor trains between Glasgow and Carlisle by No 903 *Cardean* made that engine a veritable institution on the Scottish railways.

When the London and North Western Railway built the special twelve-wheeled corridor stock for the afternoon West Coast expresses, the minimum load of the 8.13 pm down from Carlisle became seven of these palatial vehicles, and a paragraph in *The Railway Magazine* of August 1932 vividly recalls the spirit of the day:

'A handsome combination *Cardean* made with seven cars of the "two o'clock", all twelve-wheelers of a special design, and some of the smoothest-riding stock that has ever run over West Coast metals. And so, on a typical winter's night at Carlisle, with half the city—or so it seemed—making the Citadel station the venue of its evening promenade, and *Cardean* the centre of attraction, the same ritual would be gone through after *Cardean* had backed down; the fireman, usually from high up on the great tender, would wave to and fro an improvised torch consisting of an oil-can, whose spout contained a blazing wick of oily waste, to show to officials farther down the platform that the brake test had been made satisfactorily, then would come a thrilling blast on the great foghorn that *Cardean* carried in place of a whistle, and the shapely form of the "two o'clock" vanished into the night. Yes, those were great days.'

Together with Nos 49 and 50, the five engines of the 'Cardean' Class were allocated regular duties which they kept until the general changeover of workings occasioned by the major timetable changes in 1917. Apart from *Cardean* herself, No 49 was at Polmadie, No 50 was at Balornock, Nos 904 and 905 at Perth, and Nos 906 and 907 at Kingmoor. As far as I can trace, engines 904-907 were not put on to the strenuous single-home workings of the night trains between Carlisle and Perth; Nos 904 and 905 worked mainly between Perth and Aberdeen; while Nos 906 and 907 were usually seen between Carlisle and Glasgow Central. The regular turns for these two latter engines were the 6.5 am down 'sleeper' non-stop to Glasgow Central, returning on the 10 am up for Euston, and the Glasgow portion of the 10 am down from Euston. From Buchanan Street, No 50 usually took the midday Aberdeen express as far as Perth, and in the evening took over the 5.30 pm from Aberdeen, which was notable at that time in running non-stop to Glasgow, via Coatbridge, and arriving at the Central station rather than Buchanan Street. In 1913, Lord Monkswell had a footplate pass for

this train, but unfortunately in the relevant notebook he gives tantalizingly few details of what would otherwise have been an interesting run. He had been footplating since 10 am, and he was doubtless tired when he climbed on to No 50 for the last stage of the trip home.

Cardean herself, nursed and petted by the one driver who had almost exclusive use of her during the first ten years of her life, had a very sheltered existence for most of the time. Although the introduction of the huge 4-6-0 locomotives was originally intended to eliminate rear-end assistance on the Beattock Bank, the beautiful twelve-wheeled West Coast Joint Stock, which involved a minimum tare load of just over 300 tons, provided such a problem in haulage, on an all-weather basis, that arrangements were made for banking assistance for the 'Corridor' every day. With the very easy schedule of the up train, the only really hard work *Cardean* had to do, unassisted, was in running the 39.7 miles from Carlisle to Beattock station in 45 minutes. I do not think the down 'Corridor' was ever photographed in *Cardean*'s days. The late hour of departure from Carlisle, and the non-existence of 'summer time' in those pre-1914 years precluded photography with the equipment then available; and the absence of photographs undoubtedly led to an interesting feature of the appearance of the train being unrecorded. Apart from the brief stop at Strawfrank Junction just short of Carstairs to detach the Edinburgh coaches, the 'Corridor' was non-stop from Carlisle to Glasgow, and as usual with trains not needing to call at Motherwell, it took the Holytown route north of Law Junction. To indicate this, a variation of the semaphore headcode was used. Instead of the familiar 'bow tie' in front of the chimney carried on expresses

routed via Motherwell, the code for the Holytown route consisted of the left-hand arm being horizontal and the right-hand pointing downwards. The photograph on page 88 shows this applied to engine No 49 at Kingmoor shed, though whether that engine was rostered for the down 'Corridor' on that occasion I cannot say.

The well-nigh exclusive use of *Cardean* on the train leads on to the events of June and July 1909 when the engine was running experimentally on the London and North Western main line between Carlisle and Crewe, in competition with one of the 'Experiment' Class 4-6-0s. Whether the regular Polmadie driver handled her throughout the 'exchange' running I cannot say, except that on certain severe tests the performance of the engine was far-and-away superior to anything demanded on the normal out and home runs with the 'Corridor'. Southbound, *Cardean* worked the 12.58 pm from Carlisle, then allowed 109 minutes for the 90 miles to Preston inclusive of a stop at Penrith. No more than 24 minutes, start to stop, was allowed for the 17.9 miles from Carlisle to Penrith, and from the restart a modest 18 minutes was allowed to climb the 13.6 miles up to Shap Summit. The test train was made up to a tare load of 367 tons. These timings were sharper than anything worked before the Second World War (excepting the 'Coronation Scot') when the principal West Coast expresses were booked to pass the summit in 44 minutes from Carlisle, with an allowance of 19 minutes pass-to-pass up from Penrith. By dint of magnificent work on the footplate, *Cardean* succeeded in keeping to these fast times. To assess the power output necessary to achieve this, I have made a 'reconstruction' of the run, estimating the passing times and speeds. These are shown in the accom-

Left *A development of the McIntosh blue-painted '30' Class 0-6-0s used for Clyde Coast services. The 2-6-0s were used for main line goods trains between Glasgow and Carlisle.*

Right *5-ft 0-in heavy goods and mixed traffic 4-6-0 No 920, built in 1906 (British Railways).*

panying table, and it becomes reasonably clear that a sustained output of about 1,200 edhp took place between Carlisle and Plumpton, and after Penrith the output must have been between 1,400 and 1,500 edhp for 16 minutes on end.

Caledonian and LNW Railways: 12.58 pm Carlisle-Preston

Engine CR 4-6-0 No 903 *Cardean*
Load 367 tons tare, 390 tons full

Distance (miles)		Schedule time (min)	Actual time (m s)	Speeds (mph)
0.0	CARLISLE	0	0 00	—
1.4	No 13 Box		3 00	
4.9	Wreay		8 30	
13.1	Plumpton		18 30	
17.9	PENRITH	24	23 30	—
1.1	Eamont Junction		2 50	
3.3	Milepost 48		5 40	54
4.3	Milepost 47		6 49	52
5.3	Milepost 46		7 59	50
6.3	Milepost 45		9 12	48½
7.3	Milepost 44		10 28	47
8.3	Milepost 43		11 45	46
9.3	Milepost 42		13 04	45
10.3	Milepost 41		14 25	44
11.6	Shap		16 05	53
13.6	Summit Box	18	18 30	48
19.1	Tebay	24	23 45	73½ (max)
32.1	Oxenholme	38	37 30	—
44.9	CARNFORTH	51	49 30	—
51.2	LANCASTER	58	57 00	—
72.2	PRESTON	80	78 15	

In the various dynamometer car trials carried out since nationalization, with locomotives worked extremely hard under strictly controlled conditions, some power outputs have been obtained that are high in relation to the tractive power of the locomotives concerned; in some, the sustained drawbar pull in heavy hill-climbing conditions has been more than 40 per cent of the nominal tractive effort of the locomotive. Indeed, with the 'Britannia' Class 'Pacifics', in maximum conditions it rose to nearly 50 per cent. I have personally seen even this achievement exceeded for a few thunderous minutes by a large-boilered Ivatt 'Atlantic' climbing the Ardsley Bank out of Leeds; but according to my calculations, *Cardean* was exceeding it handsomely all the way from Penrith to Shap Summit, in 18½ minutes of outstanding locomotive effort, thus:

Engine Class	Rates
LNER 'V2' 2-6-2	43.0
GWR 'King' 4-6-0	42.2
BR 'Britannia'	50.0
GNR 'Atlantic'	60.0
CR 'Cardean'	61.2

Such work from *Cardean* needs no further comment from me!

Immediately after the completion of the 903-907 series of express passenger 4-6-0s in 1906, St Rollox Works continued with ten similar engines with 5-ft 9-in coupled wheels, Nos 908-917, and followed these with five having 5-ft 0-in coupled wheels, as on the Oban 4-6-0s, but with considerably larger boilers. These latter engines, Nos 918-922, like the 908-917 series, were all completed in 1906. The 5-ft 9-in engines were sometimes termed 'mixed traffic', but most of them were at first put on to express passenger duties such as the Clyde Coast boat trains to and from Gourock and certain of the Aberdeen expresses between Glasgow Buchanan Street and Perth. The leading dimensions of the three classes of 4-6-0 built at St Rollox in 1906 may be compared thus:

Class	903-907	908-917	918-922
Coupled wheel diameter (ft in)	6 6	5 9	5 0
Cylinders, diameter × stroke (in)	20 × 26	19 × 26	19 × 26
Heating surface (sq ft)			
Tubes	2,117.5	2,050	1,895
Firebox	148.25	128	128
Total	2,265.75	2,178	2,023
Grate area (sq ft)	26	21	21
Boiler pressure (psi)	200	180	175
Nominal tractive effort at 85 per cent of boiler pressure (lb)	22,667	20,812	23,269
Weight of engine only in working order (tons)	73	64	60.4

It was only the 'Cardean', or '903' Class, that had the huge bogie tenders, which were even heavier than those of the 4-6-0s No 49 and 50, 57 tons against 55 tons. The six-wheeled tenders fitted to the '908' and

One of the '908' Class of mixed traffic 4-6-0s built at St Rollox in 1906. This engine, No 917, seen here at Perth, differed from the rest in having a side-windowed cab (Author's Collection).

Right *Pickersgill '60' Class 4-6-0 No 14631 at Kingmoor shed in LMS black livery* (O.S. Nock).

Below right *Aberdeen-Glasgow express soon after leaving Aberdeen in 1938 hauled by Pickersgill 4-6-0 No 14633* (M.W. Earley).

Bottom right *Superheater 5-ft 9-in mixed traffic 4-6-0 of the '179' Class, built at St Rollox in 1913 and seen here in LMS black livery* (British Railways).

'918' Classes weighed 38 tons.

New engine No 908 was shedded at Balornock and regularly worked the 10 am 'Grampian Corridor Express' as far as Perth. Engines 909 and 911, stationed at Polmadie, were both named, the former after the Chairman of the Board, *Sir James King*, and the latter *Barochan*, after the residence of Sir Charles Renshaw, his successor, who lived near the Clyde coast line at Houston. A fine photograph was taken by R.A. Chrystal, son of one of the directors, of engine No 908 leaving Stirling with the down 'Grampian' which was made the subject of a beautiful 'F. Moore' colour plate in one of the earlier editions of the *Wonder Book of Railways*. To be slightly critical of an otherwise splendid painting, by the time all the 1906 batches of 4-6-0s were built, '903', '908' and '918' Classes alike, the light blue livery had been standardized, and photographs of engines 909 and 911 taken in 1907 show this clearly. Unhappily, the colour plate of No 908 leaving Stirling is in Prussian blue. Two interesting records of the working of the '908' Class on the down 'Grampian Corridor Express' have been preserved, both with engine No 913, and both in 1913. In May of that year, Lord Monkswell had a footplate pass, and was not only fortunate in having John Barr as his cicerone throughout the day, but also in having the privilege of McIntosh himself to see them off at Buchanan Street. Unfortunately, the

noble lord took very little detail other than noting that the 30¼ miles from Glasgow to Stirling took 40¼ minutes, and the 33 miles on to Perth took 41¾ minutes. Both these times were considerably faster than those made when I was doing my clocking on the Caledonian in the 1930s. On Lord Monkswell's trip, a stop was made at the Perth ticket platform, whence engine No 913 and the leading coaches proceeded to the Dundee line.

The second run with engine No 913 was recorded in the summer service in the meticulous detail characteristic of R.E. Charlewood. As before, the palatial twelve-wheeled 'Grampian' coaches were on the rear of the train, which at this season made a non-stop run to Perth, the four leading coaches on this occasion being for destinations on the Highland line, not to Aberdeen. With a gross load of 285 tons behind the tender, a good start was made up the 1 in 79 gradient through the tunnel to St Rollox, and on to Robroyston, speed rising to 30 mph, and the climbing of the Dunblane bank was excellent; but on a schedule of 82 minutes for the 63¼ miles from Glasgow to Perth, there was no need for high downhill

speeds, and the maximum was only 65 mph. When I travelled by this route in early LMS days, however, the smart-running '908' Class had been replaced by the purgatorial Pickersgill '60' Class outside-cylinder 4-6-0s, and the speeds were pedestrian in the extreme. I did see one of the '908' Class, the pioneer engine in fact, at Aberdeen in 1929. She was looking quite smart, still in the immediate post-Grouping livery of Midland red, with the number in large figures on the tender, 14609, but I did not discover what her workings were.

The '918' Class, a large-boilered version of the Oban 4-6-0s of 1902, were so few in number as to be scarce on the ground; and I do not recollect seeing one of them. On the other hand, the superheated development of the '908' Class, built in 1913-14, were massive express goods engines, albeit painted 'passenger blue', and were distinguished by having side-windowed cabs. They were used mainly on the heavy night goods trains from Carlisle to the Glasgow area, though I saw and photographed them at Perth and on the line north to Aberdeen.

9. Midland 1902-22: the operational paradox

The locomotive department of the Midland Railway under the leadership of S.W. Johnson entered the twentieth century full of promise of great things ahead. While the immediately preceding years had not brought forth any striking developments, but rather more the use of the single-wheeler on the fastest express duties south of Derby and Nottingham, locomotive practice had been essentially sound, and, as far as basic coal consumption went, as efficient as any in Great Britain. Then had come the great Smith-Johnson compounds, which bade fair to place the Midland ahead of all British railways in the year 1902. There will be a great deal to say of these engines in this and subsequent chapters of this book; but for the moment I wish to expand a little on the operational paradox that was fast developing in the Midland Railway as a whole, and which came to affect profoundly not only the original company in its pre-Grouping years, but also the London Midland and Scottish Railway in the earliest of its post-amalgamation days.

It is interesting to compare the revenue returns of the railways that were eventually amalgamated to make up the LMS system, because these throw a light on the motive power used. The following table gives the total traffic receipts for the year 1901 taken from the data published annually in Bradshaw's Railway

One of the 1902 batch of Johnson 'Belpaire' 4-4-0s, No 2788, with the larger size of bogie tender carrying 4,500 gallons (National Railway Museum).

Manual, Shareholders' Guide and Directory:

Railway	First half year (£)	Second half year (£)
Caledonian	2,067,469	2,188,896
Furness	252,578	282,544
Glasgow and South Western	858,951	896,652
Highland	246,798	267,786
Lancashire and Yorkshire	2,575,760	2,812,560
London and North Western	6,632,833	7,442,242
Midland	5,428,620	5,907,978
North London	273,551	277,671
North Stafford	440,294	469,162

While not approaching the massive traffic returns of the London and North Western Railway, the Midland was easily second, more than doubling the returns of the next competitor, the Lancashire and Yorkshire. In view of the prominence given to the locomotives of the Highland Railway, it is a sobering thought that they earned less revenue for their owners than those of both the North London and the Furness Railway. Reverting to the Midland, however, there was primarily a prodigious volume of mineral traffic originating in the collieries of South Yorkshire, Nottinghamshire and South Derbyshire that in the

Johnson 6-ft 6-in 4-4-0 No 2587 of the 1807 Class introduced in 1888, seen here as rebuilt by Deeley, was of a later batch built in 1900 (F. Moore's Rail Photos).

early 1900s constituted such a blockage to ordinary freight traffic, and to some extent to passenger business also, as to swamp the entire carrying capacity of the line south of Chesterfield. Despite this, no steps had been taken so far to augment the hauling capacity of the Midland freight locomotives, which until 1903 had remained of the same design that Johnson had introduced in 1875. These were powerful engines for that time, with 17½-in by 26-in cylinders. A fractional enlargement had been made since, to an 18-in diameter; but at the turn of the century, these engines seemed small alongside the large eight-coupled types that were then being introduced by other carriers of comparable mineral traffic like the London and North Western, the Great Northern, the Lancashire and Yorkshire, and the Caledonian.

Certainly the Midland had plenty of engines. In 1903 there were no less than 450 of Johnson's own design, not to mention nearly 500 double-framed Kirtley 0-6-0s of somewhat less tractive power. In the new century, also, there was evidently no move by the Midland Railway management to call for larger freight engines, because when Johnson built some new ones in the early months of 1903, the machinery and chassis were the same as the time-honoured design, but with a somewhat larger boiler. Although the *Locomotive Magazine* of 9 May 1903 published a photograph of the new goods engine, carrying the number 2736, it did not seem of sufficient importance to include the heating surfaces of the new boiler, except to remark that it was similar to those of the latest non-compound 4-4-0s but without the Belpaire type of firebox. The chimney, however, was of a new Derby design, tapered from the base upwards. Readers of that magazine had to wait until March 1904 for

details of that boiler, and then in a curiously back-handed way. Johnson had been deputed to design some new 4-4-0 locomotives for the heavily graded Somerset and Dorset Joint Railway, for which the Midland provided the motive power. Hitherto, for the main-line passenger working Johnson had built some relatively small 4-4-0s in his own style, but with 5-ft 9-in coupled wheels. The new 4-4-0s, which were completed at Derby in November 1903, were considerably more powerful, with 18-in by 26-in cylinders, 6-ft 0-in coupled wheels and the same boiler as that used on the new 0-6-0 goods built for general service on the Midland itself earlier in 1903. It then transpired that the tube heating surface was 1,302.9 sq ft, the firebox was 125 sq ft and the total thus 1,427.9 sq ft. The grate area was 21.1 sq ft and the working pressure 175 psi.

The new century was marked by many important changes in the locomotive departments of the leading railways of England. On the Lancashire and Yorkshire, Aspinall had already moved up to become General Manager, while on the Great Western and the London and North Western, Dean and Webb respectively had been replaced, though not in the happiest of circumstances, different though they were at Swindon and Crewe. On the Midland, however, Johnson was on the point of retiring with many years of well-earned leisure before him. To judge from some statements in the railway press in the early autumn of 1903, however, the succession at Derby was by no means clear; R.M. Deeley, after completing his

Johnson 6-ft 6-in 4-4-0 of the '1808' Class as rebuilt by Deeley and numbered in the new style as No 480 (British Railways).

pupilage under Johnson, had gradually risen in the locomotive hierarchy until he was appointed Works Manager at Derby in January 1902, but in the meantime another star of the first magnitude was arising in the department. In 1891, Cecil W. Paget began his pupilage at Derby. An old Harrovian, and son of Sir Ernest Paget, Bart, who was soon to become Chairman of the Midland Railway, he could have been marked out for promotion on any account; but he was a man of outstanding ability, and a terrific worker. His early duties involved inspection, at works, of contractor-built locomotives, because the demand for power was then more than the Midland Railway could meet with its own workshop capacity at Derby. One such assignment was of special interest as it involved a visit to the USA in 1899, when 'Mogul'-type locomotives were being built for the Midland at Baldwins and Schenectady. This was the prelude to another visit to the USA, this time in the company of Deeley, to examine and report on workshop methods.

In June 1902, Paget was appointed Assistant Works Manager at Derby, then no more than 28 years of age, and in the following year, when Deeley was promoted to be Assistant Locomotive Superintendent, Paget also moved up one to become Works Manager. At that time, those interested in the personalities as well as the hardware of locomotive engineering had already become well aware of certain strong cross-currents that were flowing in the higher ranks of the Locomotive Department. While Deeley was confirmed as Assistant Locomotive Superintendent

in the summer of 1903, Paget, equally as forceful a character, was the son of the Chairman of the Company. There was no doubt that a rare game of power politics was being played behind some not so securely locked doors in Derby, and the moves and counter-moves were undoubtedly caught up in the proverbial 'grape vine'. How else could the *Locomotive Magazine*, always famed for sobriety of utterance, announce on 5 September 1903: 'Midland Ry. Mr Cecil Paget has been appointed to succeed Mr S.W. Johnson, the Loco. superintendent, who is retiring after 30 years' service with the company.' No correction was subsequently printed, whereas in the January 1904 issue of *The Railway Magazine*, there was the official notice of Deeley's appointment with an interesting biography of his former career, and equally that of Paget, who had been appointed as Works Manager.

Deeley lost no time in starting to rebuild many of the erstwhile standard Johnson 0-6-0 goods engines, providing them with boilers of the same design as that used on the new engines of 1903, and those of the Somerset and Dorset 4-4-0s of November of that year. By midsummer 1904, the process of reboilering had been extended to the 6-ft 6-in 4-4-0s; with new splashers and cabs, they looked like a larger-wheeled version of the Somerset and Dorset 4-4-0s Nos 69-71. Gone, alas, were the graceful lines of the Johnson 4-4-0s, and in their place was a more modern general utility engine. In keeping with this drive to larger boilers, by December 1904 the *Locomotive Magazine* reported that more than a hundred of the older 0-6-0s had been fitted with larger boilers, as had also an increasing number of 4-4-0s. To anticipate the later power classification of Midland engines, Deeley's rebuildings were putting the Johnson goods

engines up from Class '2' to '3', and the passenger engines from Class '1' to '2'. In the meantime, construction of the Belpaire 4-4-0s was proceeding at intervals, the later examples having the newer form of chimney as on the new 0-6-0s of 1903, the Somerset and Dorset 6-ft 0-in 4-4-0s and the rebuilds of earlier Johnson engines. With the laying down of water troughs, there was no further need for the huge bogie tenders on these engines. A batch of rebuilt 4-4-0 engines of the No '2' Class was allocated to the Leeds-Carlisle line in 1905, and this reduced the double heading needed on the Scotch Expresses when loads were heavy. A few of the Belpaires were also used over that route, not to mention the two original Smith-Johnson compounds; but the bigger engines had been few and far between until 1905.

In 1906, rebuilding had also begun on the 7-ft 4-4-0 engines. In addition to the considerably enlarged boiler, these engines had an altered splasher arrangement and wide cabs. Also, in keeping with the new engines that were being turned out from Derby at the time, the brass numbers on the cab sides were removed, white metal plates were fitted on the smokebox doors and the number was painted in huge numerals on the tender. In the meantime, changes in personnel were being made. First of all, Paget had been promoted to Assistant Locomotive Superintendent, and then the Chief Locomotive Draughtsman at Derby had left to take up the post of Works Manager of the Great Central works at Gorton. This cleared the way for two men who proved to be much the most dominating influences in Midland locomotive affairs for the last decade in which the Company existed—J.E Anderson and S.J. Symes. Then, in 1906, the second phase of the Midland usage of compound express passenger locomotives began. Reference to the first phase of the development, under S.W. Johnson, was somewhat passed over in a previous chapter of this book; but now is the time to make a far more detailed reference.

Just 25 years ago, David St John Thomas, co-founder and now Chairman of David and Charles Ltd, asked me to inaugurate, and act as general editor of, a series of locomotive monographs they were planning. These were to be no lightweight *causeries*, but in-depth analyses of the design, performance and general history of famous classes and families of British locomotives. Choice for the first subject fell on the Midland compounds. The result was a weighty tome covering all aspects of the fifty years in which these engines were in traffic; but rereading what I then wrote about the pre-Grouping history, it seems that there was little to extol, so far as actual performance went. The two Johnson engines of 1902, Nos 2631 and 2632, were beautifully and scientifically designed and at first both were confined to a single crew, the first engine at Leeds and the second at Durran Hill, Carlisle. Engine No 2631 was put through a very comprehensive series of tests between Leeds and Carlisle between August and November 1902. No special runs were made to test the maximum output of which the engine was capable, and in fact most of the running was made with what would be considered very moderate loads, even in 1902. For example, on the 1.28 pm from Leeds to Carlisle, booked non-stop in 134 minutes for the 113 miles, the tare load averaged 250½ tons, while on the 3.55 pm up from Carlisle the average load on seven trips was not more than 152 tons. The coal consumption was proportionate, namely 45.5lb per mile northbound and 25.42 lb per mile southbound, on a somewhat easier schedule.

These first two Smith-Johnson compounds had independent controls for the valve gear for the high- and low-pressure cylinders; they had also the so-called 'change-valve' which regulated the transition from simple to compound working when starting. Johnson himself abandoned the independent valve gear controls when he built the three further compounds, Nos 2633-2635, in 1903, but he retained the change-valve, which of course was an essential of the Smith system of compounding. These Johnson-built compounds were all very swift runners. It is true that they did not have to carry very heavy loads on the Carlisle road, but engines 2631 and 2632 used to knock up maximum speeds of over 90 mph descending from Aisgill and Blea Moor in their early years. The three later engines were stationed at Kentish Town, and, although doing much excellent work, they did not get the opportunity for such spectacular running as those on the Leeds-Carlisle line. The indicator trials of engine No 2631, which were very fully reported in the technical press of the day, showed how the driver varied the cut-offs in the high- and low-pressure cylinders as occasion demanded, whereas on the three engines stationed at Kentish Town the valve gear provided only a fixed ratio of adjustments.

On taking over, on New Year's Day 1904, Deeley was not long in making his influence felt. He was very much of a scientific turn of mind, yet keenly aware of the perplexities posed by the rather elaborate controls of the Smith-Johnson compounds. He designed

instead a regulator valve of his own which was simplicity itself to operate and was embodied in a series
of new compound 4-4-0s, Nos 1000-1009, construction of which at Derby began in the autumn of 1905.
But, because of a rather brusque comment made by
Deeley himself on the substance of one of Rous-
Marten's articles in *The Railway Magazine*, one gathers
the changes had been made even before then. Rous-
Marten had been comparing the boiler proportions
of the new Deeley compounds with those of the original five, assuming that the only differences were those
of a larger grate area and higher working pressure,
and referred to them as 'Smith-Compounds'. Deeley wrote to him thus: 'There are no "Smith" compounds on the Midland Railway. They have all been
altered. The Smith reducing valve arrangement frequently failed, so I fitted the engines with a much
more simple starting arrangement.'

Ten of the new Deeley compounds were built in
1905 and another twenty with shallow frames at the

Midland compound boilers—non-superheated

Engine No	2631	1000
Length of barrel (ft in)	11 7	11 11
Minimum diameter (ft in)	4 8	4 7⅞
Tubes		
Number	261	216
Outside diameter (in)	1¾	1⅞
Heating surfaces (sq ft)		
Tubes	1,448	1,305.5
Firebox	150	152.8
Total	1,598	1,485.3
Grate area (sq ft)	26	28.4
Boiler pressure (psi)	195	220

front end in 1906. Then apparently Deeley, or most likely his masters at Derby, had second thoughts about compounds. At midsummer 1906, the Midland Board appointed W. Guy Granet as General Manager, and in a very short time he had reorganized the railway from top to bottom. It was not merely a case of creating new appointments, new departments and new alignments; he laid down an entirely new concept of railway management, based on a very strong central control of all activities from headquarters at Derby. One of the first departments to feel the effects of this was that of the Locomotive Superintendent. Deeley was not the most placid of individuals at the best of times, and in 1907 one can imagine his feelings when Paget, his deputy, was taken away and elevated to a post second only in stature to the General Manager himself. But this was not all. In his new post as General Superintendent, Paget took over not only all the activities previously associated with the 'Superintendent of the Line', but also all the locomotive running with control of all the footplate and shed staff. Deeley's title was changed to that of Chief Mechanical Engineer; but with his responsibilities henceforth restricted to design, construction of locomotives and overhaul in main works, the title carried considerably less scope on the Midland Railway than on some others, notably on the London and North Western and Great Western Railways.

Even so, at the height of what must have been a very trying time for all concerned with locomotives at Derby, Deeley brought out a new design of 4-4-0 that had some very interesting features. As the size and power of locomotives increased, so the space between the frames became more restricted; and since British designers still favoured the use of inside

cylinders, much thought was given in some drawing offices as to how space could be saved. Of course, the Joy valve gear did this very neatly; but some engineers would not use it, because of the need for a drilled hole in the connecting rod. An arrangement requiring no eccentrics at all had been used in Belgium, and in two known instances in the USA; and at the same time, when he was Works Manager at Derby, Deeley worked out an arrangement of his own on somewhat similar lines. At the time, Johnson would have none of it; but when he succeeded to the chair, Deeley filed an application for patent in respect of this device in 1905. Imagine, then, his consternation when the pioneer Great Western four-cylinder simple express locomotive No 40 *North Star* appeared in 1906 fitted with such a close adaptation of his 'scissors' gear as to look like a straight copy! Deeley was furious, and immediately wrote off to Churchward threatening all sorts of dire consequences for the GWR. Of course, Churchward was not the man to wilt in the face of threats, and he as good as told Deeley to go ahead, and take the case up in the Law Courts, or anywhere else he liked! But nothing came of this particular dispute, though in the following year Swindon were very amused, so the story goes, to see the 'scissors' gear used on the '999' Class 4-4-0s.

These handsome engines, of which ten were built, had the same boiler and firebox as the compounds, except that, by a rearrangement of the tubes, an additional 99 sq ft of heating surface was provided. These engines had 249 tubes of 1¾-in outside diameter, against 216 tubes of 1⅞-in outside diameter on the compounds. The cylinders were 19-in diameter by 26-in stroke, and the coupled wheels were of 6-ft 6-in diameter. They were intended to provide a straight

Top left *One of the later Deeley compounds, with shallow frames, built in 1906* (British Railways).

Above left *One of Deeley's '999' Class 4-4-0s, originally built non-superheated and classed '3', seen here superheated and Class '4', used between Leeds and Carlisle* (British Railways).

Right *Another still more drastic rebuild of the Johnson '1808' Class undertaken at Derby in 1909, with lengthened frames, a boiler with a Belpaire firebox, but still non-superheated* (British Railways).

Below right *A special example of the Fowler superheated 7-ft 4-4-0, normally No 502 of the former Johnson '150' Class of 1896, specially painted for the Midland Royal Train; the large number is omitted, and the Royal Cipher is carried on the cab side* (British Railways).

comparison with the compounds, although it is a little strange that the '999s' were classified '3' on their cab sides in their original condition.

How comparisons between the two classes went in Deeley's own time we do not know, but perhaps the fact that another ten compounds were built at Derby in 1908-9 suggests that the compounds had the best of it. But Deeley was far from happy in other respects. I suppose the root cause of the friction that developed between him and the top management of the Midland Railway was personality. Like many another brilliant inventor, he could be very 'touchy'. He was not allowed the autonomy enjoyed by his predecessor, nor yet that of many of his contemporaries on other leading railways, and in fighting to try and get it he gradually worked himself into a position from which there was no retreat save resignation. With Deeley's going in 1909, the Midland lost a very able engineer; but in the twentieth century, particularly with a man like Guy Granet at the head of affairs, no individual, however brilliant, is going to have a smooth passage unless he can settle in as one of a team. This Deeley seemed unable to do. He was succeeded by Henry Fowler, a man with a first-class brain but with a placid disposition, and an almost self-effacing temperament; and so beneath the iron hand at the top, and amid the unchanging needs of the traffic department, Midland locomotive practice, from 1909 onwards, descended into the doldrums, and stayed there until 1923.

This is not to say a good deal of careful scientific

work was not done at Derby. Fowler was indefatigable, and as—unlike Deeley— he enjoyed the company of his fellow engineers he took frequent part in the discussions of the Institutions of Civil and Mechanical Engineers, and read papers himself. To most outside observers, Derby was virtually at a standstill from 1910 onwards. The rebuilding of Johnson 4-4-0s, even though into such a useful small-power unit as the Class '2' Superheater engines from 1913 onwards, could scarcely be regarded as progress. But from some of Fowler's contributions to the technical discussions of the day one can piece together more of what was happening inside Derby. The point that stands out today is that no significant use was made of the results until 1923. When Fowler took over, the passenger engine situation could be summarized thus:

Power Class	Type	Design	Quantity
1	2-4-0	Kirtley	146
1	2-4-0	Johnson	135
1	4-4-0	Johnson	28
1	4-2-2	Johnson	95
2	4-4-0	Johnson—rebuilt Derby	235
3	4-4-0	The 'Belpaires' —Johnson	80
3	4-4-0	Deeley '999' Class	10
4	4-4-0	Johnson-Deeley compounds	45

The divorcing of the responsibility for running from the Chief Mechanical Engineer led to a reconsideration of the means of regulating train loads. The traffic authorities who took over this responsibility were not expected to be able to distinguish between the merits of one individual engine of a class and another. If a particular train was booked for a No '3' Class engine, any engine of that class that could turn a wheel was expected to be able to do the job, whatever its condition or mileage since last general overhaul.

In consequence, the loads for each power class were fixed well below the maximum capacity of that class when in good condition. The express trains were graded according to schedule, the great majority south of Leeds coming within the 'Special Limit' category. On a 'Special Limit' train, the maximum load for a No '4' Class engine was 230 tons. The corresponding limits for Class '2' and Class '3' engines were 180 and 205 tons respectively. Fowler had not been a year in office as Chief Mechanical Engineer of the Midland Railway when he took part in the discussion on George Hughes's 1910 paper at the Institution of Mechanical Engineers on 'Compounding and Superheating in Horwich Locomotives'. He told the members gathered there that he was about to try superheating as a first essay on one of the Deeley '999' Class 4-4-0s. Tests of coal consumption had been made, all with saturated steam engines, between a compound, a Johnson 'Belpaire' and a '999' between London and Leeds which gave the following results in coal per train ton mile:

Compound	0.112 lb
'Belpaire' 4-4-0	0.120 lb
'999' 4-4-0	0.115 lb

To the figures Fowler added this remark: 'These tests, however, could hardly be taken as representing the everyday consumption, as with an inspector on the footplate the enginemen naturally did better than under ordinary working conditions, but the figures could be depended upon as being absolutely comparable.'

What was not comparable, however, was the boiler pressure on the compound and the '999' used in these tests. Whereas the latter engines originally had 220 psi as on the compounds, by the time of these tests the '999' concerned was running with a reduced pressure of 200 psi, so that its nominal tractive power was considerably reduced. Even so, the difference in coal consumption between the 'simple' and 'compound' at 0.115 and 0.112 lb per train ton mile, was so slight as to make any conclusions valueless.

Four years later, Fowler himself read a characteristically erudite paper to the Institution of Civil Engineers on 'Superheating Steam in Locomotives', and as may be imagined included some comprehensive details on the work they had done by that time at Derby. The date was then January 1914, and by then all the '999' Class had been rebuilt, with boiler pressure reduced to 180 psi, and a start had been made on the second rebuilding of many of the No '2' Class 4-4-0s with superheaters. This rebuilding, involving new frames, cylinders and motion, in addi-

tion to the new boilers, virtually turned them into new engines, though they still remained in the Class '2' power class, and were therefore limited to a maximum tare load of 180 tons on the fastest trains. Fowler's mandate, so far as new construction went, evidently went no further than to renew a certain number of Class '2' engines thuswise, and to equip with superheaters some of the Class '3' 'Belpaire' 4-4-0s. Even so, the process was slow and when the Midland Railway became part of the LMS in January 1923, no less than 93 Class '2' 4-4-0s were still non-superheated, and likewise were 25 of the Class '3' 'Belpaires'. The operating department apparently did not require more powerful engines. In any case, there were plenty of Class '1' 2-4-0s and single-wheelers to provide pilot assistance if necessary.

The superheating of the '999' Class engines, despite the reduction in boiler pressure to 180 psi,

The first Midland compound as rebuilt with a superheater, and now preserved in pre-grouping livery (British Railways).

resulted in their being advanced from Class '3' to '4' in the power classification; but when the question arose of superheating the compounds, it would seem that there was considerable reluctance at Derby to take this step. Authority had actually been received to rebuild the five Johnson compounds with superheater boilers in 1910-11, but the work was not immediately proceeded with, and it was not until the end of 1913 that No 1040 was altered. In his paper to the Institution of Civil Engineers, Fowler told how coal consumption tests on engine No 1040, and on a sister engine No 1039 using saturated steam, had been made, and the results showed a saving of 25.9 per cent in coal and 22.3 per cent in water over the consumption with the locomotive using saturated steam. But the astonishing thing is that no particular advantage was taken of the greatly improved capacity of the engine in load haulage. I believe that about this time the load for Class '4' engines on 'Special Limit' loadings was advanced from 230 to 240 tons; but this was applied to all the compounds, not only to those that had been superheated.

10. Three smaller railways: the North Staffordshire, the 'Tilbury' and the Furness

These three railways, two of which maintained their independence right up to the Grouping of 1923, between them operated a remarkable number of locomotives that could be classified as 'great'. I had associations with all three of them in various ways, and can write of them with warm praise. Regarding the first of them, the North Staffordshire, although the family connections were at one time quite strong, I did not travel on the line myself in its pre-Grouping days. Of the 'Tilbury', or to give its full name, the London, Tilbury and Southend, for 12 years of my professional life I was Chief Draughtsman of the Westinghouse Brake and Signal Company under a very dedicated Chief Mechanical Engineer, Kenneth H. Leech, who had been a pupil of Robert Whitelegg, the 'Tilbury's' last Locomotive Superintendent. In the years I was associated with Leech, his erudition, enthusiasm and sheer love of engines implanted in me an interest in the Tilbury greater by far than could be imagined in one who had never seen one of its locomotives in its pristine pre-Midland glory. As for the Furness, I need only say that for 14 years my parents' home was at Barrow, and while I was away for much of the time myself, at boarding school and in London, there were many occasions, in school holidays, college vacations and suchlike, when I was at home.

First, then, to the North Staffordshire. In pre-Grouping days it was among the most prosperous of all the British railways, paying a dividend of rarely less than 4½ per cent on its ordinary shares from 1900 onwards. From what its profitability was derived is not the concern of the present book, except to comment that at the turn of the century the North Staffordshire had few passenger engines worth comment except in one important respect. In 1901, *The Railway Magazine* was still publishing monthly its illustrated interviews with leading railway officers, which were inaugurated in the very first issue of that journal in 1897. After four years, the leading General Managers had been featured, and the Editor was interviewing some eminent engineers, and in March 1901 the subject was Luke Longbottom, Locomotive, Carriage and Wagon Superintendent of the North Staffordshire Railway. He had then been in office for nearly twenty years, after having already had as long again on the London and North Western. But to me

the main feature of a very pleasant article was that it was accompanied as frontispiece in the magazine by a particularly charming example of one of the lithographed coloured plates that were included in some early issues. The subject was one of Mr Longbottom's 2-4-0 passenger engines, nothing to speak of technically, with 6-ft coupled wheels and 17-in by 24-in cylinders, but the painting style was delightful. The basic colour was a rich red-brown, plentifully lined out in bright red and yellow. The Company's coat of arms adorned the leading coupled splasher, while on the tender was the celebrated county emblem, the 'Staffordshire Knot'. A facetious tradition has it that at one time the district was so infested with felons that it was necessary to devise a noose that would enable them to be hanged three at a time!

Longbottom retired in 1902, and then it seems that there was an influx from the South Eastern and Chatham. The new Locomotive Superintendent was J.H. Adams, a son of the famous engineer whose work distinguished the London and South Western Railway for so many years. Before he went to Stoke-on-Trent in 1902, he had been Assistant Manager of Locomotive Works on the SE & CR covering both Ashford and Longhedge. His new Works Manager at Stoke was J.A. Hookham, who had been trained on the 'Chatham' under Kirtley, while A.J. Tassell, the new Chief Draughtsman, was a former South Eastern man, from James Stirling's time, but before joining the North Staffordshire he had spent a year in the drawing office of Neilson, Reid & Co of Glasgow. Adams and his new team found the Locomotive Department of the North Staffordshire generally in good shape, though the increasing goods traffic needed some more powerful 0-6-0s and some 0-6-2 tank engines with 4-ft 7-in coupled wheels for the shorter-haul duties. Neither of these new classes, nor the 0-4-4 tank engines for the local passenger trains, could aspire to be classed as 'great', however, and it was the main-line passenger services and the extensive 'foreign' workings in which the North Staffordshire was involved that provided the unusual interest in its locomotive power.

Adams, unlike his distinguished contemporary at Barrow-in-Furness, evinced a strong interest in high degree superheating. While Pettigrew's chief assis-

tant many years later confessed to me that 'We can't afford superheating on our short runs', it was another matter with some of the North Staffordshire's 'foreign' workings. It was traditional for one of their engines to work the 12.10 pm London express from Manchester which ran via Stoke, and changed engines from a North Stafford to an LNWR engine there for the non-stop run to Euston, even though the former engine did not work over more than 6 miles of its own track in the 37.4-mile run from Manchester. But that working was a mere nothing compared to the summer run of the Derby-Llandudno express, which was hauled by North Staffordshire engines throughout. One engine worked through over the 85 miles west of Stoke, although only the first 14 miles of the journey, to Crewe North Stafford Junction, were over the 'home' railway. Adams built four new 4-4-0s specially for working this service, which was accelerated in the summer of 1910 to make the run of 51 miles from Crewe to Rhyl non-stop in 63 minutes. Hitherto no passenger tender engines larger than 2-4-0s had been used on the North Staffordshire Railway. The new 4-4-0s of 1910, which were featured in a fine example of the F. Moore coloured postcards of the Locomotive Publishing Company, had cylinders 18½ in by 26 in, 6-ft 0-in coupled wheels and a boiler with a total heating surface of 1,225 sq ft working at 175 psi. The first four were non-superheated.

The new engines, like those of earlier dates that had been repaired under Mr Adams's supervision, had been turned out in a rather simpler style of painting than that used by Longbottom, albeit very attractive in itself. When the first news of the new 4-4-0s was released, in the *Locomotive Magazine* of July 1910,

with a line drawing and many dimensions, the splasher over the leading pair of coupled wheels was shown as carrying the 'Staffordshire Knot', though when the first photographs of this engine were published, the splasher was seen carrying the Company's coat of arms, with a second display of it on the tender flanked by the words 'North' and 'Stafford'. When Adams introduced his fine 4-4-2 tanks with Schmidt superheaters, primarily for the Manchester-Stoke express runs with the London trains, he also built one further 4-4-0 with a superheater for the special duty of hauling the Derby-Llandudno summer express. This duty, in addition to involving a non-stop run of more than 50 miles, gave no opportunity for getting any additional water between Crewe and Llandudno Junction. Although the large tenders fitted to these 4-4-0 engines carried 5 tons of coal and 3,200 gallons of water, they did not have water scoops. With ever-increasing loads on these popular holiday trains, the reduced coal and water consumption of the superheater 4-4-0 No 38 was important, and the engine worked that train every day during the summer service of 1913.

The superheater 4-4-2 tanks also had a strenuous job in working the noon express from Manchester London Road, as it was then called, to Stoke, because that train, in addition to the corridor restaurant car set of coaches for Euston, carried a Birmingham portion that was detached at Stoke. It often loaded up to more than 350 tons. Ironically enough, much the hardest part of the work was over the London and North Western section of the route. The train stopped at Stockport and Macclesfield, and it was after turning off the Manchester-Crewe main line at Cheadle Hulme that the hard work for the North Staffordshire engine began. The working time for the 11¾ miles from Stockport to Macclesfield was no more than 18 minutes, and when it is considered that this includes the 9 miles of continuous collar-work from Cheadle Hulme on an average gradient of 1 in 200, beginning with a sharp speed restriction in taking the junction off the main line, the NSR 4-4-2 tank engines had their work cut out in hauling trains that were never less than 330 tons and sometimes up to 380 tons. On restarting from Macclesfield, an even more severe climb had to be faced, the 1 in 102 bank up to the Moss signal box; but rear-end banking assistance was always provided with these heavy trains, and once clear of this initial two-mile bank, the rest was easy over the true North Staffordshire main line, either level or downhill. It was a point of honour with the NSR men always to bring the 12.10 pm from Manchester into Stoke-on-Trent on time.

Excellent though these 4-4-2 tank engines were, and economical in their performance, they were small for the hard work they had to do, particularly in respect of the boiler, which had only 887 sq ft of tube heating surface, although 133 sq ft in the firebox. The total heating surface, including the Schmidt superheater, was 1,281 sq ft. At the time the Stoke Locomotive Works was described in *The Railway Magazine*, November 1913, Adams and his staff had schemed out a much larger tank engine of the 0-6-4 type and a line drawing was included in the published article. By using coupled wheels of the smaller diameter of 5 ft 6 in, as against 6 ft 0 in on the 4-4-2 tanks and the 4-4-0 tender engines, it was evidently intended to use the larger engines on heavy mixed

duties in addition to express passenger trains. The onset of war in 1914, however, delayed the building of these engines, which, like all recent additions to the North Staffordshire locomotive stock, were to be built at the Company's own works at Stoke; and it was not until the end of 1916, after Mr Adams himself had died, that the first examples of the new class were completed. They were fine-looking engines, finished in the previous standard colour scheme, despite war conditions. Although austerity publishing restrictions had already made their mark on the appearance of *The Railway Magazine*, that journal's issue of April 1917 included a colour plate of one of the new 0-6-4 tank engines in the very best 'F. Moore' style.

As far as I can trace, that colour plate was the only illustration of one of the new engines in the magazine for nearly three years, after when there was a fine picture of engine No 118 about to leave Manchester London Road, heading the noon express to Euston. Naturally the 0-6-4 tanks were put on to this prestigious duty, though in describing some runs with them in a subsequent issue of *The Railway Magazine*, Mr Cecil J. Allen remarked that the schedule times over the London and North Western part of the journey between Manchester and Stoke had not been improved from their wartime decelerations, whereas those on the purely North Staffordshire had. On the difficult uphill stretch from the junction at Cheadle Hulme to the stop at Macclesfield, two runs with the 0-6-4 tank engines with loads of 335 and 365 tons gave times of around 15½ minutes for this 9½-mile length, in contrast to the 13-13¼ minutes made by

the 4-4-2 tanks in pre-war days, with comparable loads. Of course, Grouping soon ended this working of the train by North Staffordshire engines, and it was thereafter worked through from Manchester to Euston by a single Western Division engine, sometimes a 'Prince of Wales' Class 4-6-0 or one of the new standard compounds.

The London, Tilbury and Southend was a remarkable little railway. Even after it had been taken over by the Midland in 1912, its management structure profoundly changed and the colour of its locomotives changed from green to crimson lake, its character and the nature of its traffic remained altogether distinctive until 1923, when the Midland itself became merged into the LMS. Prior to 1912, all but two of its 82 locomotives were tanks, 70 indeed of only one type, the 4-4-2. Before the Midland take-over, the railway itself was imbued with a strong individuality and independence in outlook, which indeed was very necessary, having regard to the railway geography of East London at the turn of the century. Until 1880, the little railway had been dependent on the Great Eastern for its motive power. It entered its London terminus, Fenchurch Street, over 2½ miles of the Great Eastern line by running powers from Gas Factory Junction, and at one time it seemed that the 'Tilbury' itself was ripe for a take-over. But in that year, 1880, an order was placed with Sharp, Stewart & Co, then in Manchester, for twelve 4-4-2 tank engines. Before they arrived, Thomas Whitelegg, then a draughtsman in the Great Eastern locomotive department at Stratford, had been appointed Locomotive Superintendent of the 'Tilbury', and so he remained for 31 distinguished years.

In the London area, while the 'Tilbury' owned the line east of Gas Factory Junction, several other railways had running powers between Bromley and Barking, notably the North London and the Metropolitan District, and in 1902 the important step was taken of expanding the track from two to four running lines

from Campbell Road Junction, where the District Line from Whitechapel joins the Tilbury, to Barking. By the time these widening works were completed, in 1904, Whitelegg had 68 4-4-2 tank engines in service; 36 were of the original class supplied when the Company took over the working, and the others were of more modern design, introduced by Mr Whitelegg himself. The '37' Class was built in two batches, the first six by Sharp, Stewart & Co in 1897, and the second by Dübs and Co in 1898. They were handsomely proportioned engines, with 18-in by 26-in cylinders, a boiler of 4-ft 2-in diameter and a working pressure of 170 psi. Like all the Tilbury passenger engines, the coupled wheels were of 6-ft 6-in diameter. These were followed by the '51' Class, 18 engines built between 1900 and 1903, generally similar to Class '37' with the same cylinders and motion but with larger boilers and even better looking.

The painting was one of the most beautiful ever devised for a British locomotive. The basic colour was a medium green. The bunker and side tank panels were lined out in black and white, while the panels themselves were edged with a broad band of red-brown. The main frames were painted the same colour, as also were the steps, the bogie, the trailing wheel splasher and appendages such as the brake rod hangers. The Tilbury used the Westinghouse brake, and the pump was mounted on the right-hand side of the smokebox, with a wealth of polished brass fittings. The spokes of all the wheels were green, with the rims red-brown lined out in white. The coat of arms of the Company, a characteristically dignified emblem, was emblazoned on the tank side beneath the name of the engine, though curiously enough in all the various writings on railway coats of arms I have not seen an illustration or description of it. Of the names, and even the ten 0-6-0 goods tanks were included, one could write much in jest as well as approbation. It was William Stroudley when on the Brighton Railway who initiated the practice of nam-

ing every passenger engine after stations on the line. The Tilbury followed suit. There is a time-honoured story of a lady passenger who was seen in rapt admiration of engine No 53, not because of its technical merits but because it was painted such a nice colour—'Stepney Green'! At the other end of the scale, what about *Commercial Road* and *Black Horse Road* as engine names!!

The widening of the line between Campbell Road Junction and Barking had not been completed any too soon, because commuter traffic between the towns clustered around Southend itself was increasing rapidly. While the '51' Class engines could manage a 12-coach train of non-corridor bogie stock, the traffic department wanted to use the maximum length of the platforms the Great Eastern allocated to them in Fenchurch Street station. There was just room for 13 coaches of the standard bogie stock and a six-wheeler, and to cope with these maximum-load trains, which incidentally brought about a thousand season-ticket holders per train into the City, Whitelegg began rebuilding the '37' Class 4-4-2 tanks with larger boilers and 19-in cylinders. The work was done in the Railway Company's own shops at Plaistow. This Works was normally concerned only with maintenance and major repairs, and because of the extensive nature of the rebuilding of the '37' Class, progress was not very rapid. Only one engine was treated in 1905, two more in 1907, one in 1908, two in 1909, and the remaining engines of the class, making 12 in all, by 1911. Rebuilding of older engines, no matter how performance was improved, did not always beautify the appearance, but Whitelegg's treatment of his own '37' Class must be regarded as the 'exception of exceptions'. Those engines, in my view, were the most beautiful tanks ever to run the rails in Great Britain, or anywhere else for that matter. Appropriately, the *Locomotive Magazine* included as frontispiece to its January 1908 issue, after no more than four of them had been rebuilt, a sumptuous

colour plate by F. Moore, showing No 39 *Forest Gate*.

It was in that year that a pen-friend of mine for many years, J.F. Vickery, began commuting daily on the train that arrived in Fenchurch Street at 9.36 am. It ran non-stop from Leigh-on-Sea, and was one of the trains comprising 13 bogie coaches, plus a six-wheeler on Mondays. The distance from Leigh is 33.1 miles, and the start-to-stop run of 46 minutes was at that time complicated by a drastic slowing to 5 mph at Gas Factory Junction because of some extensive engineering work in progress. From June 1908, Vickery kept logs of all his journeys, and when, fifty years later, his eyesight began to fail, he bequeathed the log books of the first two years to me. On his first runs, the engine of the F. Moore colour plate was on the job, but after one week's running, the fourth engine to be rebuilt, the only one to be so treated in 1908, was substituted, No 47 *Stratford*, and this engine and No 39 *Forest Gate* had the train to themselves for several months. The timekeeping was extraordinarily good. My friend made most of his original notes in shorthand—in the year 1908—but his notes were amplified later for my benefit. The standard load of 13 bogie coaches on the 8.50 am from Leigh was 299 tons, and this was augmented on Monday mornings by the six-wheeler to 314 tons. The train usually carried about 975 passengers, so the gross load behind the engine could be reckoned at 360 tons.

The record of a week's running in September 1908 can be taken as typical of the work that those beautiful 4-4-2 tank engines did week in, week out with those heavy commuter trains. The departure from Leigh was within 30 seconds of the booked time every morning, and the engine was the current favourite No 47 *Stratford*. The line is more or less level to Pitsea, then comes a stiff climb to Laindon. There follows a sharp descent and then the going is relatively level onwards to Barking. It will be seen from the table that the average speeds from Laindon to Bark-

LT & SR: Leigh-on-Sea to Fenchurch Street
Engine 4-4-2 No 47 *Stratford*
Load 299 tons tare (314 tons tare on Monday)

Distance (miles)		Monday (m s)	Tuesday (m s)	Wednesday (m s)	Thursday (m s)	Friday (m s)
0.0	Leigh-on-Sea	0 00	0 00	0 00	0 00	0 00
6.6	Pitsea	10 28	10 02	10 16	10 25	10 28
10.3	Laindon	16 21	15 28	15 55	15 50	16 24
25.5	Barking	32 00	30 30	31 39	30 58	31 36
		pws	pws	pws	pws	pws
33.1	Fenchurch Street	44 38	44 22	44 13	45 28	45 23

ing were 58.2, 61.0, 58.2, 60.8 and 60.0 mph on the five successive runs.

In 1907 there was a move to change the painting of the Tilbury engines from green to a shade of lavender grey; but such care was taken with their upkeep that comparatively few engines had been so treated by the time Thomas Whitelegg's last four engines took the road in 1909. These were generally the same as the rebuilds of the '37' Class, but included certain improvements in detail. The new engines were built by Robert Stephenson & Co, and the Locomotive Publishing Co produced a fine coloured postcard of No 80 by F. Moore, in lavender, as it was displayed at the Imperial International Exhibition at the White City, London, in 1909. The engine was specially named *Southend-on-Sea*; but compared to the gorgeous green livery carried by nearly all other LTS engines, it would not have appeared to have gone down very well. In any case, the remaining two engines of the new series were, it is believed, painted green from the outset. Whitelegg himself retired in 1910, and was succeeded by his son, Robert, who had already given evidence of being a first class mechanical engineer in his own right. The Coronation of King George the Fifth, in 1911, gave him an oppor-

tunity to show how a Tilbury engine could be dolled up in honour of a great national occasion. Engine No 80, after her spell on exhibition at the White City in 1909, was given her intended name, *Thundersley*, and painted green; and I can only recommend the National Railway Museum postcard if anyone should disbelieve the well-nigh incredible degree of finery in which she was bedecked.

Robert Whitelegg's spell on the Tilbury was as short as it was unfortunate. He had become very much aware that while his father's beautiful engines were handling the traffic, there was precious little margin in reserve; and at an early date he approached the Managing Director of the Company, Mr A.L. Stride, who was also a civil engineer, to put forward proposals for much larger engines. He was planning the largest tank engines yet to be seen on a British railway, of the 4-6-4 type, having 20-in by 26-in cylinders, 6-ft 3-in coupled wheels, and the Schmidt superheater. Whitelegg himself, having regard to the running powers exercized over the Great Eastern

The first 'Baltic' tank engine, No 2101, as delivered (Beyer, Peacock & Co).

Railway west of Campbell Road Junction, had some doubts concerning the weight restrictions over that part of the line; but when the proposition was put to him, Stride was delighted and told Whitelegg to go ahead. A contract for eight of the huge new engines was placed with Beyer, Peacock & Co, and then the fateful year of 1912, for the 'Tilbury', broke. To the great surprise of everyone below director level, arrangements had been made for the take-over of the railway by the Midland. From time to time there had been rumours that the Great Eastern might step in, but not the Midland! But, for good or ill, before Parliament had risen for the summer recess of 1912 the legislation was passed authorizing the complete purchase of the London, Tilbury and Southend Railway by the Midland.

Robert Whitelegg became a mere divisional officer; but worse was to follow. Construction of his great 4-6-4 tank engines was well advanced at Beyer, Peacock's Works, and with the Midland antipathy to large engines it is more than likely that, Stride having retired at the time of the take-over, someone raised the question of weight restrictions over the Great Eastern line. The management of the latter railway were feeling deeply hurt at the incursion of the Midland into what they felt was their territory, and when the new owners raised the question of the route availability of their huge new engines to run over the GER line into Fenchurch Street, they met with a complete refusal. When they did arrive, painted of course in Midland colours, they could not be used on the trains that most needed the extra power. Whitelegg himself took every one of the eight

Tilbury 'Baltic' tank No 2102 on an up Midland Welling-borough to Cricklewood coal train near Elstree, piloted by Midland 2-4-0 express engine No 130 (F. Moore's Rail Photos).

engines on a trial trip; and eastwards from Barking, some fast running was done, including a maximum of more than 90 mph recorded by my friend Kenneth Leech who was on the footplate with Whitelegg on that occasion. Once the new engines were run in, Whitelegg himself did not stay much longer. He resigned early in 1913, and soon afterwards the eight 4-6-4s were transferred to the Midland Railway proper, where they eventually found a niche working maximum-load coal trains between Wellingborough and Cricklewood, though always with a pilot engine in front.

The Furness Railway could well be described as a microcosm of the industrial and commercial development of Great Britain itself as a world power in the Victorian era. At the time when the great Queen was crowned, Barrow was unknown, not even a name on the map of north-west England; but seven years before she celebrated her Golden Jubilee, in 1880, the engineering activities of the town had become so important that the Institution of Mechanical Engineers held their Summer Meeting there. It was at this meeting that David Joy read his memorable paper on 'A new Reversing and Expansive Valve-Gear', and F.W. Webb of the London and North Western Railway nobly supported him by having on display at Barrow the first of his new 18-in express goods engines fitted with the Joy valve gear. At that time, and for several years thereafter, the Furness Railway did not design any of its own locomotives, preferring to rely on the standard products of manufacturers, principally Sharp, Stewart & Co, who also supplied locomotives to the Cambrian Railways. In 1897 all was changed by the appointment of W.F. Pettigrew as Locomotive Carriage and Wagon Superintendent. Having been Works Manager for the London and South Western Railway at Nine Elms since 1886, and much more than a mere assistant to

William Adams in his last years, Pettigrew might well have looked forward to succeeding him in the chair; but then, at the critical moment, Dugald Drummond was looking out for an opportunity to re-enter railway service, and he got the job at Nine Elms.

At Barrow, Pettigrew took on far greater responsibilities than Locomotive, Carriage and Wagon Superintendent of a relatively small railway. The dock machinery was his responsibility. Not only this, but there were also the ships. The pleasure craft on Lakes Windermere and Coniston and their machinery came within the job of the Locomotive Superintendent, as also did the tugs used for manoeuvring large vessels into and out of the Barrow docks; and last, but by no means least, were the sea-going pleasure steamers that plied between Barrow and Fleetwood, and Barrow and the Isle of Man. But this is a book about locomotives, and it was as a locomotive engineer that Pettigrew's reputation already stood very high even before he went to Barrow. When he was at Nine Elms he took a dominant part in the trials of one of the Adams 7-ft outside-cylinder express passenger 4-4-0s; and in the paper which he jointly with Adams presented to the Institution of Civil Engineers. On the Furness Railway, his first locomotives were 0-6-0s for the heavy mineral traffic that was the life-blood of the railway, but naturally, from his experience on the London and South Western, he was anxious to improve the passenger workings. The Furness had taken delivery of six 4-4-0s of the latest Sharp, Stewart design in 1896, and, while Pettigrew's own 4-4-0s were being designed, two more of the 1896 type were purchased in 1900. They were handsome and hard-working engines, with 18-in by 24-in cylinders, 6-ft 0-in coupled wheels, and 150 psi boiler pressure.

Pettigrew's own 4-4-0 engines introduced in 1901 were unusual among Furness Railway locomotives in having 6-ft 6-in coupled wheels. The cylinders were 18-in by 26-in, but the boilers had little more evaporative heating surfaces than the largest of the preceding Sharp, Stewart design, though they worked at a higher boiler pressure of 160 psi. They were very handsome engines and looked well in the characteristic Furness livery. This has been described in some books I have seen as a dark red somewhat akin to that of the Midland, but this is not so; the Furness colour was a light red, iron-ore red as it was aptly described. Recalling how Pettigrew had been intensely engaged in road tests of express locomotives on the London and South Western Railway, it may well be imagined that he was keen to run some trials with his own new 4-4-0s, and of this I have a story to tell. One of his senior assistants, E. Sharples by name, became a family friend when my parents were living in Barrow, and one evening when we were talking about engine tests he recalled those made on the

Right *Furness Railway: one of the Pettigrew's standard 0-6-0 heavy freight engines of 1913 working a coke train from the North Eastern Railway over Tebay troughs, LNWR,* en route *to Barrow via Hincaster Junction and Arnside* (Loco Publishing Co).

Below right *The last Pettigrew 0-6-0 to retain its original boiler, No 12494* (British Railways).

Bottom right *Furness Railway: Pettigrew's 6-ft 6-in 4-4-0 express design of 1901* (British Railways).

'126' Class. He was riding in the shelter at the front taking indicator diagrams and, in his own words, 'We were tearing along at a terrific speed, for this part of the world, at about 65 mph near Silecroft, and all I could hear through the ''intercom'' from the footplate was the driver swearing because the engine would not go faster!' The '126', or 'K3', Class had been taken off the faster trains before my own stopwatching days, but Mr Pettigrew's later 4-4-0s of the '130', or 'K4', Class were still taking turns with the ex-LNWR non-superheater 'Precursors' in the late 1920s.

The first of the '130' Class were built by the North British Locomotive Company in 1913. They differed in outward appearance and in their technical details from their predecessors in having 6-ft 0-in coupled wheels and a larger firebox. The most noticeable outward characteristic was a very prominent extended smokebox, looking as if a superheater was included. They had the same-sized cylinders as the 'K3s' and the same simple front end with Stephenson's link motion actuating valves between the cylinders. The boiler pressure was 170 psi, again a slight advance upon the Class 'K3'. Despite their smaller coupled wheels, I found the 'K4s' free running engines on the straighter lengths of the southern part of the line between Ulverston and Carnforth. They used to run at up to 60 mph with the up afternoon express from Barrow, which sometimes loaded to about 300 tons. On one occasion when I was an engineering student at Imperial College, and was privileged to pay a visit to the Locomotive Works at Barrow, I asked Sharples if they had ever considered superheating. He laughed and said, 'We can't afford superheating on our short runs.' Later I learned that Pettigrew had actually made some trials with superheating using apparatus of the Phoenix type.

When we first went to Barrow in 1916, I can recall seeing an occasional 0-6-0 goods engine with an extended smokebox and the chimney mounted out on the furthest point. They looked very ugly, quite out of keeping with the usual comely outline of most Furness locomotives. This apparatus was also tried on two of the so-called 'Cleator' tanks, used for shunting in the heavily industrialized area at Cleator Moor

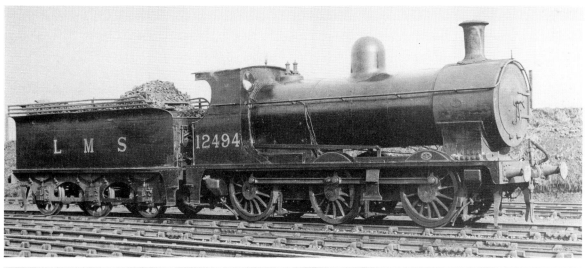

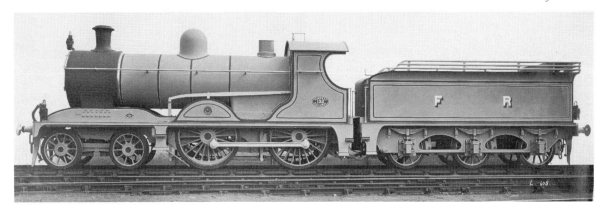

Left *Furness Railway: Pettigrew 6-ft 0-in 4-4-0 of 1913 design* (North British Locomotive Co).

Below left *Furness Railway: the first of the 4-6-4 tanks designed by E. Sharples* (Kitson & Co).

Bottom left *Furness Railway: one of the Sharples 4-6-4 tanks, No 11102, in LMS red, on an up stopping train near Dalton Junction* (O.S. Nock).

inland from Whitehaven. It was also used briefly on one of the largest Sharp, Stewart 4-4-0s originally built in 1896. The Phoenix superheater differed in principle from the more familiar types like the Schmidt, the Robinson and the Swindon by being of the smokebox, rather than the smoke-tube, type. It had its origin in the apparatus used by J.A.F. Aspinall on some of his Lancashire and Yorkshire 'Atlantics', as long previously as 1899. The Phoenix, like the Aspinall, was of the waste heat type and was accommodated entirely within the smokebox. The form of superheater was no more than a passing phase in the development of Furness Railway motive power for, in the summer of 1914, three new classes appeared, all having the same boilers and cylinders. The passenger engines were a development of the '130' Class, with 6-ft 0-in coupled wheels, while the 0-6-0 goods and 0-6-2 tanks both had 4-ft 7-in wheels. All three classes were very successful, and several additions were made to the 0-6-0s while the Furness Railway retained its independence. All three classes exemplified Pettigrew's addiction to the simplest and most straightforward design practice, with direct-acting Stephenson link motion, and using saturated steam at a pressure of 170 psi.

In the early months of 1918, however, there were important changes in the top management of the Furness Railway occasioned by the retirement of the General Manager, Alfred Aslett, and of Pettigrew himself. The new General Manager came from the London and North Western Railway, but in replacing Pettigrew there was a complete and not altogether welcome change in management. Since 1909, D.L. Rutherford had been Engineer of the Furness Railway, and in 1918 it was decided to include the locomotive, carriage and wagon department, and also the

ships, under one officer with the title Engineer and Locomotive Superintendent. In Barrow it quickly became known that the new Chief knew nothing about locomotives, their design and their running; but after things had settled down after the war, it was evident that he wanted to make a big 'splash'. One evening, when Sharples and his wife were at dinner with my family and, as was more often than not the case, the conversation turned to railways, he said simply, 'Rutherford said he wanted a 4-6-4; so we had to design one for him.' The design was in the best Pettigrew tradition, with 19½-in by 26-in cylinders, 5-ft 8-in coupled wheels, and piston valves operated by the ordinary link motion through rocking levers. The boiler was of ample proportions, non-superheated, with a tube heating surface of 1,850 sq ft, firebox 153 sq ft and a grate area of 26 sq ft. The working pressure was 170 psi. An important feature in an engine with such a long overall wheelbase was its ability to negotiate curves. There were not all that many on the main line, but in the approaches to the stations at Carnforth and Whitehaven, and in the locomotive sheds, there were some exceedingly bad ones. These the new engines rode elegantly and with ease.

In passenger traffic, the 4-6-4s made short work of the severe gradients of the main line between Roose and Plumpton Junction, it being particularly noticeable how they got away from rest on the up trains calling at Furness Abbey and Dalton, and on the down trains, all of which stopped at Ulverston. I did not travel on the early morning mail train until later years; this train, calling only at Ulverston between Carnforth and Barrow, really had to run to keep time, whereas the trains on which I clocked the 4-6-4s rarely had to touch as much as 50 mph between stations. The engines themselves had a share of the railway press in 1921, with the name of D.L. Rutherford, Engineer and Locomotive Superintendent, subjoined. But in the following year, with the Grouping already agreed, one can well imagine that he did not relish the fractionalizing of his all-embracing department on Midland Railway lines, and he resigned, and went back to Edinburgh whence he had come in 1909; there he set up in private practice as a consulting engineer. Sharples remained as Divisional Mechanical Engineer, Barrow.

11. Glasgow and South Western

The 'Sou-West', as it was affectionately known by all who worked on it and by its countless supporters in south-western Scotland, could hardly claim to aspire to any real greatness in phases of its locomotive history, yet the spirit of the railway itself and the inbred loyalty and enthusiasm characteristic of all its men, from the highest to the most humble, gave it a verve and panache that lasted long after the initials G & SWR, and indeed LMS, had ceased to exist on British railway rolling stock. To many railway enthusiasts of the pre-Grouping era, the Glasgow and South Western was a mere name, that was if it registered at all. There was an instance in the autumn of 1910 when the Diamond Jubilee of its Act of Incorporation was attained. In *The Railway Magazine,* which at that time catered far more for the business side of railways than later, there was not the slightest mention of that important event, and it was not until April of the following year that a group of rather stodgy articles, clearly strung together from official sources, did appear. *The Railway Magazine* was then at the height of its pre-war opulence, with 88 pages and a colour plate every month, all for sixpence, and the 27 pages of rather dull stuff allocated to the G & SWR were completely overshadowed in interest and variety by the rest of the magazine.

South of the Border, and indeed in most places where railway 'buffs' foregathered, 'Scotland' meant the Caledonian, with a mild taste of the Highland and the North British; but in the Lowlands, interest, partisanship and sometimes fierce antagonism raged unabated between the 'Caley' and the 'Sou-West'. It was not only in centres like Ayr, Kilmarnock and Dumfries that the traditional animosity persisted. In Glasgow, and particularly on the Clyde Coast, preferences were deep-seated among the regular patrons. When I am feeling nostalgic over past holidays in Scotland, I enjoy rereading George Blake's fine book on the Firth of Clyde, and particularly his 'Rhapsody by way of Introduction to the Firth'. I could not imagine his own father, who features largely in that opening chapter, travelling by any other way from Glasgow to their holiday retreat on the Kyles of Bute than by the G & SWR, first by a fast express train from St Enoch station to Greenock Princes Pier, and then continuing across the firth by one of the same company's fine steamships. There were those who would opt for the Caledonian making for Gourock and the inevitable steamer race across the Firth, and Blake's father tells of his satisfaction that the *Mercury* beat the Caledonian *Duchess of Fife* in the race to be first at Kirn pier. That run was in 1908, but there had been several well-loved designs of 'Sou-West'

locomotives before then.

In the early 1880s, the Glasgow and South Western was still a domeless-boilered line. The practice dated from Patrick Stirling's time. It continued with his brother James, until he went to the South Eastern in 1878, and with his successor Hugh Smellie to 1890. By this latter date, the locomotive practice of the 'Sou-West' could be regarded as among the foremost of any in Great Britain, Smellie having developed the epoch-marking Stirling No '6' Class 4-4-0 of 1873 into his own '153' Class 4-4-0 of 1886. But it was not only because of his main-line 6-ft 9-in express engines that Smellie was revered on the 'Sou-West', because before building those graceful and supremely fast engines at Kilmarnock, he had introduced a class of generally the same proportions but with 6-ft 1-in coupled wheels. There were 22 engines in that class, built at Kilmarnock between 1882 and 1885, and they were designed more particularly for the Greenock route, over which the 'Sou-West' was always in hot competition with the Caledonian, and had an immeasurably harder road to the west of Paisley. Smellie's 4-4-0s can be described thus:

Class	119	153
Year built	1882-5	1886-9
Cylinders, diameter × stroke (in)	18¼ × 26	18¼ × 26
Coupled wheels (ft in)	6 1¼	6 9½
Heating surface (sq ft)	1,065	1,198
Grate area (sq ft)	16	17.5
Boiler pressure (psi)	140	150

The '153' Class, much as they were appreciated by all who had to use them, suffered to some extent by being superseded relatively soon on the more important main-line runs by Manson's No '8' Class; but the '119' Class, the much loved 'Wee Bogies', had a much longer spell on top-class work.

It is rather remarkable that these very splendid little engines received so very little notice in the railway press until the late David L. Smith, of Ayr, started his annual contributions to the January issue of *The Railway Magazine*: 'G & SWR Nights Entertainments'. It was my privilege to know David and his father and to visit them in their home, and to learn much of the background of the stories that he eventually published in book form, *Tales of the Glasgow and South Western Railway*. The 'Wee Bogies' were originally introduced for the Greenock line, and to give some idea of the work that involved I can commend to my readers' attention the gradient profile of the line from where it leaves the Glasgow to Ayr main line at Elderslie No 2 Junction. It is important to bear in mind the deadly rivalry that existed before 1914 between the 'Sou-West' and the Caledonian, and to recall that after running on parallel tracks from Glasgow to Paisley, the 'Caley' route onwards to Gourock Pier was as near as possible level throughout. The distance from Glasgow to Princes Pier was about two miles less than that of their rivals; but what of the gradients! Fortunately, the G & SWR route was well aligned, and Smellie's 'Wee Bogies' had not only to climb the hard gradients efficiently but they had to run like stags once the summit was passed. It must have been an exciting business descending from Upper Port Glasgow cabin at anything up to 80 mph knowing that little more than two miles ahead was the dead end right on the water front!

There were 22 of the 'Wee Bogies', and nine or ten of them were stationed at Ayr. They were the maids of all work right up to the outbreak of the First World War. They were very much in demand for giving assistance to trains on the steeply graded line running southwards from Ayr to Stranraer, and when I

One of Hugh Smellie's '153' Class of 1886 used on the Midland Scotch Expresses between Carlisle and Glasgow, seen here at Dumfries shed (F. Moore's Rail Photos).

come to the later stages of the 'Sou-West' story, piloting becomes a major issue. Then, in 1890 Dugald Drummond somewhat prematurely resigned from his post on the Caledonian Railway with the prospect of a still more glittering appointment in Australia, and Hugh Smellie got his job at St Rollox. Unfortunately we were not to know if this was the beginning of a domeless boiler era on the Caledonian, for after no more than a few months in office he caught a chill, which turned to pneumonia, and he died. In the meantime, the Glasgow and South Western Railway had appointed James Manson of the Great North of Scotland to succeed Smellie. The new chief, however, was no stranger to Kilmarnock, because after his early training there, under the Stirlings, and experience at sea, he had returned to become Works Manager before going north to Kittybrewster. On the GN of S, Manson had developed a style of his own in locomotive lineaments, markedly different from that of Smellie, and this he continued throughout the 22 years that he was in the chair at Kilmarnock. Other than that the new engines, the No '8' Class, had a domed boiler, there was not all that much difference between them and Smellie's '153' Class. The tube heating surface was the same, and the grate area and the firebox heating surface were slightly increased, but the boiler was the same.

The first engine of the No '8' Class was built at Kilmarnock in 1892, and construction of them continued to the same design until 1904, by which time

there were 57 of the class. Manson's policy in this respect has been compared, not very favourably by some commentators, to the contemporary practice of St Rollox, where having produced a highly satisfactory 4-4-0 engine, as the G & SW No '8' Class certainly was, they subsequently enlarged it, stage by stage, as the demands of the traffic increased. Manson kept to the same design, and had recourse to double heading in any case of no more than moderate loading. As engines, the No '8' Class were beautifully designed and very popular with the enginemen; but they did not represent any real advance upon the Smellie '153' Class, and certainly did not justify perpetuation of the design into the twentieth century. Manson also produced his own version of the 'Wee Bogies', primarily for use on the Greenock road. In this case he built a rather more powerful engine than Smellie's, having the same-sized cylinders and motion but a larger boiler and grate area and a higher boiler pressure of 165 psi instead of the 140 psi of the 'Wee Bogies'. The '336' Class, as they were known, 25 strong, were built by Dübs & Co in 1895-9. Like the No '8' Class, they were popular and successful engines, and because of their more restricted usage they rarely had to be double-headed. The platforms at Princes Pier station, Greenock, could not accommodate any very long trains, and despite the steep gradient leading out of the station and up the hill to Upper Port Glasgow cabin, the boat trains were taken by one engine.

At this point, may I inject a personal recollection of these engines, even though it was far ahead of Manson's time. In the summer of 1930, in connection with resignalling work, I was resident at St Enoch station for a time, and had ample opportunity to observe the locomotive working. I saw that the former G & SWR engines had virtually disappeared from

the main line and Ayrshire Coast workings to be replaced by Midland compounds, and new LMS Class '2' 4-4-0s with Caledonian 4-4-0s were used for piloting. There were a number of ex-G & SWR engines still about, but they were on humdrum jobs—with one notable exception. The Manson 6-ft 1-in 4-4-0s of the '336' Class were still on the boat trains to and from Greenock Princes Pier and, after a Saturday steamer trip on the Firth of Clyde, I was pleased to see that our engine for the return trip to Glasgow was one of these, No 14215, formerly No 362, of the G & SWR. With a train of six non-corridor bogie coaches amounting to 175 tons behind the tender, that little engine started away in great style on the 1 in 70 through the tunnels to Greenock Lynedoch, and continued, without any slipping, till the speed had reached a steady 27 mph on the gradient. When higher up the bank the inclination eased to 1 in 98, there was a smart acceleration to 28½ mph before the summit was reached half a mile beyond Upper Port Glasgow cabin. Once past this point we went like the wind, reaching and sustaining 73 mph until the need to slow down for Elderslie Junction where the main line from Ayr was joined. The 17.8 miles from Princes Pier to Paisley were run in 28¼ minutes—a smart performance over so steeply graded a line.

Reverting to the main line to Carlisle, at the turn of the century practically all the Midland Scotch Expresses needed double-heading, frequently by two Manson No '8' Class locomotives. Although the railway itself was prosperous enough, earning dividends on its ordinary shares that were usually better than those of the Caledonian, it was a matter of engineering prestige, particularly at a joint station like Carlisle, and Manson designed a 4-6-0 to keep in step with McIntosh's giant Nos 49 and 50 of the

Caledonian. Some careful design work was put into the '381' Class at Kilmarnock Works, and the contract for ten engines was placed with the North British Locomotive Company. They were built in 1903 at the Atlas Works, formerly owned by Sharp, Stewart & Co, and in view of the considerable changes in design practice evidenced from Manson's previous work one would be curious to know to what degree, if any, the manufacturers influenced the basic design. Why, for example, did Manson change to the Belpaire type of firebox, and use outside cylinders, with an unusually long connecting rod of 11 ft? The general dimensions were conventional, with cylinders of 20-in diameter by 26-in stroke, coupled wheels of 6-ft 6-in diameter, and a total heating surface of 1,852 sq ft. The grate area was 24½ sq ft and the working pressure 180 psi.

Although differing so much in appearance from all previous G & SW locomotives, the new 4-6-0s were handsome in every respect, and admirably supported by the double-bogie tenders. Lovers of the artistic in locomotive lineaments were glad Manson had not perpetuated the ugly arrangement he had initiated

while on the Great North of Scotland, of having a single bogie with inside frames at the leading end of the tender, with the third and fourth axles being fixed, with ordinary axle-boxes and bearings outside. This type of tender was used in one or two instances on the G & SWR. There was an amusing editorial slip-up in the *Locomotive Magazine* in 1911 when a further batch of the 4-6-0s was built at Kilmarnock Works. I had noticed from one or two Mackay photographs taken in the Carlisle area that some of the latest engines had six-wheeled tenders, and in a supplement to its issue of 15 April 1911, the *Locomotive Magazine* had a 'portrait' photograph of engine No 126, thus equipped. But the accompanying write-up, which was acknowledged to Manson himself, stated: 'The double bogie tender weighs 50 tons with 4,100 gallons of water'! How many of the seven Kilmarnock-built 4-6-0s had six-wheeled tenders I cannot say, but the earliest of them, No 119, had a bogie tender.

The first ten of the 4-6-0s, numbered 381 to 390, were allocated seven to Corkerhill and three to Currock Road, Carlisle. They all had their own drivers, and the proprietary sense was, as never before on the

'Sou-West', manifested in the handling of these engines. Manson himself selected the drivers and briefed them in their duties, and at the shed the locomotives were groomed like greyhounds, and serviced with the best quality lubricating oil and first class coal. Manson impressed on his drivers the need to economize on coal on the long through workings between Glasgow and Carlisle, and this incidentally led to the 4-6-0 drivers earning the reputation of being professional 'coal dodgers'. They would economize by going easily up the banks, and use the speedworthiness of their engines to regain the time they had lost uphill by going their fastest downhill. In this they were often helped by the frequency of provision of assistant engines on the steeply uphill sections of the line. Until the introduction of the 4-6-0s, double heading had been the rule rather than the exception with the Midland Scotch Expresses, and so it was nothing new to couple on a 4-4-0, either a Manson or a Smellie from St Enoch, and very often take it as far as New Cumnock. It was the same going north from Dumfries, where the uphill work started. The maximum loads taken without a pilot appear to have been about 250 tons, and the running in all circumstances, judging from contemporary reports, was generally poor and involving loss of time, apart from that occasioned by signal checks and temporary restrictions of speed due to engineering works on the line.

I find it somewhat significant that in a book like David L. Smith's *Tales of the Glasgow and South Western Railway*, otherwise steeped in the lore of the railway, all its men and their engines, an author of scholarship and nigh-lifelong devotion to the subject should have so little to say about the 4-6-0s. After all, they were the premier engines of the line, and while other designs by Manson came in for a fair share of praise or otherwise, annotated by numerous asides about the enginemen and their merits and foibles, it almost seems that D.L.S. felt that the less said about the 4-6-0s the better. On the several occasions when I was welcomed into his family circle at Ayr, the talk was mainly about the Stranraer line. Arising from his experience of many journeys between Carlisle and Glasgow, Cecil J. Allen has singled out one engine for praise, No 129, one of the two fitted with superheaters, 21-in diameter cylinders, and a lower boiler pressure of 160 psi, but the runs he described were made with loads of 200 tons and less, loads which a famous railway littérateur once described as no more than 'an engine and a handcart'! Going southbound out of Glasgow on one such occasion, the superheater 4-6-0, hauling exactly 200 tons, fell to 14 mph going up the 1 in 70 of Neilston bank, but descending through Stewarton towards Kilmarnock a maximum of no less than 85 mph was reached. This was perhaps the extreme limit of 'coal dodging'; but

Right *One of the two Manson superheater 4-6-0s, originally numbered 128, seen here in Midland red leaving Glasgow St Enoch in 1928 with an express for the south* (P. Ransome-Wallis).

Below right *Manson superheater 4-6-0 No 129 with Weir feedwater heating apparatus* (F. Moore's Rail Photos).

Bottom right *Manson non-superheater 4-6-0 No 511, as rebuilt by Whitelegg, entering Carlisle on a London express shortly before the Grouping* (Author's Collection).

high speeds on the line between Kilmarnock and Glasgow were quite usual in G & SWR days.

It seems, however, that the Manson 4-6-0s were too lightly built for the heavy work in hauling the Midland Scotch Expresses. The 17 built non-superheated weighed only 67 tons without their tenders, which was in some contrast to the 73 tons of the 'Cardean' Class of the Caledonian Railway, which had the same cylinders and coupled wheels, and a slightly higher boiler pressure when saturated. The Manson 4-6-0s were proved to have front ends of insufficient strength and rigidity. The framing was too light, and with cylinders and valve chests working loose, and smokeboxes drawing air, they were a constant trouble to those who had to maintain them in service for express traffic. Manson retired in 1912, at the relatively early age of 66 for one in apparently good health, and was able to continue with many of his quiet, unobtrusive social activities. His biographer felt he might have continued much longer in office, seeing that there was no general age limit at which senior officers retired at that time. But admirable as was his attitude to life, one feels that he had had enough of the railway by 1912, and he left others to sort out the weaknesses of his 4-6-0s. It was left to Robert Whitelegg to attempt a rebuilding of some of them, but they were all taken off main-line passenger work when the LMS began introducing the Midland compounds in Scotland, on both the Caledonian and the G & SW lines. They were used to some extent on the Glasgow-Ayr trains, but not with any distinction.

At Kilmarnock, Manson was succeeded by Peter Drummond from the Highland. In a subsequent chapter of this book, it will be told how the 15 years when he was at Inverness were anything but characteristic of his style and engineering aspirations. Some very fine engines were introduced, but the largest of these were not of his design at all. Manson's retirement and Peter Drummond's move to Kilmarnock came at roughly the same time as Dugald Drummond's death. On the Highland, his younger brother's work gave the impression that when he was not perpetuating David Jones's 4-6-0 designs in principle, he was just copying Dugald's practice on the London and South Western. Manson's biographer

is somewhat scathing of Peter's first efforts to remedy the lack of power in the main-line engines of the G & SWR. Certainly he had a much freer hand at engine designing than he had at Inverness. While the drivers and firemen of the 'Sou-West' had very pronounced ideas as to what constituted a good engine, and they had been nurtured in this respect by Manson's fatherly interest in all their work, things had never reached the stage, as they did on one occasion at Inverness, of the men overruling the Locomotive Superintendent as to what type of engine should be used for a special assignment.

On the 'Sou-West', in 1913, huge new engines began to arrive from the North British Locomotive Company incorporating fittings that were quite new to Kilmarnock, including tender feed water heaters, duplex feed pumps, marine-type big ends, and the Eastleigh-type steam reverser. These would have been accepted, though not without a certain amount of seething discontent over changes that the men thought unnecessary; but what really did set the heather on fire was when the new engines were found to have the driver's position changed over to the left-hand side of the cab. It was useless for the new authority to point out that this was bringing the 'Sou-West' into line with the other major railways of Scotland. The enginemen of the 'Sou-West' could not have cared less, indeed the less like the Caledonian they were, the better they were pleased. Moreover, Peter Drummond did not exactly excel in the design of his big engines. His large 0-6-0s of the '279' Class, of which there were 15, and which were intended for the main-line goods trains between Glasgow and Carlisle, were about the most hated engines in Scotland, for their outrageous coal consumption and the many faults that led to failures while running.

It is indeed remarkable that a locomotive engineer of Peter Drummond's experience and family associations could have produced such a bad design as that of the '279' Class, and then within two years follow it with such a good one as the '16' Class 2-6-0s of 1915. Both Classes were built by the North British Locomotive Company, and ostensibly differed, apart from in their wheel arrangement, in that the later engines had superheaters and the earlier ones had not. In British locomotive practice, many examples can be quoted of the improvements wrought in what were generally considered as successful designs by superheating, notably the 'Precursor' Class of 4-4-0s on the London and North Western Railway, which in their original form were certainly dividend earners *in excelsis*, but which were far surpassed by the superheated version in the 'George the Fifth' Class. On the Glasgow and South Western, however, while the '279' Class were the most utterly 'dead' of all dead losses in the locomotive works it would be pos-

sible to conceive, the '16' Class were lively and free running, and did their work on the very minimum coal consumption. In later years, I saw a number of them in the Carlisle area, many years after Grouping, and they were very popular with the running staff, even though there were many new LMS engines on the sheds by that time.

Peter Drummond, like his elder brother Dugald, died in harness, in the early summer of 1918. While the '16' Class 2-6-0s were undoubtedly his best engines, but for the constraints put on new locomotive construction by war conditions they would not have been his largest or most impressive. At Kilmarnock, the design was worked out in full detail for a super-express passenger four-cylinder 4-6-0, on very similar lines to brother Dugald's 'Paddleboat' Class on the London and South Western; but after the 'Sou-West' with unfortunate early troubles on the 'Sou-West' with non-superheater engines, the big new 4-6-0s were to be superheated from the start. I have had an opportunity to study the general arrangement drawing, and in outline it bears a strong family likeness to the 'Paddleboats' before Dugald's successor at Eastleigh fitted them with extended smokeboxes, as part of the process of fitting them with superheaters. Had Peter Drummond lived to enter the post-war era on Scottish railways, there is no doubt that a strong move would have been made to get one or two prototypes of the new design built, before Grouping swamped everything!

The G & SWR Board lost no time in appointing a successor to Drummond. It was fortunate that so able an engineer as Robert Whitelegg was almost immediately available. In the previous chapter of this book, it has been told how his former responsible task on the London, Tilbury and Southend Railway was virtually liquidated after the Midland take-over in 1912, and during the war he was on various Government services. The vacancy in the engineering department of the Glasgow and South Western Railway was of such importance that he was released from his wartime duties to take over at Kilmarnock on 1 August 1918. Quite apart from the overriding war conditions, the general situation in the locomotive department had deteriorated since Manson retired at the end of 1912. Peter Drummond had not been long in letting everyone know that he had little time for the existing locomotive stock *in toto*, and was advocating a policy of 'scrap and build' as ruthless as any pursued by the LMS in the 1930s. But the finances of the G & SWR at the outset did not permit of such a drastic programme of stock replacement, and the onset of war in 1914 still further hampered any grandiose plans in this respect. When Whitelegg took over in 1918, he found a situation that could well have daunted the most energetic and

Great Locomotives of the LMS in colour: 1866-1945

Midland Railway: Kirtley 6-ft 2½-in 2-4-0 No 158A, built in 1866 then rebuilt with a Johnson boiler and mountings and renumbered 2 in the 1907 renumbering of the entire locomotive stock. In 1948 she was given her Johnson duplicate number 158A and set aside for preservation, and is seen here in Derby Works Yard in 1961. The locomotive is now at the Midland Railway Centre at Butterley, Derbyshire (R.C. Riley).

Above *Midland Railway : one of the penultimate batch of the famous Johnson 'Spinners', No 673, in the last style of painting as a working engine on the Midland Railway. It was built at Derby in 1896, as No 118, and as first restored to working order after preservation this number and the original style of painting was also restored. Now the engine is to be seen at the Midland Railway Centre at Butterley, Derbyshire* (J.A. Coiley).

Below *Ex-North London Railway: Park-designed 0-6-0 goods tank engine of 1879. This 1895 example, seen on the Bluebell Railway at Sheffield Park in 1962, bears the number 2650 with which it was allocated when the North London Railway stock was incorporated with that of the London and North Western shortly before Grouping in 1922* (R.C. Riley).

Above *Midland Railway : the first of the celebrated Midland compounds, originally built by S.W. Johnson in 1902 as No 2631, later renumbered 1000, and superheated in 1914. Seen here at Derby in 1957, it is normally based at the National Railway Museum at York* (R.C. Riley).

Below *North Staffordshire Railway : 0-6-2 tank engine No 2, one of the last engines built at Stoke Works before the NSR was absorbed into the London, Midland and Scottish Railway in 1923. The engine is seen at Walkden Colliery, Manchester, in 1961, but it is now based at the National Railway Museum at York* (J. G. Dewing).

Below *Highland Railway: the first ever class of 4-6-0 locomotive to run on a British railway. Designed by David Jones, No 103 was the first of a batch of fifteen engines built by Sharp, Stewart & Co in Glasgow in 1894. This engine was retired for preservation in July 1934, and after nationalization was restored to running condition and original yellow livery, and worked many railtour trains, as shown here, for example. at Stranraer in April 1963 (Roy Hobbs).*

Inset *London and North Western Railway: Hardwicke still in active service. This record-breaking 2-4-0 bears a Crewe Works plate dated August 1873, but the engine now familiar to many was actually a renewal of a Ramsbottom 'Newton' of that date, and was an almost new engine at the time of her record breaking 67 mph dash from Crewe to Carlisle on the last night of the 1895 'Race to the North'. She is here seen at Grange-over-Sands with a railtour train from Carnforth (Roy Hobbs).*

Inset *Caledonian Railway : the 'Caley Single' was originally a 'one-off' job built by Neilson & Co in 1886 specially for exhibition at the International Exhibition of Industry Science and Art held in Edinburgh that same year. Afterwards she was purchased by the Caledonian Railway and became a famous engine through her fast running between Carlisle and Edinburgh in the 1888 'Race to the North'. She has been preserved as an historical relic since 1933 and was restored to running condition in BR days. She is here seen climbing a 1 in 80 gradient near Cleland on the former Caledonian line between Edinburgh and Glasgow on a railtour in April 1965* (Roy Hobbs).

Below *Lancashire and Yorkshire Railway : the first of the Aspinall 2-4-2 tanks, No 1008, and the first engine to be built at Horwich Works, in February 1889, here seen outside the National Railway Museum at York* (J.A. Coiley).

Above *Somerset and Dorset Joint: one of the 2-8-0 freight engines, designed and first built at Derby in 1914, here seen at Bath in July 1960, when these engines were used in passenger service to assist in working the very heavy weekend traffic over the line. This engine is now on the North Yorkshire Moors Railway (R.C. Riley).*

Below *Somerset and Dorset Joint : One of the 6-ft 9-in Class '2' 4-4-0s No 40700 built to Midland design since the Grouping, piloting the 9.55 am Bournemouth-Leeds express northward from Evercreech Junction near Midford in September 1959 (R.C. Riley).*

Above *One of the last batch of Fowler 2-6-4 tanks with a side-windowed cab leaving Birmingham New Street in March 1961 (R.C. Riley).*

Below *A rather dingy 'Patriot' in passenger green livery, No 45511 Isle of Man at Willesden sheds in August 1959 (R.C. Riley).*

Below *Stanier 2-8-0 No 48619 at Coalville shed in May 1963* (R.C. Riley).

Inset *'Duchess' Class 4-6-2 No 46235* City of Birmingham *as a working engine in the dark green livery at Camden shed in February 1963* (Roy Hobbs).

Above *LMS 'Jubilee' Class 3-cylinder 4-6-0 No 5690 Leander as restored to pre-war livery, and seen at Carnforth in July 1976* (R.C. Riley).

Below *Stanier 'Jubilee' Class 3-cylinder 4-6-0 No 45588 Kashmir in BR green livery at Newton Stewart in April 1963* (Roy Hobbs).

Above *Stanier 'Black Five' 4-6-0 No 45239 at Worcester shed in June 1963* (R.C. Riley).

Below *Stanier 'Black Five' 4-6-0 No 44795 at St Rollox shed in May 1959. This engine has the later form of top-feed apparatus on the boiler* (R.C. Riley).

Inset *The first Stanier 4-6-2, No 46200* The Princess Royal, *emerging from Watford Tunnel* (J.A. Coiley).

Below *Stanier 4-6-2 No 6201* Princess Elizabeth *restored to LMS livery approaching Park South Junction at the northern end of the Barrow avoiding line with a tour special on the Furness Line in August 1980* (R.C. Riley).

Above *'Duchess' Class 4-6-2 No 46251* City of Nottingham *at Leicester Central in May 1964 while working a special train from Nottingham to Swindon* (R.C. Riley).

Below *The preserved 'Duchess' Class 4-6-2 No 46229* Duchess of Hamilton *with the headboard of the 'Caledonian' Euston to Glasgow express* (J.A. Coiley).

courageous of men. Fortunately he was endowed with both of these qualities in full measure; but at this particular juncture, the discernment that he displayed towards the personal foibles of his new command was not long in being widely appreciated by the men.

When he had relinquished his former railway command some five years earlier, he had left a department in first class shape, but at Kilmarnock he found it was far otherwise. On the main line from Glasgow to Carlisle the schedule of loads for the most powerful express locomotives, the Manson 4-6-0s, was:

Glasgow to Kilmarnock	225 tons
Kilmarnock to Dumfries	235 tons
Dumfries to Carlisle	335 tons
Carlisle to Dumfries	335 tons
Dumfries to Kilmarnock	240 tons
Kilmarnock to Glasgow	270 tons

These modest loads for 4-6-0 engines naturally involved a great deal of double heading; but from details of actual running published in *The Railway Magazine* and elsewhere, it was in any case usual for time to be lost on occasions even when the loads were well within the maximum limits laid down for unassisted 4-6-0 engines. One of the first things Whitelegg had to do was to rebuild these ill-starred express engines into a more workman-like shape. Nevertheless, the Clyde Coast services must have brought him more than an occasional pang for what he had necessarily had to give up on the 'Tilbury', and in between the urgent tasks of rehabilitating the existing G & SW stock, he began planning for a large express tank engine.

The Tilbury 'Baltics' were to have been his pride and joy, and there was no doubt that a Scottish version was early in his mind. The 'Sou-West' development, as it materialized in 1922, was an even larger and more powerful engine. The following comparison of leading dimensions is striking in itself:

Whitelegg 'Baltic' tank engines

Railway	LT & SR	G & SWR
Cylinders, diameter × stroke (in)	20 × 26	22 × 26
Coupled wheels (ft in)	6 3	6 0
Heating surfaces (sq ft)		
Tubes	1,155	1,574
Firebox	141	156
Superheater	319	255
Total	1,615	1,985
Grate area (sq ft)	25	30

Railway	LT & SR	G & SWR
Working pressure (psi)	160	180
Tractive effect at 85 per cent boiler pressure (lb)	18,900	26,741
Water capacity (gal)	2,200	2,400
Coal capacity (tons)	3	3½
Weight, in working order (tons)	94.2	99.05

The 'Sou-West' 'Baltics', six of which were built by the North British Locomotive Company at their Hyde Park Works, were very handsomely styled, and the product of a carefully designed process in which every detail was subjected to the closest scrutiny. An unusual feature was the clothing of the boilers with blue planished steel, to avoid the normal paint burning off and giving a shabby appearance. It was stated that the boilers of the new engines were very easily kept clean, although I did not see one of them in its original livery; by the time I first visited the G & SW line, they had been painted in Midland red. The new engines were put into traffic on the Clyde Coast trains in the spring of 1922, and made short work of the smartest-timed trains, those running over the 41.4 miles between St Enoch and Ayr non-stop in 50 minutes. When they were first put on, the trains were conveying their winter loading, about 210 tons behind the engine; but when the summer service began, with corridor stock throughout and a new Whitelegg 12-wheeled tea car, the load was increased to 320 tons. The remarkable thing then was that even experts with the stop-watch, like the late Cecil J. Allen, could not detect any difference in the running with these large 4-6-4 tank engines, whether they were hauling 210- or 320-ton loads. The drivers obviously used much skill in managing their huge machines to observe the point-to-point times specified in the working timetable.

While the Clyde Coast services were thus comfortably mastered with maximum summer loads, Whitelegg was thinking also of the Anglo-Scottish traffic, but on very different lines to those of Peter Drummond. In his 'Baltic' tanks he had an express passenger engine with a higher tractive effort than most British passenger engines, and it would have been relatively easy to build one as a 4-6-0 tender engine. Not long after the 'Baltics' were introduced, a test was made with one of them from Glasgow to Carlisle and back with loads very much heavier than anything previously attempted with unpiloted

engines, but, because of the limited water capacity of the tank engine, some time was taken topping up the tanks at Kilmarnock and Dumfries. The running times of the outward and return journeys were taken by a member of the drawing office staff at Kilmarnock Works, not in the meticulous detail practised by Cecil J. Allen in *The Railway Magazine*, but certainly enough to show a very fine performance. For comparison, a few years later I was a passenger by the 12 noon London express from St Enoch, and, for a tare load of 277 tons, a Midland compound, working through to Carlisle, took a pilot over the heavy gradient to Kilmarnock. Continuing southwards, then unassisted, the compound made very heavy weather of the long 1 in 100 climb south of Hurlford,

not being able to do better than 25 to 27 mph, with the result that the 4-6-4 tank engine beat her by 5½ minutes to New Cumnock, even though the latter engine had her load increased to 340 tons at Kilmarnock. South of Dumfries, with the load still further increased to no less than 440 tons, the big tank engine easily kept the current schedule of 42 minutes for the 33.1 miles to Carlisle.

Returning in the afternoon, no difficulty was found with the 440-ton load as far as Dumfries, and with the reduced load of 325 tons for the long toilsome ascent to Carronbridge, the 'Baltic' tank engine made times much the same as were usual with the 4-6-0 engines, although the latter were hauling loads of 100 tons or less. North of Carronbridge, the test train was stopped by adverse signals and lost about five minutes in running, despite which a good recovery was made on the upper part of the bank above Kirkconnel. On the final stage of the run, with the load increased to 360 tons, good work was done on the very severe ascent past Stewarton, where the gradient is 1 in 75, to pass Dunlop at an average of 30.7 mph from the restart at Kilmarnock. Some brisk running in conclusion down the Barrhead bank would have seen the train into St Enoch in about 36 minutes had it not been for some final signal checks. One could well imagine that Whitelegg and his staff were well pleased with the result of this test; though by that time the overshadowing cloud of Grouping, and the forthcoming amalgamation with the powerful English companies, precluded any thought of a new 4-6-0 express engine.

G & SWR: 1922 test train
Glasgow St Enoch-Carlisle

Engine 4-6-4 tank No 545
Load St Enoch-Kilmarnock   310 tons
       Kilmarnock-Dumfries   340 tons
       Dumfries-Carlisle   440 tons

Distance (miles)		Time (m s)	Average speed (mph)
0.0	St Enoch	0 00	—
4.6	Kennishead	8 12	33.7
7.6	Barrhead	12 00	48.0
14.4	Lugton	24 45	32.1
16.7	Dunlop	27 30	50.0
24.4	Kilmarnock	36 11	53.1
1.8	Hurlford	3 50	28.3
9.4	Mauchline	16 15	36.7
21.1	New Cumnock	30 25	49.2
40.5	Carronbridge	51 25	55.2
54.6	Holywood	64 45	62.9
58.0	Dumfries	69 30	41.0
8.5	Ruthwell	13 05	38.1
15.6	Annan	20 22	59.1
24.5	Gretna Junction	29 40	58.1
33.1	Carlisle	40 40	47.0

Carlisle-Glasgow St Enoch

Engine 4-6-4 tank No 545
Load Carlisle-Dumfries   440 tons
       Dumfries-Kilmarnock   325 tons
       Kilmarnock-St Enoch   360 tons

Distance (miles)		Time (m s)	Average speed (mph)
0.0	Carlisle	0 00	—
8.6	Gretna Junction	12 15	44.1
17.5	Annan	23 54	46.7
24.6	Ruthwell	31 36	55.6
33.1	Dumfries	41 30	55.2
3.4	Holywood	6 15	32.7
7.6	Auldgirth	11 15	50.3
11.4	Closeburn	16 08	47.5
14.2	Thornhill	19 58	44.0
17.5	Carronbridge	25 02	39.0
		sig stop	—

Top left *Peter Drummond's superheater 2-6-0 express goods engine of 1915 (F. Moore's Rail Photos).*

Above left *Whitelegg 'Baltic' tank-engine No 541 in original livery on a local train near Troon (Author's Collection).*

Right *One of Whitelegg's huge 4-6-4 tank engines at Ayr station in LMS colours (Author's Collection).*

Distance		Time	Average
(miles)		(m s)	speed (mph)
26.1	Sanquhar	42 35	—
29.4	Kirkconnel	47 15	42.3
36.9	New Cumnock	55 15	56.0
		sig stop	—
58.0	Kilmarnock	79 45	—
7.7	Dunlop	15 30	30.7
13.2	Shilford Cabin	23 10	42.7
14.7	Neilston	24 55	51.2
16.8	Barrhead	27 10	55.7
21.1	Pollokshaws	31 00	66.7
24.4	St Enoch	38 30	—

Whitelegg's large-boilered and superheated rebuild of Manson's experimental four cylinder simple 4-4-0 of 1897 No 11, Lord Glenarthur, *seen here in LMS black* (F. Moore's Rail Photos).

The closing months of Kilmarnock's independence as a locomotive-building establishment were, however, marked by the production of a new and remarkably successful express passenger engine. It was in 1897 that Manson had built the first-ever British passenger engine with four high-pressure cylinders. It was a very carefully designed variant of his No '8' Class two-cylinder 4-4-0, of which a great many were built as a G & SWR standard. From all accounts, the four-cylinder engine, No 11, gave a certain amount of trouble from the rocking shafts that connected the inside and outside valve spindles, although it continued in the top-link Anglo-Scottish services from Curragh Road, Carlisle, until the introduction of the 4-6-0s on those trains. Engine No 11 remained as built, but for the substitution of one of Manson's larger boilers in 1915, until Whitelegg's virtual renewal of the entire engine in 1922. Why he should have singled out this odd engine for such treatment could well be one of the mysteries of British locomotive history; but leaving the whys and wherefores on one side, the fact remains that in the rejuvenated No 11, or 394 as she became in 1922, Whitelegg produced the fastest and most efficient express passenger engine the 'Sou-West' ever had. Nominally a 'rebuild', there can, however, have been precious little of the original engine left, except for the wheel centres and some parts of the motion, but No 394 made history in that it was the first and only engine of the 'Sou-West' to be named, *Lord Glenarthur*, after the last Chairman of the Company.

In its renewed form, the outside cylinders remained with a 24-in stroke and the inside with 26-in, but the diameter was in both cases 14 in. The inside cylinders were formed in a single casting, though the outside pair were separate. Cross ports were introduced, thus making it possible for one piston valve to control the steam to both cylinders at one side. The front piston valve head served the front port of the inside cylinders and also the back port of the outside cylinders, and vice versa, and by that means the rocking shaft with valve, valve spindle and valve connecting rod of the original locomotive No 11 were eliminated. An outstanding feature of the new locomotive was the size of the piston valves— no less than 10-in diameter, exceptionally large for cylinders no larger than 14-in diameter. This feature undoubtedly contributed to the free running of the engine at express speed. The larger boiler, which had the following proportions, was a mixture of the Drummond designs used on the superheater 4-4-0s and the 2-6-0s:

Large tubes	357.41 sq ft
Small tubes	1,086.59 sq ft
Elements	211.00 sq ft
Firebox	148.00 sq ft

The superheater was of the Robinson type, with 22 elements, and the grate area was 27.6 sq ft. The boiler pressure was 180 psi and the nominal tractive effort 18,390 lbs at 85 per cent working pressure. The engine was completed at Kilmarnock Works just in time to have been registered as a Glasgow and South Western engine and to be finished in the traditional green livery. Unlike the Whitelegg 'Baltic' tank engines, *Lord Glenarthur* had a conventionally painted, and not a blued-steel, boiler.

The engine was allocated to Ayr shed and at once put on to the Glasgow expresses, including the non-stop trains which were booked to run the 41.4 miles in 50 minutes start to stop. The 'Baltic' tank engines and their crews kept very strict times on those trains, no matter what the load might be; but when *Lord Glenarthur* was on the job, it seemed as if there was no limit to how early the 8.25 am up from Ayr would arrive at St Enoch! There is no doubt that the large diameter of the piston valves played a major part in the free running of that engine, and it was universally popular with the men at Ayr shed. One of the finest runs with a G & SW engine on record was logged by my great friend the late David L. Smith with *Lord Glenarthur* on the 8.25 am up from Ayr with a 260-ton load. Paisley, 33.7 miles, was passed in 36 min 28 sec after a maximum speed of 69 mph, and St Enoch was reached in 45½ minutes, 4½ minutes early. The engine continued to take turns on this train with the 4-6-4 tanks and on the equally fast 5.10 pm from St Enoch to Ayr until the new standard compound 4-4-0s arrived on the scene.

12. Highland: twentieth-century developments

When ill-health following an accident on the footplate compelled the resignation of David Jones, and the appointment of Peter Drummond to succeed him in 1896, it was not long before the Highland Railway management found that tradition in locomotive design was deeply ingrained in all grades down to the humblest cleaner on the strength. Peter Drummond, following the family tradition, began by ordering eight new 4-4-0 passenger engines from Dübs and Co, and when the first of them arrived in Inverness it was damned at first sight by the enginemen for not having outside cylinders! It was, of course, a product of the Drummond family design, very similar to brother Dugald's '290' Class on the London and South Western Railway, but with smaller coupled wheels. Peter Drummond had been spared the ignominy of a change of name, however, before the first engines left Dübs' Works. It had been decided to name the new engines after mountains, this being a natural sequel to the series of 'Straths', 'Glens' and 'Lochs' used on the Jones 4-4-0s; but I became aware of the first of the 'Ben' series in an indirect way.

In the year 1927, my parents spent a month at Nairn, and on joining them for my own annual leave I was greatly intrigued to find in the massive, single-storied house in which they were staying, a large framed photograph of a 'Small Ben' Class 4-4-0 over the mantelpiece. The presence of a locomotive photograph was easily explained— the owner of the house was a daughter of the late stationmaster at Nairn— but the photograph, a builders' 'official', depicted engine No 1 *Ben Nevis*. After my return south, I checked up on the lists of Highland locomotives, and found that no such name existed! It was not until many years later that the mystery was solved—so far as I was concerned. Apparently the engine was named, and its official photograph taken. Then someone pointed out forcibly to Peter Drummond that while Ben Nevis was undoubtedly a very eminent mountain, it happened to be in North British territory, and would he please change the name at once. As the name was changed to *Ben-y-Gloe* in the same month as that in which Dübs & Co delivered the engine, there is a strong probability that she never ran as *Ben Nevis*.

Peter Drummond's 'Small Ben' Class, as they later became known to distinguish them from the larger-boilered variety which followed in 1908, differed from the Jones designs that preceded them in many respects other than having inside cylinders. They had

Stephenson's link motion instead of Allan's gear, and the regulator was of the double slide type, instead of the double beat type favoured by Jones. The tractive effort was slightly greater than that of the 'Lochs', but the new engines were put to work on the northern section of the main line, and there they became popular with the men. In one of his very earliest books, my late friend and very esteemed co-author C. Hamilton Ellis has a good story to tell of engine No 8 *Ben Clebrig*. 'Ye'll never find an easier an' more straightforward engine than our "Sma' Ben". I tell ye, man! Your mither could drive her an' get sixty out of her too!' On the Highland Railway they certainly came to reflect the fame won by their larger-wheeled counterparts, the 'T9s' on the London and South Western Railway. I had a good run behind *Ben Vrackie* on the afternoon train from Inverness to Aberdeen, as between Forres and Keith; and although it carried a load of no more than 175 tons, I was very impressed with the way the engine climbed the steep gradients on that route, particularly the 2½ miles of 1 in 60 from the Spey viaduct at Boat o' Bridge, without falling below 24 mph. The first eight engines of the class were built by Dübs & Co in 1898-9. Then came nine more built at Lochgorm Works in 1899-1900, and the final three came from the North British Locomotive Company in 1906.

Before his resignation in 1896, David Jones had prepared the design of an express passenger equivalent of his celebrated 'Big Goods' 4-6-0. There was certainly need for more powerful passenger engines on the main line south of Inverness, and there was no doubt that Peter Drummond scrutinized the design minutely. The two brothers always studied each other's work, but at that time Dugald had not advanced as far as a 4-6-0 on the LSWR. So Peter had nothing from him to copy; it was a case of using the Jones design with certain Drummond amendments, fortunately items of detail rather than of basic principles. The very celebrated 'Castle' Class had outside cylinders, Allan straight link motion valve gear, and the Jones design of boiler and firebox. Drummond added marine-type big ends, Richardson-type balanced slide valves, and Dugald Drummond's steam reverser. Whether the original Jones design included such features as smokebox wing plates and the double chimney with the louvred front I cannot say, but so far as external details such as cab and boiler mountings were concerned, the 'Castles' looked like a Drummond locomotive. The appear-

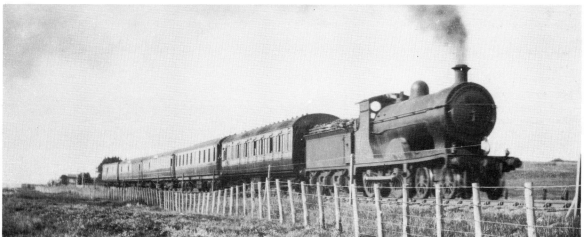

Top *One of Peter Drummond's 'Small Ben' Class, No 2 Ben Alder, at Inverness; the likeness to contemporary London and South Western 4-4-0s is very apparent* (W.J. Reynolds).

Above *One of the 'Large Bens', No 14419 Ben Mholach, in LMS days, working the Nairn and Forres section of the combined Euston and King's Cross sleeper across Dava Moor* (O.S. Nock)

Right *One of the 'Small Ben' Class in LMS days, No 14416 Ben A'Bhuird at Kyle of Lochalsh* (O.S. Nock).

ance was accentuated by use of the large bogie tenders with inside frames which were than coming into use on the 'T9' 4-4-0s on the London and South Western Railway.

The first order placed with Dübs & Co in 1900 was for six engines, all named after residences of directors of the Company:

140 *Taymouth Castle* (Marquis of Breadalbane, Chairman)
141 *Ballindalloch Castle* (Sir George Macpherson-Grant, Deputy Chairman)
142 *Dunrobin Castle* (Duke of Sutherland)
143 *Gordon Castle* (Duke of Richmond and Gordon)
144 *Blair Castle* (Duke of Atholl)
145 *Murthly Castle* (W. Stuart Fotheringham)

These engines were immediately successful and were put on to the Inverness-Perth run, each engine making five double trips weekly. By the time they had been introduced, the direct line, via Carr Bridge, had been opened for more than a year, and most of their duties were over that route, rather than over the original main line via Forres. Four more 'Castles' were purchased from Dübs and Co in 1902, namely:

146 *Skibo Castle*   148 *Cawdor Castle*
147 *Beaufort Castle*   149 *Duncraig Castle*

These engines were the last to be painted new in the beautiful apple green livery which Drummond inherited from David Jones, which included claret valances and cylinder covers and the elaborate lin-

The first of the very successful 'Castle' Class 4-6-0s of 1900, No 140 Taymouth Castle *on the roundhouse turntable at Inverness (W.J. Reynolds).*

ing of of the boiler bands with broad olive green edging to the central black stripe.

Technically, the 1902 batch of 'Castles' was interesting in that the locomotives were dual fitted, enabling Westinghouse-braked trains to be worked if necessary. Seeing that both the Caledonian and North British Railways used Westinghouse, this was a useful addition to the equipment, although the through trains from the south, composed of East and West Coast Joint Stock, were themselves dual fitted. On the 'Castle' Class engines Nos 146-149, the familiar Westinghouse pump was mounted on the right-hand side of the engine between the middle and rearmost splasher. When first introduced, both the 1900 and 1902 batches of 'Castles' had the name 'Highland Railway' in full on their large tenders. Jones did not display the Company's name or any initials on any of his engines, but Peter Drummond began the use of HR on the 'Small Ben' Class 4-4-0s, and some of the older 4-4-0s, when repainted in Drummond's time, received the full title like the 'Castles'. Before the economy drive which played such havoc with their external finish, the Highland engines in their gay green livery were the most attractive of all the engines working into Perth station, because the Caledonian, in their original very dignified Prussian blue, had not yet touched the heights of locomotive sartorial elegance that they attained when, as an economy measure, white was mixed with the blue! On the Highland, not long after the second batch of 'Castles' had been put to work, the edict went forth that all engines would be painted dark green, devoid of any lining, and many even had the buffer beams painted green. Fortunately, the economy drive did not extend to cleaning, and the Highland engines, though robbed of their gay colours, remained as smartly turned out and immaculately maintained as any entering Perth in pre-Grouping days.

Nigh on 80 years ago there was a reverend gentleman named Warburton who travelled extensively on the Highland Railway, throughout the main line from Perth right up to Wick, and he took a great many notes of locomotive working. His were not the detailed loggings of trains and speeds of individual runs in the style of Charles Rous-Marten, but some years ago, through the kindness of another enthusiast, I became the possessor of the original notebook in which Warburton recorded his observations. But it is tantalizing in what it omits to comment upon. In 1913, writing under the pen name of 'Scrutator', he published at his own expense a 16-page pamphlet called *Behind the Highland Engines*. It was attractively produced from the office of the Inverness *Courier* and had an excellent portrait photograph of engine No 146 *Skibo Castle* on the cover. Judging from the bill that was enclosed in the copy that came into my possession, only 250 copies were printed, and they were priced fourpence. In this pamphlet, he summarizes many runs on the main line south of Inverness with the original ten 'Castles', mostly showing very smart

One of the second series of 'Castles', No 146 Skibo Castle, *at Perth, ready coaled up for the run to Inverness* (Author's Collection).

climbing of the heavy gradients; and despite the brevity of the treatment, he had a word deploring the elimination of the old colours of the engines.

In the brief notes that 'Scrutator' makes on all of the runs, engine No 141 *Ballindalloch Castle* figures prominently; remarkably, because that building was not on the Highland Railway at all but instead on the Speyside branch of the hated Great North of Scotland Railway, the line running south-westwards in Strath Spey to its junction with the Aviemore-Forres line of the Highland at Boat of Garten. But the castle was the residence of Sir George Macpherson-Grant, who had become Chairman of the Highland by the time *The Railway Magazine* featured Peter Drummond in the 'Illustrated Interview' series. In any case, *Ballindalloch Castle*, with her regular driver, Will Tulloch, was the star engine of Perth shed, never more so than when decked out for the Royal Train when King Edward VII and Queen Alexandra visited the Northern Highlands. Not even the Tilbury 4-4-2 tank, dolled up for the Coronation celebrations of King George V and Queen Mary in 1910, surpassed the turn-out of *Ballindalloch Castle* on this earlier occasion, with a magnificent placard 'ROYAL TRAIN' surrounding the crest of the smokebox, the Royal Arms on the smokebox door, flags waving above each buffer shank, and a stag's head surrounded by a garland of heather in bloom centrally on the buffer beam. As was to be expected, Peter Drummond himself rode on the footplate. Those were the days when an advance pilot ran some minutes before the Royal Train itself, and on this occasion the pilot was the 4-4-0 engine No 130 *Loch Fannich*, again beautifully groomed, though naturally not decorated to any extent.

Two more engines to the original design were built

by the North British Locomotive Company in 1910-11, namely No 30 *Dunvegan Castle* and No 35 *Urquhart Castle*. The first is the historic residence of Macleod of Macleod at the northern end of Skye, while the latter is the picturesque ruin familiar to all who have travelled the length of Loch Ness by steamer. At the same time as these two engines were delivered, the builders received an order for no less than fifty more of exactly the same design, not from the Highland Railway but from the State Railway of France. The origin of this remarkable affair can be traced to the bad traffic situation into which the Western and State Railways of France had deteriorated, in contrast to the railways elsewhere in France, and it led to the Amalgamation of the West system with the State. New engines, and plenty of them, were urgently needed, and apparently the new management went shopping around the locomotive manufacturers of Europe to seek a design that was generally suitable and which could be produced quickly. So far as the Highland 'Castles' were concerned, the North British Locomotive Company was in an ideal position, except in one respect—the speed at which the French demanded delivery. To maintain the contract date, not only had all three works, Hyde Park, Queens Park and Atlas, to be involved, but also a considerable amount of overtime had to be worked at all three.

The design was exactly the same as that of the first twelve 'Castles' that had been built by the Company, and its earlier constituent Dübs & Co, except that the French engines were fitted with the Westinghouse brake only. It was remarkable that the fifty built for the Etat also had the double-bogie tender with inside frames, a fact that would have pleased Dugald Drummond!

At the end of the same year that saw the building of the fifty engines of the 'Castle' Class for France, Peter Drummond resigned, having been appointed Locomotive Superintendant of the Glasgow and South Western Railway, as related in the previous chapter of this book. His natural successor at Inverness was F.G Smith, who had been Works Manager at Lochgorm since 1904. Four more engines of the 'Castle' Class were purchased from the North British Locomotive Company in 1913, which had certain changes in design. Instead of the marine big end favoured by the Drummonds, he used a solid type, after the Great Western style, but what appeared to be provision for a superheater in an extended smokebox was not so. Smith tried the hideous Phoenix type, disfiguring the prestigious *Ballindalloch Castle* of all engines, and one of his own design on one other engine; but the new 'Castles' always used saturated steam. Like their predecessors, they were always splendid engines on the road. They carried the plain style of painting, and the Drummond style of cast numberplate on their cabs, but on their tenders the full name was displayed even to the extent of having 'THE' before 'HIGHLAND RAILWAY'. They were named thus:

| 26 | *Brahan Castle* | 28 | *Cluny Castle* |
| 27 | *Thurso Castle* | 29 | *Dalcross Castle* |

The last of the four was originally numbered 43, but was renumbered 29 after only a few months in service. On my own first visit to the Highland, in 1927, *Brahan Castle*, then painted LMS red and numbered 14687, was on top-link work between Inverness and Perth, and I logged her running on the 3.50 pm up mail.

Coming to Smith's own engines, the 'Rivers', there can be little doubt that these were the finest express passenger engines that ever ran the rails in Scotland in pre-Grouping days. I have written at length of the sad events that led to their being prohibited from use on their own line in my own book on the Highland Railway; so I will deal with their technical features rather than mull over the human side of their introduction once again, perhaps adding an amusing addendum to the story at the very end of my references to them. Smith wanted a much more powerful engine than the non-superheated 'Castles' to eliminate much of the bank engine mileage needed with heavy trains. The new main line via Carrbridge was always a serious proposition, because not only were the gradients themselves steeper than anything on the original line, 1 in 60 against 1 in 70, but also the tremendous southbound ascent to Daviot began

immediately after the trains left Inverness, giving no time for the engines to warm up to their work. From Forres up to Dava Moor on the old line, and on the down run from Blair Atholl up to Drumochter, things were more advantageous in this respect. The 'Castles' were allowed a maximum tare load of 220 tons in Drummond's day before a bank engine could be claimed, though I have a note of *Ballindalloch Castle* taking 240 tons out of Inverness on the more easily timed 5 pm sleeping car express, which in pre-1914 days was allowed 65 minutes for the non-stop run of 34.7 miles to Aviemore. The up mail was scheduled in 62 minutes.

As I have already stressed, the 'Castles' were grand engines, and as if to emphasize the quality of performance that would have to have been surpassed on that fearful start out of Inverness, I append my log of the run recorded on the 3.50 pm up mail. The load hauled by No 149 *Duncraig Castle* was not excessively heavy, and the engine and her crew seemingly made light work of it and arrived at Aviemore 3½ minutes early. The gradients are worth recalling. The ascent begins just a mile out of Inverness, with 2¾ miles at 1 in 60, followed by 2½ miles at 1 in 70 to just before Culloden Moor station. Then follows a sharp descent of no more than three-quarters of a mile across the stately Strathnairn Viaduct, and then the climbing is resumed, 1 in 60 at once, and this is continued without a break for six miles, to a point 2 miles beyond Daviot station. The next stage, to Tomatin, includes some breaks in the rising tendency, and even some lengths of level and downhill; but from the summit of the 1 in 60 above Daviot to Tomatin, the average rising gradient is nevertheless 1 in 180. Then, from the crossing of the Findhorn Viaduct by Toma-

tin station, there is a solid 3¼ miles at 1 in 60 up to Slochd Summit, at an altitude of 1,315 ft above ordnance datum. On my run with *Brahan Castle* on the mail in 1927, when we had a load of 345 tons out of Inverness and a Jones 4-4-0 'Goods' as pilot, we took 49 min 50 sec to reach Slochd, and after a stop of 1½ minutes to detach the pilot, the 'Castle' ran fast down to Aviemore, taking only 14 min 40 sec for the 11.9 miles.

Highland Railway: 3.50 pm Inverness-Aviemore

Engine 4-6-0 No 149 *Duncraig Castle*
Load 175 tons

Distance (miles)	Time (m s)	Average speed (mph)
0.0 Inverness	0 00	—
6.7 Culloden Moor	14 40	27.4
11.2 Daviot	23 15	30.8
14.9 Moy	31 00	28.7
19.0 Tomatin	36 30	44.7
22.8 Slochd South Box	44 35	28.2
28.0 Carrbridge	50 45	50.7
34.7 Aviemore	58 30	51.9

Smith wanted a big powerful 4-6-0 that could take loads of at least 280 tons up the steepest banks

One of the three 6-ft 'Castles' built by the North British Locomotive Company in 1917, Brodie Castle, *seen here double heading* Clan Munro *on the 4.35 pm up sleeper from Inverness in 1927* (O.S. Nock).

without assistance. If the top-link drivers like Will Tulloch would take 240 tons with a 'Castle' if need be, then the new engines might manage 300 when in their prime. So they were designed with two cylinders of 21-in diameter by 28-in stroke, piston valves of 10-in diameter, and Walschaerts gear with an excellent setting, and coupled wheels of 6-ft 0-in diameter. The boiler was a large one and had a Belpaire firebox, a feature new to the Highland; and after his experiments with superheaters, Smith chose the standard Robinson type for his new 4-6-0s. In keeping with current practice on certain other British railways at that time, in their first applications of superheating the boiler pressure was lowered from the 175 psi on the 'Castles' to 160 psi, although the boilers were designed to take a pressure of 180 psi. Against a nominal tractive effort of 21,350 lb on the 'Castles', the new engines with their original pressure had 23,250 lb, but their full potential with 180 psi was 26,200 lb. At this reckoning, they were more powerful than a Stanier 'Black Five', and enginemen who had handled both classes at Perth Caledonian shed always said the Highland engines were equally as good and speedy.

When it came to designing big heavy engines, however, there was much more to it than establishing the proportions of cylinders, heating surfaces, grate areas and coupled wheel diameters. My old teacher at Imperial College, Professor W.E. Dalby, wrote a mighty tome of 750 pages on *Steam Power* which we were expected to study; but before he produced this *magnum opus*, published in 1915, he had written many learned treatises for professional bodies, and one of his major subjects was the 'Balancing of Engines'. The physical implications of the running of locomotives of greater total weight, with the great increase in boiler diameter and a higher centre of gravity, needed important consideration. The behaviour of locomotives as 'vehicles' was dependent to a large extent upon the balancing of the revolving and reciprocating parts, and the implications of this, and its effect upon the riding and on the track, were by no means fully realized by most locomotive engineers and certainly not by the great majority of civil engineers in the early 1900s. Even Professor Dalby, for all his learned analytical studies of the problems, did not seem aware of the deep significance of the different ways of effecting the requisite balance. At that time, the most customary practice was to concentrate the whole of the balance of the reciprocating parts into the driving axle. This was done on the large new 4-4-0, 4-4-2 and 4-6-0 locomotives then being introduced on the London and North Western, Caledonian, Great Northern and North British Railways. It was simple from the drawing office point of view, but very unkind to the track. The Highland 'Castle' Class engines were balanced in the same way.

At that same period in railway history, British civil engineers, without exception, made their assessments of the effect locomotives would have on the track and underline bridge structures entirely by the dead weight carried on each axle when stationary. In locomotive drawing offices, it was conventional to compensate for the disturbing effect of the reciprocating parts by inserting balance weights in the driving wheels of a value usually two-thirds the weight of the reciprocating parts themselves. While this balanced the riding and made the locomotive reasonably comfortable to ride upon, it produced what was technically called a 'dynamic augment', or 'hammer-blow' effect, on the track and underline structures, and the effect naturally got worse as the speed rose. Dalby calculated that a locomotive carrying a dead weight on its driving axle of 15 tons might have a combined effect of 24 tons at a speed of 60 mph. On the Highland, Smith had obviously studied Dalby's theories, including those parts that analyzed the effect of dividing the balance weights between two axles, instead of putting all the weight into the driving axle. He embodied this practice in his new 4-6-0s and rightly assumed that although they had a heavier dead weight on the track, they would have a much reduced hammer-blow at full express speed. In the row that blew up following the first arrival of *River Ness* and *River Spey* at Perth, such considerations, if they were ever advanced, counted for nought, and Smith resigned, and all six locomotives were sold to the Caledonian.

The dénouement came 12 years later. In 1923, the Bridge Stress Committee was set up jointly by the Railway Engineers Association, the Ministry of Transport and the Department of Scientific and Industrial Research. The principal job of that committee, as its name implied, was to investigate stresses on bridges under rolling loads at varying speeds. But there was a very important subdivision of the work, that of measuring the stresses produced by different types of locomotive, and particularly the hammer-blow effect at high speed. As a basis for comparison, a standard rate of 6 revs per second of the driving wheels was taken as representing the maximum road speed the various classes of locomotive were likely to attain. At 6 revs per second an engine with 6-ft 9-in coupled wheels would be travelling at 87 mph and a 6-ft 0-in engine at 77 mph. In the report, which was published in 1929, calculations of the hammer-

Railway	Engine Class	Type	Max axle load (tons)	Speed at 6 rps (mph)	Hammer-blow at 6 rps (tons)		Max combined load at 6 rps
					Whole engine	Axle	
LNWR	'George the Fifth'	4-4-0	19.15	87	9.7	14.1	33.2
Caledonian	Pickersgill '60'	4-6-0	19.30	78	23.5	11.7	31.0
Great Northern	'251'	4-4-2	20.00	86	9.2	10.4	30.4
North British	'868'	4-4-2	20.00	87	16.1	11.6	31.6
Highland	'Castle'	4-6-0	15.15	74	16.3	6.2	21.2
Highland	'River'	4-6-0	17.75	77	1.7	4.2	21.4
Highland	'Clan'	4-6-0	15.33	77	15.3	7.1	22.4

blow effect were included for a whole range of loco-motives, and those of designs mentioned earlier in this chapter are quoted together with those of three classes of Highland 4-6-0s in the table on p153.

Although the report on the findings of the Bridge Stress Committee was not published until 1929, the data that it contained was generally known in the engineering departments of the railways concerned some little time before that date, and one result was that the six 'River' Class 4-6-0s were transferred from the South to the North shed at Perth during the winter of 1927-8. While then painted in LMS red, they began to take up with distinction the work for which they were originally intended, although I have not been able to trace whether there was ever a sug-gestion that their intended names should also be added. For the record these were: *River Ness, River Spey, River Tay, River Findhorn, River Garry,* and *River Tum-mel.* Only the first two engines were painted in High-land livery. In 1927-8, the irony of the affair was that the man who had banned their use in 1915, David Newlands, was then Chief Engineer of the whole LMS.

The postscript to the story came another ten years later when arrangements were in hand for the clos-ing of the former Highland Railway engine shed at Perth and transferring the locomotives there accom-modated to the former Caledonian shed at the south end. At that time, all six 'Rivers' were still there, but they had been reinforced by six Stanier 'Black Five' 4-6-0s. One of my railway friends, a headquarters man from Euston, was interested in the transfer, and, in the clearing out of the debris which any old estab-lishment collects over the years, he was intrigued to

see what appeared to be a pair of loading gauge tem-plates. A casual enquiry led him to a very old man who had a very clear recollection of how they came to be there. 'Ay, the templates,' was all this man uttered in almost a hushed whisper. It then appeared that the templates were made to represent the pro-file of Killiecrankie Tunnel, notably the single-track bore with apparently the most restricted clearance of any on the Highland line. After the disclosures that the weights of the 'River' Class engines were greater than could be accepted, the civil engineer determined to give them the final *coup de grâce* by demonstrating that they were out of gauge. To see this, the templates were erected at the outer end of Perth shed and when *River Ness* was propelled slowly forward, she fouled the templates and knocked them down. No more con-vincing evidence that the new engines were unsuit-able could possibly have been produced. The civil engineer then emphasized what a disastrous accident would have occurred had one of the engines attempted to enter Killiecrankie Tunnel.

The Caledonian attended to the lateral clearances, and cut down the height of the chimney, and when the time came for the 'Rivers' to be used on the High-land, they passed the gauge limits satisfactorily. No one thought of bringing out the tell-tale templates. Then, when they were unearthed during the prep-arations for demolishing the old shed, someone out of curiosity set them up again. A 'River' Class engine was produced and promptly knocked them down. More than this, one of the few 'Clan' Class 4-6-0s that had not then been transferred for service on the Oban line happened to be on the shed at the time, and again out of curiosity the templates were re-

Left *'River' Class 4-6-0 restored to the Highland line in 1928 leaving Aviemore with the up Mail* (O.S. Nock).

Right *Two 'Clans' at the original High-land shed at Perth in pre-Grouping days,* Clan Cameron *on the left with No 55* Clan Mackinnon (Author's Collec-tion).

erected. Believe it or not, the 'Clan' also knocked them down! It seems clear that there were evil machinations against Smith's new engines in 1915!

Cumming took office as Locomotive Superintendent in succession to Smith in the autumn of 1915, and he lost no time in preparing the way for new engines. Actually, the first three of these were ordered by the wartime Railway Executive Committee in 1915, of the 'Loch' Class 4-4-0s, because of the acute shortage of power on the Highland line. These were intended to be built quickly at the Queens Park Works of the North British Locomotive Company, where the 'Loch' Class engines had been originally built, when the ownership was Dübs & Co. But other wartime commitments precluded rapid delivery, and it was not until the very end of 1916 that the 4-4-0 engines, 'Lochs' *Ashie*, *Garve* and *Ruthven*, were delivered. A curious point about them was shown in the sumptuous memorial volume issued by the North British Locomotive Company after the war, in that the illustration marking their construction was not one of the wartime engines at all, but of the very first of the original batch, No 119 *Loch Insh*, in the finery of the decorative Jones livery. The very next engines turned out by the Queens Park Works, at the beginning of 1917, were three more 'Castle' Class 4-6-0s differing from the previous in having coupled wheels of 6 ft 0 in instead of 5 ft 9 in, and six-wheel tenders in place of the Drummond 'water carts'.

To what extent Cumming himself was responsible for these changes in design one cannot say, because his own very original new designs were already in production at the works of R. & W. Hawthorn, Leslie & Co at Newcastle at the same time. In fact, Cum-

ming's first Highland engines, the very handsome outside-cylindered *Snaigow* and *Durn*, preceded the arrival of the 6-ft 'Castles', *Brodie*, *Darnaway* and *Foulis*, from the North British Locomotive Company by several months. In contrast to the 'cloak and dagger' situation surrounding the arrival and subsequent destiny of the 'Rivers', the new Cumming 4-4-0s enjoyed some interesting publicity in the first months of 1917. Not only was a 'portrait' photograph of *Snaigow* published in the January issue of *The Railway Magazine*, but the same engine was also shown elsewhere in the issue on the Inverness roundhouse turntable with women cleaners at work on it. Then, if this was not enough, the very next issue of the magazine included a very beautiful colour plate of the engine in typical parkland setting, in the best 'F. Moore' tradition. *Snaigow* and *Durn* were the first superheater engines ever to run on the Highland Railway. They were powerful units, having 20-in by 26-in cylinders and, like the 'Loch' Class, 6-ft 3-in coupled wheels. Originally the boiler pressure was 160 psi, but this was subsequently increased to 175. They were designed specially for the 'Farther North' mail trains, which were of vital importance at the time, and the two of them worked daily in each direction between Inverness and Wick for many years.

The handsome Cumming style of design was followed in 1918 in his 4-6-0 express goods engines, which were also built by Hawthorn, Leslie & Co, for the heavy goods traffic between Perth and Inverness. By retaining the same coupled wheel diameter as on the celebrated Jones 'Big Goods', it was doubtless intended that the new engines should take a share in the passenger working on the most heavily graded

Top *The last-built of the 'Clans', No 57* Clan Cameron, *in original Highland livery at Perth (Author's Collection).*

Above *The later duties of the 'Clans' : a Glasgow-Oban express entering Strathyre behind No 14768* Clan Mackenzie *(O.S. Nock).*

sections by providing pilot assistance. Their most familiar territory was, however, on the Dingwall and Skye line where their enhanced tractive effort was welcome after the LMS had introduced corridor stock and the occasional dining car on the trains between Inverness and the Kyle of Lochalsh. The picturesque

little 'Skye Bogie' 4-4-0s had managed splendidly until the bigger loads came. The Cumming 4-6-0 goods engines, of which there were eventually eight, preceded the introduction of the last Highland locomotive design, the express passenger version of the Cumming goods, but with larger all-round proportions.

Highland superheater 4-6-0s

Class	'Goods'	'Clan'
Coupled wheel diameter (ft in)	5 3	6 0
Cylinders, diameter × stroke (in)	20½ × 26	21 × 26
Heating surfaces (sq ft)		
Tubes	1,068.75	1,328
Superheater	241.0	256
Firebox	130.25	139
Total	1,440	1,723
Grate area (sq ft)	22.5	25.5
Boiler pressure (psi)	175	175
Weight in working order (tons)		
Engine	56.45	62.24
Tender	36.75	42.05

The 'Clans', which were built in two batches in 1919 and 1921, were grand engines. I saw only one of them when Inverness engines were working through to Glasgow in the first year of the Grouping, 1923. Two of the 1921 batch painted in the paler green and looking brilliantly distinctive among the blue Caledonians had this prestigious job to themselves during the summer of that year, *Clan Chattan* and *Clan Mackinnon* working down and up on alternate days. The Inverness men worked through and they had a Caledonian pilotman between Perth and Glasgow. As Grouping came so soon after they were built, the engines became better known by their LMS numbers than their original ones. The full list (with earlier numbers in brackets) was:

14762 (49) *Clan Campbell*	14766 (54) *Clan Chattan*
14763 (51) *Clan Fraser*	14767 (55) *Clan Mackinnon*
14764 (52) *Clan Munro*	14768 (56) *Clan Mackenzie*
14765 (53) *Clan Stewart*	14769 (57) *Clan Cameron*

I had a good run behind *Clan Campbell* from Aviemore down to Perth on the Edinburgh train that followed immediately behind the up mail, and with a gross load of 295 tons behind the tender we were unpiloted throughout, though the gradients in this direction are not so severe, nor the worst of them so long as in the down journey. But by far the most impressive examples of 'Clan' performance I noted were after those eight engines had been transferred to the Oban line, and made a welcome relief from the puny non-superheated Pickersgill 4-6-0s, which in my experience were among the most useless engines ever put on to British rails!

The 'Clans' were very strongly built engines, and would steam freely in the most severe working conditions. The Oban men, having taken the measure of them, pounded them without mercy on the fearsome gradients west of Callander, and up they went with the white feather always showing at their safety valves. I had good runs with 'Clans' *Munro*, *Mackinnon* and *Mackenzie*, some of them on the footplate, from which I could amply assess their quality; but the most impressive of all, even though it was a short one, came one day when we were on holiday in the West Highlands at Balquhidder and made to join the midday train from Glasgow for an afternoon excursion to Killin. The train came in on time hauled by the *Clan Chattan*, and in the brief stop while the engine was taking water I found that the load was no less than 302 tons tare, about 320 tons loaded. Immediately on starting the gradient was 1 in 60, and this continued without a break for 5.2 miles to the summit at Glenoglehead Crossing, 941 ft above sea level. We got away without a trace of slipping and went pounding up the bank at a steady 17 mph. I estimate the drawbar horsepower thus involved was about 850, a very fine performance for a locomotive of 23,600 lbs tractive effort at so low a speed as 17 mph. On shorter inclines of this mountainous route, I have noted brief spells at almost 900 horsepower with those grand engines. Recalling that in the all-out trials made by the nationalized Railway Executive from 1950 onwards with 4-6-0s of much more modern design, locomotives of considerably higher tractive power barely reached 1,000 drawbar horsepower at 20 mph, those efforts by the Highland 'Clans' are highlighted as all the more praiseworthy.

13. LNWR: Crewe at its zenith I
The 'George the Fifth' Class

The true development of LNWR locomotive practice was already under way before *Worcestershire* was launched on her 'mission impossible' down in the West Country. On Sunday 24 July 1910, the first superheater 4-4-0 engine No 2663 *George the Fifth* was taken out for a spin with the new dynamometer car from Crewe to Euston and back. It was a full dress trial, with indicator diagrams taken at numerous points. The engine was then not a month out of the shops, no more than nicely run in, and still in 'shop grey'. The load was no more than moderate, amounting to 360 tons behind the tender, and on the southbound journey the engine was not unduly exerted. They ran the 75.5 miles from Crewe to Rugby in 84¼ minutes, start-to-stop, and went on to cover the 82.6 miles to Euston in 85 minutes. This latter showed a good average of 58¼ mph. Then, with all going well on the footplate, a fast non-stop run was made back from Euston to Crewe, covering the 158 miles in 156½ minutes. Apart from the regular slowings at Rugby to 36 mph and round Stafford curve, the engine was worked uniformly hard throughout. A total of 37 sets of indicator cards was taken, and they gave values of indicated horsepower varying between 995 and 1,223, with an average of 1,082. By the uniformity of the results, it was evident that the engine was being skilfully driven, and there was no let-up on the favourable stretches. Indicator cards taken at 77 mph showed an output of 1,111 ihp.

The overall time of 156½ minutes was 14½ minutes faster than that of the 10.30 am from Euston, and 18½ minutes faster than that of the 12.10 pm, on which the working of the Great Western engine

Polar Star was noted earlier. For such a performance, the coal consumption of 45.7 lb per mile was very good, and represented 2.56 lb per indicated horsepower hour. No individual figures for drawbar horsepower were quoted at the time, but from the close study of many subsequent performances of the 'George the Fifth' Class, it can be estimated that the average on this July 1910 test occasion corresponding to the average of the 37 indicator cards was around 800. This would indicate a coal consumption per drawbar horsepower hour of around 3.5 lb. Few if any British locomotives of that era, other than those of the Great Western, would have yielded such economical results in fast and hard sustained performance.

This was a most gratifying technical achievement, and an impressive christening for the splendid new dynamometer car that had been completed in Whale's time. But it was nevertheless not the kind of data that Bowen Cooke needed in order to 'sell' superheating to the top management, and it was in the building and running of the second new non-superheated 4-4-0 of July 1910 that the 'power to his elbow' came to be derived. The two engines, No 2663 *George the Fifth* and No 2664 *Queen Mary*, working from Crewe North shed, were operated turn and turn about on the heaviest main-line service for several months. Like the majority of top-link North Western engines at that time, they were double shifted, and

No 2663 George the Fifth, *in shop grey with an indicator shelter at the front end and the testing crew complete with bowler hats ready for the test run of 24 July 1910* (British Railways).

often ran more than 6,000 miles a week. By the end of October they had each run about 40,000 miles, and while both engines were putting up admirable performances in the day-to-day handling of the traffic, the close check that was being kept on fuel consumption was already showing an outstanding advantage to the superheater engine of more than 26 per cent—*26 per cent*—on workings between Euston and Crewe. As a check, a series of specific test runs was made between Preston and Carlisle, and the saving in favour of No 2663 was 25.77 per cent. In the meantime, new engines were needed, and while these results were being presented to high authority, another nine engines of the 'Queen Mary' Class were built at Crewe, as follows:

Number	Name	Date
238	*F.W. Webb*	October 1910
896	*George Whale*	,,
1195	*T.J. Hare*	,,
1550	*Westminster*	,,
1559	*Drake*	,,
2151	*Newcomen*	,,
2271	*J.P. Bickersteth*	,,
2507	*Miles MacInnes*	,,
2512	*Thomas Houghton*	November 1910

It was a gracious act on Bowen Cooke's part to name the first two after his predecessors in office, but one can note with no little astonishment the productivity of Crewe Works at that time in turning these engines out at the rate of two per week!

By November, Bowen Cooke had his authority to build more superheater engines, and, following the completion of the 'Queen Marys', the Works was switched immediately to production of more 'George the Fifths', as follows:

Number	Name	Date
1059	*Lord Loch*	November 1910
1294	*F.S.P. Wolferstan*	,,
1583	*Henry Ward*	,,
1725	*John Bateson*	,,
2155	*W.C. Brocklehurst*	,,
2025	*Sir Thomas Brooke*	December 1910
228	*E. Nettlefold*	January 1911
445	*P.H. Chambres*	,,
2168	*Henry Maudslay*	,,

Apart from anything else, the superheater engines 'had the edge' on the 'Queen Marys' because of their larger cylinders, and so ample was the steaming capacity of the boiler that on No 2168 *Henry Maudslay*, the cylinder diameter was further increased to 20½ in. This was the future standard for the class as a whole, when multiplication of them began in earnest in April 1911.

By any standards, the 'George the Fifth' was an outstanding locomotive design; but it is important to emphasize even at this early stage that Bowen Cooke did not regard it as more than an interim stage in his programme of development. He had secured a remarkable advance in tractive power over the 'Precursors' and 'Experiments' at a negligible increase in overall weight, and a reduction in coal consumption enough to satisfy the hungriest of managements. But the 'Georges' were, after all, very small engines by the standards of 1910. One last reflection upon the events of the year; I wonder what would have happened if Bowen Cooke had really challenged Churchward to a return match, with superheater engines? There is no doubt that a 'George the Fifth' could have walked away with anything then asked of the Great Western 'Stars'—apart

Queen Mary *of 1910 as built, non-superheated (British Railways).*

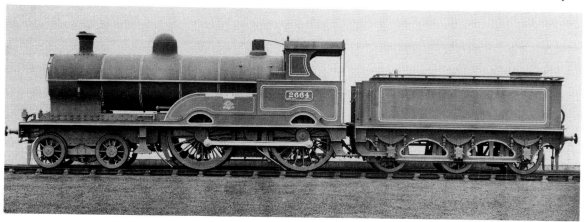

Left *The* Coronation *engine of 1911, 'George the Fifth' Class No 5000* (W.J. Reynolds).

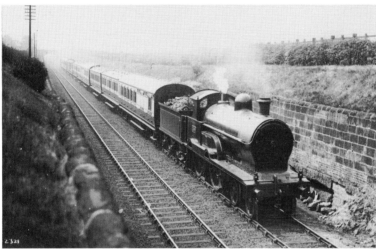

Left *A down express hauled by 'George the Fifth' 4-4-0 No 2168* Henry Maudslay *(Real Photos Ltd).*

Below *One of the first 'Precursors' to be rebuilt with piston valves and Schmidt superheater, No 2062* Sunbeam *(British Railways).*

from exceptional weekend holiday loads—and one imagines that 'G.J.C.' might have had some difficulty in explaining why it was necessary for him to build such large and expensive engines! Partisanship ran riot in 1910, as it did in 1925, and in writing about Crewe I must be forgiven for becoming partisan for just a few sentences.

The design of the 'George the Fifth' locomotives, as finalized in January 1911 by the construction of engine No 2168 *Henry Maudslay*, with 20½-in cylinders, can now be studied in detail. The main frame plates were 1-in thick, and were built up in two parts. The rear portion, spaced 4 ft 2 in apart, extended forward from the drag box to a point roughly in line with the smokebox tube plate. The forward portion extended backwards from the buffer beam, spaced 4 ft 0 in apart, and overlapped the rear portion for a length of 4 ft 9 in, thus making a very strong section in this area. It was at the rearward end of this 'double thickness' portion that one of the most important cross-stays was fixed. London and North Western locomotives were designed for hard work, and to do it reliably one needed large bearing surfaces for the driving axles. When David Joy took the design of his radial valve gear to F.W. Webb, and showed him that it needed no eccentrics, it presented great advantages in making extra space for bearings. Webb was then planning the famous '18-inch' express goods 0-6-0s, which in later years we all knew so well as the 'Cauliflowers', and it was on these that Webb first put in a central bearing on the driving axle.

All of George Whale's engines had the Joy valve gear and central bearings on their driving axles, and this feature was naturally incorporated in the 'George the Fifth' Class. On these latter engines, the main journals in the frames were of 8-in diameter by 6 in long, while the centre bearing was of 7½-in diameter by 5½ in. The total bearing area was thus increased by no less than 43 per cent by the use of the central bearing. The design of the latter was a piece of traditional 'Crewe'. Of course the use of an axle with three bearings in line required very careful methods of erection, and subsequent maintenance, but the standards of workmanship at Crewe were unsurpassed, and no difficulty seems to have been experienced. In any case, the rapid production of locomotives maintained throughout the Whale era, when all new locomotives had the central bearings, would have laid bare its weaknesses, had any of these been of a serious nature. The rear coupled axle, which had no centre bearing, had journals of 7½-in diameter by 1 ft 1½ in long.

The boiler was that of the 'Precursor', modified by the inclusion of high-degree superheating. Its most distinguishing feature was the very deep, narrow firebox. Whale, a running man for nearly all his life, knew only too well which of the various North Western boilers steamed most freely—undoubtedly those of the 2-4-0 'Precedents' and 'Whitworths', and that of the 'Precursors' was very much a simple enlargement. Some theorists among the many connoisseurs of locomotive design are apt to take the grate area as a measure of the capacity of a locomotive; but while fundamentally all depends upon a capacity to boil water, one can take this dictum still further back to a capacity to burn coal—and burn it efficiently. The 'Precursors', and still more so the 'George the Fifths', could certainly burn coal effectively. While not having large grates, they had a high firebox volume. Moreover, they were extremely easy to fire. After the Grouping of 1923, when a lot of heart-searching comparisons were being made between North Western and Midland engines, a Derby man once remarked, a little enviously one felt, that a 'George' drew its fire into such a furnace that it would 'steam under the efforts of a navvy'. Navvies or not, the LNWR firemen certainly had no difficulty in giving their drivers plenty of steam for the toughest of assignments.

The adoption of the Schmidt superheater and all its trimmings was a nodal feature in the design of the 'George the Fifth' Class. By the year 1910, the distinguished Prussian designer, Dr Wilhelm Schmidt, had developed the practice of high-degree superheating to an advanced extent of finality, including details of piston valves and other adjuncts that were considered essential to the effective use of highly superheated steam. An engineer who was very much in touch with British locomotive practice at the time told me that Schmidt visited Crewe at the time that *George the Fifth* was nearing completion, and personally set the valves. But whether this was so or not, members of Mr Bowen Cooke's family have told me that hospitality to the German designer did not extend to an invitation to Chester Place, the official residence of the C.M.E. of the LNWR. Be that as it may, Schmidt's design of piston valve was accepted as standard on the LNWR with the addition of Alexander Allan's trick ports; and these features combined to provide a kind of supercharging effect, which when all was new and in good shape provided some phenomenal results in load haulage in traffic. Another feature introduced on the 'George the Fifth' Class was the superheater damper. In a discussion at the Institution of Civil Engineers in 1914, Bowen Cooke remarked that:

'After considering very carefully the question of providing an automatic damper, he had come to the conclusion that it was not necessary, and he therefore fitted a control lever with which the driver could work the damper when required. The suitability of such an arrangement was proved, he

thought, by the long life of the superheater tubes. As to the wear of superheater elements, in the case of one of his engines after completing 224,441 miles of heavy main line work, the superheater elements were taken out and were found to be in such a condition that they were all replaced in the boiler, with one exception. In this one tube, of which he had a section made, it was noticeable that there was very little sign of wear in that part of the tube where most wear and tear would be expected to take place; in fact the wear and tear occurred chiefly at the ends of the tubes, where they came to and from the header castings'.

In the same discussion at the 'Civils', Bowen Cooke had some interesting points to make about 'cold' starting with superheater engines. He said:

'The question whether an engine fitted with a superheater was to any appreciable extent less powerful than the ordinary saturated-steam engine in starting a train was one of the points which had had to be considered on the main line of the London and North Western Railway, because on leaving Euston there was a gradient of 1 in 70 for about 1¼ miles, so that the heaviest initial work was put on the locomotive before the fire had been worked up by the blast, and its starting power was soon tested. When superheaters were first introduced some of the drivers complained that for the first part of the way they found that they were not "getting hold" of their trains quite so well as with a saturated-steam engine. He thought that was true to the extent that, in general, in starting before the engine was warmed up there was a little in

Superheater 'Precursor' No 2164 Oberon *on an up Liverpool and Manchester express near Kenton* (F.E. Mackay).

favour of saturated-steam; but his experience of the 1 in 70 gradient from Euston to Camden showed that it was nothing that had to be reckoned with seriously.'

The test run made with engine No 2663 *George the Fifth* in July 1910 was justifiably regarded as very good but something rather special, akin to the exhibition runs made on occasions with Webb compounds and not likely to be repeated in ordinary service. There was therefore some excitement among students of locomotive performance when in the January 1912 issue of *The Railway Magazine* Cecil J. Allen reported a remarkable run on the 10.30 am down Liverpool and Manchester express from Euston to Crewe with one of the newest engines of the class, No 1595 *Wild Duck*. Because of an unforeseen stop on Camden Bank, the train was 11 minutes late in passing Willesden Junction; but by a most praiseworthy effort by the enginemen, the whole of the lost time was recovered, and but for a signal check at the finish, Crewe would have been reached 2 minutes early. Up till that time, runs on the 10.30 am down from Euston, allowed 171 minutes non-stop for the 158.1 miles to Crewe with 'Precursors' and 'Experiments' on maximum-load trains, had shown little or no improvement on schedule time, and yet here was an engine gaining *13 minutes* between Willesden and Crewe. More than this, if one compared the running times with those of the test run with *George the Fifth* in July 1910, it could be seen that the two locomotives had run

The 2pm West Coast 'Corridor' express near Kenton hauled by 'George the Fifth' Class 4-4-0 No 1294 F.S.P. Wolferstan (Real Photos Ltd).

almost on equality as far as Rugeley, by which time the driver of *Wild Duck* had regained all the time lost by the stop on Camden Bank and was beginning to ease down.

Since the publication of details of the *Wild Duck* run in *The Railway Magazine*, which caused something of a sensation among train-timing enthusiasts, a number of expert recorders, in addition to Mr Cecil J. Allen, made many runs on the London and North Western Railway, and from their observations I have prepared a summary of twenty down journeys on the most critical adverse section from Watford Junction up to Tring. Heading the list is the dynamometer test with *George the Fifth* and afterwards the runs are in ascending order of loads. The estimated value of the equivalent drawbar horsepower is shown in the last column of the table, and it will be noted that the test run of July 1910 is one of the lowest of all. The average of all the twenty runs works out at the remarkable figure of 963, and the individual run of *Wild Duck* only just above the average, at 985. The important point to note about all the horsepower values in the table is that they were the unsolicited efforts of the individual engine crews, in ordinary traffic conditions. No previous advice was given to the drivers that any detailed note taking was being done, and except for runs 12 and 18 no reference was made to them afterwards. Other than that, the drivers remain anonymous. Many of the runs were made on the 10.30 am from Euston to Crewe, with Crewe North shed men who on this turn worked through to Man-

chester; some were also made on the sharply timed 5.30 pm Belfast Boat express. Two runs with the engine *F.S.P. Wolferstan* were made on the 2 pm 'Corridor', the second of which, run No 18, claimed the record for power output. Delay was expected late in the journey from extensive permanent way work, and the Camden driver was going hard to gain time to offset the effect of the subsequent slowings. The only one of the tabulated runs that was made after the 1917 decelerations, and after the restoration of the two-hour Euston-Birmingham service in 1921, was No 2 on the 9.10 am down, which called at Willesden Junction only. The engine, notably, was a 'Precursor', built in 1906, but subsequently rebuilt with superheater and piston valves.

LNWR: Performance of superheater 4-4-0s, Watford-Tring (14.2 miles)

Engine No	Name	Gross load (tons)	Time (m s)	Average speed (mph)	Estimated edhp
2663	George the Fifth	360	15 15	55.9	857
282	Alaric	320	14 20	59.5	840
1489	Wolfhound	380	14 40	58.1	900
2494	Perseus	390	14 30	58.7	920
1481	Typhon	395	15 35	54.7	885
1417	Landrail	400	14 35	58.4	945
5000	Coronation	400	14 45	57.8	965
1417	Landrail	400	14 50	57.4	965
2089	Traveller	400	16 03	53.0	845
2495	Bassethound	400	15 56	53.4	845
1294	F.S.P. Wolferstan	410	15 20	55.5	910
1595	Wild Duck	410	14 45	57.8	985

Engine No	Name	Gross load (tons)	Time (m s)	Average speed (mph)	Estimated edhp
1733	*Grouse*	415	14 35	58.4	1,025
2279	*Henry Crosfield*	420	15 15	55.9	955
1713	*Partridge*	425	15 05	56.5	995
404	*Eclipse*	425	14 46	57.7	995
5000	*Coronation*	430	16 10	52.7	920
1294	*F.S.P. Wolferstan*	435	13 57	61.1	1,170
1481	*Typhon*	440	16 30	51.5	935
2279	*Henry Crosfield*	445	15 50	53.8	1,000

The 'star turn' by *F.S.P. Wolferstan* on the 'Corridor', which yielded the remarkable output of 1,170 edhp was logged by R.E. Charlewood, one of the most precisely accurate observers I have personally known. There can be no doubt about the average speed of 61.1 mph between Watford and Tring, with the load of 435 tons. Whether the boiler would have been able to provide steam for the continuation of this effort for much longer than the 14.2 miles from Watford to Tring cannot now be said, but that these engines could sustain between 950 and 1,000 horsepower for much longer distances is evident from the many logs on which the summary of individual performances is based. Inevitably, I suppose, in my dual capacity as a life-long locomotive enthusiast and a professional engineer of nigh on sixty years' experience, I should find myself making detailed comparisons between these runs of the 'George the Fifth' Class 4-4-0s and some other recent performances of modern engines of which intensive study has been made with the aid of one or other of the stationary testing plan's operated by British Railways and supplemented by controlled road dynamometer test runs on certain specified routes. As a result, I have prepared a tabular summary of the maximum efforts of six classes of modern engines at the same speed as that of the

twenty average 'George the Fifth' runs previously referred to. The difference is that the twenty were, with one exception, efforts of individual drivers when no one was looking over their shoulder, while all the modern instances were when a swarm of test engineers, and once or twice VIPs, were watching their every action.

The last line in the table is remarkable, because it shows that the equivalent drawbar horsepower figures of the 'George the Fifth' Class on this basis of comparison are 20 per cent higher than their nearest rival and more than 40 per cent better than some. The results tabulated are exclusively those of locomotives representing the best of British practice in the post-Grouping period. The Great Western 'Manor', for example, covers the performance of those engines after the modification to their draughting had been carried out at Swindon in the early 1950s. All the engines of recent design had differing valve gears, though of the most up-to-date versions of their respective railways. The Great Western engines had Churchward's setting of the Stephenson link motion, while the LMS and BR types had the arrangement of the Walschaerts radial gear standardized under Stanier. The 'B1' 4-6-0 which gave such excellent results had the Doncaster setting of the Walschaerts developed by B. Spencer, one of Sir Nigel Gresley's personal assistants. The odd one out was, of course, the 'George the Fifth' itself which had the Joy radial gear, and which in LMS days under Lancashire and Yorkshire and Midland influence was denigrated to be beneath consideration. It is true that in the period when the standards of maintenance were allowed to fall, certain mishaps occurred with the gear, but the resulting denigration seemed to take no account of the immense mileage successfully performed in former years. Apart from that, the 'George the Fifth' Class 4-4-0s stand pre-eminent in the comparison made, and that could well be from the efficient working of the Joy valve gear, allied to other sterling features of the design.

Maximum power comparisons at 56 mph

Engine Class	'George the Fifth'	'Hall'	'Manor'	'Mogul'	BR'4'	BR'5'	'B1'
Railway	LNWR	GWR	GWR	LMS	BR	BR	LNER
Type	4-4-0	4-6-0	4-6-0	2-6-0	4-6-0	4-6-0	4-6-0
Total engine weight (tons)	59.8	75.8	68.9	59.20	67.9	76.0	71.3
Tractive effort at 85% of boiler pressure (lbs)	20,000	27,275	27,340	24,172	25,515	26,120	26,878
Drawbar horsepower	963	1,030	900	830	1,020	1,020	1,100
Dhp per 100 lbs of tractive effort	4.81	3.80	3.30	3.44	4.00	3.80	4.10

Top *The last-built of the 'George the Fifth' Class 4-4-0s, No 2370* Dovedale, *at Crewe Works in July 1915, seen here in wartime plain black without lining or crest* (British Railways).

Above *Just after Grouping, the up 'Manxman' is seen on Castlethorpe troughs with a 16-coach load hauled by superheater 'Precursor' No 5294* Druid *piloting a 'Prince of Wales' Class 4-6-0 No 5680* Loadstone (L.J. Thompson).

Comparisons may be odious, but I think it is very safe to assert that during those years from 1911 to the time of wartime decelerations of train service from January 1917 onwards, the performance of the 'George the Fifth' Class engines was incomparable among British 4-4-0 engines, and that there were moreover no 'Atlantics' and very few 4-6-0s that could equal it. Close analysis and comparison with work done in different parts of Great Britain during the Grouping era shows that the 'Georges' were undoubtedly at their best on the Southern Division, in climbing the 1 in 330 gradients at high speed and running freely on the level and gently falling gradients. Their excellent valve gear enabled them to use steam to the best advantage, and develop sustained outputs of power considerably greater than one might expect from the value of their nominal tractive effort. With lighter loads, as on the two-hour Birmingham expresses, they ran very freely and economically.

Their work in the North Country requires a special mention. The Oxenholme-Carlisle piloting arrangements of 1908 had enabled heavy train formations to be worked over Shap by the 'Experiment' Class engines, but runs recorded in detail seemed to suggest that the 'Experiments' were overloaded on occasions between Crewe and Oxenholme. On theoretical grounds, the 'George the Fifth' Class engines were not ideal for the entire Crewe to Carlisle run. On the moderate gradients to Carnforth, they could naturally make good time with any load up to about 400 tons. But the reliability of their steaming, and their capacity for high cylinder performance, enabled them to climb the banks in such style that the 'equal to 17' Oxenholme-Carlisle piloting rule was immediately waived for superheater engines, and there are recorded instances of gross loads of 390 tons being

taken unassisted over Shap, not only within the scheduled end-to-end times from Preston to Carlisle, and from Crewe to Carlisle, but with accurate point-to-point timekeeping between Carnforth and Shap Summit.

Details are given in the accompanying table of four runs between Preston and Carlisle. The first was on the Glasgow portion of the 10 am from Euston, running non-stop from Crewe to Carlisle. This was a train that varied considerably in its loading. Its minimum, in the winter, was a five coach set including a 12-wheeled dining car from Euston and one brake composite from Birmingham to Glasgow, about 200 tons in all. But at busy times, the Birmingham portion included its own dining car, and in the following chapter of this book, when dealing with the work of the 'Claughton' Class engines, I record one occasion when this train loaded up to 440 tons, and still no pilot. The other three runs in the present table were made on the 2 pm down 'Corridor' after that

LNWR: Preston-Carlisle

Run no		1	2	3	4
Engine No		2155	2663	2242	1188
Engine name		*W.C. Brocklehurst*	*George the Fifth*	*Meteor*	*Penmaenmawr*
Load, empty/full (tons)		327/340	330/345	346/360	372/390

Distance (miles)		Schedule time (min)	Actual time (m s)	Actual time (m s)	Actual time (m s)	Actual time (m s)
0.0	PRESTON	0	0 00*	0 00	0 00	0 00
4.8	Barton		7 10	8 40	8 00	8 20
12.7	Scorton		14 55	16 20	15 10	16 40
21.0	LANCASTER	23	22 55	24 00	22 40	24 10
27.3	CARNFORTH	30	28 25	29 15	28 30	30 30
34.6	Milnthorpe		35 35	36 15	35 30	37 30
40.1	OXENHOLME	44	42 45	42 35	41 35	43 50
47.2	Grayrigg		54 30	53 40	52 35	55 05
53.2	Tebay	62	60 55	60 20	59 40	61 40
58.7	Summit	72	69 30	70 20	70 30	72 15
60.7	Shap		72 25	72 55	73 20	75 15
72.2	PENRITH	86	82 40	84 10	83 50	85 05
79.3	Calthwaite		89 05	90 45	90 55	92 15
85.2	Wreay		93 45	95 45	95 35	97 30
				sig stop	sigs	pws
90.1	CARLISLE	104	99 05	103 30	102 40	103 55
Net times (min)			100*	100¾	100¾	102¾
Max speed to Carnforth (mph)			—	75	70½	74
Min speed to Grayrigg (mph)			33¼	33	31½	33
Min speed to Shap (mph)			22½	22½	19½	19½
Max speed to Carlisle (mph)			—	—	79	83½
Edhp on Grayrigg bank			910	905	890	1,030

* 10 am train Euston-Glasgow, times from Preston at 15 mph

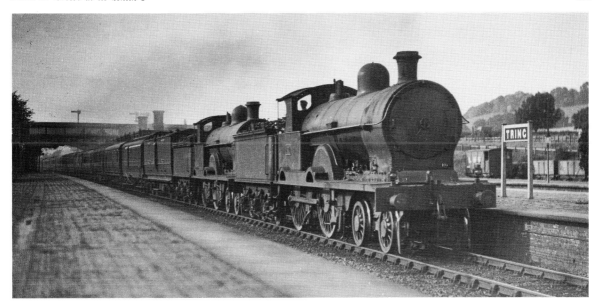

Two superheater 'Precursors', Titan *and* Delamere, *on the up Irish Mail passing Tring in 1927* (Rail Archive Stephenson, photo F.R. Hebron).

train had detached its Aberdeen and Whitehaven portions at Preston. The minimum load of this train was seven sumptuous 12-wheelers, weighing loaded about 300 tons, so that all three engines whose work is tabulated had considerably over the normal load. It is important to note also that even in the case of the heaviest loading, that of *Penmaenmawr* with no less than 390 tons behind the tender, exact time was kept on the uphill section from Carnforth to Shap Summit.

The values of equivalent drawbar horsepower are given only for the ascent of the Grayrigg bank. While the individual figures on the Shap incline would probably have been higher still, the speed, even at the summit, was still inclined to be falling and calculations of the edhp would not be as reliable as those on the Grayrigg bank, where speeds on the upper reaches were sustained. On the southbound climb to Shap, I have a record of engine No 1631 *Racehorse*, hauling a load of 325 tons, sustaining a speed of 42½ mph on the long 1 in 125 gradient between Clifton and Shap station, which works out at the remarkable edhp value of 1,190. This, indeed, was the pinnacle of performance in an outstanding run. Study of the log tabulated herewith shows that far from there being any deficiency in the 'cold' start out of Carlisle, the engine was already developing more than 1,000 edhp by the time Wreay was passed. The uphill working times booked to this train were very severe, and, despite the magnificent performance, time was not

kept between Penrith and Shap Summit; but despite the effort put forth uphill, there was evidently no lack of steam, by reason of the positively hurricane descent that followed, with 86½ mph before Tebay, and speed in the high seventies down the Grayrigg bank. By this, the train was nearly 3 minutes early on passing Oxenholme, and 4¼ minutes ahead at Carnforth. The rest of the journey to Preston was a 'doddle' by comparison.

LNWR: 12.58 pm Carlisle-Preston (1913)

Load 310 tons tare, 325 tons full
Engine 4-4-0 No 1631 *Racehorse*

Distance (miles)		Schedule time (min)	Actual time (m s)	Speed (mph)
0.0	CARLISLE	0	0 00	—
4.9	Wreay		9 18	42¾
7.4	Southwaite		12 34	—
13.1	Plumpton		19 12	56/62½
17.9	PENRITH	24	24 30	—
4.2	Clifton		6 54	45
—			—	42½
11.5	Shap		16 54	
13.5	Summit	18	19 26	—
19.0	Tebay	24	24 01	86½
25.0	Grayrigg		29 17	—
32.1	OXENHOLME	38	35 20	75
37.6	Milnthorpe		39 50	79
44.9	CARNFORTH	51	46 49	eased
51.1	LANCASTER	58	53 14	,,
62.7	Garstang		65 53	,,
72.2	PRESTON	80	78 44	

The 'George the Fifth' Class, 1911-15

'Hound' series

956	*Dachshund*	April 1911 (renamed *Bulldog* in 1914)
1478	*Wolfhound*	,,
1504	*Boarhound*	,,
1513	*Otterhound*	May 1911
1532	*Bloodhound*	,,
1628	*Foxhound*	,,
1662	*Deerhound*	,,
1706	*Elkhound*	,,
1792	*Staghound*	,,
2495	*Bassethound*	,,

'Coronation' series

5000	*Coronation*	June 1911
502	*British Empire*	,,
868	*India*	,,
882	*Canada*	,,
1218	*Australia*	,,
2081	*New Zealand*	,,
2212	*South Africa*	,,
2291	*Gibraltar*	,,
2177	*Malta*	July 1911
2498	*Cyprus*	,,

July-August series

361	*Beagle*	July 1911
888	*Challenger*	,,
1360	*Fire Queen*	,,
1394	*Harrier*	August 1911
1623	*Nubian*	,,
1631	*Racehorse*	,,
1644	*Roebuck*	,,
2089	*Traveller*	,,
2220	*Vanguard*	,,
2494	*Perseus*	,,

'Game-bird' series

1371	*Quail*	September 1911
1417	*Landrail*	,,
1472	*Moor Hen*	,,
1595	*Wild Duck*	,,
1681	*Ptarmigan*	,,
1713	*Partridge*	,,
1730	*Snipe*	October 1911
1733	*Grouse*	,,
1777	*Widgeon*	,,
1799	*Woodcock*	,,

1913 series

82	*Charles Dickens*	January 1913
752	*John Hick*	February 1913
1138	*William Froude*	,,
2124	*John Rennie*	,,
2154	*William Siemens*	,,
2282	*Richard Arkwright*	,,
89	*John Mayall*	March 1913
132	*S.R. Graves*	,,
681	*St George*	,,
845	*Saddleback*	,,
1193	*Edward Tootal*	,,
2279	*Henry Crosfield*	,,
404	*Eclipse*	April 1913
1188	*Penmaenmawr*	,,
1481	*Typhon*	,,
1680	*Loyalty*	,,
2086	*Phaeton*	,,
2197	*Planet*	,,
2242	*Meteor*	May 1913
2428	*Lord Stalbridge*	,,

'Resorts' series

104	*Leamington Spa*	June 1915
226	*Colwyn Bay*	,,
363	*Llandudno*	May 1915
789	*Windermere*	,,
984	*Caernarvon*	,,
1086	*Conway*	June 1915
2106	*Holyhead*	,,
2153	*Llandrindod*	,,
2233	*Blackpool*	,,
2370	*Dovedale*	July 1915

14. LNWR: Crewe at its zenith II
The '375' superheater 4-6-0s

In June 1911, the *Locomotive Magazine* printed this paragraph: 'It is reported that an order for ten four-cylinder simple engines of an entirely new type has recently been placed at Crewe Works.' That journal was not always strictly accurate in the news items it published, but this was the first intimation that something big and new was in contemplation. The date is, yet is not, significant. It could be construed that the idea of a four-cylinder simple engine arose from the working of the Great Western 4-6-0 *Polar Star* in the previous summer; but we know that while Bowen Cooke was glad enough to have the loan of a 'Star' for that momentous fortnight, it did not alter the conception he was forming for his own new 'super' express locomotive. Nor was the idea of a four-cylinder simple express engine novel at Crewe. Webb had built one in 1897, the 4-4-0 No 1501 *Jubilee*, for comparison with the four-cylinder compound No 1502 *Black Prince*. But Bowen Cooke's thoughts were running deeper, and far beyond a mere 4-6-0 simple version of the 'Jubilees'.

His worldwide interest in locomotives was to stand him in good stead, and no one so minded could fail to be enthralled by what was in progress on the continent of Europe in the early 1900s. Churchward certainly had been, and the Great Western had imported three de Glehn compound 'Atlantics'. From his educational sojourn there, Bowen Cooke was equally interested in German practice, and to him the work of Maffei, in Munich, was as significant as that of de Glehn, in Belfort—perhaps even more so. The fact that Maffei was building four-cylinder compounds in which all four cylinders drove on to the leading coupled axle gave them a physical affinity with the 'Jubilees' and 'Alfred the Great' 4-4-0s of the LNWR, but that was all. As a Running Superintendent, Bowen Cooke had a surfeit of experience of the shortcomings of the Webb compounds, and if he had ever thought of building compounds of his own, one may be very sure they would have been very different from those ill-starred 4-4-0s.

Apart from compounding itself, the basic feature of all Alfred de Glehn's locomotives was the division of the drive between two axles. While reducing the stresses induced in any one axle, it also applied the driving forces to the main frames of the locomotive in two places, and if the work was being accurately shared between the high- and low-pressure cylinders, the loading on both driving axles would be the same. Maffei's system of putting everything on to the lead-

ing coupled axle imposed heavy loading at one point only, in each frame. On the LNWR compound 4-4-0s, this condition had been met by the use of a centre bearing, which in the absence of eccentrics in the Joy valve gear could be accommodated conveniently. But there was a great deal more to it than equalization of the loads on the bearings, and in this facet of his design planning Bowen Cooke was a good dozen years ahead of his time—at any rate so far as British railway engineers were concerned.

It was, of course, quite an unconnected coincidence that the first news of Bowen Cooke's 4-6-0 engines 'broke' at the same time as details were first published in England of two new designs of four-cylinder 4-6-0s in Holland—the yellow 'Zeppelins' of the Central Railway, and the celebrated Beyer, Peacock engines of the State Railway. The first-named had been built by Maffei. In 1909, the year of so much locomotive 'interchange' activity on the LNWR, the Dutch State Railways had on loan one of the beautiful Beyer, Peacock inside-cylinder 4-6-0s of the North Brabant company. For a time this ran on express trains between Amsterdam, Utrecht and Arnhem, and created a most favourable impression; but while the North Brabant engine performed work greatly superior to that of the existing 4-4-0s, and also to that of the inside-cylinder 'Atlantics' then used on the Flushing mail trains, the State Railways wanted something still more powerful. When the State Railways began to formulate plans for their own 4-6-0 locomotives, the civil engineering authorities were prepared to accept an axle load of 16 tons, on condition that the unbalanced centrifugal forces of the balance-weights could be obviated. For this reason, the four-cylinder balanced type was chosen. The absence of hammer-blow, and the thereby constant axle load of 16 tons, permitted a larger boiler to be provided on the new engines. The detail designing of the new Dutch four-cylinder 4-6-0 locomotives was done by Beyer, Peacock and Co in Manchester, and it would have been very surprising if news of what was going on there had not reached Crewe. Now, the 'George the Fifth' Class 4-4-0s had a maximum axle load of 19.15 tons, and at a speed of 80 mph they had a dynamic augment, due to the balance-weights, of nearly 12 tons, bringing the maximum combined load per axle to over 31 tons. Bowen Cooke argued that if the layout of the machinery in his new four-cylinder 4-6-0 was arranged like the Dutch State Railways' 4-6-0s that Beyer, Peacock had just built, there would be no dynamic augment at all, and an axle load of 21 or even 22 tons could be used safely. The Great Western 'Star', which had run between Euston and Crewe, and which had a maximum axle load of only 18.5 tons, had a maximum combined load at 80 mph of about 25 tons, despite the use of four cylinders. With all this in mind, Bowen Cooke set the Crewe drawing office to work on the design of a big four-cylinder 4-6-0 with all four cylinders driving on to the leading coupled axle.

But the most carefully prepared plans can go adrift, and we know now that the first weight diagram of the new engines was not accepted by the Chief Engineer. How the case for heavier axle loading was submitted must remain a matter for conjecture, but evidently the elimination of dynamic augment by the use of four cylinders in line cut no ice with E.F.C. Trench, and he refused to accept a static axle load of more than 20 tons—a grudging increase of only 0.85 tons over that of the 'George the Fifth' Class. In view of Trench's objections, Bowen Cooke did not press the matter, and put the drawing office on to a modified design, to keep the weight down to what Trench would accept. In the meantime, to fulfil the order for ten new superheater 4-6-0s, included in the 1911 estimates, a superheated version of the 'Experiment' Class was produced. The first engine of this new class was completed at Crewe in October 1911, No 819 *Prince of Wales*. It is ironical to recall that the 'Prince of Wales' Class 4-6-0s, which Trench accepted without demur, had a maximum axle load of 18.25 tons, which by the addition of the hammerblow (dynamic augment) went up to a maximum com-

bined load, at 80 mph, of 29¾ tons! The engineering departments of the great railways of Britain certainly worked in 'blinkers' in what has sometimes been called their golden age; one ponders not a little upon the early Grouping days when Trench was a member of the Bridge Stress Committee, set up by the then Department of Scientific and Industrial Research, and the hammer-blow effect on the track of numerous locomotives was laid bare, including that of the express passenger 4-4-0s and 4-6-0s of the LNWR. One wonders if there were any pangs of conscience over the rejection of the original weight diagram of the Crewe four-cylinder 4-6-0 of 1911! The figures published in the report of the Bridge Stress Committee in 1929 were:

Class	Max axle load (tons)	Max hammer-blow (tons)	Max combined axle load (tons)
'George the Fifth'	19.15	14.1	33.2
'Prince of Wales'	18.25	11.4	29.7
'Claughton' (as built in 1913)	19.75	nil	19.75

The above figures related to a uniform speed of 6 rev per sec which is equivalent to 87 mph for the 'George' and the 'Claughton' and 80½ mph for the 'Prince of Wales'.

The ten new 4-6-0s of 1911 took the road almost incidentally, and were immediately successful. The

Left *One of the 1911 batch of 'Prince of Wales' Class 4-6-0s, No 2021* Wolverine, *ascending Shap with the Glasgow portion of the 10 am ex-Euston* (F.E. Mackay).

Above right *Up Irish Mail passing Colwyn Bay hauled by 'Prince of Wales' Class 4-6-0 No 2285* (H. Gordon Tidey).

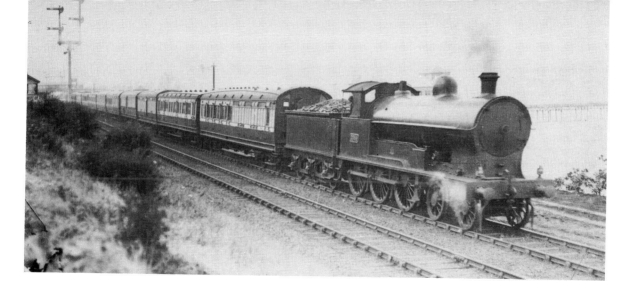

form of the firegrate which had caused some of the men difficulty in firing the 'Experiments' had by that time been mastered, and the 'Princes' quickly became well-liked engines. To the outside world, however, their advent was scarcely noticed. Their introduction was something of an anti-climax to the 'build-up' towards the four-cylinder engines that enlivened the railway technical journals in the early summer of 1911, and following the success of the 'George the Fifth' Class, as superheated developments of the 'Precursors', the superheated versions of the 'Experiments' were taken for granted. The *Locomotive Magazine* published a list of their names, but in *The Railway Magazine*, where Cecil J. Allen used to present each January a commentary on the locomotive activities of the previous year, in 1912 they were not even mentioned. The first reference to their actual work did not come until more than a year later. So far as I can ascertain, no dynamometer car trials were run with them. In such unobtrusive fashion did what was eventually the most numerous and most generally successful passenger locomotive class on the LNWR make its début.

As to their technical features, apart from the extended smokebox, the boiler barrel and firebox were the same as those of the 'Experiments' and the modification of the tube heating surfaces was as follows:

	'Experiment'	'Prince of Wales'
Small tubes (no)	299	152
Small tubes, external diameter (in)	1⅞	2⅛
Heating surfaces (sq ft)	1,908	969.9
Flues (no)	—	24
Flues, external diameter (in)	—	5

	'Experiment'	'Prince of Wales'
Heating surface (sq ft)	—	405.9
Superheater (sq ft)	—	304.4
Firebox heating surface (sq ft)	133.0	135.8
Combined total heating surface (sq ft)	2,041	1,816
Grate area (sq ft)	25.0	25.0

It is interesting to see that in the 'Prince of Wales' Class, the ordinary tubes were of larger diameter, but in both the 'Precursors' and the 'Experiments' a very large heating surface had been attained by a rather crowded arrangement of the tubes. The distance between the tube plates on both 'Experiment' and 'Prince of Wales' Classes was 13 ft 0 in.

The cylinders on the 'Princes', of 20½-in diameter, were inclined at 1 in 16 as on the 'Experiments', but the new engines had 8-in diameter piston valves, with 'indirect' Joy's motion, as on the 'George the Fifths'. The valve gear dimensions were:

Travel of valves in full gear	5⅜ in
Lap	1¼ in
Lead (inside)	⅛ in
Exhaust clearance	1/16 in

They had the Schmidt type of piston valves, with trick ports, and could produce a high output of power when occasion demanded it. All ten engines were, I believe, originally stationed at Crewe North, and worked mostly on the Carlisle road. So far as traffic working was concerned they were classified, for loading regulations, with the 'George the Fifth' Class, under the collective term 'superheater engines', and the official load limit between Euston and Oxenholme was 400 tons. What they attempted to take unassisted up the Grayrigg bank, and southbound from Carlisle up to Shap Summit, seems to have been left to the discretion of individual drivers; but the actual records, which have been searched through carefully, do not include any bigger gross load than 375 tons, taken southbound from Carlisle by No 1388 *Andromeda*. There is no doubt that until the introduction of the 'Claughtons' in 1913, the 'George the Fifths' had the limelight to themselves, throughout between Euston and Carlisle.

In the meantime, the Crewe drawing office was busy preparing the revised design for the boiler of the four-cylinder 4-6-0, to bring the axle loading down to a level that would be acceptable to the Chief Engineer. Between the new parameters they were set, Sackfield and his men in the Crewe drawing office made an extraordinarily fine job of that boiler. In retrospect, the Churchward superheated 'Stars' of the Great Western Railway are generally considered to represent the zenith of British locomotive practice in pre-Grouping days, noting also that the first Gresley 'Pacifics' that just came within that era had certainly not found their true form by the end of 1922. So, it is interesting to compare the 'Claughton' boiler with that of the superheated 'Star', noting in the accompanying table the vital ratio between the free gas area through the tubes, and the grate area. So far as tube heating surface was concerned, the amounts were almost equal, with a shorter distance between the tube plates, though Sackfield had reverted to the 'Experiment' size of tube, 1⅞-in external diameter, against the 2⅛-in he used on the 'Prince of Wales' Class. The 'Claughton' had a considerably larger firebox, but the outstanding difference was in the superheaters. The 'Claughtons', like the 'George the Fifths', reached steam temperatures of 630 to 650°F compared to 500 to 550°. This would not only impart a much greater fluidity to the steam, and enable it to

flow more freely through the valves and ports, but the total energy of the steam in lb calories per lb would be 745 in the 'Claughton' against 710 in the 'Star'. Of course, there still remained the difference in boiler pressures, and in conditions of full regulator working the steam chest pressures would be about 160 psi on the 'Claughton' and about 210 psi on the 'Star'.

	'Claughton'	'Star'
Small tubes (no)	159	176
external diameter (in)	1⅞	2
Superheater flues (no)	24	14
external diameter (in)	5¼	5⅛
Superheater elements (no)	96	84
external diameter (in)	1½	1
Heating surfaces (sq ft)		
Tubes	1,647.2	1,687
Firebox	171.2	155
Superheater	413.6	262
Combined total	2,232.0	2,104
Distance between tube plates (ft in)	14 10½	15 3
Grate area (sq ft)	30.5	27.1
Free gas area as percentage of grate area	14.7	15.1

Taken all round, although this boiler was not so large as Bowen Cooke had hoped to use, it was, as I shall show later, no mean steam raiser. The firebox was something new in Crewe locomotive practice, and included one feature that might have been inspired by the Great Western 'Star', namely a grate that was

Below left *One of the first batch of 'Claughtons' in shop grey, No 163* Holland Hibbert *(British Railways).*

Below left *One of the first batch of 'Claughtons' in shop grey, No 163* Holland Hibbert *(British Railways).*

Right *One of the first 'Claughtons' outside Euston, No 1191* Sir Frank Ree.

level at the back and with the front part sloping forward. As when the 'Experiments' were new, and some of the firemen found difficulty in finding the best technique for firing, so it was with the 'Claughtons'. Men who worked on them told me one had to fire 'all round the box', rather then dumping it in thick in the deep narrow grate of a 'George' or a 'Precursor', or projecting it in almost horizontally to hit the tube plate, as on an 'Experiment' or a 'Prince of Wales'. The first 'Claughtons' also had superheater dampers worked by the driver, as on the 'Georges', and this accessory was often used with great effect by the most experienced and regular drivers when starting away 'cold'. Engines working the 'crack' turns from Crewe North were supplied with Welsh coal, which takes a little time to burn through. Even though a fireman may have built up a big fire, an engine starting south from Crewe and pounding up the Madeley bank with a heavy train might begin to lose pressure, while still maintaining superheat. The technique then was to close the superheater damper to deflect all the exhaust gases through the small tubes. It was fascinating then to watch the pressure gauge needle rise, while the pyrometer needle dropped back. Once pressure was restored, the damper would be opened again, and the boiler would steam freely.

In these preliminaries about the 'Claughton' engines, I have dwelt extensively upon the boiler, because it was the feature that had to be altered, and purely on outward appearances came in for a good deal of criticism. No less important, of course, was the engine proper. Here, within the general specifi-

cation, Sackfield produced a very simple and straightforward design. The decision to abandon the Joy valve gear was interesting. It would have been practicable to fit this on to the inside connecting rods, and drive the valves of the outside cylinders through rocking shafts. This had been done on the four-cylinder compound 4-4-0s, and with the 'Claughtons' there would have been none of the complications arising from Webb's original design for the simultaneous linking up of the high-pressure and low-pressure motion. The connecting rods were the same length as those of the 'Experiment' and 'Prince of Wales' Classes, namely 6 ft 6 in. Use of Walschaerts valve gear outside made a simple and accessible arrangement with the valves of the inside cylinders driven by rocking shafts ahead of the cylinders. There was nothing of Great Western influence here, because one could hardly imagine a greater contrast between this neat arrangement, and the highly ingenious, but highly inaccessible, layout on Churchward's 'Stars', designed in the sacred Swindon cause of keeping all the motion well out of sight, and having the centre-lines of the cylinders horizontal. The basic dimensions of the Walschaerts valve gear on the 'Claughtons' were:

Travel of valves in full gear	$4^{5}/_{16}$ in
lead	$^{5}/_{32}$ in
steam lap	1 in
exhaust clearance	$^{1}/_{16}$ in

It will be noticed that the valve travel and the steam lap were less than on the Joy valve gear fitted to the

'Georges' and 'Princes', but the maximum steam port area in relation to the cylinder volume was made larger than on either of the earlier classes of superheater engine.

Another departure was the abandoning of the centre bearing on the driving axle. With cylinders of no more than 16-in diameter, there would have been plenty of room to get this in, but instead Sackfield put extra-massive journals in the main frames. These latter were 1 in thick, as on the 'George the Fifths', and lapped in the traditional Crewe style for about 3 ft in the region of the motion plate. At the end of January 1913, engine No 2222 *Sir Gilbert Claughton* left the erecting shop at Crewe, and little more than a fortnight later, on Sunday 9 February, there was a test run with the dynamometer car from Crewe to Rugby and back. The load was 'equal to 20½', which would be about 400 to 420 tons, and although delayed by two permanent way checks, the train ran the 75½ miles back to Crewe in 82 minutes. The engine was then in shop grey, and it remained the only one of the class for just over three months. No technical details of this test run were made public, but after the engine had been lined out in white for the official photographs, it was painted in the standard running colours and took up its first regular duties—haulage of the 2 pm 'Corridor' between Crewe and Carlisle, returning with the 1 am up sleeper from Carlisle to Crewe. Working thus mainly in the hours of darkness, No 2222 remained largely occulted from public gaze in her early days. After the completion of this engine, Crewe Works continued

with the production of 'George the Fifth' 4-4-0s, and twenty more were turned out by the beginning of May 1913, an average of between five and six a month.

Construction of the 'Claughtons' began in earnest in May 1913. The first batch were all named after directors and the names and completion dates were:

Number	Name	Date
1161	*Sir Robert Turnbull*	May 1913
1191	*Sir Frank Ree*	,,
1159	*Ralph Brocklebank*	,,
1319	*Sir Frederick Harrison*	,,
1327	*Alfred Fletcher*	,,
21	*Duke of Sutherland*	,,
163	*Holland Hibbert*	June 1913
650	*Lord Rathmore*	,,
2046	*Charles N. Lawrence*	,,

After being run in, engines 1161 and 1191 went to Camden, and No 1327 to Edge Hill. The remaining seven were all at Crewe North. The two London engines worked on the heavily loaded single-home turns to Crewe, the 12.10 pm Liverpool and Manchester express, and the 2 pm 'Corridor'. Engine No 1327 *Alfred Fletcher*, named after the Chairman of the Traffic Committee and a prominent member of the Liverpool section of the Board, had the 11 am Lime Street to Euston, returning with the 5.55 pm down, non-stop to Edge Hill. The Crewe North engines worked mainly on the Carlisle road.

The pioneer engine, No 2222, was a favourite on

the 5.19 pm down from Crewe (the 2 pm 'Corridor' from Euston), but in those first months, so far as outstanding performance went, the palm would seem to have gone to the Edge Hill engine *Alfred Fletcher*, worked on alternate days by two supremely competent drivers. Some of the individual feats of haulage with trains regularly loaded to over 400 tons matched even the Class '40' diesel electrics when these were going all out! But in its issue of December 1913, *The Railway Magazine* carried this brief note:

'On a recent Sunday afternoon a special test run was made from Euston to Crewe with engine No 1159 *Ralph Brocklebank*, one of the new 4-6-0 'Sir Gilbert Claughton' Class. A train, chiefly of sleeping saloons and dining cars equal to 22, and representing a load of 434 tons, was made up, and the dynamometer car was attached. The train left Euston at 1.30 pm and in spite of three serious checks, made an exceptionally fine run. There were slacks at Tring and Milford, and the train was stopped for 5 minutes outside Crewe. Yet Crewe station was reached at 4.8 pm, the 158 miles having been covered in 158 minutes, a net time of virtually 2½ hours. The same engine recently completed a notable trial run with an ordinary train, the 141 miles from Crewe to Carlisle being covered in 142 minutes, with about 360 tons.'

Surprisingly, it was not until more than thirty years later that readers heard anything more of these trials, which actually represented engine performance the like of which had never previously been seen in Great Britain. Full details were certainly released to *The Engineer* in February 1914, and Bowen Cooke himself presented much additional information when he opened the discussion at the Institution of Civil Engineers on a paper by Henry Fowler on 'Super-

Left *Officially 'G2' Class, the 'Super Ds' were the longest lived of all the Crewe main line engines with Joy valve gear. An up express goods passes Lancaster in 1951 hauled by No 49267 (Derek Cross).*

Right *Euston-Liverpool express near Kenton, hauled by unnamed 'Claughton' No 1335 (Author's Collection).*

Right *An unnamed 'Claughton', No 2097, on the West Coast 'Corridor' express near Kenton (Real Photos Co Ltd).*

heated Steam in Locomotives'.

In my book *The LNWR Locomotives of C. J. Bowen Cooke,* I reviewed the reports comprehensively, including the detailed logs of the running, indicator diagrams, some speed charts and particulars of all the indicator diagrams taken by Tommy Sackfield and his men riding in the shelter on the front of the engine. At the Institution of Civil Engineers, Bowen Cooke gave the following summaries of the results on the two days:

2 November 1913, Euston-Crewe

Mean drawbar pull over whole trip	855 hp
Average indicated horsepower from diagrams taken at 25 points	1,358 hp
Average drawbar horsepower at the above 25 points	975 hp
Average drawbar horsepower per ihp	71.8%

4 November 1913, Crewe-Carlisle

Mean drawbar pull over whole trip	1.83 tons
Mean power at drawbar over whole trip	663 hp
Average indicated horsepower from diagrams taken at 17 points	1,387 hp
Average horsepower at the 17 points where the indicator diagrams were taken	920 hp

In contrast to the run of 2 November, however, there were lengthy stretches during the second run over which the engine was being worked under very easy steam, as from Coppull down to Preston, and from Shap Summit down to Carlisle, where for much of the distance the engine was running without steam at all. On the other hand, between Carnforth and Shap Summit, where in this distance of 31.4 miles there is a vertical rise of 885 ft, the average speed was 54 mph, and the horsepower records thus:

Milepost (past Lancaster)	Ascending gradient (1 in)	Speed (mph)	Drawbar horsepower	Indicated horsepower
9	134	60½	1,015	1,504
14	173	67	950	1,407
20	104	52½	980	1,494
24	131	47	996	1,526
32	146	69	1,082	1,669
34	75	58	1,082	1,606
36	75	42½	1,092	1,593
37½	75	37	1,187	1,496
Average			1,045	1,535

Reading again the report of that discussion at the Institution of Civil Engineers, in which Aspinall, Churchward, Gresley, Hughes, Raven and several

engineers connected with Dominion and Colonial Railways took part, and to which Dr Schmidt, the designer of the superheater, made a written contribution, it is, in retrospect, a little surprising that not one of those distinguished participants—not even Churchward—fastened on to the astonishing figures that Bowen Cooke had released. In 1914, superheating was still something quite new, and almost without exception those who spoke in warm praise of Fowler's paper were concerned with the practical details of superheater construction and maintenance, problems of lubrication, and so on. It was only Bowen Cooke who referred to any extent to the 'end-product', and with the *Ralph Brocklebank* engine it was an end product with a vengeance.

In 1913, the same year as the first 'Claughtons' were built, the Traffic Department of the LNWR replaced the old method of reckoning train loads by 'coaches' by the logical tonnage system, and decreed that the maximum load for any express train throughout the system would be 420 tons. The 'Claughtons' were rostered to take this maximum anywhere on the line, except northbound between Tebay and Shap Summit, where rear-end banking was always available; but if things were going well on the footplate, drivers disdained any assistance and took Shap in their stride. This was frequently the case in conditions of maximum loading with the Glasgow portion of the 10 am from Euston, when the one Birmingham 'through carriage', attached next to the engine at Crewe, sometimes consisted of four or even more coaches including their own restaurant car. This was taken by an unaided 'Claughton' on a schedule planned in the days of the 'Experiments', 159 min from Crewe to Carlisle, when the loads were rarely as much as 275 tons. From 1913 to the end of 1916, at peak periods the train was made up to the full 420 tons.

With maximum loads, drivers aimed at getting a little time in hand by the time Carnforth was passed, because the uphill allowance, 39 minutes for the 31.4 miles up to Shap Summit, planned for much smaller loads, was very severe and not usually maintained. Even so, the uphill running was uniformly very fine, with power outputs on the Grayrigg bank almost equal to the maximum obtained in the 1913 trials on *Ralph Brocklebank*. Details of three 'Claughton' ascents of the bank are given herewith, the third in very bad weather:

Engine No	856	2222	163
Engine name	E. Tootal Broadhurst	Sir Gilbert Claughton	Holland Hibbert
Gross load (tons)	420	440	440
Time, Oxenholme to Grayrigg (m s)	12 30	11 52	11 30

Engine No	856	2222	163
Engine name	*E. Tootal Broadhurst*	*Sir Gilbert Claughton*	*Holland Hibbert*
Min speed on 1 in 106 (mph)	32	31	34
Equivalent dhp	1,120	1,135	1,260

The third run was made in the early days of the First World War when not only was the weather bad, but also the train was much delayed by a troop special which had to be given priority. Fortunately, the road was clear after Carnforth and a magnificent climb of the Grayrigg bank was made. In such weather, however, the driver stopped at Tebay for rear-end assistance up Shap. The first of the three runs was also subject to some delays, but the second was favoured by an almost clear road throughout and reached Carlisle in 157½ minutes from Crewe, a splendid run.

In October 1913, production started in earnest with the 'Prince of Wales' Class, and the thirty engines were all named, except for the last one of all, after poets and men of letters. Those honoured were not confined to British subjects, because *Victor Hugo*, *Mark Twain* and *Bret Harte* were included—while the catholicity of taste was also displayed by *Sir W.S. Gilbert* and *Felicia Hemans*. One wonders if the fireman of No 1400 sometimes felt things were getting so hot on the footplate that the deck might begin to burn! The exception to the poetic gallery was engine No 2520 which was named after the great Superintendent of the line who retired in 1895, *G.P. Neele*; when

the engine was built, in March 1914, he was approaching 90 years of age. Building of the 'Prince of Wales' and 'Claughton' Classes continued through the war years, such was the need for more engines to cope with the increased traffic; indeed, such was the pressure on Crewe Works itself that a contract had to be made with the North British Locomotive Company for twenty 'Prince of Wales' Class 4-6-0s in 1916. Crewe itself built thirty more of the class, also in 1916, and no less than fifty 'Claughtons', ten each in 1911 and 1915, and the last thirty in 1917. It was on this batch that the practice of naming all LNWR express locomotives was temporarily stopped as a wartime measure to save brass. The names of the 'Princes' and 'Claughtons' built from 1914 onwards are listed at the end of this chapter.

The Armistice of 1918 found the LNWR and its men as exhausted as the rest of the nation. The General Manager, Sir Guy Calthrop, was a victim of the terrible flu epidemic that swept across Europe, and although Bowen Cooke himself escaped that particular post-war hazard, his death in 1920 occurred at the relatively early age of 62. He had been looking forward to getting back to locomotive work, but in the event new engines were required very urgently, not only to make up the arrears of wartime production at Crewe, but also to provide work in the engineering industry to absorb the labour force becoming redundant by the cessation of armament production. Orders were placed on Crewe for 65 more 'Prince of Wales' Class 4-6-0s, and for seventy more 'Claughtons'; the building of the boilers for the last-named engines was subcontracted to Vickers Ltd at Barrow-in-Furness.

Though I believe Bowen Cooke had in mind more modifications to the design of the 'Claughtons' for the post-war batches, the only major alteration that

Last of the 'Poet' series of the 'Prince of Wales' Class 4-6-0s built in 1913-4, No 2520 G.P. Neele (British Railways).

Left *Liverpool and Manchester Scottish Express on Tebay troughs, with 'Prince of Wales' 4-6-0 No 1400* Felicia Hemans *(Real Photos Co Ltd).*

Left *The LNWR War Memorial engine No 1914* Patriot *leaving Euston with the 1.15 pm West Coast 'Corridor' express in 1920 (F.E. Mackay).*

Right *Up Irish Mail passing Penmaenmawr hauled by 'Renown' Class 4-4-0 No 1968* Cumberland *and 'Prince of Wales' Class 4-6-0 No 833* Suvla Bay *(Rail Archive Stephenson, photo F.R. Hebron).*

there was time to make to meet the urgency of the programme was to the firebox. The Great Western type of grate, level at the back and sloping down in front, which was the only feature in which the original engines of 1913 could be said to resemble the 'Star' was abandoned in favour of a continuous sloping grate. There were changes to the method of cylinder and piston valve lubrication, and Ross 'pop' type safety valves were used instead of the traditional Ramsbottom type. Except for the first of the new 'Claughtons', all the new 4-6-0 locomotives of 1919-20 were at first unnamed. The exception was the very celebrated No 1914 *Patriot*. It was a happy inspiration to dedicate the first of these engines as a kind of mobile war memorial, and to transfer the significant number, 1914, from the 'Renown' Class 4-4-0

Invincible which had previously carried it. *Patriot* had a specially large nameplate that carried the additional words: 'In memory of the fallen L & NWR employees 1914-1919.' With appropriate sense of occasion, *Patriot* was put on to regular daily haulage of the 'Corridor' express from Euston to Crewe. It then left at 1.15 pm, and the new engine made an impressive sight at the head of the magnificent rake of twelve-wheeled coaches that had so distinguished the train in peace and war.

In the summer of 1920, the last of Bowen Cooke's life, an interesting modification was made to the valve gear of one of the 'Prince of Wales' Class 4-6-0s, No 479 *Thomas B. Macaulay*. These engines, like the 'George the Fifths', had the indirect version of Joy's gear, which had three more pin joints than that of the direct arrangement, used on the 4-6-2 superheater tank engines. The drawing showing the alteration applied to the 'Prince of Wales' Class is dated April 1920, but also includes some changes in the basic dimensions, namely a reduction in the valve travel in full gear from $5^{11}/_{32}$ in to $4^9/_{16}$ in, and an increase in the exhaust clearance from $1/_{16}$ in to as much as $1/_4$ in. On theoretical grounds, these might seem retrograde steps, except that the 'Claughtons', with no more than $4^5/_{16}$ in travel in full gear, had proved very fast and powerful engines. It would seem that Crewe was satisfied with the results obtained from the modified 479, because when an order was placed with Beardmore's for a further ninety engines of the 'Prince of Wales' Class, they were specified with direct motion, as on No 479. The names of the 'Prince of Wales' and 'Claughton' Class engines were as follows:

'Prince of Wales' Class
1911 series

819	*Prince of Wales*	1691	*Pathfinder*
1388	*Andromeda*	1704	*Conqueror*
1452	*Bonaventure*	1721	*Defiance*
1454	*Coquette*	2021	*Wolverine*
1537	*Enchantress*	2359	*Hermione*

Poets' series, built 1913-4

362	*Robert Southey*	1134	*Victor Hugo*
892	*Charles Wolfe*	2040	*Oliver Goldsmith*
1081	*John Keats*	2075	*Robert Burns*
1089	*Sydney Smith*	321	*Henry W. Longfellow*

479	*Thomas B. Macaulay*	979	*W.M. Thackeray*
951	*Bulwer Lytton*	1400	*Felicia Hemans*
2198	*John Ruskin*	964	*Bret Harte*
2205	*Thomas Moore*	985	*Sir W.S. Gilbert*
2213	*Charles Kingsley*	1321	*William Cowper*
1679	*Lord Byron*	2152	*Charles Lamb*
2249	*Thomas Campbell*	2293	*Percy Bysshe Shelley*
2283	*Robert L. Stevenson*		
86	*Mark Twain*	2377	*Edward Gibbon*
146	*Lewis Carroll*	2443	*Charles James Lever*
307	*R.B. Sheridan*		
637	*Thomas Gray*	2520	*G.P. Neele*

North British Loco Co series, built 1915-16

136	*Minerva*	90	*Kestrel*
173	*Livingstone*	401	*Zamiel*
257	*Plynlimmon*	525	*Vulcan*
446	*Pegasus*	610	*Albion*
1749	*Precedent*	867	*Condor*
2063	*Hibernia*	1132	*Scott*
2175	*Loadstone*	1466	*Sphinx*
2203	*Falstaff*	1744	*Petrel*
2300	*Hotspur*	2055	*Milton*
2392	*Caliban*	2399	*Samson*

1915-16 series, built at Crewe

27	*General Joffre*	877	*Raymond Poincare*
88	*Czar of Russia*	1333	*Sir John French*
122	*King of the Belgians*	2275	*Edith Cavell*
160	*King of Serbia*	2396	*Queen of the Belgians*
185	*King of Italy*	2408	*Admiral Jellicoe*

1915-16 series, built at Crewe

606	*Castor*	95	*Gallipoli*
745	*Pluto*	126	*Anzac*
810	*Onyx*	833	*Suvla Bay*
1084	*Shark*	849	*Arethusa*
1346	*Trent*	1100	*Lusitania*
1352	*The Nile*	1324	*Falaba*
1379	*Witch*	2092	*Arabic*
1484	*Smeaton*	2276	*Persia*
2417	*Atlas*	2295	*Anglia*
2442	*Odin*	2340	*Tara*

Post-war named series

2392	*Caliban*	1290	*Lucknow*
940	*Richard Cobden*	1325	*Disraeli*
621	*Telford*	1178	*Prince Albert*
1584	*Scotia*	1542	*Marathon*
504	*Canning*	1694	*Premier*
974	*Hampden*	2516	*Dalton*
522	*Stentor*		

'Claughton' Class
1914 and 1916 batches

250	*J.A. Bright*	668	*Rupert Guinness*
260	*W.E. Dorrington*	856	*E. Tootal*
1131	*Lord Faber*		*Broadhurst*
1429	*Colonel Lockwood*	1567	*Charles J. Cropper*
2239	*Frederick Baynes*	2401	*Lord Kitchener*
209	*J. Bruce Ismay*	511	*George Macpherson*

'Claughton' class

695	*Sir Arthur Lawley*	2204	*Sir Herbert Walker*
968	*Lord Kenyon*	2221	*Sir Francis Dent*
1093	*Guy Calthrop*	2338	*Charles H. Dent*
1345	*James Bishop*	2395	*J.A.F. Aspinall*
2174	*E.C. Trench*		

1917 series, first three

37	*G.R. Jebb*	1552	*Sir Thomas Williams*
154	*Captain Fryatt*		

Post-war named series

2230	*Clio*	2059	*C.J. Bowen Cooke*
1019	*Columbus*	2430	*Vindictive*
2373	*Tennyson*	30	*Thalaba*
2420	*Ingestre*	42	*Princess Louise*
2427	*Duke of Connaught*	110	*Lady Godiva*
2445	*Baltic*	150	*Illustrious*
986	*Buckingham*	158	*Private E. Sykes VC*
1177	*Bunsen*		
1407	*L/Corpl J.A. Christie VC*	169	*Breadalbane*
1599	*John O'Groat*	179	*Private W. Wood VC*
2499	*Patience*		
2511	*Croxteth*	180	*Llewellyn*
12	*Talisman*	192	*Bevere*
2268	*Frobisher*	207	*Sir Charles Cust*

15. Into the Grouping era

The railway casualties from the First World War were not only on the battlefields. The London and North Western Railway suffered more severely from loss of top management than any other British company, from the unremitting strain of war conditions and the 'delayed action' that set in afterwards. Although he was no older than his early sixties, Bowen Cooke suffered a general breakdown in health in the summer of 1920 and died in the autumn of that year. The Chairman, Sir Gilbert Claughton, had a severe illness in the middle of the war, but carried on until the beginning of 1921, but the greatest loss, not only for the LNWR but the entire future of the LMS Group, was the death of Sir Guy Calthrop, the General Manager, in 1919. Sir Guy, who was not then 50 years of age, had already had a distinguished railway career even before he became General Manager in 1914. He was trained on the LNWR, then went to the Caledonian as General Superintendent and then General Manager, after which he went to the Argentine, as General Manager of the Buenos Aires and Pacific Railway. In 1917 he had been temporarily relieved of his vital railway duties to take on the national duties of Coal Controller, as which he was such an immediate and outstanding success that no more than a year later he had a baronetcy conferred on him. The mind inevitably dwells on the influence this brilliant and still relatively young man would have had on the post-war railway scene had he lived.

Sir Thomas Williams, the Chief Goods Manager of the LNWR, who had been Acting General Manager during Sir Guy's absence on wartime duties, succeeded him in 1919, but unlike Sir Guy he was nearing the age of retirement. It might seem that I have dwelt, albeit briefly, on the change of General Managers of the LNWR in a book wholly concerned otherwise with locomotives; but the changes in top management personnel following the retirement of Sir Thomas Williams were profound, and came to affect every department on the railway, most of all that of mechanical engineering. The underlying reasons were entirely political. The post-war Coalition Government of David Lloyd George, and his brilliant protégé Eric Geddes, was set on some form of transport unification, even eventual nationalization, and the top managements of some of the major railways began to consider how they might be aligned in some future grouping scheme. The Lancashire and Yorkshire was associated with the LNWR in much more than geography; indeed, in 1873 a Bill was presented to Parliament for complete amalgamation, but then rejected on the grounds that it would create too great a monopoly of railway business. It was far

otherwise in 1920. At the end of that year, the railway world was astonished to learn that the successor to Sir Thomas Williams was to be Arthur Watson, who had but recently succeeded the great Sir John Aspinall as General Manager of the Lancashire and Yorkshire. More than this, in addition to taking over the LNWR he was to retain also his previous command. The formal amalgamation of the two companies followed a year later, a year ahead of the Government Grouping which resulted in the LNWR and LYR forming part of the London Midland and Scottish Railway.

Much has been written of the vicissitudes experienced by the locomotive departments of the various Grouped railways and their men in the subsequent years; but until the top management intervened in 1926 and countermanded the project to build a huge four-cylinder compound 'Pacific' in the French style, the story was mostly that of warring personalities and strong-minded subordinates who swayed the susceptibility of their genial but too scientifically minded chief hither and thither. On the formation of the combined LNWR/LYR in 1922, George Hughes of the Lancashire and Yorkshire was already 67 years of age and could have looked forward to some years in retirement. But with Arthur Watson as General Manager, preference would undoubtedly be given to a LYR man, even though the likelihood of his retaining the post for long was no more than brief. In other circumstances one could have thought that a younger man in the person of Bowen Cooke's successor at Crewe, Capt H.P.M. Beames, would have been more suitable, and able to guide the new group through its formative stages, particularly as Beames had already given ample proof of his administrative and technical ability while acting as assistant to Bowen Cooke. Unfortunately, it seems that anything North Western was anathema to Watson, as witness his treatment of the headquarters staff at Euston. In years gone by it was said of the great Chairman, Sir Richard Moon, that he personally briefed every new officer on his appointment with the words 'Remember first of all that you are a gentleman; and then that you are a London and North Western Railway Officer'. I wonder if some of the older men remembered this earlier admonition, particularly in respect of their new boss!

In the last years of the Lancashire and Yorkshire Railway, Horwich made some amends for the dismal failure of its four-cylinder 4-6-0 engines, originally built in 1908. The rebuilding of them began in 1920, with 16½-in cylinders, superheaters, Walschaerts valve gear, and a greatly improved motion. General

Top *The first LYR four-cylinder 4-6-0 to be rebuilt by Hughes in 1920, with a superheater and new front end* (British Railways).

Left *One of the LYR-type four-cylinder 4-6-0s built new in 1921, leaving Carnforth on a West Coast Main Line train to Crewe* (O.S. Nock).

Below *The first Horwich mixed traffic 2-6-0 introduced in 1926, of which the first examples were painted in Midland red. Nicknamed 'Crabs', a total of 245 were built between 1926 and 1932, seventy at Horwich and the rest at Crewe* (British Railways).

satisfaction was expressed over the results, and, after the merger with the LNWR and the appointment of Hughes as Chief Mechanical Engineer, comparative trials convinced Horwich that the rebuilt engines were superior to the 'Claughtons', and orders for more of the Class '8' 4-6-0s, as they were termed, were issued. As rebuilt, on the basis of nominal tractive effort they were the most powerful express passenger engines in Great Britain, at 28,879 lb surpassing the Great Western 'Stars' and *The Great Bear* at 27,800 lb and substantially beating their Crewe rivals, the 'Claughtons', which had no more than 24,100 lb. In the first years of the LMS it seemed that the policy was to build sufficient Class '8' 4-6-0s to take over all the principal West Coast Main Line duties. Beginning in August 1921, a total of 55 new engines of the class had been built down to February 1925, but it did not work out as Horwich had intended. The results of the trials of 1922, as 'leaked out' to certain technical journalists, certainly favoured the Lancashire and Yorkshire engines, but the Horwich people were very 'touchy' on the subject, and my own travelling experiences behind Class '8' engines were not all edifying. Then, in 1924 at the World Power Conference, C.B. Collett, who had recently succeeded Churchward as Chief Mechanical Engineer of the Great Western Railway, read a paper on 'Testing of Locomotives on the Great Western Railway'. Then the fat was in the fire with a vengeance in Horwich circles.

In the various dynamometer tests against LNWR 4-6-0s conducted in 1922 between Manchester and Blackpool, Manchester and York, and between Crewe and Carlisle, the LYR 4-6-0s had returned an average coal consumption of rather more than 5 lb drawbar horsepower hour. This had been gratifying enough to Horwich, seeing that the original saturated engines of 1908 burned more than 7 lb—when they were in good condition. But here was Collett claiming that in some maximum load tests between Swindon and Plymouth, at the highest express speeds then scheduled, the coal consumption of *Caldicot Castle* was no more than 2.83 lb per dhp hour! To make this figure a true basis for comparison with the work of engines burning different grades of coal, allowance must be made for the difference in calorific value. For top quality Northern hard coals, the equivalent to that 2.83 would be about 3.0 lb, although the top-link engines at Crewe North shed and working on the Carlisle road used to be supplied with Welsh coal. Even so, there was a world of difference between 2.83-3.0 lb and the 5 lb plus of the LYR 4-6-0s. It was certainly an anxious time in the drawing office at Horwich while comparisons were being made between what were thought to be the chief differences in design, and what had created the wide difference

in working efficiency between the two designs of four-cylinder 4-6-0. Regrettably, the opinion was formed at Horwich that the Swindon figures had got to be taken with the proverbial 'pinch of salt'. But as one engineer who was involved in that original investigation said ruefully, many years later, 'We've learned better now!'

In the meantime, while Horwich was busying itself with designs for still larger engines in the new-found post-LYR style, the Operating Department of the newly established LMS was thinking on quite different lines. The LNWR was not the only railway in the new Group to have lost an outstanding officer in the immediate post-war years. On the Midland, the General Superintendent, Cecil W.S. Paget, after his monumental reorganizing of the Operating Department in pre-war years, and his brilliant wartime career in command of the Railway Operating Division of the British Army on the Western Front, decided to resign from his post on the Midland Railway in 1919, and enter into business management. He was then no more than 45 years of age, and, unlike the LNWR men previously referred to, in excellent health. We must spare a thought as to how much the LMS might have benefited from the driving power of his dynamic leadership in the years that then lay ahead. One of his protégés from Midland days, J.H. Follows, had developed sufficiently to be appointed Acting General Superintendent during Paget's war service, and he succeeded him in 1919. When the Grouping came four years later, Follows was appointed Chief General Superintendent of the LMS, and another Midland man, J.E. Anderson, formerly Deputy CME of the MR, was appointed Superintendent of Motive Power, thus completing the divorcing of responsibility for locomotive running from the Chief Mechanical Engineer. The close association of Follows and Anderson was to have some interesting sequels in the next few years.

Follows had been brought up on the Paget system of train operation and control, which was designed to suit the Midland pattern of traffic. It would seem as though he visualized none other, because after Grouping his organization at Derby was at one time scheming how the passenger train services of the former LNWR lines south of Liverpool and Manchester could be reorganized on Midland lines, substituting a swarm of light-formation 55-mph trains for the previous 'heavyweights'. Follows and Anderson together visualized that nothing larger than Class '4' engines would be required to haul these trains—in other words, Midland compounds. So, irrespective of what the drawing office was cooking up, a series of dynamometer car trials was organized between Carlisle and Leeds with Class '4' engines, ostensibly to prove that the Midland compound was the most suitable and the most economical engine for the job. At the time of the Grouping, only 24 of the compounds had been superheated, and although the rest of the class were graded as Class '4' by the Midland Railway, there was no comparison between the work they could do and that of the locomotives which had been superheated. In addition to these latter, the ten simple 4-4-0s of the '999' Class, also superheated, were Class '4'. Against these 34 Midland 4-4-0s were ranged the six Caledonian 'Cardean' Class 4-6-0s, the Highland 'Clans', and no fewer than 245 LNWR 4-6-0s of the 'Prince of Wales' Class.

The dynamometer trials between Carlisle and Leeds, which began in mid-December 1923 and continued for a month in the worst of the winter weather on the Settle and Carlisle line, involved only three of the Class '4' engines owned by the LMS: a 'Prince of Wales' 4-6-0, a '999' Class 4-4-0, and, of course, a Midland compound. While the two first mentioned, though in good condition, were taken out of the regular link workings at Carlisle, from Upperby Bridge and Durran Hill sheds respectively, the compound, No 1008, had only just been worked in after a major overhaul at Derby. She was not only in first class condition but she had also the reputation of being a 'star' engine in every way. With any class of locomotives there were always variations due to very minor details of their erection, valve setting, and so on; and while there would undoubtedly be 'black sheep', even among the Midland compounds, at Derby, among those who had anything to do with running, engine No 1008 was acknowledged to be the 'flower of the flock'. There was, therefore, every reason for putting her forward as the chosen protagonist of the Midland against the North Western. She did them proud indeed, hauling trains of tonnages unheard of on the Midland over Aisgill Summit, and gaining time in the process; indeed, the brilliance of her work became something of an embarrassment to Derby afterwards, when none of the many compounds tested on various examinations, though excellent engines in themselves, could approach, let alone surpass, the results turned in by No 1008.

Even before the outcome of these trials was known, however, a series of twenty new compounds had been authorized, and, beginning with No 1045 in February 1924, Derby turned out these engines at the rate of one per week. By the time this order was well on the way to completion, the report on the trials of December 1923 and January 1924 had been completed and digested, so much so that Derby was instructed to continue at once with a second batch of twenty compounds. The 1045-1064 batch differed from the original Midland engines in having 6-ft 9-in coupled wheels, and both the high-pressure and low-pressure cylinders were ¾ in larger in diameter.

Apart from their numbers, these engines could be distinguished immediately from Nos 1000-1044 by the shape of the dome cover. This was slightly flattened at the top, as on the Class '2' superheater rebuilds, whereas the original Midland engines had a very handsome rounded top to their domes. But the 1045-1064 batch were in every way true Midland engines, with Ramsbottom lock-up safety valves and the tall, characteristic Derby chimney.

Those in command of the locomotive department had, by the summer of 1924, developed such as superiority complex where the compounds were concerned that they seemed ready to back them against all comers. Use of them in Scotland was already envisaged, and in the late autumn of 1924 a further series of trials over the Settle and Carlisle line was organized, in which compounds would be tested against Caledonian 4-4-0s and North Western 4-6-0s. Although in the earlier trials the going had been fairly close, so far as power output was concerned, between the compound and the North Western 'Prince of Wales' 4-6-0, Derby were evidently convinced of the overwhelming superiority of their own engine; and in November 1924 they decided to challenge one of the much larger and heavier 'Claughton' Class 4-6-0s of the LNWR on equal terms—equal, that is, so far as haulage tasks set to the competing locomotives were concerned.

On paper, the trials seemed unequal from the start, for whereas in the earlier series, in 1923-4, the engines engaged were all Class '4', in the November and December trials of 1924 the compounds were matched against a Class '5' 4-6-0 and a Class '3' 4-4-0 simple from the Caledonian. Events contrived to make the trials unequal in other respects too.

As in the previous trials, the trains concerned were to be the 12.10 pm from Carlisle to Leeds and the 4.3 pm down. Since the time of the first series, the latter train had been retimed to include a stop at Hellifield. The engines and men concerned were based on Durran Hill shed, Carlisle, and this introduced a factor that in November 1924 considerably affected the results and led to a lot of wrong conclusions being drawn. The West Coast Main Line, despite the introduction of a number of new Lancashire and Yorkshire four-cylinder 4-6-0s, was very short of engine power. The LMSR authorities had reduced drastically the maximum tonnages that could be taken unassisted, not only over Shap, but throughout between Euston and Carlisle. The result was an enormous amount of double heading and a consequent shortage of engines. The North Western shed at Carlisle could not spare a 'Claughton' for trials over the Midland line to Leeds, so Edge Hill shed was instructed to transfer one of its own stud. Whether the shedmaster was told why, I cannot say, although from subsequent events I very much doubt it.

When one shed is instructed to part with one of its engines to another depot, it is no more than human nature to send the worst that will comply with the instructions, and on 19 November Edge Hill transferred No 2221 *Sir Francis Dent*. This engine had been out-shopped at Crewe in July 1924 after a general repair. It was then worked hard, for those days, averaging 6,000 miles a month, before it was sent to Carlisle. The driver and fireman who were to work it in the trials made two return trips with it from Carlisle to Leeds in the following week, and then on 2 December came the first of the dynamometer car trials. The Caledonian engine was completely outclassed and apparently one return trip was enough to show that she was not up to the haulage of 300-ton trains, let alone anything heavier. The 'Claughton' steamed badly throughout, and although the engine had sufficient reserve of power for the driver to work these trains to time, the record of coal consumption suffered in consequence, and the results were not representative of the class as a whole. It will be seen, however, that three different compounds were used at different times, two being of the new short-chimneyed series, and one a standard Derby 7-ft superheater engine. The latter, engine No 1023, far from emulating the work of her sister engine No 1008, put up a consistently shocking performance on the banks. Against a schedule of 67 minutes from

Up West Coast express soon after the Grouping passing Lancaster, hauled by four-cylinder 4-6-0 No 695 Sir Arthur Lawley *('Claughton' Class) (Real Photos Co).*

Carlisle to Aisgill, she took 76 min 49 sec on her first trip with 350 tons, and 74 min 55 sec on the second; these efforts were followed up by losses of roughly another minute in each case from Aisgill to Blea Moor, thus totalling losses of 11 minutes and 9 minutes from Carlisle to Blea Moor. Against these totals by No 1023 of 89 min 47 sec, and 87 min 53 sec engine No 1008 a year earlier had made times of 76 min 54 sec, 78 min 59 sec, 79 min 36 sec and 79 min 54 sec on the four runs she made with 350-ton trains. The coal consumption figures obtained with engine No 1023 are not quoted herewith because she was in effect running to a slower schedule.

Before passing on to the trial runs made between Preston and Carlisle in 1925, I must refer back in detail to two of the runs made by engine No 1008 in December 1923, because they probably represent the finest all-round performances ever achieved with the true Midland compounds. The logs are tabulated herewith, and some notes on the working follow. There is a gruelling start out of Carlisle, with 6 miles out of the first 8.4 inclined at 1 in 133, and in such conditions it was astonishing work, by previous Midland standards, to pass Low House Box in 15¼ minutes with a load not far short of 400 tons gross behind the tender. Then came the sharply undulating length on the wooded hillsides above the River Eden, where it makes so picturesque a course deep in the rocky gorges of Armathwaite and Barons Wood. Even with such hammering as was meted out to No 1008 she could not, even with the 300-ton load, keep the sectional time to Lazonby, but on the downhill stretch to Lazonby itself, and on the gradual rise to Long Marton, the initial loss of time was recovered—in fact, on the second trip, with the heav-

LMSR: 12.01 pm Carlisle-Leeds

Engine 4-4-0 Compound No 1008

Date			17 December 1923		18 December 1923	
Loads empty/full (tons)			306/320		355/370	
Distance (miles)		**Schedule** time (min)	**Actual** time (m s)	**Speeds** (mph)	**Actual** time (m s)	**Speeds** (mph)
0.0	CARLISLE	0	0 00	—	0 00	—
2.7	Scotby		6 23	32¼	6 15	31
—			—	41½	—	42
8.4	*Low House*		15 42	34	15 40	37½
13.5	*Summit*		21 19	50	21 08	53
15.4	Lazonby	21	23 19	66	22 51	69½
19.8	Langwathby		27 36	51	26 47	56½
23.4	Culgaith		30 53	59½	30 38	64½
27.9	Long Marton		36 05	64½	34 51	63½
30.8	APPLEBY	39	39 00	55½	37 51	52½
33.2	Ormside		41 19	69½	40 20	64½
36.5	*Top of 1 in 100*		45 12	42½	44 39	37
38.3	Crosby Garrett		47 30	50	47 13	47
41.5	Kirkby Stephen		51 46	38	51 45	35
44.8	*Mallerstang*		57 23	32	58 03	27
			—	41	—	37½
48.3	Aisgill	68	63 03	32	64 35	27
51.4	Hawes Junc		66 47	61	68 21	62½
59.5	*Blea Moor*	80	75 20	55	76 58	53
73.5	*Settle Junc*	93	86 58	78*	89 14	76*
			sigs		sigs	
76.8	HELLIFIELD	97	90 13	—	92 21	
—			—	63½	—	61
86.8	SKIPTON	109	102 48	—	105 48	—
—			sigs		sigs	
102.1	Shipley (Bingley Junc)	129	126 55		126 19	
—			—	63½	—	65
113.0	LEEDS	143	140 24		139 40	

*Max speed between Blea Moor and Settle Junction

ier train, the crew of No 1008 were substantially improving on their efforts of the previous day.

Then, after the welcome respite afforded by the falling gradients from Appleby to Ormside viaduct, there comes the main ascent. There is 15 miles of it, though it certainly does include two appreciable breaks in the climbing. From a point near Griseburn signal box, the 1 in 100 eases to 1 in 162, and this further eases to the crossing of Smardale viaduct, near Crosby Garrett. Then comes the worst pitch, a solid 5 miles of 1 in 100 through the wildest of moorland and mountain country, till Mallerstang Box is neared. The speed usually falls to its lowest figure anywhere on the ascent from Carlisle at the south end of Birkett tunnel, and at this point there is the welcome ¾ mile at 1 in 302 past Mallerstang before entering upon the final 3 miles at 1 in 100 up to Aisgill summit.

Magnificent though the work of No 1008 was on her second trip, one could hardly expect her to maintain the lead over the 300-ton run in arduous mountain conditions, and the 350-ton trip had dropped down to level going at Kirkby Stephen, and fell behind to the extent of 1½ minutes at Aisgill summit. Even so, on a schedule planned for a 260-ton maximum load, they were 3½ minutes early passing the summit, with a 370-ton train. There was some brisk running down to Settle Junction on both trips, but by that time the train was close on the tail of the preceding express from Glasgow to St Pancras, and signal checks prevented the making of any further fast time.

The test results obtained successively with engines 1008, 1065 and 1066 over the Settle and Carlisle line had justifiably put Derby 'on top of the world' so far as engine performance on the LMSR was concerned, and with the North Western people disappointed and dispirited it was the Midland that was definitely stealing the honours in a way that its most fervent admirers would scarcely have believed two years earlier. One wonders, indeed, if the astonishingly successful performance of the superheated compounds between Leeds and Carlisle had not taken Derby itself by surprise. But in any case, the prowess of the compounds fitted in so completely with the Midland idea of train operating, as envisaged for the entire LMSR system, that it was eventually to place the locomotives in a role for which the Chief Mechanical Engineer was not prepared to back them. From being most carefully nurtured 'pets', they seemed likely to become the strenuously used maids-of-all-work for the whole line.

The prelude to their general introduction on the North Western main line, and their simultaneous invasion of Scotland, was a little publicized but very important series of dynamometer car trials between Preston and Carlisle, held in May 1925. There are two reasons why this event almost completely escaped attention in the railway press of the day: first, that the tests were carried out on special trains of empty stock, and were run at times when travellers by ordinary Anglo-Scottish expresses were unlikely to see the 'specials'; and secondly, the tests took place in the fortnight immediately following the great interchange trials between the LNER 'Pacifics' and the Great

Left *One of the standard Midland compound 4-4-0s No 1167 on an up 2-hour Birmingham express at Castlethorpe troughs* (Author's Collection).

Below right *The Midland 'magnum opus', the four-cylinder 0-10-0 No 2290 built in 1919 by Sir Henry Fowler. Only one engine of this design was ever built, and the principal task of assisting trains up the Lickey Incline still continued to be fulfilled by 0-6-0 tank engines used in multiple.*

Western 'Castles'. The latter event had attracted the attention of vast numbers of railway enthusiasts, many of whom spent days of their annual leave travelling behind the rival engines.

It is thus not altogether surprising after the attention that had been given to the contest of giants farther south, that this purely domestic affair in the Westmorland hills, of which no advance information had leaked out, remained almost completely unknown. I have seen, many years afterwards, some oblique references to the results, which rather indicate that this particular set of trials was being confused with a series that took place in 1922 between Crewe and Carlisle, when Lancashire and Yorkshire and London and North Western engines were involved.

In May 1925, four locomotives were tested: a Lancashire and Yorkshire Hughes rebuilt 4-6-0, known as Class '8'; London and North Western 4-6-0s of both the 'Prince of Wales' and 'Claughton' Classes; and a Midland compound. In 1926, a Caledonian Pickersgill 4-6-0 of the '60' Class was put through the same set of tests in identical conditions of loading. So far as the rivals of the compounds were concerned, there was no mistake about the North Western engines this time, and a 'Claughton' in excellent 'nick' was put on to the job. The choice of a compound fell once again upon No 1065, which by that time had amassed a mileage of 28,063 since new out of Derby. At the time of the Preston-Carlisle trials of May 1925 she had run a little over 10,000 miles since her cylinders had been lined up to 19-in and 21-in diameter. The two Class '4' engines—the 'Prince of Wales' and the compound—ran two return trips from Carlisle to Preston and back with 300- and 350-ton trains, the two Class '5' engines ran similar tests with 350- and 400-ton trains. As on the Settle and Carlisle line, the 'specials' were timed to the same schedules as the fastest ordinary expresses of that period over the route, namely 114 minutes for the 90 miles southbound, and 103 minutes for the northbound trip.

The enginemen chosen for this job all belonged to Carlisle. The compound was worked by Durran Hill men, who had learned the road to Preston previous to the tests; but, according to the report, engine No 1065 had never been over the route before. This, of course, was of no consequence providing that her driver knew the road sufficiently well to run with confidence. The conditions laid down were that each engine should take its load without assistance, and that every effort should be made to conform to the working times allowed throughout the run, especially between Carlisle and Shap Summit on the outward trip and between Preston and Shap Summit on the return. There is no doubt, however, that the four engine crews concerned entered into the spirit of things in such a way as to make something of a sporting contest of it. The North Western man on the Horwich 4-6-0 did some very spectacular hill-climbing on certain trips, rather confusing the issue by getting well ahead of time, though he paid the penalty in overtaxing the capacity of either his boiler or his fireman—or both—and in heavy coal consumption.

The compound, No 1065, ran true to the magnificent form one had come to expect from this engine, though in the tests with 350-ton trains her actual coal consumption in pounds per mile exceeded that of the North Western 'Claughton'. This was indeed a reversal of events from November 1924, but the latter engine, No 30 *Thalaba*, was clearly driven and fired with great skill and enthusiasm.

When it came to comparing the coal consumption in relation to actual work done, in the coal burnt per drawbar horsepower hour, the compound once again came out on top, as follows:

300-ton trains	Coal per dhp hr (lb)
'Prince of Wales' 4-6-0	5.10
Compound No 1065	4.29

350-ton trains	
'Prince of Wales' 4-6-0	5.05
Compound No 1065	4.25
Horwich 4-6-0	5.07
'Claughton' 4-6-0	4.78

The coal consumption figures for the compound confirm the exceptional nature of the results obtained on some of the runs with engine No 1008 in the first set of trials, and the overall figures for the complete series are appended, neglecting those with the ineffective 1023.

Engine No	Route	Load (tons tare)	Coal per dhp hr (lb)
1008	Leeds-Carlisle	220	4.22
1008	,,	230	4.50
1008	,,	250	3.94
1008	,,	300	3.80
1008	,,	300	4.02
1008	,,	350	3.78
1008	,,	350	4.20
1008	,,	350	3.71
1008	,,	350	3.80
1065	,,	300	4.46
1065	,,	300	4.39
1065	,,	350	4.33
1065	,,	350	4.45
1066	,,	300	4.68
1066	,,	350	4.48
1060	,,	300	4.72
1060	,,	300	4.65
1060	,,	350	4.47
1065	,,	300	4.22
1065	,,	300	4.18
1065	,,	350	4.15
1065	Preston-Carlisle	300	4.29
1065	Preston-Carlisle	350	4.25

About the time that the Preston-Carlisle trials ended, Hughes himself retired, and was succeeded by Sir Henry Fowler. CME headquarters was moved from Horwich to Derby, and the design staff there became doubly immersed in plans for bigger and better compounds, even up to a 'Pacific'. The Operating Department was not impressed by the prospect, and neither were the ex-North Western men. There grew up, indeed, a kind of unholy alliance between the West Coast running men and the 'old guard' of Midland operating men, who for some reason had a rooted objection to the 'Pacific' type. Then, in January 1926 at a meeting of the Graduates Section of the Institution of Mechanical Engineers, one of Sir Henry Fowler's former pupils, E.L. Diamond, read a most scholarly paper, 'An investigation into the cylinder

Left *The larger-boilered Somerset and Dorset 2-8-0, of which five were built by Robert Stephenson & Co in 1925. These, and the smaller boilered variety introduced in 1914, were essentially freight engines; but in the peak holiday traffic that developed after nationalisation they were regularly used for Saturday special trains, taking loads of ten coaches over the Mendips without assistance. The 'Black Five' 4-6-0s and the Southern Bulleid 4-6-2s were limited to a maximum of eight* (British Railways).

Left *The post-Grouping development of the Midland '2P' 4-4-0 with 6-ft 9-in coupled wheels, introduced in 1928* (British Railways).

Below *The Fowler 2-6-4 tank engine as originally built in 1927 and painted Midland red. A total of 95 of this type were built, followed by thirty more with side-windowed cabs* (British Railways).

losses in a compound locomotive'. This related to the working of 4-4-0 engine No 1065 on the Leeds-Carlisle route in February 1925, and the paper was notable not only for its content but also for the distinguished audience, including Sir Henry himself, and for the remarkably comprehensive written discussion that followed. I fancy, however, it was the trenchant phrasing of Diamond's peroration that really made Fowler sit up:

'Perhaps the most important fact of all those set forth is that in the cylinders of the locomotive under investigation which is known to be of high efficiency, the total losses due to restricted passages given to the steam at admission and exhaust increase from 17.6 per cent at 24 miles an hour to no less than 67.6 per cent at 68 miles an hour, of which probably not more than 15 per cent is necessary for the production of draught; that is to say, an amount of power equal to half the work that is actually being exerted on the train is wasted in throttling losses at this speed. In view of this fact the Author unhesitatingly recommends the universal adoption for compound as well as simple-expansion locomotives of the long-lap valves by means of which the port opening to steam at admission and exhaust can be materially improved.'

After the meeting, Fowler asked if he might borrow the script of the paper, and he took it back to Derby next morning. The design for the new 2-6-4 tank engine of the '2300' Class was then on the drawing boards, and he told the Chief Draughtsman, Herbert Chambers, to scrap the valve gear and modify it to Diamond's recommendations, with the happy result told in a later chapter of this book. Meanwhile, a most distinguished contributor to the written discussion on the paper was Monsieur A. Bréville, L'Ingénieur en Chef du Matériel et de la Traction of the Northern Railway of France. He, as the designer of the brilliantly successful post-war 'Super Pacifics' of that railway, sent a fascinating account of tests they had made, not only with his own engines, but with the 'Pacifics' and 'Atlantics' of his predecessors. Fowler was nothing if not a copyist, and from the 'grape-vine' it was learned that the super-LMS compound was to be based on the principles of de Glehn rather than of Smith-Deeley. The 'unholy alliance' had got to work fast. Unknown to Derby, the Crewe drawing office had prepared a design for an improved 'Claughton' with a larger boiler, which could go into production at short notice, while the big guns of the Operating Department succeeded in impressing the Chairman to such an extent that Sir Henry Fowler was instructed to stop all work on the compound 'Pacific'. It was certainly not too soon, for the frames for the first two engines had already been cut at Derby. The sequels to these moves were as unexpected as they were eventually far-reaching.

16. The 'Royal Scots': origin and development

In the early autumn of 1926, two giants of the British railway world met for a private luncheon party: Sir Guy Granet, Chairman of the LMS, and Sir Felix Pole, General Manager of the Great Western. How their conversation ranged is the purest conjecture, but one may be fairly sure that Sir Guy confided to his companion something of the bitter internal dissensions with which the locomotive department of the LMS was racked at that time. Granet's immense strength of character and breadth of outlook strode far beyond any partisanship remaining from pre-Grouping days, staunchly Midland as he had always hitherto been. The situation in 1926 had become far more serious than any old-fashioned inter-railway rivalry. On hearing of the immediate locomotive crisis on the LMS, it is not hard to imagine Pole, that most ardent of Great Western propagandists, saying, 'Well, try one of ours.' However, when it was arranged for GWR 4-6-0 No 5000 *Launceston Castle* to make a number of experimental runs over the West Coast Main Line between Euston and Carlisle, the CME's department at Derby took it as a *coup d'état* on the part of the senior men of the Operating Department, and at first took a very poor view of it.

As a man of such high professional status and scientific attainments, it was an affront to Sir Henry Fowler, and a man of more volatile temperament would have resigned forthwith. He had been told to stop work on a major project which had previously been authorized, and to arrange for the testing of a foreign engine, the loan of which had been arranged largely behind his back. As expected, *Launceston Castle* did very well on LMS metals until on her very last trip north to Carlisle when she encountered such a storm of wind and rain north of Lancaster that the standard GWR sanding gear was virtually useless, and a good deal of time was lost through slipping on the steep gradients. To those without any partisan leanings, the work of the Great Western engine, both at the time and retrospectively, would have been applauded more wholeheartedly had it not been for the unfavourable and often inaccurate comparisons made to locomotive work done over the route by London and North Western engines, and the fact that some people who were in a position to have access to the dynamometer car records should subsequently have made assertions that were just not true. In a paper presented to no less authoritative a body than the Institution of Locomotive Engineers, for example, in reference to the experimental running of the

GWR 4-6-0 No 5000 *Launceston Castle,* it was stated: 'The GWR engine performed with quiet mastery all the work on which the 'Claughtons' lost time, dropped their steam pressure, and made the welkin ring with their reverberating exhaust'. The speaker was a Horwich man and possibly had some partisan feelings; but one had only to go back 18 months to find data to cast into his teeth his further assertion that 'so far in advance was the performance over anything yet seen on LMS metals, that a profound impression was made'. I cannot resist setting alongside the details of the best run *Launceston Castle* made between Crewe and Carlisle the uphill performance of *Thalaba* in May 1925, with a 400-ton train, thus:

Engine No	5000	30
Engine name	*Launceston Castle*	*Thalaba*
Load (tons)	415	395

Distance (miles)		Actual time* (m s)	Actual time* (m s)
0.0	Carnforth	0 00	0 00
12.8	Oxenholme	13 50	14 18
19.9	Grayrigg	26 20	25 39
25.9	Tebay	33 00	32 32
31.4	Shap Summit	43 00	41 29
Minimum speeds (mph)			
	Grayrigg	26½	34
	Shap Summit	20	28½
Average speed (mph)			
	Oxenholme-Grayrigg	34	37½

*Times from passing Carnforth at 65 mph

The upshot of the 'Castle' running was that Fowler was instructed to get fifty 4-6-0 engines of comparable power built for the summer traffic of 1927 — *fifty!* The last of the dynamometer car trials, those between Crewe and Carlisle, were not completed until 20 November, and the five weeks between then and Christmas were ones of the most feverish activity. None of the railway workshops was in a position to build fifty locomotives of such dimensions, and of an entirely new design, in the time originally stipulated, and there was no cohesion in the locomotive department of the LMS that would have allowed the design to be shared out between establishments like Crewe,

Derby, Horwich and St Rollox, as was done with the new BR standard locomotives from 1948 onwards — one doing the boiler, another the frames, and so on. The job had to be put out to contract, but at mid-November 1926 no one knew what the new engines were to be like.

An immediate approach was made to the Great Western asking if Swindon could build fifty 'Castles' at once, and when this was refused, negotiations were opened with the North British Locomotive Company, whose vast experience and massive design potential held out the best prospects. Again, the Great Western was asked to furnish drawings of the 'Castle', and again the request was refused. While the Operating Department of the LMS had by that time specified that it wanted a 4-6-0 of comparable tractive power to a 'Castle' but with only three cylinders, to minimize the amount of machinery between the frames, the headquarters drawing office at Derby had little or nothing to assist the probable contractors in preparation of a quotation for the job. After the 'Castle', the nearest English equivalent to the desired locomotive was the Southern Railway 4-6-0 No E850 *Lord Nelson,* then brand new and so far the only one of its class. An appeal was made to R.E.L. Maunsell, which met with more success than the previous one to Swindon. H. Chambers, the chief locomotive draughtsman of the LMS, went to Waterloo and had discussions with Clayton and Holcroft, and a com-

plete set of drawings of *Lord Nelson* was sent post-haste to Glasgow. It is amusing to recall that in contemporary LMS internal correspondence, the new engines were referred to as 'Improved Castles'.

The North British Locomotive Company must have worked like lightning, because on 7 December 1926, less than a month after the end of the *Launceston Castle* trials, the firm submitted its quotation. Construction was to be shared between the Hyde Park and the Queen's Park Works, 25 to each; delivery was to commence 25 weeks after acceptance of the quotation, and to be completed in 35 weeks. The contract price was £7,725 per engine, a total of £193,125 to each works. The quotation was accepted on 23 December 1926, and then the race was on! So far as basic design was concerned, despite the availability of the Southern drawings and the brief running experience with the 'Castle', the new engines could be described as neo-Derby, but they were very far from a mere enlargement of the Midland compound, with the long-travel valves that had proved so successful on the 2-6-4 tanks of the '2300' Class. Because of the holidays at Christmas and New Year, the orders were not placed at the two works until 7 January 1927, and 25 weeks from then brought the promised delivery date for the first engines to 2 July, just a week before the summer service was to come into operation; but in the event things did not work out quite so expeditiously.

The locomotive building programme for 1927 announced in February included this item: '50 4-6-0 locomotives of a new design intended for dealing with heavy fast passenger traffic between Euston and Scotland'. After that, a great silence descended, and

The 'Royal Scot' in its first summer, before the new engines were ready, passing Tring southbound with 'George the Fifth' Class 4-4-0 No 5384 S.R. Graves and unnamed 'Claughton' No 5958 (Rail Archive Stephenson, photo F.R. Hebron).

The 'Royal Scot' in the first summer, northbound near Burton and Holme, hauled by two Polmadie compounds, Nos 900 and 903 (Rail Archive Stephenson, photo F.R. Hebron).

Engine No 6100 Royal Scot posed for the official picture at Queen's Park Works, Glasgow. This was not the actual first engine, which had been sent to London unnamed for the official inspection (British Railways).

Engine No 6126, newly arrived from Glasgow Hyde Park Works in 1927 at Crewe (British Railways).

when on the approach to the summer service, which was to come into operation on 11 July, it was announced that the morning express from Euston to Glasgow and Edinburgh was to be named 'The Royal Scot', nobody apparently knew what was going to haul it. For the first time in the history of the service, it was to be limited to through passengers only, and the only intermediate stops were to change engines at Carnforth and to detach the Edinburgh portion of the train at Symington. With a tare load of 417 tons it had to be double-headed throughout, by a 'Claughton' and a superheated 'Precursor' on the first stage, and by two Midland compounds north of Carnforth. The first of the new 4-6-0s was not delivered to Derby until 14 July. It was then unnamed, and it remained so when it made its first bow, to the directors, the press, and the public, at Euston. It was another three weeks before any further engines of the class were delivered from Glasgow.

One's first impressions of the new engines were of the gigantic girth of the boiler, and of the almost non-existent chimney. Even a Gresley 'Pacific' had a slender look compared with No 6100. Although of such massive appearance, the engine was handsomely proportioned, the tender, wholly in the Midland style, was much narrower than the locomotive. The tenders were in fact of the standard 3,500-gallon LMS type, carrying 5½ tons of coal, and while the engine cab was built out almost to the maximum width of 8 ft 7 in over the platform, the width of the tender body was only 7 ft 2 in. How disconcerting this could be to a visitor I discovered when I made my first footplate journeys on these engines.

Before passing on to a detailed discussion of the design, I must speak in warm praise of the men who carried it through. Even with the huge organization, wealth of experience and manufacturing facilities of the North British Locomotive Company, it was no small achievement to have the first engine in steam in 25 weeks from the placing of the orders at the works, and that included all the detailed drawing office work, too. Herbert Chambers, chief locomotive draughtsman at Derby headquarters, acted as liaison, and laid down the basic features of the design, with the overall requirement of a three-cylinder 4-6-0 with a nominal tractive capacity roughly equal to that of a Great Western 'Castle'. As things turned out, the working of the Euston-Carlisle non-stops, with gross loads of about 440 tons, was a task considerably more arduous than anything then required of Great Western engines. In the trials of 1926 that created such a favourable impression on the LMS, *Launceston Castle* was not required to make any non-stop runs longer than 158 miles.

In the records of the North British Locomotive Company, the order for the fifty locomotive engines is shown as having been received on Christmas Day 1926, and details of the allocation to the two works, dated 27 December, are shown on the relevant sheets from the order book. One notes that they are specified as having the Midland type of superheater, while it was not until 5 May 1927 that they became known as the 'Royal Scot' Class. Furthermore, NBL was not notified of the names that the locomotives were to bear until 18 January 1928, presumably to enable the nameplates to be made. The last of the fifty locomotive engines had actually been delivered two months previously. The leading dimensions and general proportions of the engines can be appreciated from the accompanying table:

'Royal Scot' Class: leading dimensions

Boiler		
Barrel, outside diameter (ft in)	5	9
Tubes, small		
Number		180
Outside diameter (in)		2
Superheater flues		
Number		27
Outside diameter (in)		5⅛
Length between tube plates (ft in)	14	6
Heating surfaces (sq ft)		
Small tubes		1,892
Superheater flues		
Firebox		189
Superheater elements		416
Combined total		2,497
Grate area (sq ft)		31.2
Cylinders (three)		
Diameter (in)		18
Stroke (in)		26
Motion (Walschaerts)		
Piston valves, diameter (in)		9
Max valve travel (in)		
Outside cylinders		$6^{13}/_{32}$
Inside cylinders		$6^{3}/_{16}$
Steam lap (in)		$1^{7}/_{16}$
Exhaust clearance		nil
Lead (in)		¼
Cut-off in full gear (per cent)		75
Tractive effort at 85% working pressure (lb)		33,150
Factor of adhesion		
$\dfrac{\text{Adhesion weight}}{\text{Tractive effort}}$		4.22

A very important feature is the design of the motion which, as the tabulated particulars show, provides for a maximum valve travel of $6^{3}/_{16}$ in in full gear, and a steam lap of $1^{7}/_{16}$ in. Another important fea-

Left *The first 'Royal Scot' Class 4-6-0 No 6100, as yet unnamed and ready for the first inspection at Euston* (Loco Publishing Co).

Left *'Royal Scot' Class No 6100 dressed up for the North American tour. The engine actually used on the tour was originally No 6152* (British Railways).

Below right *Engine No 6116* Irish Guardsman *passes Tring with the up 'Royal Scot' in June 1928* (Rail Archive Stephenson, photo F.R. Hebron).

ture was the large diameter of piston valve, 9 in, in relation to cylinder diameter, with consequent large ports and their contribution to a free-running engine. The great advantage of this characteristic had been appreciated from the astonishing speedworthiness of the 2-6-4 tank engines of the '2300' Class which were the first Derby-designed engines to have long-lap, long-travel valves.

The design of the boiler and firebox shows clearly the influence of *Lord Nelson*. The diameters of the small tubes, superheater flues and superheater elements were the same. In the barrel, the 'Royal Scot' was slightly longer between the tube plates, 14 ft 6 in as against 14 ft 2 in, and there were 180 small tubes against 173, but the shapes of the fireboxes were practically identical. Structurally, of course, the 'Royal Scot' boiler had to be designed to carry the higher working pressure of 250 psi. The 'Nelson' had

the Maunsell superheater; on the 'Scot', what was referred to in the specification as the 'Midland' type of superheater was the Derby version of the Schmidt. After the boiler barrel and the firebox, any resemblance between the 'Scot' and the 'Nelson' ceased.

Apart from the basic layout of the machinery, which was soundly and robustly designed, the engines had initially certain Midland specialities like the Fowler and Anderson bypass valves on the cylinders, and brakes on the bogie wheels, both of which were subsequently taken off. Standard Midland practice was also perpetuated in the use of the Schmidt type of piston ring, a single wide one originating from the pre-war German design, but without the elaboration and complication of trick ports, as used in contemporary Crewe designs. Taken all round, the 'Royal Scot' was an excellent design, made all the more notable by the circumstances in which it originated, and the speed of production. Comparisons may be odious, but even to the compiler of logs from the confines of the passenger accommodation of trains, it seemed evident that the 'Scots' had got the edge on the 'Nelsons', although in the early days there were times when the acoustics of their going suggested that they were not being handled to the best advantage.

The introduction of the record non-stop schedules between Euston and Carlisle in September 1927 was marked by a tremendous burst of publicity and, may I add, 'ballyhoo'. On the inaugural day, 26 September, J.H. Follows, who under the reorganization of the top echelons of the Company had been made a Vice-President, addressed a number of press representatives in the late afternoon of that day, and then they accompanied him to the station to witness the arrival of the up 'Royal Scot', which, hauled by engine No 6104, obligingly came in 3 minutes early. Then, of course, there were photographs of Follows shaking hands with the Carlisle driver, who at that time did not know the road south of Crewe well enough to go on his own and had a road pilot. In the crowd around the engine at Euston, however, I did not recognize a single member of the Chief Mechanical Engineer's Department. It was a party for the Operators. Sir Henry Fowler came into it towards the end of October when a series of dynamometer trials were run with engine No 6100. He was then President of the Institution of Mechanical Engineers, and on 16 December of that same year he took the opportunity of a paper by the distinguished American engineer, Lawford H. Fry, 'Some Experimental Results from a Three Cylinder Compound Locomotive'—a giant of the 4-10-2 type—to broadcast, from the Chair, an elaborate summary of

the LMS tests on the 'Royal Scot'. The results were extraordinarily good, some even better than the 'Castle' figure of 2.83 lb dhp hour which had set the Horwich heather on fire in 1924. Actually, the 'Royal Scot' figures were not quite as good as they looked, because it was afterwards revealed that the recording apparatus in the Horwich dynamometer car was not reading accurately, and the total of horsepower hours was not as large as recorded.

However, the glory in which the 'Royal Scots' originally took the road did not last long. It was soon evident that the dynamometer car test results obtained with No 6100 in the late autumn of 1927 were not representative of the sustained performance of the class as a whole. It was supremely fortunate that the introduction of the class coincided so closely with the installation of the late Lord Stamp as President of the Executive of the LMS. As a master statistician, he quickly appreciated that the locomotive department was one of the biggest spenders on the railway. It was spending about £3 million a year on repairs, to say nothing of the coal bill, and he wanted to know where the money was going. So there was instituted the system of individual costing, to see how much money was spent on each locomotive. Compared to previous practice it might have seemed like bureaucracy run mad, but in fact it proved a magnificent tool of management. But for its introduction, the 'Royal Scots' might well have passed into the realm of engines that showed a deterioration in performance with advanced age, and superficial observers could have glibly attributed it vaguely to senility, which they had a habit of doing with other engine classes—not by any means all of them on the LMS.

The 'Royal Scots' very soon began to show an

The up 'Royal Scot' leaving Carlisle hauled by No 6139 Ajax (Rail Archive Stephenson, photo F.R. Hebron).

alarming increase in coal consumption. In the ordinary way this might have passed by the running department, or been acknowledged as just one of those things, had the working diagrams been those of LNWR and Caledonian days, and the longest continuous runs those between Euston and Liverpool. But with Euston-Carlisle non-stops, and other runs between Crewe and Glasgow, and some between Crewe and Perth, it was a very different matter. With those small tenders there was a definite risk of running short of coal, and many of my earlier experiences with the 'Royal Scots', when travelling as a passenger, while beginning well, showed a marked falling-off in the effort towards the end of the journey. I remember particularly a run on the up 'Midday Scot', when we were worked from Glasgow to Crewe by No 6123 *Royal Irish Fusilier*. The load was progressively increased from the initial 265 tons from Glasgow to 395 from Symington, and finally to 475 tons after the Stranraer coaches had been added at Carlisle, and the whole run bore unmistakable evidence of the need to save coal wherever possible. The uphill work was slow, but downhill the driver let the engine go for all it was worth. Speed fell, for example, to 28¾ mph at Beattock summit, and a clear 4½ minutes were lost from Carlisle to Shap. Equally, no higher speed than 58 mph on the level between Lancaster and Preston was indifferent work with the train falling behind time.

Going north, one of the Polmadie men on No 6128 had begun quite brilliantly out of Crewe with the 'Midday Scot', again with a 475-ton load, passing Preston in 54½ minutes and reaching Lancaster in 81½ minutes (72 miles), or 79 minutes net allowing for three slight checks. The crew did no more than hold their own onwards to Carlisle, although the train was running late, and did poorly on to Carstairs; they lost time to Beattock, stopping there for a banking-engine, and passed the summit in 72½ minutes instead of the 67 minutes scheduled from Carlisle. The train then ran very feebly downhill, eventually taking 96¾ minutes to Carstairs. Furthermore, it was not only on the lengthy double-home turns that the 'Scots' were disappointing. No 6103, leaving Euston 10 minutes late one evening with the 5.20 pm down with a load of 345 tons, did no better than keep booked point-to-point times to Crewe, and it was left to the 'Claughton' that took over there to regain something of the loss onwards to Preston. When loads were not much over 400 tons, many drivers of that period preferred to have a 'Claughton' rather than a 'Scot', while acknowledging that they needed the bigger engines for heavier loads.

The reasons for this disturbing increase in coal consumption with increasing mileage were sought with diligence and skill. In some cases, the increase was nearly 80 per cent which would mean consumptions of something like 70 lb of coal per train mile on the hardest duties. No wonder the drivers were skimping and saving wherever they could, when supplies were limited by those small tenders. It was through systematic and scientific testing that the Schmidt type of wide piston ring was found to be the villain of the piece. With moderate steam pressures and light usage, its bad effect, with increasing wear, had not been readily discernible on Midland engines. However, a boiler pressure of 250 psi, and the work that the 'Scots' had to do, caused excessive leakage past the rings when wear began to take effect, and this was largely responsible for the inordinate increase in coal consumption. One engine had the original valve heads and Schmidt rings replaced by solid valve heads and six narrow rings, and on the same duties the coal consumption was brought down from 70 to 35 lb per mile! The revised arrangement thereafter became standard. The average consumption for the whole class including lighting-up, stand-by, and all else for the first six years of its existence showed clearly how things were improved by this change in the valve design.

During the winter of 1927-8, the Euston-Carlisle non-stop runs with a 15-coach train, and the need to run a second train in the down direction carrying the Aberdeen portion and providing the intermediate service, proved an uneconomic luxury, and there were times when the 10.00 am running non-stop to Carlisle carried fewer than 100 passengers. From the autumn of 1928, the train called additionally at Rugby and Crewe, and carried the Aberdeen por-

The down 'Royal Scot', a 17-coach load, restarting from Oxenholme having attached a pilot for the North Country banks; non-superheated 'Precursor' 4-4-0 No 5263 Oceanic *and 4-6-0 No 6109* Royal Engineer *(Rail Archive Stephenson, photo F.R. Hebron).*

tion to Crewe, where the latter was combined with the Birmingham Scotsman. With the Edinburgh section of 'The Royal Scot' reduced to four coaches, the load became 15 from Euston to Crewe, and 13 onwards to Symington. One engine still worked through from Euston to Carlisle, and with little short of 500 tons gross load from Euston, about 390 tons onward, and sharper point-to-point timing than during the non-stop period, the duty was a severe one, while the locomotives were suffering from their original piston valve design.

The 'Royal Scots' reached their zenith of performance in the years 1934-9. At that time I was travelling a good deal on the West Coast Main Line and I would not have to look beyond my own notebooks to find many runs of superlative quality. Some of the more arduous turns were being taken over by 'Pacifics', but on their normal allocations, and sometimes when deputizing for the 'Princess Royals', the work was unsurpassed by any locomotives of comparable tractive effort in Great Britain. Their work at that time could be divided into four broad categories: the shorter English turns, going no farther from Euston than Crewe, Liverpool, or Manchester; the purely Scottish allocations to and from Carlisle; the difficult double-home turns from Crewe to Glasgow and to Perth; and finally the Euston-Carlisle double-homes, worked on a variety of trains. Mention could also be made of the Irish Mails, worked with one engine throughout between Euston and Holyhead, 263 miles. In terms of distance, these were longer than the Crewe-Glasgow turns, but over an easy road throughout and with easier schedules,

Details of one of the best runs I had on the 6.05 pm are tabulated herewith and relate to the Friday before Whitsun 1935, when the 6.00, 6.05 and 6.10 pm were all running in two parts. The regular 'Merseyside Express' did not have rear-end banking assistance out of Euston, and rarely got anywhere near the initial allowance of nine minutes to Willesden, but after that, as the table shows, we got away in tremendous style, so much so that our driver began sighting adverse distant signals from Boxmoor, and eased up considerably. Our attained speed of 58½ mph on the 1 in 339 from Wembley represented an output of about 1,360 equivalent drawbar horsepower. Good and completely unchecked running followed to Stafford, despite an increasingly strong cross wind, and then there came a remarkable effort on the rising gradient to Whitmore summit. On the 1 in 650 to Standon Bridge, speed rose to 64 mph, equivalent to 1,280 edhp. The train was heavily checked in the approach to Crewe, but a clear road and fast running afterwards gave an arrival 1½ minutes early at Mossley Hill.

LMS: 6.05 pm Euston-Mossley Hill

Engine 'Royal Scot' 4-6-0 No 6142 *Lion*
Load 473 tons tare, 505 tons full

Distance (miles)		Schedule time (min)	Actual time (m s)	Speed (mph)
0.0	EUSTON	0	0 00	No banker
1.0	Milepost 1		3 50	
5.4	WILLESDEN JUNC	9	10 13	56
11.4	Harrow		16 42	54½
14.8	Carpenders Park		20 48	58½
17.5	WATFORD JUNC	22	22 48	
—			eased	—
31.7	Tring	38	38 45	44
46.7	BLETCHLEY	51	51 49	74½/69
52.4	Wolverton		56 33	74½
59.9	Roade	63	63 23	57½
69.7	Weedon		72 42	64½
76.2	*Kilsby Tunnel South*		79 24	54
82.6	RUGBY	89	85 44	slack
91.3	Shilton		95 34	63/61
97.1	NUNEATON	103	100 37	77½
102.4	Atherstone		104 54	69/75
—			pws	47
110.0	TAMWORTH	116	112 49	54/60
116.3	Lichfield		118 47	54
124.3	Rugeley	129	126 40	68
133.6	STAFFORD	139	136 15	35*

Distance (miles)		Schedule time (min)	Actual time (m s)	Speed (mph)
143.4	Standon Bridge		147 02	64
147.6	Whitmore		151 05	60½
153.3	Betley Road		156 07	75
—			signals	—
158.1	CREWE	165	164 00	25*
166.9	*Winsford Junc*	175	173 38	77½
174.3	*Weaver Junc*	182	179 45	54*
177.4	Sutton Weaver		183 31	43½
182.8	Ditton Junc	191	190 10	58
189.6	MOSSLEY HILL	200	198 37	—

Net time 195¾ minutes
*Speed restrictions

The vastly improved, and indeed almost spectacular, running sometimes put up on the Crewe-Glasgow double-home turns could not be better illustrated than by the run of No 6108 *Seaforth Highlander* on the down 'Midday Scot' as tabulated herewith. The start was vigorous, and following the permanent way slack at Kirtlebridge there was a tremendous effort to Beattock summit. The acceleration uphill, on 1 in 200, to 50 mph at Castlemilk summit involved 1,280 edhp, and then came a very fast run from Lockerbie to Wamphray. Having already gained three minutes to Beattock despite the Kirtlebridge slack, there came a remarkable ascent of the bank itself. Speed had fallen to 23½ mph by Greskine box, halfway up, when the driver opened out to make a recovery to 26 mph by Beattock summit. This gave the value of 1,300 edhp, notable at so relatively low a speed.

LMS: Carlisle-Carstairs

Engine No 6108 *Seaforth Highlander*
Load 408 tons tare, 430 tons full

Distance (miles)		Schedule time (min)	Actual time (m s)	Speed (mph)
0.0	CARLISLE	0	0 00	—
4.1	Rockcliffe		6 25	67
8.6	Gretna Junc	11	10 40	—
13.0	Kirkpatrick		15 15	52
16.7	Kirtlebridge	20	19 20	—
—			pws	—
20.1	Ecclefechan		23 37	50
22.7	*Castlemilk Box*		26 40	50
25.8	LOCKERBIE	30	29 25	—
28.7	Nethercleugh		31 40	78
34.5	Wamphray		36 25	—
39.7	BEATTOCK	44	41 00	60
42.3	*Auchencastle*		44 27	—
45.4	*Greskine*		50 40	23½

The down 'Royal Scot' ascending Shap hauled by No 6160 Queen Victoria's Rifleman (O.S. Nock).

Distance (miles)		Schedule time (min)	Actual time (m s)		Speed (mph)
47.8	*Harthope*		56	30	24
49.7	*Beattock summit*	64	61	15	26
52.6	Elvanfoot		64	37	—
57.8	Abington		69	17	—
63.2	Lamington		73	42	79
66.9	SYMINGTON	81	76	45	62/73
73.5	CARSTAIRS	89	83	50	

Net time 82½ minutes

Coal having been one of the major headaches in the first years of the long double-home turns with the 'Royal Scots', some trials were made late in 1934 with the 'Midday Scot' in each direction between Crewe and Glasgow to see what could be done, after the working of the engines had been so greatly improved by the fitting of the modified piston valves. No 6158 *The Loyal Regiment* was driven to maintain schedules that demanded something near to maximum boiler capacity. At that time, the ordinary schedule of the 'Midday Scot' between Symington and Carlisle was 73 minutes, but for these trials it was cut to 64 minutes. In the accompanying table the normal schedule times of the faster 'Royal Scot' train are shown, and the extent to which they were surpassed is impressive. The average speed over the 13.5 miles from Lamington to Beattock summit was 56.2 mph and the average edhp was around 1,250.

Then came a fast descent to Carlisle in which the 43.4 miles between the Greskine and Kingmoor signal boxes were covered in 35 min 27 sec—an average of 74.7 mph. Driver Garrett of Crewe North was responsible for this fine run.

LMS: Symington-Carlisle

Engine No 6158 *The Loyal Regiment*
Load 427 tons tare, 455 tons full

Distance (miles)		*Schedule time (min)	Actual time (m s)		Speeds (mph)
0.0	SYMINGTON	0	0	00	—
3.7	Lamington		5	50	65
9.1	Abington		11	20	56/60
11.6	Crawford		14	05	—
14.3	Elvanfoot		17	00	51/60
17.2	*Summit*	22	20	16	45
21.5	*Greskine*		24	10	—
27.2	BEATTOCK	32	28	30	85
32.4	Wamphray		32	20	69
38.2	Nethercleugh		37	08	74
41.1	LOCKERBIE	45	39	40	—
44.2	*Castlemilk*		42	43	56
46.8	Ecclefechan		45	15	—
50.2	Kirtlebridge	54	48	03	77
53.9	Kirkpatrick		51	13	67
58.3	Gretna Junc	62	54	30	88
62.8	Rockcliffe		57	53	—
64.9	*Kingmoor Box*		59	37	72
—			signals		
66.9	CARLISLE	71	64	05	

*Normal schedule. Test schedule 64 minutes

Engine No 6143, originally named Mail, *here seen as* The South Staffordshire Regiment (British Railways).

Experimental work with Sir Henry Fowler's high-pressure compound 4-6-0 No 6399 *Fury* came to an end with a grievous fatal accident from the bursting of one of the boiler tubes while passing through Carstairs station during a trial run, and for some years the engine languished in the paint shop at Derby. In 1935 it was decided to scrap the original boiler and cylinders, and use the frame and wheels for a new 'Royal Scot', but fitted with a taper boiler. While the rebuilding work was in progress, an interesting investigation was carried out in the drawing office at Crewe into the possibility of this rebuilt engine hauling 400 tons behind the tender at an average speed of 70 mph between Euston and Manchester (or Euston and Liverpool); it was assumed that a non-stop run would be made, in either case. It was concluded that an average of 75 mph would have to be maintained over the 171 miles of road where there were no speed restrictions, and it was estimated that a continuous output of around 2,000 indicated horsepower would be needed. This, it was realized, was far beyond the capacity of a 'Royal Scot' even with the improvements that were planned to be included in the rebuilt engine. Even with the load reduced to 300 tons, the margin of power in hand would be too small for regular working. But the investigation had one interesting side issue in 1939.

One of the most brilliant 'Royal Scot' performances I personally recorded was made not many weeks before the outbreak of war in 1939, on the Edinburgh section of the up 'Royal Scot' non-stop from Carlisle to Euston. On this occasion the weather was perfect, and an 11-coach train of 355 tons would not have proved a very severe task. But from Wigan southwards we got behind a slower train, and were so delayed as to pass Crewe 10½ minutes late. From there we went like the wind, as the accompanying tabulation bears witness. Between Crewe and Willesden we cut the schedule of the 'Liverpool Flyer' by 10 minutes and clocked into Euston exactly on time after an easy run in from Watford. From Stafford for 115 miles the engine was worked at high capacity, averaging 74 mph over the 113.5 miles from Milford to Bushey. Even before that, the effort was eased, because the speed downhill from Tring, usually the fastest stretch of the whole journey, was less than that from Lichfield to Hademore troughs, and from Roade to Castlethorpe.

LMS: Carlisle-Euston, 'The Royal Scot'— Edinburgh portion

Engine No 6132 *The King's Regiment (Liverpool)*, Driver F. Brooker (Camden)
Load 339 tons tare, 355 tons full

Distance (miles)		Schedule time (min)	Actual time (m s)	Speed (mph)
0.0	CARLISLE	0	0 00	—
4.9	Wreay		9 47	40
7.4	Southwaite		13 05	52/50
13.1	Plumpton	19	19 52	60/54
17.9	PENRITH	24	24 48	62½
26.1	*Milepost 43*		34 45	37
29.4	Shap		39 52	47

Distance (miles)		Schedule time (min)	Actual time (m s)	Speed (mph)
31.4	*Summit*	41	42 32	44½
36.9	Tebay	46	47 07	82
42.9	Grayrigg		52 07	66
50.0	OXENHOLME	58	58 12	77
55.5	Milnthorpe		62 11	86½/76
62.8	Carnforth	69	67 39	82
69.1	LANCASTER	74	73 35	60/46
80.6	Garstang	85	84 45	72½
90.1	PRESTON	95	94 50	15
95.6	*Euxton Junc*	102	102 38	54/61½
—			pws	—
105.3	WIGAN	113	113 42	—
—			signals	—
117.0	WARRINGTON	125	129 17	—
—			signals	—
124.9	*Weaver Junc*	133	139 50	—
—			signals	—
141.1	CREWE	148	158 32	—
149.1	Madeley		168 28	53
155.7	Standon Bridge		174 35	79
—			signals	50
165.6	STAFFORD	174	183 27	75/45
169.7	Milford		188 04	66
174.9	Rugeley	183	192 30	80½
182.9	Lichfield	190	198 30	77
189.2	TAMWORTH	195	203 07	86½
196.9	Atherstone		209 05	73/81
202.1	NUNEATON	207	213 07	77½
205.7	Bulkington		216 09	70½
211.1	Brinklow		220 28	81
216.6	RUGBY	222	225 18	38*
220.4	*Kilsby Tunnel North*		229 58	56
229.5	Weedon		237 46	83½
236.4	Blisworth	240	242 56	79
239.3	Roade		245 16	72½
244.4	Castlethorpe		248 58	88
252.5	BLETCHLEY	254	255 02	76/79
259.0	Leighton Buzzard		260 12	74
267.5	Tring	268	267 36	64
274.7	Hemel Hempstead		273 31	82
281.7	WATFORD JUNC	280	278 50	77½
283.2	Bushey		280 03	72½
—			eased	
287.8	Harrow		284 42	56
293.8	WILLESDEN JUNC	291	290 27	69
296.8	South Hampstead		293 18	—
299.2	EUSTON	299	298 33	—

The investigation regarding the proposed acceleration of the Manchester service had one side-thrust

as a result of the examination of the data of this run. It is the effort over the 32.9 miles from Rugeley to Brinklow that on analysis appears so outstanding. There the average speed was 77.2 mph against a slight rising gradient averaging 1 in 1,600 over the 32.8 miles. Over this stretch the engine appears to have been developing an average of about 1,810-1,820 indicated horsepower, while some individual readings give the following:

Speed (mph)	Gradient (1 in)	Equivalent dhp	Estimated ihp
77	766	1,273	1,978
78	654	1,346	2,056
73	321	1,477	2,107
70½	320	1,428	2,013
81	Level	1,095	1,875

The effort was relaxed a little after Rugby, and still more after Tring; on the former section, readings at Blisworth, Castlethorpe, Leighton Buzzard and Tring showed approximate outputs of 1,770, 1,512, 1,749 and 1,673 indicated horsepower. In calculating these values, I have used the modern graph that relates to British Railways stock. Horsepower apart, this run did show that one of the original 'Royal Scots' in first class condition and expertly driven and fired, could make the required average of 75 mph over the open stretches of line with a tare load of 340 tons, made up as follows:

Section	Miles	Time (m s)	Speed (mph)
Betley Road-Great Bridgeford	16.5	12 45	77.7
Milford-Rugby No 7 Box	46.2	36 09	77.0
Kilsby Tunnel North-Bushey	62.8	50 05	75.3

This gave a total of 125.5 miles covered at an average speed of 76 mph, but even before passing Bushey the effort was being very much relaxed. On the previous form, there would have been no difficulty in averaging 80 mph from Tring to Willesden and this would have increased the aggregate high-speed mileage to 136.1 and the average speed over it to 77 mph. Quite apart from the comparisons with the investigations of 1935, the remarkable point about the performance of No 6132 and its crew was that it came at the end of a non-stop run through from Carlisle. No more striking evidence of the capacity of the 'Royal Scot' locomotives could be found than this run, and the recollections of it are among my most cherished railway memories.

17. Changes in command

Although the memories of the rather ignominious end of Fowler's adventure towards a de Glehn compound 'Pacific' had been more or less expunged by his apparent enthusiasm for the 'Royal Scots', and no less by his installation as President of the Institution of Mechanical Engineers, the backwash of the affair of 1926 remained, notably in a definite loosening of the stranglehold Derby had sought to maintain over locomotive affairs since 1925. Soon after the 'Royal Scots' were established on the West Coast Main Line, Crewe was allowed to go ahead with the project of the enlarged 'Claughton', though not to the extent of building new engines, but instead to reboiler a batch of the existing ones. The first few to be treated retained their original front end, with Walschaerts valve gear, though having solid valve heads and narrow rings, as used in the modifications made to the 'Royal Scots'. The rebuilt 'Claughtons' had boilers providing heating surfaces as follows: tubes, 1,550 sq ft; firebox, 183 sq ft; superheater, 365 sq ft. The grate area was 30 sq ft as on the original engines. With a working pressure of 200 psi, against the original 175 psi, the nominal tractive effort of the reboilered engines was 27,577 lb.

In July 1926, one of the original 'Claughtons', No 5908 *Alfred Fletcher,* was the first British locomotive to be fitted with the Caprotti valve gear, and dynamometer test runs between Crewe and Carlisle in January 1927 showed a notable saving in coal and oil consumption over a standard engine of the class. In 1928 it was decided that engine No 5908 should be one of the 'Claughtons' to be fitted with the enlarged boiler, and that nine more of the class earmarked for rebuilding should also be fitted with Caprotti valve gear. So the Western Division of the line eventually had twenty rebuilt 'Claughtons', ten retaining their original valve gear. Like the original engines of the class, they all proved very speedy machines, and with their higher tractive effort they were a welcome addition to the motive power stud. Dynamometer tests between Euston and Manchester on heavily loaded trains showed that the Walschaerts valve gear engines, with their improved piston valve design, were rather more economical than the Caprottis, thus:

Valve gear	Caprotti	Walschaerts
Average weight of train (tons tare)	418	419
Average running speed (mph)	52.9	52.7
Coal consumption		
lb per mile	39.9	38.2
lb per dhp hour	3.53	3.25

In regular service, the Caprotti engines were divided between Longsight and Holyhead sheds, at which latter depot they worked the Irish Mails throughout between Holyhead and Euston with the Welsh crews working through on a double-home basis. Most of the Walschaerts valve batch went to Preston where for a time they monopolized the working of the Liverpool and Manchester Scottish expresses. I had a number of good runs with them between Preston and Carlisle, particularly as they took heavy trains of up to 400 tons unpiloted over Shap on timings that were as fast as the pre-war trains over that route. When the Stanier '5X' 4-6-0s were introduced, some of the '5X' 'Claughtons' were transferred to Carnforth shed to take a share in the working of the residential trains to Morecambe, and the 'Ulster Express', to and from Crewe. I had a certain amount of business in Northern Ireland in the later 1930s and used to travel by the latter train when *en route* from London to Belfast, and one night in the summer holiday season we had a very heavy and crowded train of 475 tons loaded. One of the Crewe North 'Scots' brought us down from Euston in good style, and then for continuation of the run one of the '5X' 'Claughtons' backed on, No 5970 *Patience.*

We made one of the most brilliant northbound starts from Crewe I have ever recorded with a steam locomotive, and that includes very many runs with 'Pacifics'. The detailed log of the journey is appended herewith. It was unfortunate on that busy night that there were signal checks that interfered with punctuality, but the quality of the locomotive performance was as fine as anything I have subsequently noted with an LMS '5X' Class engine of all various classes. The schedule north of Preston was very sharp, and the only time out of a number of runs on that train I have seen only net time kept was when we were hauled by two Midland compounds, Nos 1171 and 1099. From Crewe the load was 440 tons, but at Preston a substantial increment brought it up to no less than 550 tons. With two compounds both resol-

Top left *The first 'Claughton' to be rebuilt with large boiler, but retaining the Walschaerts valve gear, No 5999* Vindictive (British Railways).

Above left *'Claughton' No 5927* Sir Francis Dent *as rebuilt with a large boiler and Caprotti valve gear* (British Railways).

Left *Rebuilt 'Claughton' No 5986 with Walschaerts valve gear, stationed at Preston and used on the Carlisle road* (F. Moore's Rail Photos).

LMS: 9.05 pm Crewe-Morecambe, 'The Ulster Express',

Engine Rebuilt 'Claughton' Class 4-6-0 (Walschaerts valve gear) No 5970 *Patience*
Load 439 tons tare, 475 tons full

Distance (miles)		Schedule time (min)	Actual time (m s)	Speed (mph)
0.0	CREWE	0	0 00	
2.7	*Coppenhall Junc*	5	4 40	51
4.9	Minshull Vernon		6 57	60
8.8	*Winsford Junc*	11	10 31	70½
—			—	75
11.8	Hartford		12 58	72½
13.5	Acton Bridge		15 09	71½
—			—	75
16.2	*Weaver Junc*	18	16 45	51 (slack)
18.8	Preston Brook		19 40	64
21.2	Moore		21 50	69
22.4	*Acton Grange Junc*		22 58	61
24.1	WARRINGTON	26	24 37	62
			sigs dead slow	
27.5	*Winwick Junc*	30	30 30	
29.8	*Golborne Junc*		35 15	37
31.0	Golborne		36 54	44½
33.2	Bamfurlong		39 32	61½
35.8	WIGAN	39	42 10	60
38.1	Boars Head		44 46	41½
			pwr	35
39.1	Standish	43	46 27	45
41.6	Coppull		49 52	42
44.3	Balshaw Lane		52 16	73
45.5	*Euxton Junc*	50	53 19	67½
47.0	Leyland		54 37	71
48.7	Farington		56 01	74
50.7	Preston home signals		58 33	
			stop	
			59 33	
51.0	PRESTON	58	61 53	
0.0		0	0 00	
1.3	*Oxheys Box*	3	3 55	
4.7	Barton		8 41	56
7.4	Brock		11 26	64½
9.5	Garstang	11	13 23	63
12.7	Scorton		16 25	64½
15.3	Bay Horse		18 52	65
16.6	Galgate		20 04	65½
19.9	*Lancaster Junc*		23 15	—
			signals	
21.0	LANCASTER	22	25 22	—
22.9	*Morecambe Junc*	25	28 36	—
			sig stops	
25.0	MORECAMBE PROMENADE	30	42 08	—

utely driven, we bowled along the level of the North Lancashire plain at 70 to 72 mph, and in the dining car a party of Erin-bound travellers were enjoying a convivial 'noggin' before going on board at Heysham. But our two drivers were evidently intent on giving them their money's worth, because they took the turnout at Lancaster Old Junction at an unchecked 69 mph and glasses, bottles and all else in that dining car suddenly became airborne! As we rushed down the bank to the Castle station, touching 74 mph, I wondered if this exuberance was going to be extended to our negotiation of the 20 mph curve at Morecambe South Junction, but all was well in that case. Despite our running between Preston and Lancaster, we were only *6 seconds* up on the schedule between those two points.

Just before Crewe produced the first reboilered 'Claughtons', in December 1927, Derby was ready with the first of the new 2-6-4 tanks, the valve gear of which benefited greatly from that now famous meeting of the Graduates Section of the Institution of Mechanical Engineers. Their basic dimensions were: cylinders, 19-in diameter by 26-in stroke; coupled wheels, 5-ft 9-in diameter; boiler pressure 200 psi. This provided a nominal tractive effort of 23,125 lb. With a maximum axle load of no more than 18¼ tons, they had a high route availability. The boiler was a shortened version of that used on the new Midland compounds, using the same tube plates and arrangement of superheater; but the distance between the tube plates was 11 ft 4⅝ in against 12 ft 3⅜ in on the compound, and the heating surfaces were reduced accordingly. The grate area was 25 sq ft. The outstanding feature was, of course, the use of long-lap, long-travel valves, which made them extraordinarily free-running engines. Although it is carrying the story several years forward, I shall never forget the impact they made on their first arrival on the Euston-Watford suburban trains. In the early 1930s I was living at Bushey and travelled daily to Euston. Originally we had the 'Precursor' tanks, non-superheated, and by then they were a bunch of very tired old ladies. The periodic overhauls at Crewe, which had kept so many of the ex-LNW 4-4-0s and

Top right *One of the rebuilt Caprotti 'Claughtons', No 6013, on the up 'Lancastrian' at Castlethorpe troughs* (Leslie J. Thompson).

Above right *A rebuilt Walschaerts valve gear 'Claughton' climbing Shap with the midday Liverpool and Manchester Scotsman : engine No 5993* (O.S. Nock).

Right *The original 'Claughton' with improved valves, still hard at work in the early 1930s. No 5985 is seen here with the up 'Lancastrian', a 13-coach train, at Castlethorpe troughs* (Leslie J. Thompson).

4-6-0s in excellent condition, did not seem to have reached the 'Precursor' tanks, and most of them were very poor tools. Then, from the beginning of 1934, we got the 2-6-4 tanks. The 8.53 am non-stop from Watford to Euston originated at Bletchley on weekdays, and consisted of a six-coach corridor set, strengthened by three non-corridors at the rear. But on Saturdays it originated at Tring, and was a six-coach suburban set worked by the Watford tank engines, and when Nos 2375, 2378 and 2379 came on to the job, we travelled up to Euston on the wings of the wind!

The first record I have of a 2-6-4 on the trains is from January 1934, and although it was vastly better than the work of the 'Precursor' tanks, with sustained speeds of 69 to 71 mph, it was no more speedy, with 180 tons, than I had come to expect daily with 'Georges' and 'Prince of Wales' 4-6-0s hauling 285 to 315 tons on the weekday trains. But by the early summer of that year the Watford men had fully taken the measure of these splendid engines, and on Saturday we used to pass South Hampstead, 15.1 miles from the start, in less than 'even time'. A critic might suggest that this stretch is 'all downhill'; in fact, it is level for the first 3 miles, then downhill for 7½ miles, and level for the remainder. The maximum speeds, with the engines always travelling bunker first, were around 77 to 78 mph, and the exhaust completely silent after the first half-mile or so. The climax, so far as my own recording was concerned, came on 16 February 1935 when engine No 2387 was on the job, with the usual Saturday load of 185 tons (see the accompanying table). The start was a little slower than usual, but we were doing 75 mph at Harrow, and then dashed up to a maximum of 83½ mph at Brent Junction. A tremendous pace was kept up on the subsequent level track, and we were still doing 79½ mph at Queens Park, and 74 mph on entering Primrose Hill Tunnel. Passing Milepost 1 in the record time of 16 min 2 sec from the Watford start we could, with a normal finish, have been at rest in Euston in 18 minutes. But the staff were not quite ready for the arrival of a commuter train 3 minutes early and we were checked outside.

The years do not seem to have slowed the paces of these engines, and a friend sent me details of a run with one of the erstwhile Watford engines, made in December 1963 on the 1.15 pm from Windermere to Lancaster. On this fairly recent occasion, the load was no more than three coaches, but the old warrior 'flew' to some purpose. The schedule was a fairly sharp one, allowing only 13 minutes to pass Carnforth from Oxenholme, 12.8 miles, and 20 minutes to the stop at Lancaster, 19.1 miles. Engine No 2378 (then numbered 42378) was doing 86 mph at Milnthorpe at the foot of the Grayrigg bank, increased this to a full 90

LMS: 8.53 am Watford-Euston (Saturdays)

Engine 2-6-4 tank No 2387
Load 168 tons tare, 185 tons full

Distance (miles)		Schedule time (min)	Actual time (m s)	Speed (mph)
0.0	WATFORD JUNCTION	0	0 00	—
1.5	Bushey		2 54	—
2.7	Carpenders Park		4 20	55
4.2	Hatch End		5 54	66
6.1	Harrow		7 30	75
7.5	Milepost 10		8 36	78
9.4	Wembley		10 02	81
10.5	Milepost 7		10 50	83½
12.1	WILLESDEN JUNCTION	13	12 00	80½
13.9	Queens Park		13 21	79½
15.1	South Hampstead		14 19	74
16.5	Milepost 1		16 02	—
—			sigs	—
17.5	EUSTON	21	19 00	—

mph on the level towards Holme, and passed Carnforth at 85 mph, almost 2 minutes inside the exiguous point-to-point booking of 13 minutes. With easy running afterwards, Lancaster was reached in 18½ minutes. The load was certainly a featherweight, but a six-coupled tank engine, with 5-ft 9-in wheels, that can attain 90 mph on level track is a very good advertisement for the valve gear recommended by the late E.L. Diamond. There were eventually 125 of these engines, of which the last thirty had side-windowed cabs.

Before leaving the period of Sir Henry Fowler's chieftanship and returning to the story of the new main-line 4-6-0s, there is another important locomotive class to be mentioned. From the very moment of his appointment as President of the Executive, Sir Josiah Stamp began to take a keen interest in locomotive matters. It was not that he was interested in locomotives as such; but their maintenance and running costs represented such a large proportion of the total expense of running the railway that he, with the critical mind of an economist and statistician, was at once drawn towards the problem involved. One can readily imagine that he found the methods of working one of the most potentially lucrative traffics on the line—the Toton-Cricklewood coal trains—somewhat archaic, in that practically every load was double-headed, with two ex-Midland 0-6-0s. Whether or not Stamp himself suggested a trial of the Beyer-Garratt type of locomotive I cannot say; but one can be sure that the adoption of a type that would do the

One of the Beyer-Garrett 2-6-0 + 0-6-2 heavy mineral engines, with the revolving self-trimming tender (British Railways).

work of two existing engines would have received his warm approbation.

The first three engines of this new series were put to work in 1927. They are sometimes referred to as the direct incorporation of two Horwich 2-6-0s into the Garratt principle, but although the coupled wheelbase is the same, this is about the only dimensional similarity between the Garratt and the tender engines. On the former, the cylinders were of 18-in diameter by 26-in stroke, and the coupled wheel diameter 5 ft 3 in. With a boiler pressure of 190 psi, this provided a tractive effort of 45,620 lb, or roughly the same as a '4F' superheater 0-6-0 and a non-superheated pilot. It is nevertheless one thing to provide tractive effort on paper; what the statistician may not always appreciate is that the development of that tractive effort depends upon the man with the shovel! The firing of a Garratt with a grate area of 44.5 sq ft was needless to say a vastly different proposition from firing a '4F', the most puissant partner in the previous standard combination on the coal trains between Toton and Cricklewood. It is interesting to compare the boiler proportions of the two locomotives, noting how the inherent features of the Beyer-Garratt make possible a boiler of almost ideal proportions for free steaming at high rates of evaporation. A study of these dimensions shows that the Garratt had virtually double the steaming capacity of a '4F' 0-6-0, but would of course need very careful firing to make such proportions a reality in actual traffic. The firebox was not greatly longer than that of the '4F', being 8 ft 5 in as opposed to 7 ft. The '4F' boiler was, of course, identical to, and interchangeable with, that of the Class '2' standard 4-4-0.

The three original Beyer-Garratt locomotives were subjected to a long period of testing against the double-headed method of working, including coal consumption trials with the dynamometer car, with

Comparison of boiler proportions between '4F' and Beyer-Garratt

	'4F'		Garratt
Distance between tube plates (ft in)	10	10½	12 5
Tubes:			
Large, outside diameter (in)	5½		5½
number	21		36
Small outside diameter (in)	1¾		2
number	146		209
Heating surfaces (sq ft)			
Tubes	1,034		1,954
Firebox	124		183
Superheater	246		466
Combined total	1,404		2,603
Grate area (sq ft)	21.2		44.5

loaded trains of 1,450 tons in the southbound direction, and 100-wagon trains of empties taken on the return. The test results proved remarkably in favour of the Beyer-Garratt type of locomotive, and in 1930 a further thirty were ordered. At that time, Sir Josiah Stamp stated that 'in addition to saving one set of men per train, they will displace 68 old freight tender engines'! On these later engines, Messrs Beyer, Peacock & Co were able to incorporate their patent self-trimming coal bunker. There had been many cases on overseas railways where the inclusion of this device would have been welcome on Beyer-Garratt locomotives, but where it was impracticable because of strict limitations upon maximum axle load. The use of this device considerably eased the fireman's work, by eliminating the tiresome necessity of getting coal forward manually. This was a very welcome accessory

on locomotives having a grate area more than double that of the largest locomotives with which the freight enginemen of the Midland Division had previously been familiar.

In view of this epoch-marking change in the working of the Toton-Cricklewood coal traffic, the design and operating of the self-trimming coal bunker is worth a detailed description. It consisted of a closed container of conical shape, the axis of which was inclined towards the footplate end of the bunker. The top side of the container was thus horizontal, and the floor had a slope sufficiently steep to work the coal forward when revolving. The front end was fitted with suitable doors and a shovel plate to suit the standard footplate practice of the LMS, while the top of the container was provided with a set of double doors for coaling. Rotation of the bunker was controlled from the footplate through worm gearing from two reversibly-driving steam engines. The bunker could be revolved in 30 seconds, or less, but in actual practice it was found that three or four revolutions sufficed to bring up any amount of coal required on the shovelling plate. With the introduction of these engines into general service it will be appreciated that the working of the coal trains between Toton and Cricklewood was well on the way to modernization.

At the beginning of 1930, consequent upon the death of R.W. Reid in the previous year, Sir Harold Hartley, an eminent scientist, though not previously in the railway service, had been appointed a Vice-President, and Director of Scientific Research. Reid's death at a relatively early age had left a serious gap in Sir Josiah Stamp's carefully planned reorganization of the top-level management, and Reid, who as Carriage and Wagon Engineer until his promotion to a Vice-Presidency at the end of 1926, had been

considered as one of the brightest stars of the future. He was a son of W.P. Reid, the Locomotive Superintendent of the North British Railway and designer of the 'Atlantic' engines. One of the first results of the top-level changes on the LMS in 1930 was that Sir Henry Fowler was 'moved sideways', as it were, to become Assistant to Sir Harold Hartley and that E.J.H. Lemon, the Carriage and Wagon Engineer, was to be Chief Mechanical Engineer of the Company.

One of Fowler's last acts as CME was to authorize a more extensive rebuilding of two of the 'Claughton' 4-6-0s than had been recently carried out at Crewe. One can sense that the age-old rivalry between the two establishments was still very much alive in 1930, because it seemed that Derby could not see Crewe producing a very successful '5X'-powered 4-6-0 without wanting to do one of their own. The two prototypes of what eventually became a new class were very simply produced by taking the Crewe design for the enlarged 'Claughtons' boiler and putting it on to the 'Royal Scots' chassis and machinery. It was a true rebuild, for, although the wheel spacing was altered, the original frames were used, as well as the bogie and the original reversing gear. The two engines so treated were No 5902 *Sir Frank Ree* and No 5971. As rebuilt they were fitted with the standard Midland 3,500-gallon tenders and in this guise they certainly looked neo-Midland engines. The cylinders, valves and valve gear were the same as those of the 'Royal Scot', but, because of the lower boiler pressure, the nominal tractive effort was 26,520 lb as against 27,150 lb on the '5X' 'Claughtons' reboilered at Crewe. Engine No 5971 was stationed at Leeds, Whitehall Junction shed, and soon came into the limelight of publicity in *The Railway Magazine*. At that

Left *One of the Beyer-Garrett 2-6-0 + 0-6-2 engines on a maximum-length up Midland coal train near Radlett (O.S. Nock).*

Right *One of the first two three-cylinder converted 'Claughtons' nicknamed 'Baby Scots', No 5902* Sir Frank Ree *(British Railways).*

time, a number of unrebuilt 'Claughtons' had taken over the principal express train workings from Midland compounds over the Settle and Carlisle route, and with the modified type of piston valves they were doing good work economically. Actually, the early work of the rebuilt No 5971 showed nothing better, if as good, as the unrebuilt engines were then doing. But to those who had the job of detailed observation, the two 'three-cylinder converted Claughtons', as they were officially first known, gave ample evidence of their quality.

In January 1931, when E.J.H. Lemon became Chief Mechanical Engineer, it subsequently became evident that the latter was, however, no more than a 'caretaker' appointment on the part of Sir Josiah Stamp, because although Lemon was a strong personality and a first class organizer, he had up till then been a 'carriage and wagon' man, and in any case Stamp had him marked down for still higher things. The choice of a true and lasting successor to Fowler as Chief Mechanical Engineer eventually fell upon Stanier, who took office on 1 January 1932. While still larger engines were contemplated, there was a pressing need for more passenger locomotives in the '5X' category, and largely as a stop-gap while new designs to Stanier's own requirements were prepared, authorization was given for another forty 'Claughtons' to be replaced by the rebuilds. The first 15 of these were built at Crewe in 1932; in 1933, of the remaining 25 of the batch, ten were built at Derby and the rest at Crewe. Although taking the numbers of those they replaced, they were virtually new, with a minimum of old parts incorporated. The new engines of 1932-3 were distributed between the Western, Midland and Northern Divisions, and although everywhere doing good work, it was par-

ticularly on the ex-LNWR services between Euston, Birmingham and Wolverhampton, and between Euston and Manchester, that they came to shine so markedly. On the Midland they took over duties and schedules that had been satisfactorily worked by Midland compounds, mostly with light loads, while in Scotland they worked from Polmadie mainly on the Liverpool and Manchester Scottish trains as far south as Carlisle. In England, between Preston and Carlisle, those trains were being very competently handled by large-boilered 'Claughtons' of the Walschaerts gear series. As they became widely distributed over the line, the enginemen soon found a more appropriate name for them than the rather ponderous 'three-cylinder converted Claughton'. They called them the 'Baby Scots', and this is just what they were.

In referring to the building and allocation of the production batches of the 'Baby Scots', I have side-stepped the year of Lemon's session as Caretaker CME. It was a year in which he was called to play a vital part in LMS locomotive history. While he himself had been chosen by Sir Josiah Stamp to succeed J.H. Follows as a Vice-President, he had to carry out the preliminary moves in the appointment of a permanent CME. I have told elsewhere what those moves were; but the news of Stanier's appointment was not everywhere welcomed on the LMS, not least by one of the Vice-Presidents who had vetted him. It was known in high railway circles that Sir Harold Hartley would have preferred someone of ace-high intellectual attainment, 'another blue-eyed boy from Balliol', as another railwayman sarcastically put it! Sir Harold might have had cause to doubt their choice of a CME in the early stages. It was well known that D.C. Urie, who had succeeded Anderson as Superintendent of Motive Power, had a deep-rooted antipa-

Top *One of the later 'Baby Scots' after renumbering from 5500 upwards, No 5538* Giggleswick *(British Railways).*

Above *No 5538* Giggleswick *on the down Thames-Clyde Express near Radlett* (E.D. Bruton).

thy to anything or anybody who came from the Great Western, and he had some reason for this antipathy when some of the first Stanier locomotives, both 4-6-2 and 4-6-0, had a way of 'going off the boil' at critical stages in their long runs. Fortunately, Crewe, through the magnanimity of H.P.M. Beames, was solidly behind Stanier. When Fowler left, Beames had been appointed Deputy Chief Mechanical Engineer, and

after Lemon's brief stay he felt that his turn had arrived at last. But it was not to be. He wrote to Stanier, expressing his own disappointment, but saying there was no one he would prefer more to serve under. In the new set-up, the Midland faction was admirably represented at Stanier's Headquarters by S.J. Symes, as Personal Assistant to the CME.

18. Stanier's first four years

Stanier began his memorable 12 years as Chief Mechanical Engineer of the LMS by accepting *in toto* the organization set up by Lemon in 1931. The positions held by Beames and Symes were noted at the end of the previous chapter and H. Chambers remained as Chief Locomotive Draughtsman at CME Headquarters at Derby. Stanier himself was in no way an engine designer. His outstanding speciality was in workshop practice, apart from his genius in leading men and his unerring skill in getting the right men on to the job. Before he came to the LMS, he had opportunities of appraising the work Beames was doing in the thorough modernization of all the manufacturing facilities at Crewe, and that great work had his complete approbation. He brought with him from Swindon a large wooden chest full of blueprints of Great Western locomotives and their details, and in his early months at Euston he was in the habit of handing selected ones out to Chambers at appropriate times. One change in organization he made in the early months was to detach Riddles from his existing job as Assistant Works Superintendent at Derby and to install him as Locomotive Assistant to the CME.

No one who had held a position of high responsibility in the locomotive department of the Great Western Railway would deny that one of the kingpins of the successful performance of the locomotives and their high thermal efficiency was the taper boiler

developed by Churchward to a high state of perfection by the time the 'Prince' and 'Princess' series of 4-6-0s were introduced just before the outbreak of the First World War. There was the development of the valve gear as well; but in going to the LMS in 1932, Stanier would be doubtless well aware that the lesson of long-lap, long-travel valves had been well and truly learnt at his new headquarters at Derby several years previously, and that in the new standard range of locomotives that it was his mandate to get built as quickly as possible, it was the boiler rather than the chassis and machinery that was to be his first consideration. Yet his first introduction of what was the Swindon standard No 1 boiler could well have proved fatal to his stay on the LMS had it not been for the resolute action of two of his most loyal supporters. In 1934, more '5X' 4-6-0s were urgently needed. Because the drawings and tools for the new taper-boilered engines were not quite ready, a further batch of ten 'Baby Scots' was ordered and the new Stanier '5Xs' followed them into the erecting shop at Crewe. They also were three-cylinder engines, and it is interesting to compare the boiler proportions of these, as originally built, with the GWR No 1 standard:

	GWR	LMS
Heating surfaces (sq ft)		
Tubes	1,686.60	1,463.0
Firebox	154.78	162
Superheater	262.62	228
Grate area	27.07	29.5

Although the firebox and grate areas were larger, the tube heating surface and the superheater were con-

One of the latest of the parallel-boilered 2-6-4 tanks, No 2400, built at Derby in 1933. This class, the earliest examples of which were painted red, was introduced in 1927. The total, all built at Derby, was 125 (British Railways).

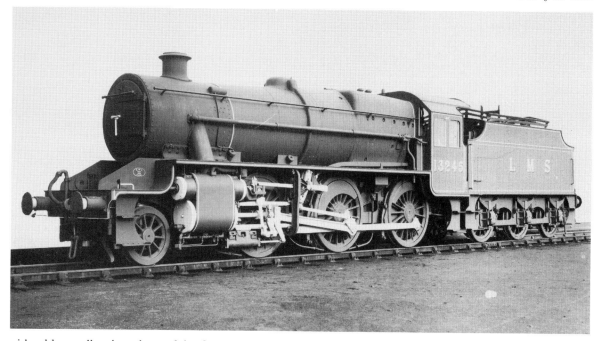

One of the first Stanier engines for the LMS: 2-6-0 No 13245, built at Crewe in 1933 (British Railways).

siderably smaller than those of the GWR No 1, and the latter was used with complete success on the 'Saints', 'Stars' and 'Hall' Classes. The LMS taper-boilered '5Xs' had the same tractive effort as the 'Baby Scots', a little below that of the 'Stars'; but when they were put to work on the Western Division of the LMS, particularly on duties previously worked by 'Baby Scots', the footplatemen damned them at once—they would not steam. The word had got round that the two prototype 'Pacifics' were affected in the same way, and Stanier's men suffered some awkward times. Riddles, a Crewe man himself, suggested putting them all on the Midland until the initial fracas on the Western had died down. But the Midland had received a quota of 'Baby Scots', and north of Leeds the unrebuilt 'Claughtons' were very popular and hard-worked engines. As for the taper-boilered '5Xs', I can only pass on the comment made to me by the driver of one of them at the end of a disastrous run down from St Pancras to Leeds one night on the 6.15 pm express: 'Superheaters,' he fumed, 'they can't heat water, let alone steam.'

Of course, the proportions of Great Western boilers and superheaters had been arrived at after much investigation and constant riding on the footplate by drawing office staff and locomotive inspectors. Once introduced, they were backed up by very careful firing of the picked coals reserved for top-link duties. On the LMS, not only were the combustion characteristics of the various coals different, but on top-link duties the standards of firing varied. Even after the

Western Division men had 'got the hang of' the Stanier '5Xs' in their original condition, there were wide variations in the running. It was a characteristic of all Great Western express locomotives when they were starting 'cold', particularly on the dead level out of Paddington, that they took a long time to get into speed, 'getting their superheat' as one driver expressed it. The old LNWR men were just the reverse when they had their own familiar engines, like the man who was driving the 'Ulster Express' out of Crewe as mentioned in the preceding chapter, who had his 475-ton train running at 60 mph before it was five miles out of Crewe. Great Western drivers on heavy West of England or South Wales expresses rarely attained 60 mph by Southall, nine miles out.

Readers of *The Railway Magazine* in the latter half of the year 1934 may well be perplexed at the foregoing criticisms of these engines, because certain articles by Cecil J. Allen showed them in a far different light. In their first months of service on the Western Division, a number of dynamometer car tests were carried out on ordinary service trains, and the running times of these, though not any technical data, were noted by correspondents of Mr Allen. It was clear that some very special and vigorous methods were used on these test occasions, so much so that their like was never seen again in the history of these engines, at any rate while they had the original boilers and low-degree superheat. I can quite imagine that enthusiasts of the train timing art were often bitterly disappointed when their own runs so frequently failed to come up to the standard of the 1934 test runs.

Two instances of very slow starts by Stanier '5Xs' that were the prelude to very good runs may be quoted. The first was on the up 'Midday Scot' when engine No 5592, then unnamed, had on a very heavy load of 469 tons tare out of Crewe. The load, incidentally, was 54 tons over the 'Special Limit' for a '5X' engine, and the crew made very heavy weather of it up to Whitmore, taking no less than 20¾ minutes for this first 10½ miles. Then they bucked up, to such an extent indeed that the 145.2 miles from Whitmore to South Hampstead were covered at an average speed of 59.5 mph, and the 158.1 miles from Crewe to Euston were completed in 171½ minutes. Another instance was on the 11.30 am from Euston to Birmingham, one of the trains that had 5 minutes cut from its overall schedule and was allowed only 1 hr 55 min inclusive of a stop at Coventry. With a load of nine coaches, 291 tons tare, we made a very laboured start out of London, and were doing no more than 53 mph on passing Willesden Junction. Then the pace hotted up so that we covered the 65.1 miles from Watford to Rugby in 56¼ minutes, and averaged 72 mph for the 48.6 miles north of Tring. We were dead on time at Coventry, and our overall time from Euston to Birmingham was, to be very exact, 115 min 12 sec. But these were exceptional runs in my experience while the engines were in their original low-superheat condition.

Their mixed traffic equivalents, the ever-celebrated 'Black Fives', got off to a much better start than the '5Xs'. Why this should have been so I cannot say. The tube heating surface and the superheaters were almost the same, and the fireboxes were smaller. Alongside the Great Western 'Halls', which had the same diameter of coupled wheels, 6 ft 0 in, the cylinders were 18½ in by 28 in and the valve gear was Walschaerts. The first order in 1934 was for no less than seventy engines, twenty from Crewe and fifty from the Vulcan Foundry, the running numbers being 5000-5019, and 5020-5069 respectively. Vulcan's were first off the mark; engine No 5020 was featured in the initial publicity literature for the class, and it figured in some of the dynamometer car trials carried out in the same year. The rest of the first ten of the Vulcans went to Perth, and, fitted with tablet exchanging apparatus, worked mainly on the Highland line. In the meantime, the pioneer engine No 5020 had been doing excellent work between Crewe and Euston. Incidentally, the twenty engines bearing the lowest numbers, namely Nos 5000 to 5019, were not completed at Crewe until the early months of 1935.

LMS: 2.40 pm Euston-Crewe

Engine Stanier Class '5' 4-6-0 No 5020
Load 468 tons tare, 495 tons full

Distance (miles)		Time (m s)	Speed (mph)
0.0	EUSTON	0 00	
1.0	Milepost 1	3 23	—
5.4	Willesden Junc	9 52	—
8.1	Wembley	12 29	58½
11.4	Harrow	16 10	—
13.3	Hatch End	18 15	—
17.5	WATFORD JUNC	22 35	—
21.0	Kings Langley	25 57	—
24.5	Hemel Hempstead	29 29	—
28.0	Berkhamsted	33 09	—
31.7	TRING	37 14	54½
36.1	Cheddington	—	77
40.2	Leighton Buzzard	44 27	
46.7	BLETCHLEY	49 42	—
52.4	Wolverton	54 27	—
59.9	Roade	61 43	57
62.8	BLISWORTH	64 43 sig check	
82.6	RUGBY	85 56	
5.5	Brinklow	7 53	—
14.5	NUNEATON	16 03	75
19.7	Atherstone	20 25	—
27.4	TAMWORTH	27 37	—
33.7	LICHFIELD	33 41	55
41.7	Rugeley	41 32	
51.0	STAFFORD	50 41	
56.3	Norton Bridge	56 32	63
65.0	Whitmore	64 54	61½
70.7	Betley Road	69 59 sig stop	78
75.5	CREWE	78 19	

The dynamometer car test run on the 2.40 pm Euston-Liverpool express included some excellent running as will be seen from the accompanying log. There seems to have been no hesitation in starting on this fine run, either from Euston or from Rugby, and, in my own early runs with the 'Black Fives', I always found them very smartly off the mark. I had the privilege of some footplate passes for them on the Highland line, but unfortunately they were loaded so heavily as to always need pilot assistance. But as I was returning one Sunday from such a trip on the 'Royal Scot' train, one of the new 4-6-0s, No 5028, took over at Crewe and gave us an exhilarating, if somewhat delayed, run to Euston. We were twice stopped for signals before we even reached Stafford, but in between these two both crew and engine showed their form with a maximum speed of 79 mph

near Norton Bridge. From Stafford, with a load of 380 tons, we ran the 78.8 miles to passing Castlethorpe in 78¼ minutes, and on passing Roade had recovered 3 minutes of the 6 minutes lost by the initial signal checks. But a long permanent way check near Wolverton seemed to put the engine 'off the boil', so to speak, and the recovery past Bletchley and up to Tring was not up to the standard shown earlier in the run. Nevertheless, we came smartly down the bank to Watford, and although we eased markedly afterwards, we finished into Euston only 31½ minutes late in a total of 173 min 32 sec from Crewe. The net time for the 158.1-mile run was 159½ minutes.

On 2 and 3 May 1935, the LMS staged a Jubilee exhibition of locomotives and rolling stock at Euston which presented a cavalcade of progress during the 25 years of the reign of King George V. The locomotives included were the famous ex-LNWR 4-4-0 *Coronation,* built at Crewe in 1911, and the first of the Stanier '5X' 4-6-0s No 5552, built in 1934, but repainted in a special Jubilee finish of black and silver which involved the use of a special chromium plating process. The engine was appropriately named *Silver Jubilee,* and made a strikingly ornate pair with the *Coronation* of 1911 at the head of platforms 6 and 7 at Euston. The last-named engine was also in black, but of course carrying her LMS number 5348. Subsequently, the Stanier '5X' 4-6-0s naturally became known as the 'Jubilee' Class. Crewe certainly 'dolled up' No 5552 with a plethora of chromium plating,

even including a special cover for the top feed apparatus on the boiler barrel. But at the time *Silver Jubilee* was turned out, plans were well under way for a modified boiler for the '5Xs'. Stanier's mandate from the outset had been to 'scrap and build'; but the management was in such a hurry to get the new engines into traffic that there was no time to get any prototype tested out before the bulk orders were placed. No fewer than 113 of the 'Jubilees' were ordered straight off the drawing board, and it was not as if they were a straight copy of the Great Western 'Star' so far as the boiler was concerned. The modified '5X' boilers had the same tube heating surface though a larger firebox and grate area, and a much larger superheater, the respective dimensions being 181.1 sq ft firebox, 31 sq ft grate, and 307 sq ft superheater. It proved amply adequate for the hardest work the engines were required to do.

Before referring to the modifications made to the 'Black Five' boilers, mention must be made of the difficulties Stanier had with some of the engines that he inherited. One of Bowen Cooke's former pupils, Kenneth Cantlie, who had considerable locomotive experience in the Argentine and then China, on one of his home visits called on Stanier at Euston and was alarmed to learn of the frequency of cracked frames and hot driving axle boxes on the 'Prince of Wales' 4-6-0s. While these were one of the classes that were gradually being phased out, there was still much work that could be done by these engines, and Stanier, coming from a railway on which hot boxes were the once in a lifetime, was perplexed. He asked Cantlie if it had always been the case with those engines, and in response to an indignant 'no', invited him to go to Camden shed and have a word with the District Superintendent. Then, to Cantlie's astonishment, when he climbed into a pit beneath one of the 'Princes', he saw that the centre bearing on the driving axle had been removed. No wonder that many of them ran hot and sometimes cracked their frames when being heavily worked, seeing that roughly one-third of the designed bearing surface had been removed! Fulminating, Cantlie rushed back to Stanier, who inevitably knew nothing about it. Obviously it was one of the Derby 'improvements' on Crewe standard design and had been done in Fowler's time, and there was nothing at that late stage in the history of the 'Prince of Wales' Class that could be done about it.

But another epidemic of hot boxes could be, and was effectively, dealt with by Stanier. On the Midland Railway, manganese bronze axle-boxes had always been standard on the larger engines, and naturally Chambers had specified these for the 'Royal Scots'. As the material was too soft to take a pressed-

in brass and was not itself a bearing metal, it was necessary to confine the white metal by bronze strips dovetailed into the parent metal. These strips, even if carefully fitted into their grooves and suitably located with pegs, tended to come loose in time and disturb the white metal. Where inside collars were fitted to the axles, this was particularly likely to happen, and where an engine was a heavy one with big side thrusts on the boxes, disintegration was inevitable. It gave reasonably good service on the lightly-used Midland engines, but not on a class worked like the 'Royal Scots', and in 1932, among the seventy engines of the class, there were no fewer than 102 cases of hot boxes.

In coming to the LMS, Stanier was naturally interested in the Crewe design of steel box with pressed-in brasses, because it was nearest in principle to the Great Western type, with which he was very familiar. He was surprised, however, at its bad record in 1931-2, particularly on the 'George the Fifth' and 'Prince of Wales' Classes, still more so on being assured by more than one old Crewe man that it had not been so in LNWR days. Investigation suggested beyond much doubt that the trouble in 1931-2 and earlier had arisen from the removal of the centre bear-

Above left *A typical 'Black Five' goods duty: southbound near Falahill on the Waverley Route with a mixed freight between the Millerhill and Kingmoor yards* (Derek Cross).

Right *One of the later 'Jubilees', No 5696* Arethusa *(built at Crewe in 1936), climbing Beattock Bank with an excursion from Manchester to Glasgow* (M.W. Earley).

ing on the driving axle of the Joy valve gear engines, thus throwing an inordinately heavy load on to the driving boxes in the main frames. Stanier then introduced on the LMS the Great Western conception of a steel axle-box with a thin layer of white metal not shrouded at the sides but only at the ends. This allowed the brass to be machined before the metal was applied. To give increased surface for effective bonding, this machining took the form of a series of serrations, and so an almost perfect bond was achieved.

This design of axle-box had many advantages. The tendency of the white metal to spread, which took place with the older designs of thick liners, almost vanished, and this enabled the end shrouding to be dispensed with. At the same time, the actual bearing surfaces were made very large, to permit of low bearing loading per square inch, while another notable and successful feature was to have the thin white metal lining unbroken by any oil grooves. The oiling was done entirely from an underpad, housed in a withdrawable keep of sufficient depth to contain an auxiliary supply of oil. There was some concern at the time this design was introduced on the LMS, because it was considered that the underpad on its own could not adequately lubricate the bearing. Stanier knew, however, that on the GWR the elimination of the upper feed on all the modern engines had brought no troubles. He had no hesitation in applying it to all his new standard engines on the LMS; on the 'Royal Scots', when new boxes to the original overall dimensions were substituted, it worked like a charm. In 1939 there were no more than six cases of hot boxes among the entire seventy engines of the class.

So far as the new maximum power locomotives for the Anglo-Scottish traffic were concerned, Stanier naturally had the GWR 'Kings' very much in mind, though for the long 400-mile through runs a much larger boiler and firebox seemed desirable; this would provide for a lower rate of combustion on a large firegrate, and hopefully avoid the formation of clinker on the firebars towards the end of such runs. The boiler originally fitted to the prototype LMS 'Pacifics' Nos 6200 and 6201 had so many points of similarity with that of *The Great Bear,* that I have often wondered if Stanier included some drawings of that engine in the stack of blueprints he took with him from Swindon to Euston. The comparative dimensions were:

Engine	GWR No 111	LMS Nos 6200-1
Length of barrel (ft in)	23 0	20 7¼
Diameter, max (ft in)	6 0	6 4¾
Diameter, min (ft in)	5 6	5 9
Firebox grate area (sq ft)	41 8	45 0
Tubes		
Small		
diameter (in)	2½	2¼
number	147	170
Large		
diameter (in)	5⅛	5⅛
number	14	16
Heating surfaces (sq ft)		
Tubes	2,597	2,523
Firebox	159	190
Superheater	399	370

The dimensions quoted for *The Great Bear* are those of the third variety of boiler, after the superheater had been changed from the original 21-element type to one of 14 elements. The firebox heating surface was originally 185 sq ft by inclusion experimentally of four arch tubes. It was reported that when it was first introduced, firemen found considerable difficulty in maintaining steam pressure on 'The Bear', but this arose from unfamiliarity with the form of wide grate, and the need to keep the back corners well filled. Once this technique had been mastered, the engine steamed freely.

The engine proper also followed Great Western practice in using exactly the same dimensions for the four cylinders and the coupled wheels as on the 'King' Class, and with the same boiler pressure the nominal tractive effort was the same. But the use of four sets of valve gear was unusual. At the time it was stated that this rather elaborate arrangement had been adopted to avoid the inequalities in steam distribution that can arise when the movement of one piston valve is derived from a lever mechanism connected to the valve spindle of another. One could understand that there might have been some reluctance on the LMS to adopt the Swindon design of derived gear, having the Walschaerts valve gear inside, and driving the valves of the outside cylinders by a system of rocking levers. During the winter of 1933-4, the appearance of engines 6200 and 6201 on the 400-mile Euston-Glasgow through workings was intermittent, to say the least of it. The first of the two was based at Camden, and the second at Polmadie. I used to travel from Bushey into Euston almost daily by an electric train that passed Camden shed when the last stages in the preparation of the engine for

the down 'Royal Scot' were in progress — stacking a few extra lumps on the tender and such like — and during that winter the engine was as often a not a 'Royal Scot'. I 'chatted up' the Carlisle crew of No 6201 one day when they had brought in the up train, with no more than a moderate load of 12 coaches, about 400 tons. They were a most expert and enthusiastic pair, as I learned when I rode on the footplate with them in another connection; but they were far from enthusiastic about No 6201, more particularly at having to take over from a Polmadie crew in Carlisle station, and then continue non-stop to Euston. The fireman put it succinctly: 'The Glasgow boys come in,' he said, 'and say "she won't steam", and you've 300 miles to go!'

Then, at the Easter holiday weekend of 1934, there came an opportunity to gain some first-hand experience. To help me obtain data for a literary assignment, the LMS gave me footplate passes for the 'Royal Scot' in both directions. Engine No 6201 was not available for the down run, although she was actually on Camden shed in the morning; but I was able to ride No 6200 right through from Symington to Euston on Easter Tuesday with a 15-coach 500-ton load. It was a memorable experience— memorable in a wide diversity of ways—and so far as basic running data was concerned I was more or less on virgin ground, and in presenting my footplate pass to the Polmadie driver on No 6200 at Symington, on 3 April 1934, I was very much stepping into the unknown, so far as locomotive men outside the LMS were concerned. I was not the only novice on the engine that morning; it was the first time the

Above left *One of the Derby-built 'Royal Scots', No 6160* Queen Victoria's Rifleman, *with the later wide tender* (British Railways).

Right *'Royal Scot' Class 4-6-0 No 6124* London Scottish *on the 2.40 pm Euston-Liverpool express passing Kilburn* (E.R. Wethersett).

The first Stanier 'Pacific', No 6200 The Princess Royal, *in 1934 with the down 'Royal Scot' (a 15-coach train) near Whitmore* (Rail Archive Stephenson, photo F.R. Hebron).

driver and fireman had ever been on her, and LMS regulations then allowing no more than three men on the footplate, they had not the guidance of an inspector to help them.

The coal was soft Scottish, and we were burning a tremendous lot of it; but one of the troubles was the form of the original tender fitted to those engines. The floor of the coal space at the back was level, and the supplies just refused to come forward, and this is what our Camden driver was doing, raking it forward, so that his fireman could concentrate on getting it into the firebox. From Crewe for the next 100 miles of the journey south he took spells in the tender getting coal forward, while I and the fireman, when he could, looked forward to the signals. Had the driver not done this we should undoubtedly have had to stop. He was, of course, at the controls when passing through the large stations, but on the gently up-and-down gradients of the open line, particularly south of Rugby, the regulator and reverser positions were set and the engine allowed to find its own pace, while the driver was in the tender.

Had I been going no further than Carlisle that day with the Polmadie men I would have thought that the engine had the job very comfortably in hand. Indeed, had I retired from the footplate to the comfort of the train for the rest of the run I would have been confirmed in my first impression. Despite a number of signal checks and temporary slowings for permanent way work, we were on, or ahead of, our schedule at all important timing points, and eventually clocked into Euston 4 minutes early. Looking back on that epic journey, however, now more than fifty years ago, I do not think an average, fully experienced top-link

engine crew could have been blamed for losing quite a lot of time in the conditions that developed before we were halfway to London.

A friend, a lifelong railwayman, who was an expert recorder of train speeds, travelled by the southbound 'Royal Scot' as a passenger a week or so after I did in April 1934, and from what he noted from the train I should imagine the crew were in much the same trouble for steam as we were. The difference was that there was no third man on the footplate to help with signal sighting, if the driver should have felt inclined to help in getting coal forward; and sad to say they had a net loss of no less than 18 minutes to be booked against them on the Carlisle-Euston non-stop run. Experienced observers of train running put these vicissitudes in performance down to inexperience on the part of the engine crews, and to the various teething troubles that inevitably beset the early months of working any new design incorporating so many new features as those included in the LMS Nos 6200 and 6201.

The major problem, of course, was the boiler, with the variation in quality of coal available at the different sheds concerned with the West Coast Main Line traffic. The intensive utilization envisaged, when the class was enlarged and taking a major share in the most important long mileage duties, would result in the locomotives being handled by men from Camden, Crewe North, Carlisle (Upperby) and Polmadie sheds; and it would require that the locomotives should respond adequately to average rather than specialized management. The original tasks of working through with the 'Royal Scot' train in each direction with lengthy overnight stopovers were considered to be no more than so many preliminary canters, and turn-round times of little more than four hours in London and Glasgow were envisaged. This kind of utilization obviously could not be attempted while the engines were so 'touchy' in steam production as was demonstrated on my footplate journey on No 6200.

At that early stage in the history of the 'Pacific' engines, with only two of them available, experience in firing technique was necessarily limited, and the man I rode with was firing 'all round the box', as he would have done with the earlier 4-6-0 locomotives. In later years, the work was found more effective and much less laborious by keeping a very thick fire just under the door, and tapering it gradually towards the front. Firing technique apart, Stanier had the steam circuit very carefully examined, and he found that the cross-sectional area through the superheater formed a bottle-neck in the steam flow. The superheater was based closely upon Swindon practice and he found on examination of the Great Western drawings that the 'Kings' were equally restricted. Hoping to be helpful, he wrote to Collett to tell him what they had discovered, but his letter was not even acknowledged! The early troubles experienced with engines 6200 and 6201 convinced Stanier that with the variations in fuel that had to be used, and the diversity of duties, the medium

The second Stanier 'Pacific' No 6201, then unnamed and fitted with shelters for men taking indicator diagrams and other running tests (British Railways).

degree of superheat cherished on the Great Western was not suitable for LMS conditions, and a boiler of distinctly modified design was worked out for the production batch of ten more 'Pacifics' authorized for the 1935 building programme.

A very important change was made in the design of the tender, and the new type was fitted to engines 6200 and 6201 before there was any notification of changes to the boilers. In the new tenders, the traditional Midland style disappeared; but quite apart from the side panelling, and its upward extension and shaping to the loading gauge profile, the boon to the firemen was the continuous sloping floor to the coal space, on quite a steep slope, which ensured that the coal trimmed forward readily and the labour of getting supplies forward was greatly lessened. The capacity was the same, carrying 4,000 gallons of water and 9 tons of coal.

The nigh on two years of observation, investigation and analysis of the performance vagaries of the two prototype 'Pacifics' came to an end in the winter of 1934-5, with the decision to abandon the Great Western principle of a moderate degree of superheat, and revert to the practice of the former London and North Western Railway, which had proved so brilliantly successful on the Bowen Cooke express locomotives, though now, of course, incorporating all the sophistications of modern practice in the manner of lubrication, steamtightness of valves, and so on. And it was in the early months of 1935 that engine No 6200 got her new boiler, and authorization was obtained to build ten more 'Pacifics' of the improved design. This situation marked an important stage in the campaign Riddles and his team were waging to ride out the opposition to the Stanier locomotives

generally; and Riddles himself took a leading part in the dynamometer car trials of engine No 6200 that were conducted at the end of June.

The first of these was made on the high-speed 6.12 pm from Crewe to Willesden, but in very different circumstances from the demonstration high-speed run on the same train in April 1934. Then, a gross load estimated as 380 tons behind the tender was run over the 152.7 miles in 134½ minutes. On 27 June 1935, a load of 475 tons was taken over the same distance in 129½ minutes; and those overall average speeds of 68 mph with 380 tons, and of 70.8 mph with 475 tons, amply indicate the degree of improvement that had been built into the locomotive. But the most significant feature of the working, made clear by details of driving technique included in the information published in the technical press at the time, was that the locomotive was at no time being 'thrashed' to make this spectacular run. It was, on the contrary, being worked in a way approximating to the thermodynamic ideal. The regulator was full open for most of the time, to take advantage of the high pressure of steam in the boiler, but the reverser was linked up to ensure steam was cut off at each of the piston strokes as early as possible. On the fast undelayed

The Princess Royal with new high-superheat boiler and improved tender with a dynamometer car and extra coaches approaching Carlisle with the down 'Royal Scot' in 1936 (P. Ransome-Wallis).

stretch of 67.2 miles from Welton to Wembley, for example, the contrast between this run and my own, just over a year earlier, was profound:

LMS: Welton-Wembley (pass to pass)

Engine 4-6-2 No 6200		
Date	**3-4-34**	**27-6-35**
Load (gross trailing, tons)	500	475
Average speed (mph)	66.6	77.2

On the earlier journey, the engine was working in 20 per cent cut-off throughout, with full regulator, while on the second the cut-offs were mostly at 15 to 18 per cent. On the ascent to Tring, a brief use was made of the longer cut-off of 25 per cent, and whereas on my run speed fell away to 48 mph at the summit, on the second the minimum speed was no less than 67 mph, a remarkable difference.

On the latter run, some fast running was made on the gently favourable stretches, with eight individual maximum speeds of 80 mph and over, with a highest of 86½ mph and three other instances of 85½ mph. Riddles himself rode on the footplate of the locomotive, and the CME's department may well have been highly gratified at the vast improvement in the performance of the locomotive as manifested by this run.

Having demonstrated so brilliantly the capacity of the modified locomotive in high-speed running on the easily graded route south of Crewe, a dynamometer

The first of the 1935 batch of 'Pacifics', No 6203 Princess Margaret Rose, *passing Oxenholme with the down 'Royal Scot'* (Rail Archive Stephenson, photo F.R. Hebron).

car test run with a train of empty coaches, totalling 461 tons tare, was made from Crewe to Glasgow and back on Sunday 30 June, a round trip of 490 miles in the course of which some very hard running was made in climbing the steep gradients of the North Country. At that time, the down 'Midday Scot' was allowed 84 minutes to cover the 72 miles from Crewe to Lancaster; 83 minutes for the continuing 69.1 miles over Shap to Carlisle; and 89 minutes for the 73.5 miles to Carstairs, in each case start to stop. On the test run, with a gross trailing load of 470 tons, these times were cut to 71 min 38 sec, 68 min 24 sec, and 69 min 11 sec—in the last-mentioned case, the time was to passing through Carstairs station.

The most important feature of this remarkable Sunday's running was the economy in fuel consumption with which such outstanding times were made. The coal consumption for the round trip averaged 52.6 lb per mile, or a total of 11½ tons for the round trip. Related to the work done, it worked out at no more than 2.88 lb per drawbar horsepower hour. This is almost exactly the same as the results published for the Great Western 4-6-0 *Caldicot Castle* in 1924, which caused such astonishment and disbelief in locomotive engineering circles at the time. But there are two very important differences in the circumstances of the two sets of trials. The first is that the 'Castle', although conveying the maximum loads scheduled for each section of the route between Swindon and Plymouth, was worked at normal rates of steam consumption. *The Princess Royal* was worked exceptionally hard. The second point is that the very

great increase in the degree of superheating provided by the new boiler fitted to the LMS engine, and the fundamental divergence from long-established Great Western practice in this respect, made no difference to the basic coal consumption. The way was clear for the notable improvements in the Anglo-Scottish train service that were brought into effect in May 1936.

Early in July, the first of the new engines of the class, No 6203 *Princess Margaret Rose,* was completed and, after 'running in', working from Crewe North shed, it was allocated to Camden, for the Euston-Glasgow 400-mile turns. I was at Crewe on 6 August, and saw her come through with the down 'Royal Scot', non-stop to Kingmoor as usual in the summer service, where she would be remanned for the Scottish continuation of the run. In the official description, published in *The Railway Gazette* on 19 July 1935, the engine was stated to have a 32-element superheater, with a heating surface of 653 sq ft. But while this may have been the intention so far as all the new 'Pacifics' were concerned, more recent researches into departmental documents have indicated that the first four of the new engines had 24-element superheaters, with a heating surface of 467 sq ft. These four engines had the modified firebox, with combustion chamber, and the shorter boiler barrel, as on No 6200 in her second form. At the same time there seems to be documentary evidence that the varying types of 'Pacific' boilers were switched around between individual engines, so that short of opening smokebox doors one could not be sure of what the 'innards' were on any one occasion. In any case, it did not seem to matter much, for one of the most outstanding performances I noted in these early years was with a locomotive that, according to this later documentation, had a 24-element superheater.

19. Stanier locomotives, medium and large

It was natural that much attention should be given to the 'Pacific' engines representing the most advanced practice in British locomotive development; but after all, their numbers could, at the time, be counted on one hand, whereas the Stanier 4-6-0s could already be counted in their hundreds. So something of a digression must be made, for a few pages, to record the development of the lesser units of the LMS fleet. Following experience with the first 'Pacific' engines, and the modifications made to provide an increased cross-sectional area for steam flow through the superheater, a change was made to the boilers of new Class '5' engines built from 1935 onwards, commencing with Nos 5070-5074, built at Crewe. Following this 'pilot' batch, no fewer than 377 further engines of the class were built by contractors between 1935 and 1937, Nos 5075—5124 by Vulcan Foundry Ltd, and Nos 5125—5451 by Armstrong Whitworth. A further development, with a still larger superheating surface, was embodied in locomotives built from 1938 onwards. The three stages of development were thus:

Class '5' 4-6-0 boilers

Batch	5000-5069	5070-5451	5452 onwards*
Period	1934-5	1935-7	1938 onwards
Superheater elements (number)	14	24	28
Heating surfaces (sq ft)			
Superheater	227.5	307.0	359.0
Tubes	1,460	1,460	1,479
Firebox	156	171.3	171.0
Total	1,843.5	1,938.3	2,009
Grate area (sq ft)	27.8	28.65	28.65

*Includes engines numbered below 5000

It will be seen from the foregoing that it was not merely a case of rearrangement of the boiler in successive developments; it was an all—round enlarge-

Left *'Black Five' two-cylinder 4-6-0 No 5171 climbing Shap on a fast goods with a bank engine in the rear* (British Railways).

Right *'Black Five' No 5362 taking water at Balquhidder on an express from Glasgow to Oban* (O.S. Nock).

ment, which gave remarkably successful results in service. In these latter engines, while the top feed was retained, a dome was mounted on the boiler, with a grid-type regulator within. In view of the increasing use of the locomotives in express passenger service, I may add that the piston valves were of 10-in diameter, with a travel in full gear of 6½ in, steam lap 1½ in and exhaust clearance ¹/₁₆ in.

Very careful attention was given to the design of the running gear to ensure trouble-free service. The coupling and connecting rods were of fine-grain steel and the wheel centres were steel castings, with Gibson rings for fixing the tyres. The balance weights were of the built-up type, instead of being cast integrally with the wheels; these consisted of steel plates on either side of the spokes, filled in between, to the required weight, with lead. The locomotives were balanced to 50 per cent of the reciprocating parts. These engines had the standard Stanier arrangement of axle-box, while following the Second World War some had the additional refinement of manganese steel liners in the horn guides. The result was a locomotive singularly free from incidental trouble in service.

The Class '5s' have been referred to as 'the enginemen's friend'. This is taking too narrow a view of it; from my own experience, and from discussions with locomotive men of all grades and in all parts of the LMSR system from London to Wick, I would say they were everybody's friend. I have never known a locomotive so universally acclaimed. Up to the end of 1939, the 500 engines of the class then in service were averaging 145,000 miles between general repairs,

while in the years 1938 and 1939 there had been no more than 54 cases of heated axle-boxes. This latter represented a probability of a hot axle-box on any one engine of only once in 15 years.

So far as mileages between general repairs are concerned, the rather remarkable fact emerged that the performance seemed to be steadily improving, rather than deteriorating with the age of the locomotives. In 1952, the average mileage from one general repair to the next was approximately 160,000, though one must not forget the intermediate mileages between classified repairs. These locomotives had one or more intermediate repairs between successive 'generals'. For the year ending 31 December 1957, average mileages between repairs for the Class '5' 4-6-0 locomotives maintained on the LMR were as follows:

	Average mileage between general repairs	Mileage to intermediate repair after general	Mileage to general or intermediate repair after previous intermediate repair
Locomotives fitted with white-metalled boxes	167,069	73,014	64,286
Locomotives fitted with manganese steel liners	182,826	90,639	79,494

Above *Liverpool-Glasgow express passing Tebay hauled by 'Jubilee' Class three-cylinder 4-6-0 No 5706* Express *(Derek Cross).*

Left *Crewe-Glasgow relief express approaching Shap Summit hauled by 'Jubilee' Class three-cylinder 4-6-0 No 45629* Straits Settlements *(Derek Cross).*

Above right *'Jubilee' Class 3-cylinder 4-6-0 No 45700* Amethyst *in British Railways black livery (British Railways).*

As regards thermodynamic performance and general haulage ability on the road, the Class '5' 4-6-0s on their own showing can be regarded equally as express passenger engines, without any reservations or qualifications, and as very competent goods engines capable of heavy work on adverse gradients. A locomotive that can work a fitted freight of 600 tons between Carlisle and Sheffield at an average speed of 32 mph inclusive, and which can run freely up to 90 mph with a 300-ton express passenger train between St Pancras and Leicester, certainly qualifies for the description 'general utility'. Tests with the dynamometer car and engine No 5079 gave the following results:

	Fitted freight services	Express passenger services
Coal consumption		
lb per mile	55.7	34.7
lb per dhp/hr	3.13	3.38
Water consumption		
gal per mile	41.5	32.8
lb per dhp/hr	23.3	24.3
Evaporation		
lb of water per		
lb of coal	7.44	7.49

Having regard to the versatility of the engines and their general usefulness in any kind of service, the above must be considered as highly satisfactory results.

Turning to the 'Jubilee' Class of three-cylinder 4-6-0s, generally speaking their début was not as successful as that of the 'Black Fives'. I fancy that some of my own early experiences were typical. There were steaming troubles at first, and naturally the reaction to them from the footplatemen was unfavourable in comparison with the 'Baby Scots'. But there was nothing inherently wrong with the design of the boiler or machinery. It so happened that the draughting was not ideally proportioned. Had the need for new engines been less urgent there would have been time for a few prototypes to be built before quantity production began. As it was, 113 of them were ordered straight off the drawing boards, and it needed no more than a very simple alteration to the blast pipe orifice diameter to put their steaming absolutely right. In their early days, with the small superheaters and domeless boilers, I found them a little slow in warming up to their work.

As with the 'Black Fives', there was a similar development, so far as the boiler was concerned, on the 'Jubilees'. The later engines of the class were fitted with boilers having 24-element superheaters, domes and a separate top feed. The relative proportions, as compared with those of the original engines, were:

	Original type	Modified type
Heating surfaces (sq ft)		
Tubes	1,462.5	1,460

	Original type	**Modified type**
Firebox	162.4	181
Superheater	227.5	300
Combined total	1,852.4	1,941
Grate area (sq ft)	29.5	31.0
Working pressure (psi)	225	225

The improvement was perhaps even more pronounced than in the case of the 'Black Fives'. The latter had been a success from the start, whereas the '5Xs' had been variable. As modified, the '5Xs' became extraordinarily willing and hard-slogging engines, as well as being very swift on the favourable stretches of line. An outstanding experience of my own was on the footplate of engine No 5565 *Victoria*, working the up 'Thames-Clyde Express', when the cut-off was maintained at 42 to 47 per cent with full regulator on the ascent from Carlisle almost to Armathwaite at speeds of well above 40 mph and sustaining a drawbar horsepower (corrected for gradient) of 1,400 to 1,500. The steaming was excellent during this heavy spell, and indeed throughout the long run from Glasgow to Leeds. The '5X' engines were very reliable hill-climbers, and a test of their versatility was to be seen in the working of the St Pancras-Manchester expresses throughout from one terminus to the other.

On a train like the 10.15 am down in the year 1958, the one '5X' engine in the course of a single through run was required to average almost 60 mph from start to stop from St Pancras to Kettering, with running at 80 mph to 85 mph in places; to make a short and sharp run from Leicester to Loughborough, 12½ miles in 14 minutes start to stop; and then from Matlock to tackle, with an unchanged load of 350 tons, the heavy ascent to Peak Forest. On the long stretches of 1 in 100 gradient, continuous use of 30 per cent cut-off with full regulator was necessary to keep time to Millers Dale; but the most severe test came in the restart from the latter station, up a continuous 1 in 90, where the 4.6 miles to Peak Forest are scheduled for 10 minutes start to pass. Cut-offs never less than 40 per cent with full regulator were necessary for timekeeping. Records available of the working on this train showed highly consistent steaming throughout and a ready response to all demands for power, whether in slogging uphill to Peak Forest, or in running at nearly 80 mph on the level between Leicester and Loughborough.

The first of the Stanier standard 2-8-0 locomotives, No 8000, was completed at Crewe in the early summer of 1935. Like the earlier Class '5' mixed traffic 4-6-0s, the first batches had domeless boilers. While the cylinders and motion were the same as on the 4-6-0s, the boiler was shorter, though making use of existing flanging plates. Later engines were fitted with domed boilers, and large fireboxes—the latter exactly the same as on the 4-6-0s. With cylinders of 18½-in diameter by 28-in stroke, a boiler pressure of 225 psi and coupled wheels of 4-ft 8½-in diameter, the nomi-

nal tractive effort was 32,438 lb at 85 per cent boiler pressure. The maximum axle load on the locomotive was 16 tons, in fact less than the maximum on the tender, which was 18.6 tons. With long-travel, long-lap valves, as on the Class '5', the new 2-8-0 locomotives were surprisingly free in running, and I shall never forget my first personal experience of one of them. At the time of their introduction, and for some years afterwards, I was often travelling home by the 6.15 pm residential train from Euston, running non-stop to Bushey. Until 1935 we usually had former LNWR engines from Bletchley shed— 'George the Fifths', 'Princes', or, more often than not, an old non-superheated 'Experiment'. The Stanier 4-6-0s duly came on to the job, and one night, with the usual 215-ton train, we went out to Bushey faster than ever before, sustaining a speed of over 60 mph on the 1 in 337 rise from Wembley. Only when we arrived at Bushey did I see that the new taper-boilered engine that had worked the train was not a 4-6-0 at all, but a 2-8-0!

Freight engines are habitually much longer lived than their express passenger contemporaries—indeed, many of the old LNWR 0-8-0s remained in heavy service until the late 1960s, long after the Crewe express engines had all been scrapped. There was not

Top left *The first Stanier 2-8-0, No 8000, built at Crewe in 1936* (British Railways).

Above left *One of the 1935 batch of Stanier 'Pacifics', No 6205* Princess Victoria (British Railways).

Right *The 10.30 am Euston-Liverpool express near Bourne End in 1935 hauled by 4-6-2 No 6205* Princess Victoria (Rail Archive Stephenson, photo F.R. Hebron).

therefore in the late 1930s so urgent a need for the new 2-8-0s, and by the end of 1939 no more than 126 of them had been built. But the onset of war changed everything. How the class was then developed is recounted later in this book.

Returning now to the big engines, when I was privileged to visit Crewe Works in August 1935, work on the belt system of erection was rapid and the new 'Pacific' engines were being turned out at the rate of one every 5½ days. Their names were all of ladies of the British royal family, thus:

6203	*Princess Margaret Rose*
6204	*Princess Louise*
6205	*Princess Victoria*
6206	*Princess Marie Louise*
6207	*Princess Arthur of Connaught*
6208	*Princess Helena Victoria*
6209	*Princess Beatrice*
6210	*Lady Patricia*
6211	*Queen Maud*
6212	*Duchess of Kent*

By October, all ten of the new engines were in regular express traffic and doing consistently first class work. I was not able to accompany any of their Euston-Glasgow turns, but their working diagrams were arranged to include the down 'Merseyside Express', a heavy and fast train, and also the up 'Liverpool Flyer', with its 64.5-mph booking from Crewe to Willesden.

The 'Princess Royal' Class locomotives, the 'Lizzies' to give them their homely nickname, reached their pre-war zenith of performance in the working of the day Anglo-Scottish expresses in the twelvemonth between May 1936 and the introduction of the streamlined 'Coronation Scot' in 1937. From that time onwards, because of the alterations to the train service and the advent of the new 'Pacific' locomotives, they tended to be somewhat overshadowed. But in the revival of real express running on the West Coast route in the last years of steam traction, the 'Lizzies' rose to even greater heights of achievement, as later chapters of this book will bear eloquent witness. At this stage, however, I am mainly concerned with the 'Midday Scot', and particularly with the exacting northbound run from Lancaster to Penrith. The difficulty of this 52.1-mph start-to-stop booking, over Shap, did not by any means rest entirely on the power output required on this one section; and in comparing it with some notable hill-climbing achievements of the past, particularly with London and North Western locomotives, the markedly changed operating conditions must be borne in mind.

In North Western days, locomotives of the Anglo-Scottish expresses worked only between Crewe and Carlisle in the Northern Division. Engines were always changed at Crewe, and the daytime trains, which had the sharpest timings, were taken forward by picked engines, and men who were specialists on the road. From 1936 onwards, it was very different. The 2 pm from Euston, although from the start not carrying quite such a heavy load, had a non-stop run to Crewe roughly equal in speed to that of the 'Merseyside Express'; but whereas the engine and crew of the latter train were going no further than Liverpool, the 'Pacific' on the 'Midday Scot' was remanned at Crewe, and had a further 243 miles to go, including the exacting stage from Lancaster to Penrith. Furthermore, the load was *increased* at Crewe by the addition of the through portion from Plymouth to Glasgow. While the opening run down from Euston was always in the hands of Crewe North men, the continuation to Glasgow had Crewe and Polmadie men on alternate days. Neither was the hard work finished when the train reached Penrith. After a fast run down to Carlisle, none too easy in spite of the favourable gradients because the start had to be made with the lengthy train strung out on a relatively sharp curve, there remained the 102.3-mile non-stop run from Carlisle to Glasgow, admittedly with a reduced load, but still requiring a very high standard of locomotive work.

It is unfortunate that the fairly extensive documentation concerned with the working of this train relates only to the first few weeks of its operation, in summer weather conditions. One had also to take account of the personal factor in assessing the quality of the locomotive work actually displayed. In steam days on the railways of Great Britain, the human element intruded to a far greater extent than was evident in France or the USA in the working of exacting schedules, and the losses of time incurred on some of the journeys to be discussed were probably just as much the result of a driver's attitude to the job as were the gains in time displayed on others. The running details so meticulously recorded do not give any drivers' names, nor whether they were based at Crewe or Polmadie. It is interesting to note that one of the finest runs, and the poorest run, in the collection were made by the same engine, No 6208 *Princess Helena Victoria*. It is also notable that on the first five days on which the schedule was operated a different 'Pacific' was used each day.

The bulk of the data on which the accompanying analysis of the performance is based was recorded in meticulous detail by Mr R.E. Charlewood, a veteran railwayman whose observations of train running, particularly over the London and North Western main line, extended back to the turn of the century. His annual survey of LNWR express running in *The Railway Magazine* began as early as 1901. He rode the

The down 'Royal Scot' passing Oxen-holme in 1935 hauled by 4-6-2 No 6206 Princess Marie Louise (Rail Archive Stephenson, photo F.R. Hebron).

The down 'Royal Scot' passing Hay Fell Box in 1935 hauled by 4-6-2 No 6203 Princess Margaret Rose (Rail Archive Stephenson, photo F.R. Hebron).

The up 'Midday Scot' just over Shap Summit and racing down to Tebay hauled by 4-6-2 No 6212 Duchess of Kent (Derek Cross).

LMS: The 'Midday Scot' in 1936-7
Carnforth-Shap Summit (31.4 miles, schedule 37 minutes, 50.9 mph)

Engine No	Engine name	Load (gross trailing, tons)	Actual time (m s)	Average speed (mph)	Initial speed (mph)	Final speed (mph)	Average equivalent drawbar horsepower
6200	*The Princess Royal*	470	34 08	55.5	72	35	1,683
6212	*Duchess of Kent*	520	37 50	49.8	64	27 ⅛	1,609
6205	*Princess Victoria*	470	38 25	49.9	64 ½	30	1,428
6208	*Princess Arthur of Connaught*	470	40 14	46.9	64	23 ½	1,359
6203	*Princess Margaret Rose*	470	36 18	51.9	67	31 ½	1,555
6206	*Princess Marie Louise*	475	39 53	47.5	63	24	1,371
6210	*Lady Patricia*	530	38 42	48.9	63	29	1,573
6209	*Princess Beatrice*	470	35 31	53.0	70 ½	27 ½	1,556
6208	*Princess Arthur of Connaught*	515	35 38	52.7	71	28 ½	1,673

'Midday Scot' from Lancaster to Penrith every day in the first week of its acceleration, and had some further notable trips subsequently. His interest was purely in the running times. He was not an engineer, and regarded locomotives and their handling as quite incidental to the business of keeping scheduled time. But his records were so accurate, and so complete, that a close analysis of the engine performance, and of the horsepower involved, could be made from them. The accompanying table has been prepared from the foregoing and from two other runs logged by other observers. That with the pioneer engine, No 6200, on the 1935 test run, was recorded by Mr D.S. Barrie; but outstanding as was its climbing speed, it was practically equalled in power output by a performance of engine No 6208 in ordinary service. In calculating the drawbar horsepower, careful account has been taken of the difference between the speeds at Carnforth and Shap Summit, and the difference in kinetic energy in the start and the finish of the ascent.

I have been inclined to dwell on the severity of this schedule, not only for itself, but because of the way it was slotted into a roster of locomotive utilization more intense than anything previously set before the principal express passenger types on the West Coast route. Nevertheless, so far as the critical section from Carnforth to Shap Summit is concerned, in applauding the fine performance of the 'Princess Royal' Class locomotives, the achievements of past years must not be forgotten, relating loads and the average horsepower to the weight and nominal tractive effort of the locomotives concerned. It is the London and North Western 'Claughton' 4-6-0 Class that provides probably the most interesting example, because the 'Royal Scot' 4-6-0s, while fulfilling their difficult role admirably and economically, never seemed to rise to their highest levels of performance on the gradients of the North Country.

I have taken the two fastest climbs of the Grayrigg bank on the 'Midday Scot' on ordinary service, by engines 6208 *Princess Helena Victoria* and 6209 *Princess Beatrice,* and tabulated alongside them two notable 'Claughton' runs when high horsepower readings were obtained. The first was with a maximum tonnage load on the Glasgow portion of the 10 am from

Drawbar horsepower comparisons, Grayrigg and Shap banks

Date	Engine No	Load (tons)	Average speed (mph)	Average dhp	Dhp/te	Dhp/total weight	Dhp/engine weight
1935	6209	470	53.0	1,556	86.7	10.0	14.8
1936	6208	515	52.5	1,673	92.7	10.9	15.7
1914	2222	440	44.5	1,130	103	9.5	14.7
1925	30	405	45.5	1,075	100	9.0	13.9

Euston, when, in 1914, the pioneer engine of the class, *Sir Gilbert Claughton*, took a 440-ton load over Shap without assistance, and gained time on the 159-minute schedule then in force between Crewe and Carlisle. The second run was made during a series of comparative dynamometer car tests with various LMS types on special trains between Preston and Carlisle in 1925. The 'Claughton' Class engine concerned was No 30, *Thabala*. These LMS tests were made when economy in coal consumption was a major consideration, though not at the expense of losing time uphill and getting it back with high speed downhill running from Shap. A special requirement of the tests was that all the competitors were to endeavour to maintain the uphill times. This the 'Claughton' engine did, with the maximum test load of 405 tons. The accompanying table reveals that as far as horsepower per tractive effort was concerned, the 'Claughtons' had the advantage over the 'Lizzies', but in engine weight the ratios were reversed, albeit no more than slightly.

Going north over the Caledonian line, *The Princess Royal* on a dynamometer test run on 30 June 1935 did some notable work, producing a sustained power output greater by far than anything previously achieved over this route. It was significant, however, from the schedule times laid down as shown in the accompanying log, that the actual times over this section of the route were little more than were expected — indeed, a little time that had been gained between Carlisle and Beattock station was lost ascending the main part of the bank. Schedule times apart, however, the running was magnificent throughout from Carlisle to Beattock Summit, and a notable tribute to the remarkable improvements effected in the design of this locomotive by use of the modified boiler with the greatly enlarged superheater. There was evidently no shortage of steam after the ascent of the Beattock Bank, for a very rapid descent of the Clyde valley fol-

The down 'Royal Scot' beside the Oxford Canal near Brinklow in 1937 hauled by 4-6-2 No 6210 Lady Patricia *(Rail Archive Stephenson, photo T.G. Hepburn).*

lowed, including such speeds as 82 mph at Crawford, and 83 mph before Lamington. There had been a gain on schedule time by Symington, and with a further high maximum of 79 mph before Strawfrank Junction, Carstairs was passed a little over 3 minutes early. No significant speeds were needed in running the remaining 28.8 miles down to Glasgow in 31¾ minutes.

LMSR: Dynamometer car test Carlisle-Glasgow, 30 June 1935

Engine 4-6-2 No 6200 *The Princess Royal*
Load 461 tons tare, 470 tons full

Distance (miles)		Schedule time (min)	Actual time (m s)		Speed (mph)
0.0	Carlisle	0	0	00	—
4.1	Rockcliffe		5	51	61
8.6	Gretna Junction	10	9	40	73
13.0	Kirkpatrick		13	50	56
16.7	Kirtlebridge	18	17	32	67
20.1	Ecclefechan		20	36	57
25.8	Lockerbie	27	25	53	72
31.7	Dinwoodie		30	40	76/66
34.5	Wamphray		33	08	71
39.7	Beattock	40	37	58	58
45.4	Greskine Box		46	09	35
49.7	Summit	55	54	22	30
52.6	Elvanfoot		57	32	72
55.3	Crawford		59	33	82
57.8	Abington		61	42	76/83
63.2	Laminton		65	45	77
66.9	Symington	71	69	11	59
73.5	Carstairs	78	74	54	79/43
—			pws		—
102.3	Glasgow Central	112	106	30	—

Perhaps the most telling record of the prowess of the 'Princess Royal' Class lies in the three days of dynamometer car testing in October 1936, when engine No 6210 *Lady Patricia* was in competition with the 'Turbomotive', and the 400-mile journey between Glasgow and Euston was performed four times in

LMSR: Dynamometer car tests, London and Glasgow

Engine 4-6-2 No 6210 *Lady Patricia*

Route	Euston-Glasgow		Glasgow-Euston	
Train	10.0 am	2.0 pm	10.45 pm	10.0 am
Date (1936)	19 Oct	20 Oct	19 Oct	21 Oct
Weight of train behind drawbar (including dynamometer car)(tons)	552 tons to Crewe; 482 tons to Symington; 313 tons to Glasgow	480 tons to Crewe; 512 tons to Carlisle; 496 tons to Glasgow	534 tons to Crewe; 560 tons to Euston	336 tons to Symington; 534 tons to Euston
Train miles	401.92	401.95	402.09	402.12
Actual running time (min)	464.5	450.9	495.8	436.17
Speed Average (mph)	52.0	53.4	48.7	54.0
Maximum (mph)	80.0	82.2	81.0	83.0
Work done				
Horsepower hours	6,685.27	6,318.94	5,603.48	5,691.6
Average drawbar horsepower	863.54	840.84	678.30	782.95
Coal (excluding shed duties)				
Total weight (lb)	19,132	18,844	17,812	16,548
lb per mile	47.6	46.8	44.4	41.2
lb per drawbar horsepower hour	2.86	2.96	3.18	2.91
lb per sq ft of grate per hour (actual running time)	55.0	55.7	47.9	50.6
Water				
Total gallons	15,925	15,605	14,472	13,935
Gallons per mile	39.6	38.9	35.9	34.7
lb per drawbar horsepower hour	23.62	24.7	25.83	24.5
Evaporation				
lb of water per lb of coal	8.32	8.28	8.12	8.43

three days: down with the 'Royal Scot', up with the 'Night Scot', down with the 'Midday Scot' and finally up with the 'Royal Scot'. While the locomotive itself would be remanned as usual *en route*, I have often wondered as to what relief was provided for the testing staff in the dynamometer car. Not only were the actual runs lengthy, but the turn-round times both in Glasgow and London were not unduly long. The technical results of these four journeys, which are appended herewith, are taken from R.C. Bond's splendid paper presented to the Institution of Locomotive Engineers in January 1946, covering 'Ten Years' Experience with the LMS 4-6-2 Non-Condensing Turbine Loco 6202', to which extended reference is made in the next chapter of this book.

In respect of engine No 6210, while the figures are deeply impressive in themselves, they have a greatly added interest in the data concerning the southbound 'Night Scot', a train not normally coming within the sphere of observation of enthusiasts of the stop-watch. Although its running average speed of 48.7 mph was considerably slower than that of the daytime trains, the firing rate shows that its haulage was no mean task with the vast loads conveyed. It should also be emphasized that the tonnages quoted are the tare weights of the coaches, and that an addition of about 5 per cent needs to be added to each to assess the full load to be hauled.

The two southbound runs provide some remarkable contrasts. The actual amount of coal used on the 'Night Scot' was greater than that on the up 'Royal Scot', even though the latter train was run in such tremendous style as to be 29½ minutes less on the road, and the consumption per mile no more than 41.2 lb. This run, on 21 October 1936, with a tare load of 534 tons from Symington to Euston, must have been one of the most spectacular ever made by a 'Princess Royal' Class locomotive, with its total gain of 6 minutes on the booked running times then in operation. The northbound run on the 'Midday Scot' on the previous day was also a magnificent performance, in view of there being little reduction of load at Carlisle. Although the Edinburgh and Aberdeen sections were detached as usual, extra coaches were added to make the load up to nearly 500 tons tare for the non-stop run to Glasgow.

20. The experimental Turbomotive

In 1932, the original authorization for new maximum power express passenger locomotives was for three units of the 'Pacific' type. But with a man of Sir Harold Hartley's lofty scientific attainments, then well established as a Vice-President, it was not surprising that a drive towards greater technical efficiency in locomotive working would be strongly backed from the top. Ever since the successful application of the steam turbine to marine propulsion, railway locomotive engineers have sought means of realizing the increased thermal efficiency theoretically possible over that of the reciprocating steam engine. In other respects also, the turbine would appear to have attractions for rail propulsion, since the absence of heavy reciprocating parts would largely eliminate problems of balancing, and the resulting locomotives would be easier on the permanent way. To secure the greatest practical temperature range, and consequently the highest thermal efficiency, earlier turbine-driven locomotives had been equipped with condensers. The trouble with these experimental machines, like those tried out in various countries on the continent of Europe, was that the complications arising from the use of condensers and all their attendant equipment involved much additional maintenance work, and so reduced the availability of the locomotives in service that any reductions in fuel consumption due to increased thermal efficiency were far outweighed by the disadvantages.

At the same time, turbine propulsion in itself holds out so many inherent advantages that the idea was not finally abandoned, and for this reason a Swedish experimental locomotive, built in 1932, attracted considerable attention among locomotive engineers

Below *The Turbomotive, No 6202, as originally built with the domeless boiler as used on the 6203-6212 series of 'Princess Royal' 'Pacifics'* (British Railways).

Bottom *Turbomotive No 6202 with a domed boiler in 1937* (British Railways).

in this country. In that year, the Grangesberg-Oxelösund Railway put into service a 2-8-0 main-line locomotive using a non-condensing turbine. The railway in question had a number of 2-8-0 reciprocating steam locomotives of the same general power classification, using the same boiler, and the only difference between the turbine and the rest lay in the drive, which in the former was effected through triple-reduction gearing and a jack shaft. The extreme simplicity of the turbine drive appealed to British engineers, who were for ever seeking increased monthly mileages from their locomotives and immunity from failure, and at the invitation of the late Dr H.L. Guy, later Sir Henry Guy, then Chief Turbine Engineer of the Metropolitan-Vickers Company, Stanier visited Sweden to see the locomotive at work. Dynamometer car tests indicated savings of 7¼ per cent in coal consumption and 15 per cent in water in favour of the turbine, and serious consideration began to be given on the LMSR to the building of an experimental locomotive on similar lines. The Swedish locomotive was used in freight service, and the dynamometer car trials previously mentioned were carried out with loads of 1,500 tons.

Some very broad indications as to the advantages of turbine drive have already been outlined. One could perhaps group the respective arguments under three main headings: (1) a non-condensing turbine in place of cylinders, valves, and valve gear; (2) elimination of reciprocating parts; and (3) totally enclosed rotary gear drive, with efficient lubrication. The elimination of reciprocating parts results in the elimination of hammer-blow. With reciprocating steam locomotives, the civil engineer of the LMSR permitted a static axle load of 22½ tons maximum; but with turbine drive and a complete absence of hammer-blow, a static axle load of 24 tons maximum was permitted, thus providing for a most valuable increase in adhesion weight.

With regard to (3) above, by the use of a totally enclosed gear drive it was hoped to secure a substantial reduction in frictional losses, with a consequent reduction in wear and tear; it was also hoped to eliminate repairs to the running gear, and further to reduce the incidence of heating due to grit penetrating the work faces. All three factors, with their numerous ramifications, gave promise of a more powerful locomotive within the limits of weight laid down by the civil engineer's department, as well as greater availability and a reduced coal and water consumption over reciprocating locomotives doing the same work. With all this in mind, Stanier began active preparations for the design of an express passenger 'Pacific', generally similar to the 'Princess Royal' Class, but to be driven by a non-condensing turbine of the 'Ljungstrom' type. The collaboration of the Metropolitan-Vickers Company and Ljungstrom was obtained, and the power characteristics of the proposed new locomotive were worked out by Dr Guy and his staff.

The expectations of the new locomotive in comparison with those of the 'Princess Royal' Class were as follows:

	Reciprocating	Turbine
Boiler pressure (psi)	250	250
Steam temperature (°F)	850	650
Evaporation (lb/hr)	30,000	30,000
Output at rail (hp):		
at 30 mph	1,570	2,050
at 40 mph	1,700	2,270

Left *The left-hand side of the Turbomotive with its domed boiler at Camden shed in 1936 (P. Ransome-Wallis).*

Right *The Turbomotive, right-hand side view, showing the casing for the small reverse turbine (British Railways).*

	Reciprocating	Turbine
at 50 mph	1,770	2,350
at 60 mph	1,800	2,400
at 70 mph	1,770	2,350

It is interesting to learn that the turbine locomotive was designed for maximum efficiency at 62 mph, thus suggesting heavy hauls at relatively moderate speed, rather than the working of lightweight high-speed services. The tractive effort at starting was estimated at 40,000 lb as with the 'Princess Royal' Class, but at 70 mph the turbine was expected to sustain a drawbar pull of 5¼ tons.

Dr Guy was responsible for the design of the turbines and the gear drive, while the design of the chassis and boiler was developed by the Derby drawing office in association with Guy and his staff. There were two turbines, one for forward running and one for reverse, mounted very neatly on the running plates on the left-hand and right-hand sides of the locomotive respectively. There were 16 stages in the forward turbine, and with a view to using the locomotive (and others of her type that might be built subsequently) on the through Anglo-Scottish workings already allocated to the 'Princess Royal' engines, the internal arrangement of the blading was designed to maintain high efficiency over a wide range of speed. A high standard of performance was needed, equally when slogging up Shap and Beattock at 30 mph, and in making averages of 60 to 65 mph over long stretches south of Crewe. Steam was passed via one or more of six hand-controlled valves to the nozzle group in the turbine casing. The valves were opened in succession, and the power output of the turbine was regulated by the number of valves open. The turbine was permanently connected through double-helical triple-reduction gearing to the leading coupled axle. The reverse turbine, on the other hand, was normally not connected with the main drive; its reduction gear was connected when required through a sliding splined shaft and dog clutch mechanism. Originally there was a steam servo motor to effect engagement, but this was later discarded in favour of a simple hand control from the cab.

As originally built, No 6202 had a domeless boiler with proportions generally similar to those of the modified 'Princess Royal' type with a 32-element superheater, as in the 6203-6212 batch; but the layout of small tubes was different. A double blast pipe and chimney was fitted from the outset, and with a continuous exhaust, as compared with the pulsations of a reciprocating engine, some modifications to the draughting were necessary. The relevant boiler proportions were as follows:

Engine Nos	6203-6212, 6200 (modified)	6202 original	6202 later
Small tubes			
Number	123	112	81
Outside diameter (in)	2⅜	2¼	2¼
Superheater flues			
Number	32	32	40
Outside diameter (in)	5⅛	5⅛	5⅛
Heating surface superheater elements (sq ft)	653	653	577

The Turbomotive on the down 'Merseyside Express' passing Hatch End (C.R.L. Coles).

Engine 6202, as shown above, was later fitted with a boiler having a 40-element superheater that provided a free area through the flue tubes of 69.3 per cent of the total, as compared with 53.7 per cent in the original domeless boiler. This actually resulted in a slight reduction in superheating surface, though at a still later date a 40-element superheater with triple elements as in the 'Duchess' Class was fitted, and increased the superheater heating surface to 832 sq ft.

The locomotive was put into service in June 1935 and the most superficial observations showed that it was capable of the hardest work set to any LMSR locomotives of the day. It was used principally between Euston and Liverpool, and it is not without significance that one of the fastest among my large collection of runs on the down 'Merseyside Express' was made with No 6202. The engine rode very smoothly and was highly appreciated by the footplate staff. At first there was some trouble with exhaust steam beating down and obscuring the view from the cab glasses, but this was obviated by the fitting of deflector shields. On the journey in question, despite a relaying slack near Willesden, the 82.6 miles from

Euston to passing Rugby were covered in 83¼ minutes, with a load of 515 tons, and the average speed over the 18¾ miles from Cheddington to Castlethorpe was exactly 75 mph. Crewe, 158.1 miles, was passed in 163¾ minutes, in spite of a check from adverse signals and some enforcedly slow running for some miles north of Nuneaton, where it was foggy. North of Crewe, however, the fog was encountered in full measure, and a punctual arrival in Liverpool was not possible; but the net time to passing Crewe was equivalent to an average speed of 60 mph from leaving Euston.

With an entirely new type of locomotive, and one that remained the only example of its kind running in Great Britain, it was not altogether surprising that troubles were experienced in service. The remarkable thing is that they were so few—that is, until war conditions put an entirely different aspect upon locomotive operating in general. In a most frank and comprehensive paper presented to the Institution of Locomotive Engineers in 1946, my friend the late R.C. Bond gave a complete record of the availability of the locomotive, together with an account of all the major failures that occurred. Until the outbreak of war in 1939, the locomotive had averaged 54,205 miles per annum compared with about 80,000 miles per annum for the 'Princess Royal' Class; for a novel and experimental machine, this must be considered as a remarkably fine record, especially in that during the year 1936 a total of 73,268 miles was run. In the early days of the war, however, since this locomotive needed a good deal of specialized attention, it was taken out of traffic, and stored at Crewe.

At its best, the road performance of the locomotive was so good as to suggest that any amount of time and persistence was worth expending in order to achieve the reliability so absolutely essential in the heaviest traffic. At three different periods during 1936 and 1937, a series of dynamometer car trials was conducted on through Euston-Glasgow workings, matching the engine against standard 'Pacifics' of the 'Princess Royal' Class. These records are particularly interesting in that they represent the work of No 6202 with three different boilers, and at varying periods since last general overhaul. The majority of the tests were carried out on the 'Royal Scot', in each direction, though a few were on the accelerated 'Midday Scot', which from 1936 onwards had the remarkable booking from Lancaster to Penrith referred to in Chapter 19 of this book. For the most part, the loads conveyed were very heavy. The tabulated summaries show the average running speeds made throughout, but to present the tasks given both to No 6202 and to the competing reciprocating engines, the intermediate timings are given below:

	Distance (miles)	Schedule time (min)	Average speed (mph)
a) 10 am Euston to Glasgow			
Euston-Rugby	82.6	87	56.9
Rugby-Crewe	75.5	80	56.6
Crewe-Carlisle	141.0	159	53.3
Carlisle-Symington	66.9	81	59.6
b) 10 am Glasgow to Euston			
Glasgow-Symington	(reduced load)		
Symington-Carlisle	66.9	71	56.6
Carlisle-Euston	299.1	334	53.9
c) 2 pm Euston to Glasgow			
Euston-Crewe	158.1	163	58.2
Crewe-Lancaster	72	79	54.7
Lancaster-Penrith	51.2	59	52.1
Penrith-Carlisle	17.9	19	56.5
Carlisle-Glasgow	102.3	116	52.9

Except between Symington and Glasgow, where the load of the 'Royal Scot' express was generally lighter

LMSR Dynamometer car test runs, 2 pm Euston–Glasgow

Date	20.10.36	27.10.36
Engine No	6210	6202
Boiler	—	B
Load (tons tare):		
Euston-Crewe	480	454
Crewe-Carlisle	512	486
Carlisle-Glasgow	496	486
Length of trip (miles)	401.4	401.4
Actual running time (min)	450.9	454.9
Average speed (mph)	53.4	53.2
Maximum speed (mph)	82.2	85.0
Average drawbar horsepower	840.8	943.5
Coal consumption:		
per train mile (lb)	46.8	49.6
per dhp hr (lb)	2.96	2.78
per sq ft of grate area per hr (lb)	55.7	58.5
Water consumption (gallons per mile)	38.9	38.5
Evaporation:		
lb of water per lb of coal	8.28	7.71
lb per hour (running time)	20,750	20,280

through the detaching of the Edinburgh portions, the gross loads behind the tenders were generally above, rather than below, 500 tons. In view of this, the record of coal consumption, not only of the turbine but also of the 'Princess Royal' Class engines, is an exceedingly fine one. For easy reference, in the tables which have been set out in detail, the different boilers fitted to engine 6202 are referred to as A (domeless), B and C (both with domes), thus:

Ref letter	No of superheater elements	Superheater heating surface (sq ft)
A	32	653
B	40	577
C	40*	852

*With triple-flow elements

On two occasions, once with the 'Princess Royal' Class engine No 6210 as referred to in Chapter 19 and once with No 6202, the 400-mile run between London and Glasgow was performed four times in three days, by use of the 10.45 pm up sleeping car express, thus:

1 10 am Euston-Glasgow
2 10.45 pm Glasgow-Euston
3 2 pm Euston-Glasgow
4 10 am Glasgow-Euston

LMSR: Dynamometer car test runs, 10 am Euston-Glasgow

Date	4.5.36	6.5.36	26.10.36	22.6.37	24.6.37
Engine no	6202	6202	6202	6202	6202
Boiler	A	A	B	C	C
Load (tons tare):					
Euston-Crewe	564	556	535	484	489
Crewe-Symington	470	474	475	484	489
Symington-Glasgow	331	304	305	315	320
Length of trip (miles)	401.4	401.4	401.4	401.4	401.4
Actual running time (min)	452.16	449	442.75	448.5	436.5
Average speed (mph)	53.3	53.7	54.5	53.8	55.3
Average drawbar horsepower	831.5	787.6	828.6	851.2	858.2
Coal consumption					
per train mile (lb)	44.6	41.7	44.3	44.3	42.4
per dhp hr (lb)	2.86	3.14	2.91	2.81	2.74
per sq ft of grate area per hr (lb)	51.3	49.8	53.7	53.1	52.2
Water consumption (gallons per					
mile)	35.8	31.5	35.4	40.3	37.7
Evaporation					
lb of water per lb of coal	8.0	7.56	7.99	9.11	8.87
lb of water per hr (running time)	19,630	16,900	19,300	21,670	20,750

LMSR: Turbine loco No 6202, uphill performance

Carnforth-Oxenholme (12.8 miles)

Engine (boiler)	Load (tons tare)	Time (m s)	Average speed (mph)
6202 (A)	474	12 55	59.5
6202 (B)	475	14 55	54.5
6202 (C)	489	12 10	63.1

Oxenholme-Tebay (13.1 miles)

6202 (A)	470	16 20	48.2
6202 (B)	486	14 55	57.7*
6202 (C)	484	16 00	49.1

Tebay-Summit (5.5 miles)

6202 (A)	470	8 50	37.4
6202 (B)	486	7 10	46.1
6202 (C)	484	7 35	43.5

Beattock-Summit (10 miles)

6202 (A)	474	16 50	35.7
6202 (B)	486	15 15	39.4
6202 (C)	489	16 10	37.1

*'Midday Scot' schedule

The work performed by both engines, particularly on the difficult 2 pm down 'Midday Scot', showed that they had stood up to this severe test remarkably well. In this connection, the tests on the 2 pm down (see the tables on page 239) were perhaps the most severe of all. Apart from these two, the normal loads of the trains concerned were taken, with the addition only of the dynamometer car; but on the 2 pm, which at that time had its load reduced to about 300-350 tons for its fast non-stop run from Carlisle to Glasgow, the load was specially augmented, so that tare loads little short of 500 tons were conveyed.

Some of the individual performances involved were remarkable, especially the very fast ascents of the Shap and Beattock inclines by engine No 6202 with boilers B and C. At the same time, some of the running of this engine was unnecessarily hard over certain sections. The six valves did not permit of the fine adjustments of control that an experienced driver can exercize with the ordinary screw reverser on a reciprocating steam locomotive. On the final series of tests with No 6202 in June 1937, it would seem that the optimum performance was attained at a standard that appears definitely above the maximum achievements of the 'Princess Royal' Class. What this actually meant in running conditions can be appreciated from certain selected performances from the dynamometer car test runs made on the 'Royal Scot' in June 1937:

Speed (mph)	Load (tons tare)	Gradient (rising)	Drawbar pull (tons)	Drawbar hp	Total approx ihp
34	489	1 in 75	8.26	1,678	2,224
46¼	489	1 in 131	5.44	1,501	2,046
58	489	1 in 99	4.43	1,531	2,177
72½	483	1 in 333	3.50	1,517	2,336

On the basis of these tests and of the general performance of the locomotive during its first four years

The Turbomotive on the up 'Merseyside Express' near Brinklow in September 1937 (Rail Archive Stephenson, photo T.G. Hepburn).

of service, the results could be regarded as very encouraging, and it was certainly felt by many engineers that the experiment was worth pursuing still further. A point of considerable importance was that the uniform blast avoided any grooving of the firebox plates, and the boiler and firebox consequently had a better life than that of the reciprocating engines.

As previously mentioned, the Turbomotive was taken out of service in 1939; but when the war effort began to work up to its full intensity, and every engine that could turn a wheel was needed, No 6202 was put into service again and it was unfortunately under the stress of wartime conditions that the more serious failures took place. The overall picture, as presented in 1946 by Mr Bond, showed that since construction, but deducting the time when the engine was stored, the average annual mileage was only 28,500. In war conditions, the annual mileages of the 'Princess Royal' and 'Duchess' Classes had dropped from the pre-war 80,000 for both classes to 53,000 and 73,000 respectively, so that both were in a different category altogether from No 6202. While some of the troubles experienced with No 6202 were definitely attributable to war conditions, others were part of the price one would expect to pay for experience with a type of propulsion new on a British main-line express passenger locomotive. Lack of previous experience with turbine drive tended to make the inspection staff a little over-cautious, but while this is understandable, and a good fault, it sometimes resulted in the locomotive being 'stopped' when it actually proved to be unnecessary, and so contributed to the relatively poor availability record. Another important factor, sometimes, was the time spent in getting replacement parts. Where the turbines were concerned this meant obtaining them from the Metropolitan-Vickers Company, and with the latter very heavily engaged in vital war production it was difficult to get isolated production or repair jobs for No 6202 fitted in. The delays following upon failures were therefore much greater than they would have been in normal times, and far more than if a stud of turbine locomotives had been at work and the railway shops fully equipped to deal promptly with their maintenance. For these reasons, the availability record of No 6202 cannot be compared on any fair basis with that of the reciprocating 'Pacifics' of the LMSR. All the more serious failures took place during the war period, including the rather alarming breakage of the forward turbine spindle at 60 mph. These failures may, in part, be attributed to increasing mileage since construction, and as part of the experience that had to be obtained before a turbine locomotive of this kind could be considered as a thoroughly reliable all-round motive power unit.

In the circumstances that developed after nationalization, however, considerable expenditure would have had to have been incurred in renewing the main turbine and other parts, and it was decided to rebuild her conventionally. In the autumn of 1952, carrying the name *Princess Anne,* she took the road once more, as a very handsome variant of the 'Princess Royal' Class. In this form, however, she had the shortest of lives, being completely smashed up on 8 October in the tragic double collision at Harrow. We were not to learn what this new 'Pacific' entirely in the Stanier tradition could do.

21. The streamlined era

The announcement by the LNER of a lightweight high-speed service from King's Cross to Edinburgh for Coronation year, 1937, came as a jolt to established LMS operating philosophy for Anglo-Scottish services. The 'Royal Scot' and 'Midday scot' were popular and well patronized trains, and despite increased loading the haulage capacity of the latest 'Pacific' engines was proving not only adequate but was doing the job with notable economy. But in view of the latest LNER project, Lemon wanted a six-hour service from Euston to Glasgow, and to convince Sir Josiah Stamp and his fellow Vice-Presidents, he determined upon a demonstration run with a train of roughly the same weight as that of the 'Silver Jubilee', plus the Horwich dynamometer car. Stanier was in India at the time, one of a Committee of Enquiry into the finances of the state-owned railways, and while S.J. Symes was acting as head of the CME's department, the arrangements for this spectacular trial run rested in the eager and enthusiastic hands of R.A. Riddles, then Principal Assistant to the CME. The only person who was not particularly enthusiastic about the high-speed project was the Motive Power Superintendent, D.C. Urie, who was still rather anti-Stanier.

In retrospect, the choice of a locomotive for this very important and significant trial run was a little unusual. As will be appreciated from the details quoted at the end of Chapter 19, the 'Princess Royal' Class engine No 6210 was in tremendous form at that time, while so far as hill-climbing ability went, the

achievements of the Turbomotive, No 6202, were then unsurpassed. Instead, however, the one engine of the whole 'Pacific' series to retain the original boiler of 1933 was selected, No 6201, even though that boiler had by then been retubed and fitted with a 32-element superheater and a steam dome instead of the collector pipe used on all other engines of the class.

The revised boiler dimensions, as compared with those of the other engines of the class having 32-element superheaters, were:

Tubes	
Small	
number	119
outside diameter (in)	2⅜
Large	
number	32
outside diameter (in)	5⅛
Length between tube plates	
(ft in)	20 9
Heating surfaces (sq ft)	
Tubes	2,429
Firebox	190
Superheater	594
Total	3,213

The preludes to the two record runs were as dramatic as the runs themselves were brilliant; but it was not until I came to know Riddles and Bond personally and heard the tale from their lips that I realized how near to cancellation first the northbound and then the

southbound runs came. I have told the story in the astonishing detail in which it was related to me in the biography I wrote of Sir William Stanier and his engineering work. Abbreviated logs of the two magnificent runs made on these two successive days are set out herewith. Lemon made a festive occasion of it, and many eulogistic references to it all were made in the technical press, with many confident predictions of a regular six-hour service between Euston and Glasgow to match the promised LNER service between King's Cross and Edinburgh. But for reasons that have never been divulged, the new LMS train eventually took the road in a very much 'watered-down' form.

LMSR: Trial runs Euston-Glasgow-Euston, 16-17 November 1937

Engine 4-6-2 No 6201 *Princess Elizabeth*
Load down run 225 tons; up run 255 tons tare (260 tons in all)

Distance (miles)		Schedule time (min)	Actual time (m s)	Speed (mph)
Down run, 16 November				
0.0	EUSTON	0	0 00	—
5.4	Willesden Junc	8	7 22	66
17.5	Watford	18	18 58	80½
31.7	Tring	30	29 57	77
46.7	Bletchley	41	40 32	95½/*79
59.9	Roade	51	50 55	77
69.7	Weedon	—	58 20	82/*70
82.6	RUGBY	70	68 30	*35
97.1	NUNEATON	82	81 08	90/*83
106.5	Polesworth	—	88 20	82/*35
116.3	Lichfield	100	97 40	85/*76
133.6	STAFFORD	114	111 55	77½/*30
147.6	Whitmore	127	123 51	82/*63
153.3	Betley Road	—	128 22	93
158.1	CREWE	136	133 00	*20
182.1	WARRINGTON	156	153 39	*55
193.9	WIGAN	168	165 01	*49
199.7	Coppull	—	170 50	54
209.0	PRESTON	183	179 15	*20
230.0	LANCASTER	200	196 42	*86/57
236.3	Carnforth	205	201 38	83½
249.1	Oxenholme	215	211 45	*65
256.2	Grayrigg	—	218 10	66
262.2	Tebay	227	223 15	76
267.7	*Shap Summit*	233	228 23	57
281.2	Penrith	245	240 11	*53/88
299.1	CARLISLE	260	255 27	*20
307.7	Gretna	268	263 30	85½/*58
324.9	Lockerbie	282	277 47	90
338.8	Beattock	293	287 43	80
348.8	*Summit*	306	297 14	56
362.3	Lamington	—	309 30	81/*35
372.6	Carstairs	328	319 37	*25
388.5	Motherwell	344	336 40	many
401.4	GLASGOW	360	353 42	slacks

*Speed reduced by brakes to figures noted

Left *The down 'Coronation Scot' near Brinklow in 1937 hauled by engine No 6221* Queen Elizabeth *(Rail Archive Stephenson, photo T.G. Hepburn).*

Right *The up 'Coronation Scot' on Tebay troughs hauled by No 6224* Princess Alexandra *(British Railways).*

Distance (miles)		Schedule time (min)	Actual time (m s)	Speed (mph)
Up run, 17 November				
0.0	GLASGOW	0	0 00	many
12.9	Motherwell	16	16 47	slacks
18.3	Law Junc	22	24 31	for
28.8	Carstairs	33	34 28	curves
35.4	Symington	—	40 33	71½
39.1	Lamington	—	43 15	86½/*65
52.6	*Summit*	56	54 18	80/67
62.6	Beattock	—	62 28	75
76.5	Lockerbie	77	72 50	89/77½
93.7	Gretna	90	86 12	86½/*45
102.3	CARLISLE	97	93 22	85/*20
107.2	Wreay	—	99 17	—
120.2	Penrith	114	109 18	85/*75
133.7	*Shap Summit*	127	121 50	63/67
139.2	Tebay	132	126 18	82/*70
145.2	Grayrigg	—	131 25	69
152.3	Oxenholme	143	137 21	80/*66
165.1	Carnforth	153	147 20	86½/*65
171.4	LANCASTER	158	152 10	72
182.9	Garstang	167	161 05	87
192.4	PRESTON	175	168 15	*25
201.7	Coppull	—	178 05	76/71½
207.5	WIGAN	190	182 40	83/*48
219.3	WARRINGTON	202	193 34	77½/*51
227.1	*Weaver* Junc	209	201 31	79/*56
243.2	CREWE	223	213 15	95/*20
253.8	Whitmore	233	222 58	81/*65
267.8	STAFFORD	245	234 50	84/*30
277.1	Rugeley	253	242 29	80
285.1	Lichfield	259	248 41	92
291.4	Tamworth	264	253 02	82/*33
304.3	NUNEATON	277	264 38	90
318.8	RUGBY	289	276 10	87/*30
331.7	Weedon	—	287 15	82/*73
341.5	Roade	308	294 38	80
354.7	Bletchley	318	304 32	—
369.7	Tring	331	315 35	77½
383.9	Watford	342	325 45	91/*79
396.0	Willesden	352	335 50	*40
401.4	EUSTON	360	344 20	

*Speed reduced for curves, etc

Technical details of the two runs were as follows:

	Down 16 November	Up 17 November
Load behind tender (tons tare)	225	255
Actual running time (min)	353.7	344.1

	Down 16 November	Up 17 November
Average speed (mph)	68.2	70.15
Coal consumption		
lb per mile	46.8	44.8
lb per dbhp hr	3.68	3.48
lb per sq ft of grate area per hr	70.8	69.9
lb per hr	3,190	3,130
Water consumption		
gallons per mile	34.5	30.2
Evaporation, (lb of water per lb of coal	7.36	6.70
lb of water per hr	23,500	21,100

Weather conditions were considerably less pleasant on the up journey, with squalls of wind and much heavy rain, but despite this the task of the locomotive was lighter, notwithstanding the heavier load. It is evident from the details of the engine performance that the wind was of some assistance, as compared with conditions on the previous day when the weather was sunny. It is reported that the boiler steamed consistently well throughout both trips, and this engine, be it remembered, had the original length of barrel, though with larger tubes. It will be seen also that the average coal consumption per hour was slightly in excess of the 3,000 lb now considered the maximum to be expected with hand firing on a long continuous run.

In the past, a great deal of attention had been given to the effects of hammer-blow on the track, but under modern conditions it was by then becoming realized that the lateral forces exerted by the locomotive on the track are of no less importance than the vertical loads, and the question of the guiding of a locomotive was coming into prominence. Experiments had shown that the highest flange-forces are experienced at the leading coupled wheels, and the object of bogie or guiding wheels is not only to relieve some of the pressure on the coupled wheel flange when the engine is rounding a curve, but also by restraining the extremities of the engine to avoid oscillation and its resulting flange-forces on the straight. The de Glehn bogie, as adapted to English use at Swindon, had proved very effective in having adequate side control, by springs, and having the friction, at the point where the weight is carried, of a low and constant value. The pony trucks on the LMSR 'Pacifics' were designed with the same features, but Stanier and his staff included another interesting refinement in the design of the bogies for the later 'Pacifics'. Another point had been considered in leading up to this, namely that any arrangement of side control, whatever its nature, can only take effect after the side clearances between axle-box and horns, wheel-boss and axle-box, and wheel flange and rail have been taken up. An engine in which the sum of these clearances is great will be uncontrolled for a measurable distance on either side of its centre-line, and oscillation and high flange-forces are to be expected. Stanier therefore insisted on an extremely high standard of bogie axle-box maintenance, and on the LMSR 'Pacifics' a thicker flange was used on both bogie and trailing truck wheels to reduce the clearance between wheel and rail. The new 'Pacifics of 1937 were extremely smooth and steady riders; in the many hundreds of miles I have ridden on their footplates I have never noted the merest suspicion of hunting, or undue oscillation.

At first, the new 4-6-2 locomotives were known as the 'Princess Coronation' Class, but in this account it will be convenient to refer to them throughout by the class name by which they are known today, the 'Duchesses'. Superficially, at any rate, the differences between the 'Princess Royals' and the 'Duchesses' were only slight in regard to the engine proper. The relative dimensions that contributed to the figure of nominal tractive effort were as follows:

Class	'Princess Royal'	'Duchess'
Cylinders, diameter x stroke (in)	16¼ x 28	16½ x 28
Coupled wheel diameter (ft in)	6 6	6 9
Boiler pressure (psi)	250	250
Nominal tractive effort at 85% boiler pressure (lb)	40,300	40,000

In the fashion of the day it was perhaps inevitable that they should be streamlined, and in contrast to their LNER rivals, they were truly streamlined, in that the aerodynamic form of their outer case was very carefully fashioned so as to provide the least possible resistance to passage through the air at speed. Although I have not seen any figures to prove it, in all probability the air resistance of the 'Duchess' Class at speeds in excess of 75 mph was considerably less than that of the LNER 'A4' Class. With the streamlined form overshadowing all else, the tremendously massive proportions of the new locomotives could not, at first, be fully appreciated. At the same time, a study of the boiler proportions was enough to suggest that

careful design work had been put in to secure so large an increase in total heating surface for so small an increase in total weight. Comparison with the later 'Princess Royals' may be made as follows:

Class	'Princess Royal'	'Duchess'
Boiler:		
Tubes, small, number	123	129
outside diameter (in)	2⅜	2⅜
Superheater flues (number)	32	40
outside diameter (in)	5⅛	5⅛
Length between tube plates (ft in)	19 3	19 3
Heating surfaces (sq ft)		
Small tubes	1,272	1,545
Superheater flues	825	1,032
Firebox	217	230
Superheater elements	653	830
Total	2,967	3,637
Grate area (sq ft)	45	50
Weight of engine in working order (tons)	104½	105¼

The weight quoted above for the 'Duchess' is for the non-streamlined variety, so as to make comparison as fair as possible.

At the front end every care was taken in design to provide for the freest possible flow of steam. The diameter of the valves was increased from 8 in to 9 in and very large direct and internally streamlined passages were used. In his Presidential Address to the Institution of Locomotive Engineers in 1939, Stanier acknowledged the indebtedness of engineers all over the world to André Chapelon for drawing attention to the importance of internal streamlining, all the way through the steam circuit from the regulator to the blast pipe. Each link in the chain, regulator ports, steam pipes, superheater header and elements, and blast pipe, are subjects for separate study and investigation; but on the LMSR particular attention was paid to that part of the steam circuit involving the passage of the steam through the valves either into or out of the cylinders. A special apparatus was devised to test the effect of various forms of internal streamlining, and it was shown that the steam flow could definitely be improved. In the case of the exhaust ports, a reduction of as much as 37 per cent in the resistance to steam flow was effected.

In contrast to the four sets of valve gear on the

The Coronation *engine of 1937 at Camden shed, coaled up ready for the run to Glasgow* (C.R.L. Coles).

'Princess Royal' Class, a reversion was made on the 'Duchesses' to the Great Western arrangement of having only two sets for the four cylinders, though the layout was the inverse of that of the 'Star', 'Castle' and 'King' Classes, in having the motion outside, and a derived gear for the inside cylinders. This made a far more accessible arrangement. The rocking shafts driving the inside valve spindles were taken off at a point in rear of the outside cylinders so that the factor of expansion of the outside valve spindle did not arise. The leading dimensions of the valve motion in comparison with those of the 'Princess Royal' Class were:

Class	'Princess Royal'	'Duchess'
Piston valve diameter (in)	8	9
Maximum travel of valves (in)		
Outside cylinders	7¼	7¹/₃₂
Inside cylinders	7⁵/₁₆	7¹/₃₂
Steam lap (in)	1¾	1¾
Exhaust clearance (in)	nil	¹/₁₆
Lead (in)	¼	¼
Cut-off in full gear (per cent)	73½	75

The provision of a small amount of exhaust clearance on the 'Duchesses' is a point to notice, but by far the greatest difference lay in the increase of the valve diameter from 8 in to 9 in, and a very free-running engine resulted.

The first of the new class, engine No 6220 *Coronation*, was completed at Crewe Works in May 1937, and the unusual form of the streamlining, in contrast to that of the then well-known 'A4s' of the LNER, created much interest and comment. The blue and silver finish, with the horizontal lines continuing throughout the length of the train, certainly created a novelty. In passing, it may be mentioned that the blue colour was almost an exact counterpart of the old Prussian blue of the Caledonian Railway, and indeed a definite attempt had been made to reproduce it. In later years at St Rollox, so much white was mixed with the basic colour that the so-called 'Caledonian blue' became a very much brighter and lighter colour, approximating to a limpid summer blue sky. Then, to the disappointment of everyone concerned on the LMS, and of all their most ardent supporters, the management announced that the overall time between Euston and Glasgow by the new service would not be the expected six hours, but six-and-a-half. It reduced what would have been a real challenge to a mere 'boy's job', as it was once put to me.

Looking back to those exciting days of June 1937, and the part I was able to play, albeit as no more than a recorder, I can recall vividly the mounting public partisanship for either the LMS or the LNER. Young men engaged in heated argument over the merits of the rival forms of streamlining; older men shook their heads sadly at the publicity that was developing, and one went so far as to say, 'I wonder what old Webb would have thought of all this.' When it became known that both companies were going to stage demonstration runs with the new trains, the 'Coronation Scot' from Euston to Crewe and back on 29 June, and the 'Coronation' from King's Cross to the Barkston triangle on the following day, partisanship rose to immense heights of exciting anticipation. The LNER then held the British speed record with a maximum of 113 mph, and while the moderate schedule of the 'Coronation Scot' did not give any prospects of 100 mph running in regular service, this invitation run on 29 June 1937 was another matter. My own expectations of something unusual were heightened when I learned that no fewer than four expert 'stop-watchers' would be travelling on the train. We certainly did get something unusual, so unusual that I still wonder by what small margin we were lucky enough to survive to tell the tale!

So the special 'W700' set out from Euston, booked to run the 158.1 miles to Crewe in 135 minutes at an average speed of 70.2 mph. The driver of the new engine was T.J. Clarke, who had driven No 6201 on the trials of November 1936; and this time his fireman was C. Lewis. With them on the footplate was Inspector S. Miller of Willesden and, again, Riddles himself. The speed restrictions were generally the same as those in force at the time of the trials in November 1936; but it was a fairly open secret that the LMS were out to capture the British railway speed record. The section of line between Norton Bridge and Crewe was specially fettled up, and the line maximum of 90 mph lifted, to permit a record attempt down the Madeley bank. The terrain and alignment were ideal—except in a respect that arose in dramatic and terrifying suddenness—and those on the footplate were asked to attempt something special. The British record then stood at 113 mph, and I have since learned that the crew were asked to try to get 120. Without anything unusual in the way of running, and a very even pace uphill and down, the train passed Stafford just over 5 minutes early on the special schedule, 133.6 miles from Euston in 109 min 56 sec—73 mph. The engine was taken very quietly onwards until the 60 mph restriction through Norton Bridge was behind us, and then the attempt on the record began. Unfortunately it was ill-judged. What I write now is, regrettably, being wise many years after the event; but had a speed chart been prepared for this critical section with the same care and scientific basis as that for the Euston-Glasgow runs of November 1936, the result might have been very different.

Seeing what had been done on the latter occasion in accelerating the *Princess Elizabeth* engine away after a speed restriction, the recovery from the Norton Bridge slack on 29 June was disappointingly slow. I was travelling in the leading coach of the train, and one just could not hear the exhaust beat of the engine. As we topped Whitmore summit the speed was no more than 85 mph. I appreciate that 'no more than 85 mph' is in relative terms only; but knowing the capacity of these engines, it could easily have been 95, and that would have made all the difference afterwards. Certainly the subsequent acceleration was very swift; but we were getting perilously near to Crewe before we approached the LNER record of 113 mph. The entry to Crewe station, over three successive crossover roads, was reminiscent of the celebrated run through Portobello, Edinburgh, in the early hours of 20 August 1895, immortalized by the racy pen of Norman Doran Macdonald; and when we arrived safe and sound in No 3 of all Crewe platforms, the stop-watch reading of four independent recorders, Cecil J. Allen, D.S.M. Barrie, S.P.W. Corbett and myself, all agreed precisely that the maximum speed had not exceeded 112½ mph. No record could be claimed in this respect; but in quickly checking over his figures, while still on the platform, Cecil J. Allen remarked that the time from Milepost 157 to the stop in the station—1.1 miles in 1 min 19 sec—was a record, and of such a nature that he added, 'Nobody will believe us when we tell them!' The overall time from Euston to Crewe was 129¾ minutes, an average of 73.1 mph.

The large party of guests was entertained to lunch at the Crewe Arms Hotel; E.J.H. Lemon presided, and very wittily and successfully made light of the somewhat precipitate entry into Crewe, which as one correspondent afterwards wrote 'strewed the floor of the dining car with a mosaic of broken crockery'. In the course of his speech, however, he was handed a slip of paper; it was the result of a scrutiny of the speed-recorder chart taken off the locomotive. Up to that point he had quoted the 112½ mph agreed among the four of us, but as he read the paper a broad smile spread over his face, and he said, 'I have not been bribed, but I can now tell you that the maximum speed was 114 mph.' It is, I am afraid, no exaggeration to say that those of us who had been taking so detailed an account of the running regarded this claim with some scepticism. We would all have readily agreed that a peak of 113 mph could have occurred, although it had eluded four independent stop-watches; but 114 took some stomaching, particularly as by this the British railway speed record was snatched by one mile per hour from the LNER. We had, however, little time to reflect on the ethics of the situation. The LMS had now officially claimed 114 mph and we all made for the return special to Euston.

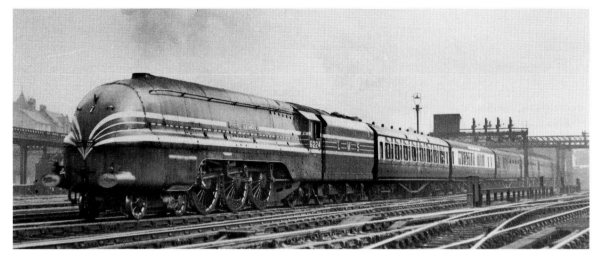

Top *The down 'Midday Scot' leaving Crewe in 1938 with through GWR coaches from Plymouth next to the engine, No 6224* Princess Alexandra *(P. Ransome-Wallis).*

Above *A red streamliner on the up 'Royal Scot', south of Tring summit in 1938; No 6228* Duchess of Rutland *(C.R.L. Coles).*

Left *A streamliner among Caledonian engines at Polmadie shed in 1938; No 6227* Duchess of Devonshire *(Rail Archive Stephenson, photo T.G. Hepburn).*

Right *The first of the non-streamlined 'Duchesses' of 1938; engine No 6230* Duchess of Buccleuch *(British Railways).*

The other four engines of the class were:

6221 *Queen Elizabeth*   6223 *Princess Alice*
6222 *Queen Mary*   6224 *Princess Alexandra*

After all the excitement of the trial run of 29 June had died down, leaving only resentment on the other side of the country that the claim for maximum speed supremacy had been made on what could only be described as controversial and unconvincing evidence, the 'Coronation Scot' settled down to a fairly humdrum existence, keeping closely to its 6½-hour schedule between Euston and Glasgow. A close friend of mine from college days, then in the steel industry, travelled on it from time to time in the course of business. He was an expert in the art of scientific measurement, and from the detailed logs he took he always considered the train very dull from the viewpoint of locomotive performance. Furthermore, a round trip from Euston to Glasgow and back with the dynamometer car showed that although the duty required considerably lighter steaming than on the preceding 'Midday Scot' schedule, it did necessarily result in greater overall efficiency, though of course involving less severe working of the machinery or of the crew. The coal consumption per drawbar horsepower hour was 3.03 lb, as compared to 2.96 lb by engine No 6210 on the 'Midday Scot' in 1936, when such a tremendous effort was made.

In 1938, a further ten 'Pacifics' were built at Crewe. They differed from the five 'Coronations' in two aspects. Only five of them were streamlined, and then in the LMS standard red rather than blue, but only four of the new engines were completed by the late autumn of that year. The names chosen for the new streamlined units were:

6225 *Duchess of Gloucester*   6228 *Duchess of Rutland*
6226 *Duchess of Norfolk*   6229 *Duchess of Hamilton*
6227 *Duchess of Devonshire*

The five non-streamlined engines were massive-looking things, emphasized by a large casing over the steam pipes above the running plate. The boiler, also, appeared much longer than on the 'Lizzies'. As first turned out, the five engines were identical, but within a year the last one of the class had been fitted with a twin-orifice blast pipe and double chimney. The five engines were named thus:

6230 *Duchess of Buccleuch*   6233 *Duchess of Sutherland*
6231 *Duchess of Atholl*   6234 *Duchess of Abercorn*
6232 *Duchess of Montrose*

In the summer service of 1938, the new engines quickly established themselves on the heaviest West Coast express trains.

At the time there was a degree of mystery about the completion of the last example of the streamlined series, No 6229. On one occasion it was reported as having been seen in Aberdeen in such a dirty condition that the paint could not be distinguished! Be that as it may, in early January 1939 I travelled behind No 6229 on the down 'Merseyside Express' in *blue*! The explanation was that *Duchess of Hamilton* had exchanged names and numbers with the pioneer streamliner, *Coronation,* to make the newest engine, No 6229, available for the American tour of the 'Coronation Scot' train, and named accordingly. About the same time, the Exhibition engine appeared magnificently turned out in LMS red, with the headlight and American bell already fitted. The train was shipped to the USA on 26 January; meanwhile, the masquerading *Duchess of Hamilton,* still smartly turned out in

The down 'Manxman' passing Camden shed in 1938, hauled by No 6234 Duchess of Abercorn before that engine was fitted with the twin orifice chimney (P. Ransome-Wallis).

blue, continued to give excellent service, as evidenced on my run on the 'Merseyside Express', when on a snowy night we were only 4 minutes late in Liverpool after delays of about 15 minutes on the way. I was then enjoying a penfriendship with a fellow rail enthusiast who lived in Chicago, Dwight Fullerton by name, and it was not long before he wrote of his impressions of the 'Coronation Scot'. He evidently made a most thorough examination, and was puzzled at how the motion parts were all stamped 6229 whereas the number of the engine was 6220!

On Sunday 26 February 1939 there was staged between Crewe and Glasgow a counterpart of the heavy load trial made in June 1935 with *The Princess Royal*, but with a still heavier load of no less than 605 tons. The test was made all the more interesting by the use of engine No 6234 *Duchess of Abercorn* which had recently been modified by the fitting of a twin-orifice blast pipe and double chimney. As in the 1935 trials, a train of empty coaching stock was made up, and the only passengers carried were testing staff in the dynamometer car. Although the engine was not indicated, sufficient data was taken on the heavy adverse stretches of the North Country to make reliable estimates of the indicated horsepower, as well as the continuous record of the drawbar horsepower registered from end to end of the outward and return runs. The estimates of the indicated horse power were highly significant, because they represented by some measure the highest that had been recorded by a British express locomotive at that time.

LMSR: Test run, 26 February 1939. Schedule and actual running times

Engine 4-6-2 No 6234 *Duchess of Abercorn*
Load 20 coaches, 604 tons tare
Crewe–Glasgow

Distance (miles)		Schedule time (min)	Actual time (m s)
0.0	CREWE	0	0 00
2.7	Coppenhall Junc	5	05 45
			pws‡
8.7	Winsford Junc	11	33 30
16.2	Weaver Junc†	18	40 40
24.0	WARRINGTON†	25	47 35
27.5	Winwick Junc	29	51 00
35.8	WIGAN	38	58 50
39.1	Standish Junc	42	63 20
45.5	Euxton Junc	49	69 50
50.9	PRESTON*	55	75 45
52.2	Oxheys	58	79 40
60.4	Garstang	66	88 00
			sigs
71.9	LANCASTER†	76	98 15
78.2	CARNFORTH	81	104 05
91.0	OXENHOLME	95	115 30
104.1	Tebay	111	130 20
109.6	Shap Summit	120	137 25
123.1	PENRITH†	133	149 00
127.9	Plumpton	137	153 30
141.0	CARLISLE §	150	165 30
0.0		0	0 00
8.6	Gretna	11	10 40
25.8	LOCKERBIE	28	28 10
39.7	Beattock	41	pass
		43	39 40
49.7	Beattock Summit	61	56 10
66.9	Symington	pass	74 00
		76	78 25
73.5	CARSTAIRS*	83	86 40
84.0	LAW JUNCTION†	94	97 20
89.4	MOTHERWELL†	100	103 20
93.9	Uddingston*	104	109 50
95.7	Newton	108	110 25

Distance (miles)		Schedule time (min)	Actual time (m s)
98.3	Rutherglen Junc	112	113 25
102.3	GLASGOW CENTRAL	118	118 25

Glasgow-Crewe

Distance (miles)		Schedule time (min)	Actual time (m s)
0.0	GLASGOW CENTRAL	0	0 00
12.9	MOTHERWELL	19	19 45
18.3	LAW JUNCTION	29	26 40
28.8	CARSTAIRS*	43	39 30
35.4	Symington	51	48 15
39.1	Lamington	—	52 08
44.5	Abington	—	57 13
47.0	Crawford	—	59 36
49.7	Elvanfoot	—	62 03
52.6	Beattock Summit	69	64 40
62.6	Beattock	79	73 35
76.5	LOCKERBIE	91	84 25
93.7	Gretna	106	97 45
102.3		116	106 30
0.0	CARLISLE§	0	0 00
4.9	Wreay	—	8 59
7.4	Southwaite	—	11 52
10.8	Calthwaite	—	15 11
13.1	Plumpton	19	17 45
17.9	PENRITH†	24	21 50
31.4	Shap Summit	43	40 15
36.9	Tebay	48	44 40
42.9	Grayrigg	—	50 23
50.0	OXENHOLME	60	56 30

Distance (miles)		Schedule time (min)	Actual time (m s)
62.8	CARNFORTH	71	67 00
69.1	LANCASTER	76	72 20
80.6	Garstang	87	84 00
90.1	PRESTON*	97	93 35
99.4	Coppull	—	105 53
105.2	WIGAN†	116	113 05
117.0	WARRINGTON†	128	126 10
124.8	Weaver Junc†	136	134 25
141.0	CREWE	153	153 05

*   Slack, severe
†   Service slack, moderate or slight
‡   Stop and single-line working
§   Stop of 4 min

Coal consumption (excluding shed duties):	
lb per mile	68.7
lb per sq ft of grate area per hour (actual running time)	75.7
lb per dbhp hr	3.12
Water consumption (excluding shed duties):	
gallons per mile (continuous blow down in operation throughout test)	53.1
lb per dbhp hr	24.15
Evaporation	
lb of water per lb of coal	7.74
Distance covered (train miles)	487.2
Actual running times (m s)	532 15
Booked running time (min)	535
Net running time (min)	516½
Average speed (mph)	55.2
Maximum speed (mph)	88.0

Crewe-Glasgow

	Carnforth-Shap Summit			Gretna-Beattock Summit		
	Carnforth-Oxenholme	Oxenholme-Tebay	Tebay-Shap Summit	Gretna-Lockerbie	Lockerbie-Beattock	Beattock-Beattock Summit
Length of ascent (miles)	12.96	13.08	5.69	17.27	13.96	10.13
Average drawbar horsepower	1,870	1,668	1,830	1,598	1,609	1,724
Maximum drawbar horsepower	2,120	1,934	2,065	1,733	1,823	2,081
Maximum indicated horsepower (calculated)	3,209	2,806	2,963	2,236	2,556	2,761
Average speed of ascent (mph)	68.0	53.0	47.9	59.3	72.5	36.8
Cut-off range, per cent of stroke	20-25	25	25-35	20-25	20-25	30-40
Boiler pressure (psi)	250	245	240	250	245	250

| | Motherwell-Law Junction | **Glasgow-Crewe** Motherwell-Beattock Summit | | |
		Law Junction-Carstairs	Carstairs-Symington	Symington-Beattock Summit
Length of ascent (miles)	5.42	10.53	6.74	17.28
Average drawbar horsepower	1,923	(a)	1,520	1,860
Maximum drawbar horsepower	1,998	1,978	1,638	2,282
Maximum indicated horsepower (calculated)	2,583	2,567	2,138	3,333
Average speed of ascent (mph)	46.7	49.4	46.1	63.4
Cut-off range, per cent of stroke	20-30	30-35	20-25	30-35
Boiler pressure (psi)	250	245	245	245

(a) Not shown, as this section includes some coasting

| | Carlisle-Shap Summit | | |
	Carlisle-to-Plumpton	Plumpton-to-Penrith	Penrith-to-Shap Summit
Length of ascent (miles)	13.03	4.77	13.68
Average drawbar horsepower	1,822	2,000	1,560
Maximum drawbar horsepower	2,511	2,394	2,331
Maximum indicated horsepower (calculated)	3,248	3,241	3,021
Average speed of ascent (mph)	43.9	71.4	44.4
Cut-off range, per cent of stroke	30-35	20-30	30-40
Boiler pressure (psi)	245	230	245

Right *Engine No 46242* City of Glasgow *was built as a streamliner in 1940, but is seen here as altered, in British Railways livery, climbing Camden Bank with the 'Midday Scot' in 1960 (Rail Archive Stephenson, photo D.M.C. Hepburne-Scott).*

Below *One of the first wartime-built streamliners, No 6244, at first named* City of Leeds *but then in 1941 renamed* King George VI *(British Railways).*

The scheduled and actual running times on that day are detailed in the accompanying tabular summary. The start from Crewe was severely hindered by the single-line working to Winsford Junction, but of the 22 minutes thus lost, 7 were regained by exceptionally fine running to Carlisle. On the Caledonian section of the line there was an interval of nearly 70 miles between successive sets of water troughs, with a hard road intermediately. It was not until after the Grouping that any water troughs had been installed on this part of the line, and then they had not been spaced as generously as on the LNW section. The Stanier tenders, although well supplied with coal capacity and having the advantage of a steam-operated coal pusher, had no greater water capacity than a 'Royal Scot', 4,000 gallons, and this placed them at some disadvantage compared with their East Coast rivals when it came to very long non-stop runs; the Gresley tenders carried 5,000 gallons. Apart from the haulage of such gargantuan loads as 605 tons, as on the February test trip, in subsequent years there were several instances when I was on the footplate when we were running short of water. The comparative coal and water consumption of the 'Pacific' engines 6210 and 6234 on dynamometer car test runs makes an interesting and thought-provoking contrast:

Engine No	6210	6220	6234
Average weight of train (tons)	522	331	605
Average running speed (mph)	52.0	60.4	55.2
Coal consumption			
lb per mile	45.0	39.2	68.7
lb per drawbar hp/hr	2.98	3.02	3.12
lb per sq ft of grate area per hr	62.2	47.3	75.7
Water consumption			
Gallons per mile	37.3	32.3	52.1
lb per drawbar hp/hr	24.7	25.0	24.1
Evaporation (lb of water per lb of coal)	8.30	8.24	7.74

The advance in capacity represented by engines 6200 and 6234 in no more than four years was remarkable, because although approximately the same overall times were maintained on both outward and return journeys, the loads were 470 and 605 tons—an astonishing difference! The maximum tonnages conveyed northbound over Shap and Beattock could well have been the largest on express passenger service, because on the Beattock bank in particular, rear-end banking was usually provided for loads of 550 tons or thereabouts. On these test runs, there is no doubt that the enginemanship was of the very highest order. Travelling experience behind the 'Duchess' Class locomotives was then very limited among the enthusiasts who were qualified to produce a reliable record of such a performance. Few, even among experienced locomotive engineers, realized how very exceptional the occasion was. It was not so much a matter of the output of power, either from the cylinders or from the boiler, high though they both were, but of adhesion on the steep gradients of the North Country. Years later, the mounting experience of the running of these engines, both from my own travelling and from that of many other observers, led to the view that slipping often accompanied bad rail conditions. These circumstances made even more extraordinary the results that were obtained on 26 February 1939, in view of the adverse weather prevailing through most of that winter's day.

The rather extraordinary feature of the statistics of these trials was the coal consumption per train mile. Seeing that engine No 6210 used no more than 45 lb per mile when working a train of 522 tons tare (at least about 545 tons full), it is surprising that one of 605 tons would need 68.7 lb per mile, though the average speed was higher, 55.2 against 52.0 mph. Again, the basic consumption was excellent at no more than 3.13 lb per drawbar hp/hr. The evaporation rate, however, was surprisingly low for a locomotive of such high superheater capacity.

Early in 1939, it was announced that twenty more 'Pacifics' of the 'Duchess' Class were to be built, though these were to be named after cities on the LMS system. The new engines were originally all to be streamlined, and to differ from the 6220—6229 batch in having twin-orifice blast pipes and double chimneys. This development was a sure sign of the success of the application of the device to the non-streamlined No 6234. The five new engines completed at Crewe in 1939 were named as follows:

6235 *City of Birmingham*   6238 *City of Carlisle*
6236 *City of Bradford*   6239 *City of Chester*
6237 *City of Bristol*

There were some additional units planned in 1939, but the outbreak of war in September postponed their construction until April 1940 and after. It was notable, however, that war or no war, work proceeded at Crewe with the conversion of earlier engines to the twin-orifice blast pipe and double chimney arrangement. In 1940, six of them were altered, namely engines 6221, 4, 7, 8, 30 and 31. Progress slowed up during the worst of the war period, but by 1944 all the original engines had been dealt with except for No 6220, which had then resumed her original number. The new engines of 1940 were:

6240 *City of Coventry*   6243 *City of Lancaster*
6241 *City of Edinburgh*   6244 *City of Leeds*
6242 *City of Glasgow*

There was a report in 1940 that the last-mentioned engine was to be stationed at Leeds, though for what duties it is not clear. Actually, the engine was named thus for only a short time. In connection with some special wartime working it was renamed *King George VI* at the end of the year. Doubtless because of some wartime security arrangements, no notice was made of this last event.

22. The war years and the finale

After the launching of the 'Coronation Scot' in 1937, some important changes were made in the senior personnel of the CME's department. Largely through the influence of Sir Harold Hartley, one imagines, his particular protégé C.E. Fairburn, who had been Chief Electrical Engineer, was promoted to combine the office of Deputy Chief Mechanical Engineer with his existing command, and at the same time Riddles was appointed Mechanical Engineer, Scotland. H.G. Ivatt was made Principal Assistant for locomotives. In 1939, it fell to Riddles to take the 'Coronation Scot' engine and train on its momentous North American tour, but a vastly more important assignment awaited him on the outbreak of the Second World War when he was seconded from his ordinary railway duties to the Ministry of Supply as Director of Transportation Equipment.

It was undoubtedly through his influence that LMS engines were chosen for war service. In 1939, the military strategists foresaw a series of campaigns in France and the Low Countries, something after the style of 1914-18, and at an early stage in the war preparations were made for large supplies of rolling-stock to be got ready for service with the British Expeditionary Force. The experience of the First World War had shown the general usefulness of the 2-8-0 in such service, and it was at first thought that a number of ex-GCR 2-8-0s would be re-equipped for the job. In the event, however, the Stanier 2-8-0 was chosen, and orders for 240 of the type, incorporating a number of modifications, were placed by

the Ministry of Supply in December 1939. Certain refinements in design for home service, such as needle roller bearings in the motion work, were not included; the tyre profiles were to conform to French, instead of British, standards, and the Westinghouse brake was fitted instead of the vacuum. It was originally intended to include such details as the Flaman-type self-recording speed indicators, and the French type of ATC.

By the time the first of these modified locomotives was delivered, in May 1940, the whole pattern of the war was swiftly changing, and with the evacuation of the British Expeditionary Force from Dunkirk, no locomotives were going to be needed in France for some time to come. The Stanier 2-8-0s were afterwards adapted for oil-burning, and sent to various countries in the Middle East, where they did heavy and important work in Egypt and Palestine. In the meantime, the ever-increasing needs of the home railways, and the almost complete cessation of new construction, led to an acute shortage of locomotives, and at a late stage in the war authorization was given for new freight engines to be built. It was felt that the new machines should be capable of service anywhere in the country, in view of the greatly altered channels of communications for war supplies to the more westerly of the ports in the English Channel, and the wartime Railway Executive Committee selected the Stanier 2-8-0 as the most suitable design. Engines of this type were in due course built at Ashford, Brighton, Darlington, Doncaster, Eastleigh and Swindon in addition to LMSR shops. At that same time, the Stanier 2-8-0 was the only one suitable for general service. The Great Western '28XX' had a

Stanier '8F' 2-8-0 as built for war service with the Railway Operating Division (British Railways).

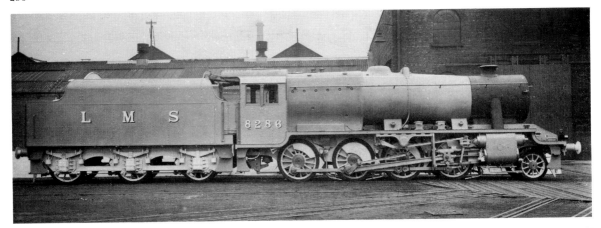

restricted route availability; the Gresley three-cylinder '02' had the conjugated valve gear which had proved troublesome in wartime conditions of maintenance; and the ex-GCR Robinson '04', though an excellent engine in itself, hardly conformed to the best modern standards. Eventually, the Stanier 2-8-0 class mustered a total of 719 locomotives.

Building of the 'Black Fives' with the 28-element superheater continued until, in 1947, the total for the class had reached 732, down to engine No 4768, but for the last hundred Ivatt introduced certain modifications in design under the auspices of the British Railways management. One isolated engine, No 4767, fitted with Stephenson's link motion outside the frames, earned the reputation of being a particularly 'strong' engine on the banks. It is one of the class now preserved in working order, and appropriately named *George Stephenson*. On the other hand, in footplate experience and otherwise I personally found those fitted with Caprotti valve gear very weak when it came to mounting steep gradients, as for example on the Settle and Carlisle line.

By the outbreak of the Second World War, the 'Royal Scots' were at the pinnacle of their performance. It was of course not often that they were called upon for such heights of power output as that involved in the run of the up 'Royal Scot' train by No 6132 as described in Chapter 16, but in general reliability, moderate coal consumption and long mileages between repairs they continued as a splendid tool of operation. But the 'Royal Scots' were then 12 years old, and the boilers were falling due for replacement. It was already evident on the LMS that among locomotives in the '5X' power class, where a direct comparison could be made, the taper boilers of the Stanier 'Jubilees' were proving considerably less costly to maintain than the parallel boilers, built-up smokeboxes and Derby-style fireboxes of the 'Baby Scots'. Thus a new design of boiler and firebox was worked out that could be fitted alike to 'Jubilees', 'Baby Scots' and 'Royal Scots'. *British Legion* served as the guinea-pig. Once the draughting was satisfactorily proportioned it was a very good engine, but the original boiler rendered it too heavy for the Midland lines, and the new standard design incorporated a considerably shorter barrel, a twin-orifice blast pipe and double chimney. The exhaust arrangements were very simple, without the system of petticoats to the chimneys that was a feature of the Kylchap design on the Paris-Orleans Railway. The following table gives the relevant dimensions and ratios of the two varieties of taper boiler:

Taper boiler class Used on	2 No 6170		2A '5X' conversion and rebuilt 'Scots'	
Tubes, small				
number	180		198	
outside diameter				
(in)	1⅞		1¾	
Flues				
number	28		28	
outside diameter	5⅛		5⅛	
Superheater elements,				
diameter (in)	1¼		1¼	
Distance between				
tube plates (ft in)	14	3	13	0
Heating surfaces				
(sq ft)				
Tubes	1,793		1,667	
Firebox	195		195	
Total evaporative	1,988		1,862	
Superheater	348		348	
Grate area (sq ft)	31.25		31.25	
Total free gas area				
(sq ft)	5.18		5.09	
Free gas area as				
percentage of grate				
area	16.6		16.3	

The total engine weight of the two 'Jubilee' Class '5X' engines fitted with the 2A boiler was 82 tons, as compared to 84 tons 18 cwt on *British Legion*, but the weight distributions on the five varieties of three-cylinder 4-6-0 were as follows:

Above left *One of the later '8F' 2-8-0s, one of a batch built by Beyer, Peacock and Co for general freight service on the British railways in the Second World War (Beyer, Peacock & Co).*

Left *'Black Five' 4-6-0 No 44709 on a Morecambe-Glasgow excursion stopping at Tebay for banking assistance up Shap (Derek Cross).*

Right *One of the later 'Black Five' standard 4-6-0s No 4784 on an Inverness to Wick mail train at Helmsdale (O.S. Nock).*

Class	Bogie		Coupled wheels						Total	
			leading		centre		trailing			
	t	c	t	c	t	c	t	c	t	c
'Royal Scot'	22	8	20	18	20	18	20	14	84	81
British Legion	22	6	20	12	20	12	20	11	84	1
'Baby Scot'	21	0	19	19	20	1	19	15	80	15
'5X' conversion	20	10	20	15	20	15	20	0	82	0
'Converted Scot'	22	0	20	7	20	9	20	4	83	0

Right *A 'Converted Scot', No 6133* The Green Howards, *in the post-war LMS lined-out livery* (British Railways).

Below right *Preserved 'Jubilee' Class three-cylinder 4-6-0 No 5690* Leander, *working a southbound enthusiasts' special on the Settle and Carlisle route near Armathwaite* (John Titlow).

The principal difference between the last two lay in the use of 17-in diameter cylinders on the '5X' conversion, and 18-in on the 'Converted Scot'.

After the successful conversion of the two 'Jubilees' Nos 5735 and 5736 in 1942, authority was given for conversion of twenty 'Royal Scots'. No 6103 *Royal Scots Fusilier* was the first to emerge in July 1943 from Crewe.

Before referring in any detail to the running of these engines, I must mention the important trials carried out on No 6138 *London Irish Rifleman*, which on leaving Crewe Works in its new form for the first time in July 1944 was already fitted with indicator shelters. Mr H.G. Ivatt, who was then Principal Assistant to the Chief Mechanical Engineer, sent me a set of indicator diagrams taken on those tests, which are of exceptional interest. They represent some of the shortest cut-off working with full regulator opening that I have ever seen on a steam locomotive fitted with piston valves and ordinary Walschaerts valve gear.

I do not know the circumstances in which the various indicator cards were obtained, but in 1944 it would have been in very severe wartime conditions, and there is no instance of a card taken at a higher speed than 62 mph. A locomotive that can give a fat enough card to yield 925 ihp in 5 per cent cut-off at 62 mph, and 1,070 ihp in 10 per cent at 60 mph, has a very excellent valve gear. In view of the investigations at Crewe prior to the building of the first taperboilered 'Scot', No 6170 *British Legion*, in 1935, it is interesting to see that no instance of 2,000 ihp was recorded with No 6138, though the ascending values of ihp with increasing cut-off and decreasing speed are impressive:

Speed (mph)	Cut-off (per cent)	ihp
62	18	1,670
56	22	1,700
52	26	1,820
44	32	1,840

These diagrams, with the engine working hard, all show a good deal of throttling of the steam at admis-

sion, the effect of which can be seen when the theoretical shape is superimposed upon the actual shape, for one of the cards taken at 22 per cent cut-off.

Mr Ivatt very kindly arranged for me to ride one of the rebuilds on the down day 'Scotsman' from Leeds to Glasgow, and the details of this run together with some logged by other friends when travelling as passengers provide a useful initial survey of the working of the class. While my own run with No 6117 gave a classic exhibition of working with a wide-open regulator and short cut-offs, it was not by any means the normal method of handling these engines. In fact, during the 1948 Interchange Trials, the engines allocated were not handled in this way at all. Like their predecessors of the original 'Royal Scot' Class, the new engines afforded yet another example of a locomotive class that seemed to respond equally well to any method of handling.

Coming now to actual details of performance, the accompanying table shows the work of Nos 6109 and 6117 between Hellifield and Carlisle on the 10.00 am express from St Pancras. The first was logged by Cecil J. Allen, travelling as a passenger, while on the second I was on the footplate. The timing of 69 minutes for the 46 miles from Hellifield to Appleby was, of course, very easy by pre-war standards, but on both occasions the train was running late, and substantial recovery of lost time took place. The maximum tare load permitted to a 'Converted Scot' over the mountain section was then 450 tons. Both trains were very crowded; indeed, on my own run an extra coach was added at Leeds, an ex-Caledonian 'Grampian' 12-wheeler, and the fact that passengers were standing in the corridors is shown by the large increase of gross over tare load of both trains. *Royal Engineer* was taken vigorously away from Hellifield, and rushed the first section of the Long Drag, but above Horton speed was allowed to fall away to 28 mph on the 1 in 100, and it did recover to more than 31 mph on the easier length over Blea Moor viaduct. On my own run, Driver Pattrick started very gently, linking up to 15 per cent cut-off as we passed the platform end at Hellifield, with the regulator one-half open. This took

us up to 62 mph at Settle Junction, and there the regulator was opened to the full. Recalling that the indicator cards taken on No 6138 had given 1,520 indicated horsepower in 15 per cent at 60 mph, it was evident that for all this apparently modest working, No 6117 was producing the power.

The ascent to Blea Moor proved to be quite impressive. When, at a point 4 miles above Settle, speed had fallen to 33 mph, the cut-off was increased to 22 per cent and we sustained 28 mph on the continuing 1 in 100 to Helwith Bridge. By this time, as the table shows, we had fallen considerably behind *Royal Engineer,* but at Horton the cut-off was increased to 30 per cent. Speed had by then begun to fall again from the 34 mph attained on the brief easing of the 1 in 100 gradient past Helwith Bridge, but that further opening out produced a marked acceleration to a sustained 36 mph, and we gained a minute on the other run between Horton and Ribblehead. On the footplate I was able to see that this fine effort, requiring about 1,420 equivalent drawbar horsepower, was easily sustained by the boiler performance in steady maintenance of pressure and water level. I judged the indicated horsepower to be about 1,750. Cut-off was reduced to 22 per cent at Ribblehead, 15 once we were into Blea Moor Tunnel, and 10 per cent at Dent Head. This took us up to 58 mph at Garsdale without any further opening out, and over Aisgill summit at 45 mph. The regulator had remained full open throughout. The two 'Converted Scots' made practically identical time from Aisgill down to Appleby. In the case of No 6117, it was made entirely without

steam, regulator closed and valves set at 54 per cent cut-off to provide cushioning and preventing speed rising too high. *Royal Engineer* made the faster running from Appleby to Carlisle, but there was no significance in the comparative figures.

LMS: Leeds-Carlisle

Engine no			6109	6117
Engine name			*Royal Engineer*	*Welsh Guardsman*
Load (tons, E/F)			380/420	416/450
Distance (miles)		Schedule time (min)	Actual time (m s)	Actual time (m s)
0.0	HELLIFIELD	0	0 00	0 00
3.3	*Settle Junc*	5	4 54	5 15
5.2	Settle		6 54	7 29
9.6	*Helwith Bridge*		13 10	15 30
11.2	Horton		15 58	18 49
13.5	*Selside Box*		20 16	22 49
16.0	Ribblehead		25 08	26 53
17.3	*Blea Moor*	33	27 37	28 57
22.2	Dent		34 31	36 30
25.4	Garsdale		37 59	40 31
28.4	*Aisgill*	49	41 12	44 09
35.3	Kirkby Stephen		47 36	50 49
43.5	Ormside		55 28	58 27
46.0	APPLEBY	69	58 41	61 27
2.9	Long Marton		4 58	5 00
11.0	Langwathby		11 59	12 41
15.3	Lazonby		15 33	16 48
20.8	Armathwaite		20 40	22 33
28.1	Scotby		27 07	29 33
—			signals	signals
30.8	CARLISLE	35	34 00	35 54

Left *A 'Converted Scot', No 46116* Irish Guardsman, *on the up Irish Mail at Penmaenmawr* (Derek Cross).

Right *During the 1948 Interchange Trials, 'Converted Scot' No 46162* Queens Westminster Rifleman, *on the 1.30 pm Paddington-Plymouth leaving Reading* (M.W. Earley).

Speeds at	6109 mph	6117 mph
Settle Junction	66	62
Helwith Bridge	34½/38	28/34
Ribblehead	28/31	36/33½
Garsdale	64½	58
Aisgill	50	45
Maximum to Appleby	71½	72½
Maximum to Lazonby	77½	68

It was nevertheless remarkable that apart from those early runs over the Midland/G & SW route, there was not a single performance by one of the 'Converted Scots' published in *The Railway Magazine* until the autumn of 1947, and then only to the extent of a single run between Carstairs and Carlisle. Over the entire main line of the former LNWR, where most of them were at work, there descended a dead silence so far as published data was concerned, and for a locomotive class that had made its début to such a blast of trumpets (from Cecil J. Allen at any rate), this could be taken as passing strange. Actually, in that relatively short time the reputation of the new engines had become somewhat tarnished, and persistent complaints from drivers of rough riding led to the matter being referred officially to the superintendent of motive power. At first it was thought that the bad riding was due to arrears of maintenance on the track from wartime conditions and the terrible winter of 1946-7. With subsequent considerable attention to the track, complaints lessened, but the opinion was still expressed that the riding was not satisfactory.

Writing now, between thirty and forty years after the actual events, I find it difficult to give a concise assessment of the quality of the 'Converted Scots'. I always found that opinion of them, professionally, depended upon how the various railwaymen had to deal with them. A very senior engineer who had been trained under Sir Nigel Gresley and who had come to the London Midland Region after nationalization to take an appointment of top-senior responsibility, once confided to me that 'they are our best engines', but I should not imagine anyone concerned with day-to-day running would have agreed with him. The ex-LNER man was, of course, concerned with statistics of yearly mileages, boiler repair costs and suchlike, and in this respect I can quite imagine that they showed up very favourably. But they became generally discredited in the eyes of the footplatemen, and drivers seemed surprised if they got an engine that was not rough. The situation became so serious that E.S. Cox of the CME's staff, famed for his writings in the professional technical press, spent some time in riding on certain engines of the rebuilt class to try and diagnose what was wrong. The original 'Royal Scots' were not the most comfortable to ride on, as I knew from my footplate experience in the 1930s; but there was none of the wild uncontrolled lurching in which the rebuilt engines all too frequently indulged.

The various remedial measures that Cox recommended in the autumn of 1947 had not had time for their effects to be generally appreciated before nationalization came, and with it the Interchange Trials of 1948, in which the 'Converted Scots' were very much involved. The individual engines used were throughout handled by one of the finest drivers I have ever known, and the vagaries in the style of running displayed on certain critical occasions would, I feel sure, be related to the engines and their riding rather than to the temperament of the crew or any trouble from the performance of the boiler. Even so, in my ordinary travelling on the West Coast Main Line around 1950, particularly on the double-home turns worked between Crewe and Glasgow, I experienced a number of cases when the symptoms seemed to indicate a shortage of steam at critical stages of the journey, involving loss of time. On the other hand, I enjoyed some runs that were exhilarating, chiefly between Euston and Crewe, though nothing to surpass or even to equal the very best I had experienced with the original 'Scots'. Then, when the converted engines seemed at last to be settling down to a normal existence, BR decided that they should be fitted with self-cleaning apparatus in the smokebox, and this, according to the official view of the motive power department, 'knocked their steaming for six'. Under BR classification, the 'Converted Scots', like the new standard 'Britannia' 'Pacifics', were Class '7P', but after fitting of the self-cleaning plates it was felt that in the case of the 'Scots', '7P' was no longer justified.

In 1955, engine No 46165 was sent to the Rugby Testing Station for a thorough examination; and the investigators came to the startling conclusion that the engines, whether original or rebuilt, that had born the brunt of so much of the heaviest West Coast express traffic for a quarter of a century had firegrates too small for the work they were called upon to do! Nevertheless, when pushed to the limit, without the self-cleaning plates, the steaming rate was found to be no less than 30,000 lb of steam per hour, and with these inserted the rate was only reduced to 28,000 lb per hour. In BR days it was stipulated, on paper, that the maximum rate of firing that a single man was expected to maintain continuously was 3,000 lb per hour, which on the 'Converted Scots' was equivalent to an evaporation of about 20,000 lb per hour. Past records with both the original and the converted engines, however, show that the engines, or rather their firemen, must have been grossly overworked on many occasions—at any rate according to the latest official reckonings!

If indeed the daily working range of the 'Scots' was regarded as between 16,000 and 21,000 lb of steam per hour, then, even within my own travelling experience, they were frequently overworked. Two very ordinary occasions, one in 1955 and one in 1956,

make this clear, the first on the 10.40 am down from Euston and the second on the 11.45 am. The following table analyzes the performance over the 68.3 miles between Brent Junction and Welton, against an average rising gradient of 1 in 1350:

Train (ex-Euston)	10.40 am	11.45 am
Load (tons, E/F)	446/475	413/445
Locomotive No	46156	46115
Weather	Fine, calm	Heavy west wind
Average speed (mph)	64*	62.4
Estimated edhp	1,140	1,060
Estimated ihp	1,620	1,540

*Net average, allowing for two checks costing 3 minutes in aggregate

The estimates of power on the second run make no allowance for any effect that the heavy west wind was having. Since the indicated horsepower for the 'one fireman' limit at 65 mph was found to be 1,330 on the Rugby tests of No 46165, it is clear that both the above engines were being 'overworked' by a considerable margin for an hour on end. On the Tring ascent, the equivalent drawbar horsepowers were 1,260 by No 46156 and 1,230 by No 46115, with indicated horsepowers about 400 greater in each case. I was not on the footplate on either occasion and had no conversation with the crews either before or after the runs.

One of the most interesting runs I had at this same period was on the 12.30 pm from Euston, then booked non-stop to Liverpool Lime Street in 3½ hours. I rode on the footplate of No 46149 *The Middlesex Regiment,* and although the load was not quite so heavy as I hoped, a series of delays made the requirements more severe than otherwise, if an on-time arrival was to be made. The driver's method of working was 15 per cent cut-off wherever possible, with the main valve of the regulator one-half open. He had used 22 per cent when getting away from the Bourne End stop, and previous to that 22 per cent from the Harrow check up to Carpenders Park. An analysis of the running from Cheddington onwards gives some interesting results:

Locomotive No 46149: Load 390 tons full

Location	Distance (miles)	Average speed (mph)	Gradient (1 in, rising)	Edhp	Ihp
Cheddington-Hilmorton	44.2	69.3	2930	913	1,470
Polesworth-Milford	23.0	23.0	2720	993	1,620
Banbury Lane	4.0	75	Level	1,010	1,660
Whitmore	Attained from slack	65	398	1,230	1,770

It would appear that for lengthy periods the engine was being 'overworked' and that use of one-half main regulator and 15 per cent cut-off was enough to do this. On the Whitmore ascent, from the slack near Great Bridgeford, 16 per cent had been used as it had been for 3 miles past Lichfield to give us the excellent minimum speed of 67½ mph after 2½ miles at 1 in 331. Neither the engine nor the fireman seemed to be overworked in the slightest, and until I came to compare the horsepower figures with those quoted in the Rugby trials of No 46165, I had passed the experience on No 46149 as an easy comfortable run. To judge from the engine working, the boiler was being steamed to produce about 1,600 indicated horsepower over practically the entire distance from Willesden to Weaver Junction, 169 miles, over which we made a net average speed of 67 mph.

This was by no means the limit of what the enginemen got out of the 'Scots' in those last splendid years. On the up 'Midday Scot', for example, No 45530 *Sir Frank Ree*, with a 530-ton load, ran the 69.9 miles from Welton to Willesden Junction in 60¾ minutes, about 1,570 ihp with one of the 17-in engines. In the North Country, No 46107 *Argyll and Sutherland Highlander*, with a 460-ton train, accelerated from a permanent way check below Oxenholme to 43½ mph on the 1 in 131 stretch of the Grayrigg bank, producing 1,770 ihp in the process, a remarkable figure at so relatively low a speed. Whatever the pundits at Rugby Testing Station may have thought about it, enginemen brought up in the traditions of the LNWR had no hesitation in going hard when occasion demanded it. Neither was the coal consumption so inordinately high when they were doing it, because outputs of 1,600 to 1,700 ihp at 70 mph or averages of that order for 40 to 60 minutes on end would not have cost more coal than about 2.5 lb/ihpr, or about 3.6 to 3.7 lb/dhp hr.

Turning now in conclusion to the 'Pacifics', it was extraordinary that at the very time when the great modernization plan for British Railways was being launched, a number of new enterprising train timings were being introduced, entirely with steam traction. On the West Coast Main Line, these, while falling some distance short of the high standards maintained before the war, were encouraging in themselves, but even more so in the spirit they seemed to engender in many engine crews to recover lost time when checks supervened. The most remarkable of the West Coast timings in the 1950s were those of the 'Royal' and 'Midday Scots' between Euston and Rugby. These two heavy trains were both allowed no more than 80 minutes, start to stop, for the 82.6 miles. The engine of the 10 am train went through to Glasgow, and was almost invariably a 'Duchess'; but the 'Midday Scot' was a Crewe North turn, and in my

travelling experience at that time worked as often as not by a 'Lizzie'. It was a very hard run, rarely loaded to much under 500 tons, particularly, as on most of my journeys, when made in hard wintry weather. The earlier series of Stanier 'Pacifics' were generally not so popular with their crews as the later ones. They were not so easy to fire, albeit having a somewhat smaller grate; and their tenders had not that inestimable boon, the steam-operated coal pusher. Nevertheless, some magnificent work was done by the 'Lizzies' in the last few years of their existence, particularly on the up 'Red Rose', as this chapter will record in its concluding pages. First, though, to the 'Midday Scot' on its 80-minute Euston-Rugby runs. I must confess I could never sense the reason behind this strenuous booking, all the more so as it was followed by the relatively easy 77 minutes for the 75.5 miles from Rugby to Crewe. Even so, I found resolute attempts being made to keep to the 80-minute booking. The only exception to this was once when I was on the footplate of No 46211, and I saw that the engine was not in the best of condition. Even so, no more than 3 minutes were dropped to Rugby, and 3 minutes were won back on the easier timing to Crewe.

Details of four first class runs on this severe assignment are shown in the adjoining tabulation. On the first, after a very quick start to Willesden, the speed was moderate as far as Watford, and even as the descent from Tring was entered upon there was a hindrance at Cheddington. Once clear of the Linslade Tunnel, however, some tremendous speed was developed, with an average of 74 mph throughout from Bletchley to Kilsby Tunnel North box. The minimum speeds of 71 mph and 72 mph were as exhilarating as the maxima of 85 mph at Wolverton and 83 mph at Weedon. The second run, with engine No 46212, was also an excellent performance, particularly in the vigorous ascent from Willesden to Tring, which put this run ahead of all others at this summit point. Further fine running, and the absence of signal or other checks, took this train well inside 'even time' when Blisworth was passed, but the permanent way check before Weedon was severe, and even without the final signal checks, overall time could not have been kept.

The third run, with the celebrated engine No 46201, set a formidable task to engine and crew. I was bound for Glasgow just after New Year in 1955 on a raw afternoon of rain and sleet, an occasion I thought the very opposite to one likely to produce good running. At Euston I found the 'Midday Scot' made up to 14 coaches, packed with passengers, so that before we left there were many standing in the corridors. When the engine came backing down, however, I was partly reassured, for on the footplate was one of the 'ace' drivers of Crewe North shed, T.

Walker. Though he greeted me cordially, I must say I was glad not to be riding with him on such a day! The engine herself was then in her third state of rebuilding, having acquired a 32-element superheater domeless boiler as fitted to the 6203-6212 series when built in 1935.

On this gloomy January occasion, speed did not quite reach 60 mph on the level beyond Willesden, but the engine was then opened out to good purpose so that the speed did not fall below 58 mph beyond Hatch End, and attained 66 mph at Watford. After that, the running was magnificent, despite the weather, with no lower speed than 63 mph over Tring Summit, an average of 74½ mph over the 18.4 miles from Tring Cutting box to Wolverton, with a maximum of 80 mph and a minimum of 61½ mph after Roade. Then the checks began. Even in view of the fine running made previously, however, I doubt if we could have reached Rugby, unchecked, in the scheduled 80 minutes on such a day. I estimate the net time as 80¾ minutes. On the easier timing north of Rugby, the driver won back 2½ minutes of the lost time.

On the fourth run, when I was on the footplate of engine No 46231 *Duchess of Atholl*, the same driver was in charge, and he gave an immaculate performance. Even granting that the latter run was made in better weather, though not free from squally April showers, the superiority of the 'Duchess' over the 'Lizzie' was absolute, particularly in the magnificent uphill work between Willesden and Tring. As far as Bushey, the engine was being worked in 25 per cent cut-off, with full regulator, and, after a spell at 15 per cent, a reversion to 20 per cent was made from Kings Langley for the rest of the ascent to Tring. Not even this quality of running, however, was able to sustain a loss of time such as that occasioned by the lengthy permanent way check before Bletchley, which cost us at least 4½ minutes. The usual checks before Rugby were, however, not severe on this occasion, and with only one appreciable check on the continuation of the run we were able to clock in at Crewe precisely on time.

Proceeding now further north, from Crewe in the late 1950s I had a number of runs on the 10.55 am from Birmingham New Street to Glasgow, though it was a train that seemed to suffer an almost chronic succession of checks from the very start. From Crewe it was a double-home 'Pacific' working, and on one occasion the train was more than 20 minutes late before the Polmadie engine and her crew took over.

LMR: Euston-Rugby, the 'Midday Scot'

Engine No			46211		46212		46201		46231	
Engine name			Queen Maud		Duchess of Kent		Princess Elizabeth		Duchess of Atholl	
Load (tons E/F)			388/410		409/440		455/490		474/510	
Distance (miles)		Schedule time (min)	Actual time (m s)	Speed (mph)	Actual time (m s)	Speed (mph)	Actual time (m s)	Speed (mph)	Actual time (m s)	Speed (mph)
0.0	Euston	0	0 00	—	0 00	—	0 00	—	0 00	
5.4	Willesden Junc	9	9 25	54	9 34	60	10 27	—	10 31	—
11.4	Harrow		15 38	58	15 16	65	16 41	58	16 07	66
17.5	Watford Junc	21	21 43	68	20 58	68	22 39	66	21 32	75
24.5	Hemel Hempstead		28 15	63	27 15		29 11	64	27 34	67½
31.7	Tring	35	35 23	60	33 58	62	36 00	60	34 12	64
36.1	Cheddington		39 30	74/55	—	—	39 44	78	37 50	75
40.2	Leighton Buzzard		43 24	71	40 57	79	42 58	80	41 00	78½
—			—	80	—		—		pws	15
46.7	Bletchley	47	48 39	79	46 11	75	48 08	75	49 59	
52.4	Wolverton		53 00	85	50 46	77	52 40	76	55 52	75½
59.9	Roade	58	59 05	71	57 10	62	59 13	61½	62 17	67½
62.8	Blisworth	61	61 32	77	59 45	72	61 54	70	64 43	76
—			—	—	pws	20	pws	20	—	—
69.7	Weedon	67	66 50	83	66 38	—	70 08	—	70 07	78
78.8	Kilsby North Box		74 10	72	77 45	—	79 29	60	77 35	69/72
—			—	79	sigs	—	sig stop		sigs	
82.6	Rugby	80	78 35	—	82 24	—	87 35		82 35	

The down 'Midday Scot' approaching Tring in 1938, hauled by No 6231 Duchess of Atholl (C.R.L. Coles).

It proved, however, the prelude to one of the most exciting and inspiriting runs I have experienced on the West Coast Main Line. It was a winter occasion, and the load was no more than 11 coaches, 382 tons tare and 405 tons full behind the tender. The engine was No 46241 *City of Edinburgh*, and not being on the footplate I had perforce to watch points from the carriage window. At first the delays seemed worse than ever, with two dead stands for signals, two further signal checks and relaying slacks; despite the ample allowance of 68 minutes from Crewe to passing Preston, we were 28 minutes late by then. Even when we got away from Preston and began to top the 70 mph mark across the level North Lancashire plain, I hardly thought that some 3 hours later I should be contemplating an on-time arrival in Glasgow! Not only did we get a completely clear road for the next 150 miles, but the men on *City of Edinburgh* went for it in such dashing style as to have recovered 26 minutes of lost time by the time we passed Symington. There came checks on the final stages of the journey, but for all that we clocked into Glasgow only 2 minutes late.

LMR: West Coast route, Crewe–Carstairs

Engine 4-6-2 No 46241 *City of Edinburgh*
Load 11 coaches, 382 tons tare, 405 tons full

Distance (miles)		Schedule time (min)	Actual time (m s)	Speed (mph)
0.0	Crewe	0	0 00	—
—			sig pwr	—
24.1	Warrington	—	40 20	—
—		—	sig pwr	—
35.8	Wigan	—	57 00	—
—			pwr	—
51.0	Preston	68	77 30	—
55.7	Barton		83 48	64½

Distance (miles)		Schedule time (min)	Actual time (m s)	Speed (mph)
60.5	Garstang		87 49	74
72.0	Lancaster	90	98 12	(eased)
75.1	Hest Bank		101 02	71
78.3	Carnforth	96	103 50	72
—	*Milepost 9½*		—	58½
85.6	Milnthorpe		110 15	76
91.1	Oxenholme	111	115 09	62
96.3	*Lambrigg Box*		120 42	52
98.2	Grayrigg		122 56	48½
104.2	Tebay	128	128 18	77
107.2	*Scout Green Box*		131 07	51
109.7	*Shap Summit*	138	134 40	37
119.0	Clifton		143 47	74
123.3	Penrith	151	147 34	—
128.0	Plumpton	156	152 07	69
—			pws	15
139.7	*Carlisle No 13 Box*		164 30	72
141.1	Carlisle	169	167 05	
0.0		0	00 00	
4.1	Rockcliffe		5 55	68
8.6	Gretna Junction	12	9 40	77
13.1	Kirkpatrick		13 38	64½
16.7	Kirtlebridge		16 54	76½
22.7	*Castlemilk Box*		21 49	68
25.8	Lockerbie	30	24 27	76/66
28.7	Nethercleugh		26 54	72
31.7	Dinwoodie		29 27	69
34.7	Wamphray		31 47	79
39.7	Beattock	43	35 56	71
45.0	*Milepost 45*		41 30	45½
49.7	*Summit*	63	48 50	37
52.5	Elvanfoot		51 48	69
63.2	Lamington		60 55	77½
—			sigs	—
66.9	Symington	79	64 38	20

Distance (miles)		Schedule time (min)	Actual time (m s)	Speed (mph)
68.5	Thankerton		66 42	64
—			sigs	—
73.5	Carstairs	87	74 13	

The log of the run will be studied with interest by all who delight in the finer points of train running; but its more notable features lay in the high uphill speeds, as for example from Milnthorpe to Grayrigg with its minimum speed of 48½ mph, and the approach to Beattock from the Solway Firth, averaging 71 mph from Floriston. The final ascents to Shap and Beattock Summits were, of course, equally first class, though the downhill speeds towards Carlisle, and again in Upper Clydesdale, were no more than moderate. For a wintry occasion, the weather was calm and reasonably fine, and from a continuous record of the milepost timings, and data of the coach resistance, I was able to make a reasonably accurate estimate of the equivalent drawbar horsepower maintained between Milnthorpe and Grayrigg summit, and on the upper reaches of the Beattock bank. These were 1,800 in the first case, and 1,860 in the second.

By that time in West Coast history, the preparations for the changeover to electric traction south of Crewe had reached such a stage that deceleration of service had begun, while, in the hope of providing more margin for recovery of time on the unaffected stretches of track, the drastic step was taken of limiting the loads of the day Anglo-Scottish expresses from Euston to Glasgow to no more than 8 coaches.

Before the alterations in loading took place, there were occasions when some outstanding performance was put up in Scotland on the 'Royal Scot' and 'Midday Scot'. I have chosen four for special mention, the first two being on the 'Midday Scot', stopping at Carstairs to detach the Edinburgh portion, and the others on the 'Royal Scot' non-stop from Carlisle to Glasgow. On the first of the tabulated runs, the start was on time, though advice of two relaying checks to come north of Beattock Summit prompted the driver to get some time in hand; and he did so by a fine climb of the Beattock Bank itself. Although the speed was no more than 62 mph through Beattock station, the bank itself was climbed in only 14 min 9 sec. The second run, although on this occasion leaving Carlisle 15 minutes late, was very similar, with a better road from Beattock Summit; however, the gaining on time continued and the train reached Carstairs only 3 minutes late. From detailed timings, I have been able to make estimates of the equivalent drawbar horsepower put forth on these two runs, and they work out at 1,885 by *City of Birmingham*, and 1,830 by *Duchess of Norfolk*.

The loads hauled on the 'Royal Scot' were much heavier, with engines that had worked through from Euston, and had been remanned at Carlisle. On the third run in the table, *Princess Alexandra* was leaving Carlisle 5 minutes late, but with three permanent way

Up 'Royal Scot' passing Penrith, hauled by engine No 46235 City of Birmingham (Derek Cross).

LMR Scottish Region: Carlisle-Glasgow

			'Midday Scot'		'Royal Scot'	
Engine No			46235	46226	46224	6232
Engine name			*City of Birmingham*	*Duchess of Norfolk*	*Princess Alexandra*	*Duchess of Montrose*
Load (tons E/F)			371/400	369/400	444/465	473/510
Distance (miles)		Schedule time (min)	Actual time (m s)	Actual time (m s)	Actual time (m s)	Actual time (m s)
0.0	Carlisle	0	0 00	0 00	0 00	0 00
8.6	Gretna Junc	12	10 27	11 07	pws 14 33	pws 13 40
16.7	Kirtlebridge		18 33	20 09	24 42	23 17
25.8	Lockerbie	30	27 12	28 07	pws 35 00	pws 32 52
28.7	Nethercleugh		29 40	30 18	37 26	35 10
34.5	Wamphrey		34 40	34 52	42 23	39 53
39.7	Beattock	43	39 12	39 20	47 00	44 22
45.3	Greskine		46 23	46 10	53 42	51 38
49.7	Summit	63	53 21	53 30	60 05	59 39
55.3	Crawford		pws 59 30	pws 58 52	pws 67 04	64 59
63.2	Lamington		pws 67 45	65 28	73 58	71 25
66.9	Symington	79	71 15	68 37	77 18	74 31
70.0	Leggatfoot		74 14	71 10	80 02	77 12
73.5	Carstairs	86	79 15	75 05	83 25	80 35
84.0	Law Junc	97			sigs 94 15	sigs 93 55
89.4	Motherwell	104			99 45	pws 99 45
102.3	Glasgow	122			pws 117 20	sigs 115 50

Speeds		mph	mph	mph	mph
Beattock		62	67	62	63
Greskine		39	40/34	42	35
Summit		36	37	39	31

Equivalent dhp					
On Beattock Bank		1,885	1,830	2,335	2,045
Net time (min)		76	74	103½	109

checks in less than 20 miles, the train was a further 5 minutes late on passing Lockerbie. But a superlative effort then followed. On the easy gradients up Annandale, speed was worked up to well over 70 mph with a maximum of 73 mph crossing the river north of Wamphray. Beattock station was passed at 62 mph and the bank climbed in the astonishing time of 13 min 3 sec. The minimum speed with this 465-ton load was 39 mph, sustained on the 1 in 75 gradient, which was equal to an output of 2,335 equivalent drawbar horsepower. It was a remarkable achievement to pass Beattock Summit in no more than 5 seconds over the

even hour from Carlisle in view of the checks that had been experienced south of Lockerbie. Further checks came on the downhill run to Glasgow, but the determination of the crew was beyond praise, and the 'Royal Scot' clocked into Glasgow Central exactly on time. The net time of 103½ minutes for the 102.3 miles from Carlisle makes this one of the finest ever runs over this route with a steam locomotive.

There was also some grand running by *Duchess of Montrose* on the second of the trips by the 'Royal Scot', with an even heavier load of 510 tons gross behind the tender. Although there were three permanent way

checks in the early stages, their combined effect was not unduly severe, and the loss of time between Carlisle and Lockerbie was only 7¾ minutes. Then the men on *Duchess of Montrose* got going in style, averaging no less than 72 mph throughout from Lockerbie to Beattock station, with maxima of 78 mph at Nethercleugh, and 77½ mph at the crossing of the River Annan north of Wamphray. A further mighty effort was made up the Beattock Bank proper, taking no more than 15 min 17 sec for this critical 10 miles, and a minimum speed of 31 mph. The equivalent drawbar horsepower on the climb works out at 2,045—another magnificent performance. Some fine speed was maintained through Upper Clydesdale,

touching 80 mph near Lamington and, despite the earlier checks, 5½ minutes of the late start of 13 minutes had been won back when passing Carstairs. Delays came thick and fast afterwards, but there was a recovery of six minutes of the late start on arrival in Glasgow. The net time of 109 minutes establishes this as another outstanding performance.

In the 'limited load' period, while there were times when little advantage seemed to be taken of the locomotive power available for making up lost time, certain instances occurred that were outstanding, and it was fortunate that there were expert recorders on the trains in question. Two examples are shown in the table appended. The first, behind engine *Queen*

Elizabeth, began badly, with the train slowed to 20 mph through Lancaster, and then brought to a dead stand beyond Carnforth. Then the road was clear to the outskirts of Carlisle, and the crew made full use of their opportunities. Working up to 75 mph at Milnthorpe, speed did not fall below 66½ mph anywhere up the Grayrigg bank; a maximum of 83½ mph was attained at Tebay, while on Shap itself the lowest rate was 51 mph. Descending to Carlisle, speed was not unduly high as far as Penrith, where a careful slowing to 60 mph was made round the curve; then they blazed away to no less than 92 mph near Southwaite. The second run began with an undelayed passage through Carnforth, and a minimum at Milepost 9½ of 66 mph. The lower part of the Grayrigg bank was taken no more than moderately, but a noticeable opening took place above Oxenholme. It was after Tebay that the really phenomenal effort came, with an absolutely sustained minimum speed of 60 mph up the last 1¾ miles of the 1 in 75 gradient of Shap.

I cannot be sure if the time of 4 min 55 sec is an all-time record with steam traction for the 5.5 miles from Tebay to Shap Summit. The previous fastest of which I have any record is the 5 min 7 sec on the test trip of 16 November 1936 with engine 6201 *Princess Elizabeth*; but the load was only 230 tons, compared to 295 tons hauled by *City of Liverpool* on the ordinary service run on the limited load of the 'Royal Scot'. On the maximum-load test runs of *Duchess of Abercorn* in 1939, the highest sustained values of drawbar horsepower were about 2,500, and from the dynamometer car records and other data it was deduced that the maximum indicated horsepower was around 3,300. A careful calculation on the performance of *City of Liverpool* climbing Shap at a sustained 60 mph with a gross trailing load of 295 tons indicates a drawbar horsepower of about 2,600, and thus slightly surpassing the maximum efforts in the 1939 tests, albeit briefly.

So, I come finally to 'The Red Rose', and to some of the finest post-war performances of the Stanier 'Pacifics' of either variety. At the zenith of post-war speed in the pre-electrification era, that train was booked to run the 158.1 miles from Crewe to Euston non-stop in 155 minutes. The gross load behind the tender was never less than about 450 tons, and sometimes topped the 550 mark. It was remarkable that the 'Lizzies' were used as often as the 'Duchesses', and on these shorter runs frequently turned in some outstandingly fine work. When I was writing the 'British Locomotive Practice and Performance' articles in *The Railway Magazine*, many correspondents were kind enough to send me details of fast runs on this train, and I append herewith summary reference to six of these. The interesting point about all of them is that the net start-to-stop times from Crewe to

Above left *The down 'Midday Scot' near Kenton in 1939 hauled by No 6232 Duchess of Montrose* (C.R.L. Coles).

Left *'Duchess' Class 4-6-2 No 6247 City of Liverpool as first de-streamlined, at Camden shed in 1947* (O.S. Nock).

LMR: Lancaster-Carlisle

Engine no			46221		46247	
Engine name			*Queen Elizabeth*		*City of Liverpool*	
Load (tons E/F)			264/280		277/295	
Distance (miles)		Schedule time min	Actual time (m s)	Speed (mph)	Actual time (m s)	Speed (mph)
0.0	Lancaster	0	0 00	20	0 00	72
—			sigs		—	—
6.3	Carnforth	5	7 05	60	4 55	82
—			sig stop		—	66
13.6	Milnthorpe		17 32	75	10 48	77
19.1	Oxenholme	17	22 00	70	15 50	60/56
26.2	Grayrigg		28 10	66½	23 17	57
32.2	Tebay	32	32 47	83½	28 20	77
35.2	Scout Green		35 21	—	30 49	63
37.5	Shap Summit	40	38 05	51	33 15	60
47.0	Clifton		45 52	80	40 37	84
—			—	—	pwr	30
51.2	Penrith	52	49 33	60	45 25	—
61.7	Southwaite		57 31	92	—	83
64.2	Wreay		59 30		55 45	—
—			sigs		—	
69.1	Carlisle	69	65 42		60 32	
Net times (pass to stop) (min)			57½		57½	

LMR: Rugby-Euston

Engine No		46200		46208		46209	
Engine name		*The Princess Royal*		*Princess Helena Victoria*		*Princess Beatrice*	
Load (tons E/F)		457/475		449/490		449/490	
Distance (miles)		Actual time (m s)	Speed (mph)	Actual time (m s)	Speed (mph)	Actual time (m s)	Speed (mph)
0.0	Rugby	0 00		0 00		0 00	
7.3	Welton	7 29	67	7 58	67	8 54	54
12.9	Weedon	11 38	85½	12 31	86	13 31	82
19.8	Blisworth	16 53	75	17 47	74	18 52	75
22.7	Roade	19 18	71½	20 11	72	21 19	70
27.8	Castlethorpe	23 15	81¾	23 54	88	25 06	90
35.9	Bletchley	29 34	75	30 29	70	31 03	80
42.4	Leighton Buzzard	34 51	72	35 46	75	36 03	78
50.9	Tring	42 07	67	43 14	63	42 53	71
54.6	Berkhamsted	45 12	79	46 27	77	45 52	80
58.1	Hemel Hempstead	47 41	86½	49 04	91	48 19	96
65.1	Watford Junction	52 46	81¾	54 07	80/78	53 03	85
71.2	Harrow	57 14	75	58 37	83	57 11	88
74.5	Wembley	59 43	85½	60 56	90	59 24	93
77.2	Willesden Junction	62 24		62 51		61 10	
82.6	EUSTON			70 04		68 50	
Average speed, Weedon-Wembley (mph)		76.8		76.2		79.0	

Euston give no lower average, in any case, than 64.5 mph. Above all, however, rank the performances of engines 46208 and 46209. Both runs were heavily delayed between Crewe and Rugby, but afterwards the work was peerless.

To emphasize the quality of the work south of Rugby on the two runs behind 46208 and 46209, I have tabulated in the accompanying table the times and speeds made on the dynamometer car test run on the 6.12 pm from Crewe to Willesden in June 1935 when the performance was considered to be the utmost that the 'Lizzies' could put forth. Until I received these two runs on 'The Red Rose', I believed this was so. These two latter journeys were both delayed in getting through Rugby, the second of the two particularly so; thus, in comparison with the 1935

exploit, it is after passing Weedon that the times become fairly comparable. Then they are astonishing! For a 'Lizzie' to average 79 mph over the 61.6 miles from Weedon to Wembley with a load of 490 tons, including a top speed of 96 mph on the descent from Tring, is breathtaking enough, but it poses the question as to what the 'Duchesses' might have done if equally opened out.

By the year 1959, the English Electric diesels were coming into regular use between Euston and Liverpool, and at the same time the deceleration in train times prior to electrification was also taking effect. The up 'Red Rose' was one of the trains that had been slowed down, with an increased allowance of 170 minutes, non-stop, from Crewe to Euston. In connection with signalling work, I was on the line fre-

LMR: 'The Red Rose'

Run No	1	2	3	4	5	6
Engine No	46250	46239	46208	46209	46253	46237
Engine name	*City of Lichfield*	*City of Chester*	*Princess Helena Victoria*	*Princess Beatrice*	*City of St Albans*	*City of Bristol*
Load (tons, E/F)	430/460	446/490	449/490	449/490	457/500	503/550
Overall time (m s)	149 21	152 15	145 36	153 09	153 25	160 34
Net time (min)	146¼	147	139	140½	144¾	146¾
Net average speed (mph)	64.8	64.5	68.2	67.4	65.5	64.6
Max speed (mph)	86	82	91	96	90	85

The first Stanier 'Pacific' The Princess Royal in BR livery, ascending Beattock Bank with a Euston to Dundee and Aberdeen express, with a bank engine in the rear (Derek Cross).

quently at the time, and returning from Crewe late one afternoon I had an unexpected treat. Arriving on No 3 platform only a few minutes before the up 'Red Rose' was due, I was surprised to see it come in from Liverpool headed, not by the expected diesel, but by a 'Lizzie', *Princess Margaret Rose*. The train was very crowded, and for some time after we had started, and I had clocked the moment of departure, I was still making my way along the corridors trying to find a seat. Gravitating towards the front end, I was heartened by the full-throated roar of the exhaust beat; and to cut a long and joyous story short, I experienced one of my finest ever runs behind one of those engines, on the eve of their withdrawal for scrapping. It is good to reflect that the engine of what proved to be my own farewell behind one of them was one saved for preservation.

The running was top class from the very outset, and the acoustics as we climbed the Madeley bank, succeeded by the downhill dash towards Stafford on the very easy gradients from Standon Bridge, were exhilarating to record, and set the pattern for the whole run. Note should be taken of the uphill work from the Trent Valley, with minimum speeds of 63 mph at Atherstone, and no less than 67 mph at Bulkington, and of the sustained high speed to the

outskirts of Rugby. There was no let up afterwards, either, with further maximum speeds of 80½ mph at Weedon and 84 mph at Castlethorpe. Despite the check at Rugeley, the train was 13 minutes inside schedule time at Roade, and would have been still more so but for the severe signal check at Bletchley. The men on 46203, however, were proof against any form of discouragement, and their ascent to Tring, with a sustained minimum speed of 66½ mph on the 1 in 335 gradient, with an equivalent drawbar horse-power of 1,495, was the climax of the run, as far as power output was concerned. The signal stop at Bourne End was very time-consuming, because it involved a warning to go carefully for some miles ahead in view of a report of possible obstructions on the line. Once clear of this area, the crew resumed their previous style of running and gave us a final burst of high speed from Watford to Willesden.

LMR: 'The Red Rose', Crewe-Euston

Engine 4-6-2 No 46203 *Princess Margaret Rose*
Load 13 coaches, 456 tons tare, 495 tons full

Distance (miles)		Schedule time (min)	Actual time (m s)	Speed (mph)
0.0	Crewe	0	0 00	
4.7	Betley Road		8 30	47½
7.9	Madeley		12 35	46½
10.5	Whitmore	15	15 36	—

Distance (miles)		Schedule time (min)	Actual time (m s)	Speed (mph)
14.6	Standon Bridge		19 23	72
19.2	Norton Bridge	23	22 57	80
21.2	Great Bridgeford		24 25	83
24.5	Stafford	33	27 05	53 (slack)
31.0	Colwich		33 29	69
—			pws	15
33.9	Rugeley	43	38 04	—
41.8	Lichfield	50	46 15	72
48.0	Tamworth	56	51 05	80
55.7	Atherstone		57 40	63
60.9	Nuneaton	70	62 10	72
64.6	Bulkington		65 19	67½
70.0	Brinklow		69 47	76
75.5	Rugby	86	74 50	40 (slack)
79.3	*Kilsby Tunnel North Box*		79 52	56
88.4	Weedon	100	88 01	80½
95.3	Blisworth	106	93 33	70
98.2	Roade	109	96 03	66½
103.3	Castlethorpe		100 03	84
109.6	*Milepost 48½*		104 43	73½
			sigs	10
111.4	Bletchley	121	108 02	—
117.9	Leighton Buzzard		114 53	71
122.0	Cheddington		118 23	68½
126.4	Tring	137	122 17	66½
130.1	Berkhamsted		125 19	80
—			sig stop	—
140.6	Watford Junction	150	141 30	72/69
144.8	Hatch End		145 07	72
146.7	Harrow		146 38	76
150.0	Wembley		149 10	79
152.7	Willesden Junction	161	151 13	72
155.7	South Hampstead		153 50	—
—			sigs	—
158.1	EUSTON	170	159 50	

Net time 143 minutes, 66½ mph

The net time of 143 minutes from Crewe, with its start-to-stop average of 66½ mph, is a sufficient commentary on this run in itself. But I can add that it was made in far from ideal footplate conditions, in the modern context. By that time, many of the top-link crews at Camden, Crewe North, Longsight and Edge Hill had a growing experience with the new diesels, and had, no doubt, an appreciation of the relative comfort of their cabs. While some of the tougher spirits among the firemen might feel that the absence of hard physical work would result in their 'getting soft', others were no doubt glad that the end of their days of coal-heaving was in sight. But while I clocked the grand run of *Princess Margaret Rose,* I gave more than a passing thought to conditions on the footplate; for it was a day of sweltering heat, and instead of driving his engine vigorously to make up lost time which had been incurred north of Crewe, one might have expected rather easier going to ease the labour of firing. But these two worthies, who came from Camden shed, obviously put their hearts into the job, and turned in a superb piece of work.

Engine No 46245 City of London *in the final BR livery of Midland red* (British Railways).

Appendix I: The Crewe Dinner, May 1971
Address by O.S. Nock in proposing the health of 'Crewe men, past and present'

I must first of all thank you, Mr Chairman, for the honour you have accorded me as your guest here tonight. I must admit that when I had got over the surprise and pleasure of your invitation I began thinking, 'Why ever pick on me, a mere signal contractor?', particularly as we as a breed were not exactly *persona grata* with the powers that used to be at Crewe. Now, to the sorrow of us manufacturers, not only of my generation but certainly one or two generations earlier, Crewe was a great signal manufactory in its own right. The London and North Western Railway was the progenitor of all 'do it yourself' concerns, and although the high-handed methods of John Saxby did not exactly help, it was, I suppose, inevitable that the LNWR would one day manufacture every scrap of its own signalling equipment. We signal contractors used to be a bit of a rough lot, given to telling railway managements what they *must* have, and when a personality like John Saxby comes up against one like F.W. Webb there is going to be a monumental crash. So there was, and John Saxby went out on his ear!

Now, folios have been written about Webb as an engine designer—not all of them complimentary—but having booted out John Saxby he was left with a pretty little problem on his hands. The whole gamut of signalling design was tied up hand and foot with patents. For contractors it was a case of designing something different from everyone else's, or going out of business! I don't think Webb's ingenuity as a designer was ever taxed to a greater extent than in producing a new form of interlocking frame that dodged everyone else's patents. But he did it, and produced a beautiful job. How it compared for cost was another matter.

Now, while I have every admiration for the range of signalling apparatus that was produced at Crewe, and I can view it with very much of a professional eye, it was of course a mere ancillary activity compared to the main business, and there, as you Mr Chairman have indicated, I have written a good deal about LNWR locomotives. The chap who writes what the amateur railway enthusiast reads lives with his head in a noose! I always remember the remark of a CME of another establishment to whom the amateur railway press—not the professionals—was

causing some embarrassment. He exclaimed to me once: 'If I want to know what is going on in my works I have to read "The Steam Trumpet"—I'll call it that for now—and always they're bloody well right!' Among readers of railway literature, the partisanship is at times quite incredible. It was many years ago that I wrote my first book on LNWR locomotives, and when this was nearing completion my publisher said, 'We shall have to have one on the Midland now.' I said, 'Do you want me to write it?' He snapped, 'Good God no! If you like the North Western you obviously hate the Midland and we couldn't have that in a book!' I can tell you another thing about that first North Western book. Rather against my wishes it had as its main title *The Premier Line*. Believe it or not, some perfervid partisans ordered that book thinking it was about the Great Western!

I have sometimes been asked by railway fans whose interests lie elsewhere, 'What was it that attracted you so much to the LNWR?' The engines were black, and you yourself have written—and it was quoted— 'they were a rough job.' First of all I had to explain that by a 'rough job' I did not mean the workmanship and the machinery—but it had been a rather careless way, on my part, of saying that no money was spent on lavish outward adornment, and certainly nothing on decorations, or décor inside the cab. I shall never forget finding in the little yard at Penrith, standing on adjacent roads, two 0-6-0 goods engines. One was a North Eastern 'C' Class, with its side-windowed cab, wood panelling inside, and those huge tool boxes, with padded seats for the chaps. The other was an 18-inch LNW—a 'Cauliflower'—and its stark austerity was positively startling by comparison. But having had some footplate experience of both, I know which one I'd have chosen if I'd had to work a train!

This brings me to the crunch of the whole affair. As a young engineering graduate, as well as being a lifelong railway enthusiast, the thing that drew me instinctively to the products of Crewe was that they so convincingly gave value for money. I don't think there have ever been engines that have amassed so many net ton-miles of work per pound sterling of capital investment. It was a famous son of Crewe who, when alternative forms of traction to steam were being considered, said that he was going to have the form that gave the highest tractive effort per pound sterling. I have always felt that the products of Crewe in LNW days must easily have held the record for ton-miles per pound of tractive effort.

The days when superheating was first being applied to Crewe locomotives are worth recalling, and the work done on the line really takes some believing today. The loads of the principal expresses out of Euston, in 1910-1916, were much the same as they are today, 400 to 450 tons, and although there was a growing stud of 4-6-0 locos, the great majority of those trains were taken by little superheater 4-4-0s of the 'George the Fifth' Class, which made average speeds of 55 to 60 mph between Euston and Crewe. There was nothing to be seen like it, anywhere in the country.

We chaps who study locomotive history occasionally come across projects that could be grouped together under the title of 'might-have-beens'. Now some of you may know that in 1910 there was an Interchange Trial of locomotives between the Great Western and the LNWR. It was not like the BR Interchange Trials of 1948, arranged to provide scientific information, but it arose through some high-standing business tycoons on the Great Western Board complaining of the high capital cost of new GWR locos. They had got hold of some figures from Crewe, and were aghast at the difference. Now, to these chaps a 4-6-0 was a 4-6-0, and I can quite well believe that one of Churchward's new four-cylinder jobs with 225 lb pressure would be very much more expensive than a Whale 'Experiment', the only express 4-6-0 the LNW then had. Churchward was asked, across the Board table at Paddington, and is quoted as replying: 'Because one of mine would pull two of their bloody things backwards. If you don't believe me, have one over for trial and put it on the Limited!' The trials were arranged, and the 'Experiment' didn't make a very good job of it. Churchward was entirely vindicated.

But the 'might-have-been' part of the story arises in another way. Those trials were made with non-superheater engines. I always feel that Crewe missed a trick by not challenging Swindon to a return match with superheater engines. The results could have been very embarrassing, because the tycoons who formed the anti-Churchward group in the Board were out for blood, although the Crewe engine might have used more coal in the process.

As a young engineer, my early studies of LNW practice were naturally of the end-products of Crewe—locomotives, rails, interlocking frames and so on—but history, even more than 'things', is the story of men, human nature, personalities, and all their foibles as much as their triumphs. And so far as locomotive engineering is concerned, there is surely no railway centre anywhere in the world—even in the vastly changing world of today—that has spread its influence and its precepts so widely across the world. While one can count the CMEs of the LNWR on the fingers of one hand, one can trace the careers of their pupils and assistants into Scotland, Ireland, India, Australia, South America and China, while at least one added to his North Western experience that of a great American railway before returning to England. One found Crewe men, in the Chair, on the Great Northern, Lancashire and Yorkshire and North Eastern, while the locomotive livery on the NWR of India and of the New South Wales Government showed clearly where the affections of loco men on those railways lay.

One could be accused of getting sentimental about locomotives, and I am always mindful of the way in which one of the greatest of all Crewe men, C.J. Bowen Cooke, pulled the leg of a railway *littérateur,* saying he was one of that group that 'wrote nice things about locomotives but didn't have to run them'. I could also come within that category.

A boiler suit and a dirty face have been my passport to many friendships, even though I could not speak the language of my companions on the footplate. It's just the same, whether you are running over the Semmering Pass in Austria, riding Garratts in Kenya, on the 2-ft gauge 'Puffing Billy' in Victoria, or on the Inverness Sleeper riding from Crewe to Perth. There is an immensely strong bond among loco men. I have been privileged to find it on the footplate, across the world—and I need hardly add it is a bond that has not lost any of its strength with the passing of steam.

And so, Gentlemen, I ask you to rise and drink with me the health of Crewe men, past and present...

Appendix II: Preserved locomotives of the LMS and its constituents

Caledonian
4-2-2 No 123 (Drummond design, built 1886); Glasgow Museum of Transport
0-4-4T No 419 (McIntosh design, built 1907); Scottish Railway Preservation Society, Falkirk
0-6-0 No 828 (McIntosh design, built 1899); Strathspey Railway (property of Scottish Locomotive Preservation Trust)

Furness
0-4-0 No 3 *Coppernob* (built 1846); National Railway Museum, York

Glasgow and South Western
0-6-0T No 9 (Peter Drummond design, built 1917); Glasgow Museum of Transport

Highland
4-6-0 No 103 (the first 'Jones Goods', built 1894); Glasgow Museum of Transport

Lancashire and Yorkshire
2-4-2T No 1008 (Aspinall type, built 1899); National Railway Museum, York
0-6-0 No 1122 (Aspinall type, built 1896); Steamtown, Carnforth (property of the Fairclough Corporation)
0-6-0 No 52044 (Aspinall type, built 1887); Keighley and Worth Valley Railway

London, Midland and Scottish
4-6-0 'Black Five'
No 4767 *George Stephenson*; North Yorkshire Moors Railway
No 44806 *Magpie*; Steamport, Southport
No 44871 *Sovereign*; Steamtown, Carnforth
No 44932; Steamtown, Carnforth
No 5000; Severn Valley (on loan from NRM, York)
No 5025; Strathspey Railway, Boat of Garten
No 45110 *R A F Biggin Hill*; Severn Valley Railway
No 45212; Keighley and Worth Valley Railway
No 5231 *3rd (Volunteer) Battalion The Worcestershire and Sherwood Foresters Regiment*; Great Central Railway, Loughborough
No 45379; Bristol Suburban Railway, Bitton
No 45407; Steamtown, Carnforth
No 5428 *Eric Treacy*; North Yorkshire Moors Railway
2-6-0 Class '5'
No 2700 (Horwich 'Crab'); National Railway Museum, York
No 42765 (Horwich 'Crab'); Keighley and Worth Valley Railway
No 2968 (Stanier type); Severn Valley Railway
4-6-0 'Jubilee' Class three-cylinder
No 5593 *Kolhapur*; Birmingham Railway Museum
No 5596 *Bahamas*; Dinting Railway Centre
No 5690 *Leander*; Steamtown, Carnforth (property of Leander Locomotive Ltd)
4-6-0 'Converted Royal Scot' three-cylinder
No 6100 *Royal Scot*; Bressingham Steam Museum, Diss (property of Butlins)
No 6115 *Scots Guardsman*; Dinting Railway Centre
4-6-2 Stanier 'Princess Royal' Class
No 6201 *Princess Elizabeth*; Bulmer Railway Centre, Hereford (property of Princess Elizabeth Locomotive Society)
No 6203 *Princess Margaret Rose*; Midland Railway Centre, Butterley, Derbyshire (property of Butlins)
4-6-2 Stanier 'Duchess' Class
No 6229 *Duchess of Hamilton*; National Railway Museum, York
No 6233 *Duchess of Sutherland*; Bressingham Steam Museum, Diss (property of Butlins)
2-6-4 Stanier-type tank engines
No 2500; Bressingham Steam Museum, Diss (on loan from National Railway Museum, York)
No 2073; Lakeside and Haverthwaite Railway, Cumbria
No 2085; Lakeside and Haverthwaite Railway, Cumbria
2-8-0 Stanier-type '8F'
No 48151; Yorkshire Dales Railway, Embsay, near Skipton
No 8233; Severn Valley Railway (property of Stanier 8F Locomotive Society)
No 8431; Keighley and Worth Valley Railway

London and North Western
2-2-2 *Columbine* (ex-Grand Junction); National Railway Museum, York
2-2-2 *Cornwall*; National Railway Museum, York
2-4-0 No 790 *Hardwicke*, National Railway Museum, York
0-6-2T No 1054 (design of 1880); Dinting Railway Centre (property of the National Trust)
0-8-0 No 485 (Class 'G2' superheated goods, built 1921); stored at Horsehay, Telford, on behalf of the Ironbridge Gorge Museum Trust

London, Tilbury and Southend

4-4-2T No 80 *Thundersley* (built 1909); Bressingham Steam Museum, Diss (on loan from National Railway Museum, York.

Midland

2-4-0 No 158A (Kirtley type, built 1866); Midland Railway Centre, Butterley, Derbyshire

4-2-2 No 673 (one of the 7-ft 9-in 'Spinners' built Derby 1897); Midland Railway Centre, Butterley, Derbyshire

4-4-0 No 1000 (three-cylinder compound, built as No 2631 in 1902, subsequently renumbered and rebuilt with a superheater in 1914); National Railway Museum, York

0-6-0 No 44027 (standard '4F' goods); Midland Railway Centre, Butterley, Derbyshire

0-6-0 No 4422 (standard '4F' goods); North Staffordshire Railway, Cheddleton, near Leek, Staffordshire

North Staffordshire

0-6-2T No 2 ('New L' Class, built about 1923); Chatterly Whitfield Mining Museum, near Stoke-on-Trent (on loan from National Railway Museum, York)

Somerset and Dorset Joint

2-8-0 No 88 (Goods and mixed traffic engine, built 1925); West Somerset Railway (property of the Somerset and Dorset Museum Trust)

2-8-0 No 13809 (Goods and mixed traffic engine, built 1925); North Yorkshire Moors Railway (property of 13809 Preservation Group)

Bibliography

Technical Papers

Institution of Civil Engineers
1899 Compound Locomotives, F.W. Webb
1914 Superheating Steam in Locomotives, Henry Fowler

Institution of Mechanical Engineers
1880 A new Reversing and Expansion Valve Gear, David Joy
1910 Compounding and Superheating in Horwich Locomotives, George Hughes
1926 An investigation into the cylinder losses in a compound locomotive, E.L. Diamond
1941 Presidential Address—Sir William Stanier

Institution of Locomotive Engineers
1945 Modern Locomotive History (LMS), E.S. Cox
1946 Ten years' experience with the LMS 4-6-2 non-condensing No 6202, R.C. Bond

Journals

Engineering, The Engineer, The Locomotive Magazine, The Railway Engineer, The Railway Gazette, The Railway Magazine

Books

The Aspinall Era, H.A.V. Bulleid, Ian Allan, 1967
British Locomotives, C.J. Bowen Cooke, Whitaker, 1899
British Railway Steam Locomotive
  Vol 1 1825—1925, E.L. Ahrons, Ian Allan, 1960
  Vol 2 1925—1965, O.S. Nock, Ian Allan, 1966
British Locomotives of the 20th Century
  Vol 1 1900—1930, O.S. Nock, Patrick Stephens, 1983
  Vol 2 1930—1960, O.S. Nock, Patrick Stephens, 1984
  Vol 3 1960—the present day, O.S. Nock, Patrick Stephens, 1985
Caledonian Dunalastairs, O.S. Nock, David and Charles, 1968
Lancashire and Yorkshire Railway in the 20the Century, Eric Mason, Ian Allan, 1954
Lifetime with Locomotives, R.C. Bond, Goose & Sons, 1975
LNWR Locomotives of Bowen Cooke, O.S. Nock, Bradford Barton, 1977
LNWR Precursor Family, O.S. Nock, David and Charles, 1968
Locomotives and Train Working in the latter part of the Nineteenth Century, E.L. Ahrons, Heffer, Cambridge, 1952
  Vol 2 (LNWR, LYR, Midland, North Staffordshire, Furness)
  Vol 3 (G & SWR, Caledonian, Highland)
Midland Compounds, O.S. Nock, David and Charles, 1964
Royal Scots and Patriots of the LMS, O.S. Nock, David and Charles, 1978
William Stanier—An engineering biography, O.S. Nock, Ian Allan, 1979

Index

Of further interest

British Locomotives of the 20th Century

In this three-volume major work of reference **O.S. Nock**, Britain's leading railway author, tells the story of British locomotive development from 1900 to the present day.

The first volume covers the pre-grouping era up to 1930 and the technicalities of locomotive design, construction and performance. Each chapter contains a tabular summary of the dimensions of the locomotives introduced in the periods concerned.

The second volume covers British locomotive development from 1930 to 1960 and recalls with relish the exciting advances in train speed. This volume traces the history of the British locomotive through the last years of steam and is packed with tables, line drawings and photographs.

The third and final volume covers the period from 1960 to the present day. Details include the launch of the great modernisation plan, the introduction of diesel services, the extension of main line electrification, the Inter-City 125 High Speed Trains and the IC 225 Advanced Passenger Train.

Great Locomotives Volume 1: Southern Railway

'Jubilees', 'Schools', 'King Arthurs' and many other familiar names will be found among the *Great Locomotives of the Southern Railway*, all described in **O.S. Nock**'s customary authoritative and entertaining style. Here are not only the histories and technical details of every major class of locomotive to run on the rails of the Southern Railway, but also the stories of the designers and their philosophies. A wealth of the author's personal recollections of the era and a fascinating collection of photographs make this book a must for the shelves of every railway enthusiast.

Volume 2: LNER

With a network covering the mountain lines of Scotland, the great industrial belt of the North of England and the rural reaches of the Fens, the London and North Eastern Railway and its constituents carried a huge variety of traffic and developed some of Britain's finest locomotives to do the job. O.S. Nock describes the men and the machines, from Patrick Stirling's graceful '8-footers' to Sir Nigel Gresley's East Coast 'Pacifics'. Containing many personal recollections and details of remarkable runs behind LNER steam, this book continues his account of landmarks in British locomotive development.

The up 'Royal Scot', a 16-coach load, in 1934, hauled by No 6200 The Princess Royal with the original boiler, south of Kilsby Tunnel (Rail Archive Stephenson, photo F.R. Hebron).